BEN JONSON'S POEMS

Ben Jonson's Poems

A STUDY OF THE PLAIN STYLE

by

WESLEY TRIMPI

STANFORD UNIVERSITY PRESS
Stanford, California
1962

Stanford University Press
Stanford, California

Library of Congress Catalog Card Number: 62-9564
Printed in the United States of America

FOR J. V. CUNNINGHAM
A master of the plain style

ACKNOWLEDGMENTS

I WISH TO THANK Mr. Douglas Bush and Mr. Harry Levin for their careful reading of an earlier version of this book. My debt to the editors of the Oxford edition of Ben Jonson's works, Messrs. C. H. Herford and Percy Simpson and Mrs. Evelyn Simpson, is inestimable, both in what I have learned from them about Jonson and about the Renaissance. My greatest personal debt is to Yvor Winters. Although many years ago he introduced me to the poetry of the Renaissance and to Jonson in particular, it is not specifically with regard to the material in this book that I wish to thank him. Rather, it is for the fact that he began my education in the traditionally humanistic sense and helped me to find many of the directions it was later to take. For the methods of investigation and application of the material in the book itself, I am most indebted to J. V. Cunningham, whose persuasiveness in his published work and generosity in private conversation he will often recognize in the following pages.

W. T.

PREFACE

In this book I have tried to describe a stylistic tradition and a group of poems written within the tradition. The two are inseparable, and I have taken my descriptive terminology from the historical context wherever it has been possible so that it might determine the questions to be asked about the poems and, as a result, the things that might be said about them. In order to establish the context I have devoted the opening chapters to the tradition of the classical plain style in antiquity and its adaptation by Jonson and the men he admired to the poetic and rhetorical controversies of the Renaissance.

Normally one would go to the English rhetoric books of Thomas Wilson, George Puttenham, Henry Peacham the elder, and others for descriptions of contemporary styles. With the possible exception of Wilson, however, they were primarily concerned with methods of amplification and with the more ornate literary conventions of the Petrarchans, whose candidly enthusiastic supporter, Abraham Fraunce, concludes: "Thus much of Eloquution in tropes and figures: in al which obserue this one lesson, the more the better" (*The Arcadian Rhetorike*, p. 105). Such treatises dealt with the plain style only in connection with the *narratio* of a formal oration. Jonson's main sources were the scholars of the sixteenth and seventeenth centuries such as the Scaligers, Daniel Heinsius, and Isaac Casaubon; the humanists such as Erasmus and Vives; and the anti-Ciceronians such as Lipsius and Bacon, who drew mainly upon Seneca for their stylistic principles. In the most general terms, the emphasis shifted from expression to content, from the Ciceronian comment of Ascham, "Ye know not what hurt ye do to learning, that care not for words, but for matter," to Bacon's Senecan reversal of the proposition when he lamented that "Men began to hunt more after words than matter."

The anti-Ciceronian movement was originally a reaction against those who held that Cicero was the only ancient writer worthy of imitation—those whom Erasmus makes fun of in his *Ciceronianus*. It became gradually identified with such men as Muret, Lipsius, and Bacon, who advocated the imitation of Sallust, Seneca, and Tacitus and the diction of Terence and Plautus. Jonson, influenced primarily by those who shared the sympathy of these men for the antirhetorical reaction against florid stylistic models, develops a rhetorical position in the *Discoveries* which is essentially the classical plain style. With the exception of many of the songs from the plays and masques, nearly all of Jonson's poems are written in that style, and in those genres—comedy, satire, epistle, and epigram—for which the ancient writers used the style. Although by the Renaissance the classical terms were already losing their precise meaning, Jonson would be most likely to use them almost exclusively in distinguishing between contemporary styles. His attitude would probably have been similar to that of his most important authority, the Spanish humanist Luis Vives, who admits that the qualities of the separate characters of style were used with great freedom in antiquity. They usually referred, he says, to individual members and periods rather than to complete compositions, for one meets in any part any of these qualities, as, for example, either the low may be in an elevated part, or the smooth in a rough, or the polished in an informal, and the same way in others. And in the same way he is not called bilious among men who has no other humor—for that is impossible—but he who has that humor predominating; so speech is judged by that quality which is most prevalent (*De Ratione Dicendi*, II, xi; *Opera Omnia*, II, 154-55). The persistence of stylistic qualities reflects a persistence of attitudes toward experience. When both are rediscoverable at various intervals of time, they may be called a literary tradition. In tracing the origins of that tradition, one can discover the connections between attitudes which on the surface seem incompatible. The entire tradition, for example, is reflected in the relation between the attitudes of Jonson's first epigram and those of his last. In order to describe that relation it is necessary to describe the historical origins of the style.

Following the classical discussions of style, the sixteenth-century treatises divide nearly every topic into two categories, *de verbis et de rebus*. The dichotomy between expression and content is ancient, and in one sense at least the history of criticism may be construed as the record of attempts that have been made to resolve it. Content has usually referred to what the writer wants the reader to know; expression, or the accumulated stylistic devices at the writer's command, to the means by which the reader may be persuaded to believe it. The intention to persuade has made rhetoric, the science of the means of persuasion, according to Aristotle, principally concerned with emotion rather than with an emotion's proper object and proper motivation. Either by analogy or by repeated association, the dichotomy of denotation and connotation has accompanied that of content and expression. As in the case of the latter, the distinction between the connotative and denotative qualities of language is artificial in so far as each of these qualities can properly be described only in terms of the other; any given statement is made up of both, and the relationship between them is the statement itself. Denotation usually refers to the simple referent of a word, connotation to its context and the qualifications which that context imposes. The attempt to isolate either quality has led usually to the emphasis of one at the expense of the other, and the relationship between them—the statement itself—is destroyed. Connotation has been extended to include not only associations legitimately offered by the context but any associations that the individual talent of the reader is able to provide. Such associations are usually described as feelings, and gradually the term connotation has come to mean not the qualifications imposed by a context but the emotions that are enjoyed by the reader whether they are relevant to the context or not.

In the plain style the denotative and the connotative most nearly approach each other in the exclusion of irrelevant associations from the context. The denotative statement defines the writer's experience so sharply that it will not admit further qualification other than his attitude toward the experience, which will itself be the context. Connotation, then, can only be perceived by an act of understanding, of insight into what the writer is saying about his experience and about his attitude toward it. It ceases to be a series of feelings evoked by association, as, for example, by means of figurative language, and becomes the awareness of the differences and similarities between the attitude, by which the writer qualifies what he says, and the reader's own experience; it is the commentary of the reader's experience upon what the writer is saying; it is, in a sense, the reader's experience itself. That the intensity of connotation will be in proportion to the relevance of the reader's experience explains why a poem of Jonson's in the plain style is so difficult to teach to a young student; he does not have any comparable experience of his own to help him understand the feeling that should accompany what the writer is saying, and there are few images—sometimes none at all—to evoke whatever feelings are within his grasp.

In the four chapters of Part I, I have treated the *Discoveries* as a handbook of the new authorities on matters of style, or at least of those whom Jonson considered the most interesting, and as a consistent exposition of a stylistic position, rather than as a collection of random fragments. Part II is a discussion of Jonson's poems in the terms developed in Part I. Modern scholarship on Renaissance rhetoric and its classical antecedents has been sufficiently extensive to make further summary of them unnecessary. It has been necessary, however, for me to describe certain historical developments again and to cite a certain number of familiar texts. The number of scholars, such as Morris Croll, R. F. Jones, George Williamson, and J. W. H. Atkins, to whom I have been indebted is so great that I can no longer be sure to whom I owe individual insights, terms, or suggestions for research. C. H. Herford and Percy and Evelyn Simpson in their edition of Jonson have been superlative guides and have constantly enabled me to verify or reject possible connections as they emerged.

The application of Jonson's rhetorical position, as defined in the *Discoveries*, to his poems is a critical, as well as historical, method. The relationship between the two disciplines has been incisively stated by J. V. Cunningham (*Tradition and Poetic Structure*, p. 270):

> Thus, since a work of literature is precisely the apprehension of its proper meaning, the appreciation of literature resides in historical interpretation. There are not two approaches to the study of literature, but only one: historical interpretation is aesthetic appreciation. If the two are distinguishable, they are distinguishable only as aspects of one another. The historical is that act of respect by which we recognize otherness: to this the various historical disciplines are subsidiary. The aesthetic is that act of sympathy by which we realize the other and make it our own.

In another place he comments that our purpose in the study of literature "is not in the ordinary sense to further the understanding of ourselves." It is rather "to enable us to see how we could think and feel otherwise than as we do . . . to erect a larger context of experience within which we may define and understand our own by attending to the disparity between it and the experience of others" (p. 141). Any study of style is, in the end, a study of an intention, of the expression of certain attitudes toward experience. Each attitude is the generalization of a given group of particular feelings, a process of organizing them. A style, then, in expressing an attitude, becomes a method for organizing the writer's feelings in a given situation. The reader may not approve of the organization, but, if the writing is good, he will understand it and its relationship to his own experience.

CONTENTS

CONTENTS

Part I: DISCOVERIES

But I, for my part, Phaedrus, consider such things [the verification of myths] as pretty enough, but as the province of a very curious, painstaking, and not very happy man, and for no other reason than that after this he must set us right as to the form of the Hippocentaurs, and then as to that of the Chimaera; besides, there pours in upon him a crowd of similar monsters, Gorgons and Pegasuses, and other monstrous creatures, incredible in number and absurdity, which if anyone were to disbelieve and endeavour to reconcile each with probability, employing for this purpose a kind of vulgar cleverness, he will stand in need of abundant leisure. But I have no leisure at all for such matter; and the cause of it, my friend, is this; I am not yet able, according to the Delphic precept, to know myself. But it appears to me to be ridiculous, while I am still ignorant of this, to busy myself about matters that do not concern me.

PLATO, *Phaedrus*

1

"AS *LIUY* BEFORE *SALUST,* SYDNEY BEFORE *DONNE*"

I HAVE TAKEN MY TITLE for this chapter from one of the most famous passages in the *Discoveries.* In the following pages, which may serve as a general introduction since they review some of the relevant problems and rhetorical texts in antiquity and the Renaissance, I shall try to offer a context for Jonson's comparison with regard to the characteristics of style that it suggests and the critical method it assumes. The complete passage is as follows:

> And as it is fit to reade the best Authors to youth first, so let them be of the openest, and clearest. As *Liuy* before *Salust, Sydney* before *Donne:* and beware of letting them taste *Gower,* or *Chaucer* at first, lest falling too much in love with Antiquity, and not apprehending the weight, they grow rough and barren in language onely. When their judgements are firme, and out of danger, let them reade both, the old and the new: but no lesse take heed, that their new flowers, and sweetnesse doe not as much corrupt, as the others drinesse, and squallor, if they choose not carefully. *Spencer,* in affecting the Ancients, writ no Language: Yet I would have him read for his matter; but as *Virgil* read *Ennius.**

Despite the fact that the doctrine of imitation constantly encouraged comparisons of English with classical writers, very few valuable remarks of any kind by distinguished writers on particular contemporaries have survived. It is interesting, therefore, to see what may be said about the literary situation of Jonson's day on the basis of his brief comments.

Jonson is closely adapting a passage in Quintilian, and the insertion of the names of Sidney and Donne immediately suggests their substitution in the original text for those of Livy and Sallust:

> For my part I would have them read the best authors from the very beginning and never leave them, choosing those, however, who are simplest and most intelligible. For instance, when prescribing for boys, I should give Livy the preference over Sallust; for, although the latter is

---

* *Ben Jonson,* ed. C. H. Herford and Percy and Evelyn Simpson, 11 vols. (Oxford, 1925–52), VIII, 618. All future references to Jonson will be to this edition, unless otherwise assigned, and will be included in the text. Throughout, I have retained the editors' brackets enclosing words inserted to supply an omission of the original.

the greater historian, one requires to be well-advanced in one's studies to appreciate him properly. Cicero, in my opinion, provides pleasant reading for beginners and is sufficiently easy to understand. . . . After Cicero I should, following the advice of Livy, place such authors as most nearly resemble him.

Quintilian then warns against two faults. First, "an excessive admiration of antiquity," encouraged by the study of Cato and the Gracchi, will result in "a harsh and bloodless style, since they will as yet be unable to understand the force and vigour of these authors" and content themselves with imitating only their style. Second, beginners should not "fall victims to the pernicious allurements of the precious blooms produced by our modern euphuists, thus acquiring a passion for the luscious sweetness of such authors." Both ancient and modern authors, however, may be read by the sufficiently mature students.[1] The question that immediately arises is to what extent we are justified in assuming that Jonson thought these, and possibly other, comments of Quintilian on Sallust were applicable to Donne. If the remarks of Quintilian are applicable, what of comments by other ancient writers on Sallust which would have been available to Jonson? These questions concern the difficulties in interpreting a critical method based upon the doctrine of imitation.[2]

Two of Quintilian's comments on Sallust are echoed by Jonson in his remarks on Donne to Drummond of Hawthornedon. As Sallust is a greater historian than Livy, Donne, being "the first poet jn the World jn some things" (I, 135), may be presumed a better poet than Sidney, though such an assumption needs careful qualification. Livy as well as Sallust is among the best authors, so Sidney as well as Donne. The reason for Sallust's superiority as an historian was his greater concern for historical fact, for the accuracy of his content. Such a reason immediately suggests in what way Donne may be preferred to Sidney; he, especially as satirist, is concerned with describing his own experience accurately, and such a concern reflected the fundamental attitudes of the anti-Petrarchan movement. Quintilian's second observation is that Sallust is more difficult to understand, and, as we shall see later, his imitators, especially when young, damaged their style with a mannered obscurity. Jonson felt as strongly about lucidity as he did about an allegiance to a true description of the actual world. The majority of his remarks on style in the *Discoveries* criticize Senecan mannerisms, particularly obscurity and roughness, despite the fact that in the Ciceronian controversy his attitudes toward literature and experience were

---

[1] Numbered notes will be found at the back of the book, pp. 239–85.

Senecan. And it was in these matters of expression that he told Drummond that Donne deserved hanging "for not keeping of accent" (I, 133) and that he "for not being understood would perish" (I, 138). These remarks tend to justify the extension of Quintilian's comments on the historians to the poets and to suggest that more might be implied about the poets than their place in teaching young boys to read.

Before trying to find out what more might be implied by pursuing further remarks on these historians in both antiquity and the Renaissance, it is necessary to locate Jonson's phrase in the context of the broader stylistic controversies which determined the Renaissance critical attitudes. The comparison of Livy with Sallust is made in the context of the Ciceronian-Senecan controversy of the Renaissance and of the Asiatic-Attic controversy of antiquity. The comparison of Sidney with Donne has reference to the anti-Petrarchan reaction to the sonneteers in the Renaissance and to the ancient satirical rejection of the poetic conventions of the elevated styles by Callimachus in Greece and later, in much more detail, by Horace and the other Latin satirists in Italy. In both periods the poetic controversies share the attitudes toward experience and style reflected in the rhetorical controversies, which accounts in part for the flexibility, as well as the looseness, of the critical terminology as it is applied somewhat indiscriminately to prose and verse. Drummond's comment that Jonson "recommended to my reading Quintilian (who (he said) would tell me the faults of my Verses as if he had Lived with me) and Horace, Plinius 2dus Epistles, Tacitus, Juvenall, Martiall" (I, 132) justifies the further application of Quintilian's passage to poetic conventions of the late sixteenth and early seventeenth centuries.

FORMS OF ATTICISM: PROSE

Not only did Jonson develop in detail a rhetorical position which corresponds to the classical plain style, but he wrote by far the largest portion of his work in those genres which most consistently employed that style: comedy, satire, the epistle, and the epigram. The origin of the style and its accompanying attitudes can best be described in terms of the ancient controversy between rhetoric and dialectic and in the emergence of the three ancient characters of style, the high (*genus grande*), the middle (*genus medium* or *floridum*), and the low or plain (*genus humile* or *tenue*).[3] In his opposition to the rhetoricians, whom he associated with the sophists, Socrates enlisted the plain style (or in his context the philosophical style) on the side of dialectic, whose purpose was to discover and to teach the truth. The purpose of rhetoric was to persuade, hence rhetoric claimed the high style, whose "intention" or *officium* was to move (*movere*), and the middle style, whose purpose was to delight (*delectare*). Dialectic employed the plain style, whose *officium* was simply to teach (*docere*). The conflict between dialectic and rhetoric, which Plato discusses in the *Gorgias* and the *Phaedrus,* encouraged, in the most general terms, a split between meaning and expression, between the philosopher and the orator, and between teaching and persuasion. Cicero blamed Socrates for the separation: "This is the source [the composition of Plato] from which has sprung the undoubtedly absurd and unprofitable and reprehensible severance between the tongue and the brain, leading to our having one set of professors to teach us to think and another to teach us to speak" (*De Oratore* III. xvi. 61).[4] Socrates made the separation in the name of philosophy; Cicero attempted to rejoin the two disciplines in the creation of an ideal orator, but in doing so became a partisan of an oratorically ornate or "Asiatic" style. He regarded the Socratic school as furnishing a model for the plain style,[5] which was designated *sermo* or the conversational style.[6] The philosophical style is "gentle" (*mollis*) and "academic" (*umbratilis*); it is not "rhythmical" (*vincta numeris*), but "loose in structure" (*soluta liberius*). "Consequently it is called conversation (*sermo*) rather than oratory (*oratio*)."[7] Morris Croll, describing its original intention, says, "Its idiom is that of conversation or is adapted from it, in order that it may flow into and fill up all the nooks and crannies of reality and reproduce its exact image to attentive observation."[8]

Cicero's most complete discussion of the three styles occurs in the *Orator*; that of the plain style is in *Orator* 75–90, that of the middle style, 91–96, and that of the grand style, 97ff. It is most expedient to select the main characteristics of his description of the Attic orator and let them serve as the standard classical statement of the plain style against which to measure its mannered extremes, which deviated, during the following century, into styles as ornate as the Asiatic.

> He is restrained and plain (*summissus est et humilis*), he follows the ordinary usage (*consuetudinem imitans*), really differing more than is supposed from those who are not eloquent at all. Consequently the audience, even if they are no speakers themselves, are sure they can speak in that fashion. For that plainness of style seems easy to imitate at first thought, but when attempted nothing is more difficult. (76)
>
> First, then, let us release him from, let us say, the bonds of rhythm (*vinculis numerorum*) . . . It [his style] should be loose but not rambling; so that it may seem to move freely but not to wander with-

out restraint. He should also avoid, so to speak, cementing his words together too smoothly, for the hiatus and the clash of vowels has something agreeable about it and shows a not unpleasant carelessness on the part of a man who is paying more attention to thought than to words. But his very freedom from periodic structure and cementing his words together will make it necessary for him to look to the other requisites. For the short and concise clauses must not be handled carelessly, but there is such a thing even as a careful negligence. Just as some women are said to be handsomer when unadorned—this very lack of ornament becomes them—so this plain style gives pleasure even when unembellished: there is something in both cases which lends greater charm, but without showing itself. (77–78)

The language will be pure Latin, plain and clear (*sermo purus erit et Latinus, dilucide planeque dicetur*); propriety will always be the chief aim. Only one quality will be lacking, which Theophrastus mentions fourth among the qualities of style—the charm and richness of figurative ornament. He will employ an abundance of apposite maxims dug out from every conceivable hiding place; this will be the dominant feature in this orator. He will be modest in his use of what may be called the orator's stock-in-trade. For we do have after a fashion a stock-in-trade, in stylistic embellishments, partly in thought and partly in words. (79–80)

Words when connected together embellish a style if they produce a certain symmetry which disappears when the words are changed, though the thought remains the same; for the figures of thought which remain even if the words are changed are, to be sure, numerous, but relatively few are noticeable. Consequently the orator of the plain style, provided he is elegant and finished, will not be bold in coining words, and in metaphor will be modest, sparing in the use of archaisms, and somewhat subdued in using the other embellishments of language and of thought. Metaphor he may possibly employ more frequently because it is of the commonest occurrence in the language of townsman and rustic alike. (81)

There are, as a matter of fact, a good many ornaments suited to the frugality of this very orator I am describing. For this shrewd orator must avoid all the figures that I described above, such as clauses of equal length, with similar endings, or identical cadences, and the studied charm produced by the change of a letter, lest the elaborate symmetry and a certain grasping after a pleasant effect be too obvious. Likewise if repetition of words requires some emphasis and a raising of the voice, it will be foreign to the plain style of oratory. Other figures of speech he will be able to use freely, provided only he breaks up and divides the periodic structure and uses the commonest words and the mildest of metaphors. (84–85)

But many of these figures of thought will be appropriate to this plain style, although he will use them somewhat harshly. (86)

A speech of this kind should also be sprinkled with the salt of pleasantry, which plays a rare great part in speaking. There are two kinds, humor (*facetiarum*) and wit (*dicacitatis*). He will use both; the former in a graceful and charming narrative, the latter in hurling the shafts of ridicule. (87)[9]

Because the term "Attic" gradually became a synonym for writing well and lost its descriptive efficacy, it will be helpful to return to the differentiating details which Cicero gives here whenever the plain style in the classical sense is to be distinguished.[10]

Of the four genres that employed the plain style, comedy, satire, and epigram were concerned with revealing the actions of others, and the epistle was chiefly concerned with self-examination. In their discussions of the epistle, Demetrius and Seneca describe some of the most important characteristics of the plain style. The *sermo*, which was developed for the Socratic purpose of self-knowledge, would naturally adapt itself to letter writing, since it would permit the writer to speak of himself candidly and to reveal the very process of his thought.

Demetrius' statements about both the plain and epistolary styles may be taken, together with Cicero's account of the Attic orator, as the norm for the plain style in classical prose. Demetrius first describes the plain style as having a subject matter "homely and appropriate to the style itself":

> The diction throughout should be current and familiar. The more familiar an expression is the homelier it is, while the unusual and metaphorical is elevated.
>
> Compound words should not be admitted (since they are appropriate to the opposite variety of style), nor yet newly-coined words, nor any other words which contribute to elevation. Above all, the style should be lucid. (*On Style*, 190–91)

Lucidity is achieved by avoiding extreme disjunction within a period, ambiguity, excessive terseness, which "may give pleasure but . . . fails in clearness," amplification, long members or clauses, and peculiar figures, "since all eccentricity is unfamiliar and extraordinary"; the natural order of words should be followed. Vivid description is achieved by clarity and precision, no matter how small the subject, while persuasiveness "depends on two things, lucidity and naturalness. In other words, what is not lucid nor natural is not convincing. Accordingly exuberant and inflated language must not be sought after in a style meant to carry conviction. The composition, likewise, in such a style, must be steady-going and void of formal rhythm" (221).

Then, Demetrius continues:

> We will next treat of the epistolary style, since it too should be plain. Artemon, the editor of Aristotle's *Letters*, says that a letter ought to be written in the same manner as a dialogue, a letter being regarded by him as one of the two sides of a dialogue.
>
> There is perhaps some truth in what he says, but not the whole truth. The letter should be a little more studied than the dialogue, since the latter reproduces an extemporary utterance, while the former is committed to writing and is (in a way) sent as a gift. (*On Style*, 223–24)

Demetrius had said earlier that "the period of dialogue is one which remains lax, and is simpler than that of narrative" (21). The letter, he goes on, "like the dialogue, should abound in glimpses of character":

> It may be said that everybody reveals his own soul in his letters. In every other form of composition it is possible to discern the writer's character, but in none so clearly as in the epistolary. (*On Style*, 227)

It is clear, when this passage is compared with that addressed to Cornutus in Persius' fifth satire, quoted below, that the attitudes behind satire and epistle are the same, both in theory, as stated in the satire and in this treatise, and in practice, as in Horace's *sermones* and *epistulae*. They are simply those of the plain style. Martial states them in his line *certior in nostris carmine vultus erit* (VII.84), and Seneca makes them the central principles of his own epistolary theory. Just as comedy, satire, and epigram describe what actually happens, so, Demetrius continues, the epistle should informally speak the truth:

> There should be a certain degree of freedom in the structure of a letter. It is absurd to build up periods, as if you were writing not a letter but a speech for the law courts. And such laboured letter-writing is not merely absurd; it does not even obey the laws of friendship, which demand that we should "call a spade a spade," as the proverb has it. (*On Style*, 229)

The letter should not be so long that it becomes a treatise "with the heading 'My dear So-and-So,'" nor should it be a dissertation on a complicated subject, for "a letter is designed to be the heart's good wishes in brief; it is the exposition of a simple subject in simple terms" (231). Its ornament must be kindly advice and a few proverbs, "but the man who utters sententious maxims and exhortations seems to be no longer talking familiarly in a letter but to be speaking *ex cathedra*" (232). In letters to royal personages, the tone may be slightly heightened, but not to the extent that it breaks the prohibitions listed above.

Demetrius' treatise also contains a good many shrewd observations on style in general. For example, he points out that "humour is spoiled by verbal adornment" (165), suggesting how urbane wit becomes one of the most vital qualities of the plain style. He shows how bombast is really a form of dishonesty by pointing out, first, that "frigidity" is the distortion, or corresponding fault, of the elevated style and "is defined by Theophrastus as that which overshoots the expression appropriate to the thought" (114), and hence "the most frigid of all figures is hyperbole . . . [because] it suggests something impossible" (124–25). Then he concludes:

> There is a sort of general analogy between imposture and frigidity. The impostor boasts, facts notwithstanding, that qualities belong to him which do not. In like manner, also, the writer who invests trifles with pomp resembles one who gives himself airs about trifles. (*On Style*, 119)

Still more interesting is his statement of the relationship between passion and simplicity, a relationship seldom stated and usually not perceived:

> The similarity in the members, and the antithesis between them, impairs the vigour of the expression through a trick of art. For anger needs no art; in such invectives the wording should be simple, and, in a manner, impromptu.
> Such devices, as I have shown, do not contribute to force of style. They are not appropriate to outbursts of passion, or to delineations of character. For simplicity and naturalness is the mark alike of passion and of character-drawing. (*On Style*, 27–28)

Seneca, too, however, despite his modifications of the plain style and the idiosyncrasies of his imitators in antiquity and the Renaissance, drew upon stylistic attitudes derived from the same philosophical origins as Attic oratory. His objective was the Socratic analysis of moral experience, and his method depended on the informal intimacy of the epistle to explore and reveal the intricacies of character. He says to his correspondent, Lucilius, that letters reveal the true self and bring far truer images of our absent friends than pictures (*Ep.* XL), and he goes on in the rest of the letter to describe the language proper to philosophical discourse. His recommendations may be summed up by his Socratic proposition, "speech that deals with the truth should be unadorned and plain" (*Ep.* XL).[11] The epistolary style as a method of self-analysis and self-revelation is most clearly stated in Epistle LXXV:

> Now who talks carefully unless he also desires to talk affectedly? I prefer that my letter should be just what my conversation would be

if you and I were sitting in one another's company or taking walks
together,—spontaneous and easy; for my letters have nothing strained
or artificial about them. If it were possible, I should prefer to show,
rather than speak, my feelings. . . . I should like to convince you entirely of this one fact,—that I feel whatever I say, that I not only feel
it, but am wedded to it.

Conversation on important matters, however, he continues, should not be
"meagre and dry (*ieiuna et arida*)," but should have a kind of urbanity,
though not for this should we "bestow very much attention on mere words":

Let us say what we feel, and feel what we say; let speech harmonize
with life (*concordet sermo cum vita*). That man has fulfilled his promise who is that same person both when you see him and when you hear
him. We shall not fail to see what sort of man he is and how large a
man he is, if only he is one and the same. Our words should aim not
to please (*delectent*), but to help (*prosint*). . . . It [eloquence] and
the other arts are wholly concerned with cleverness; but our business
here is the soul. (*Ep.* LXXV. 1–6)

Conversation is valuable, Seneca says in another letter, "because it creeps
by degrees into the soul" (*Ep.* XXXVIII. 1); the statement is surprisingly
close to that of Morris Croll in his description of the *sermo,* whose idiom
"is that of conversation . . . that it may flow into and fill up all the nooks
and crannies of reality." Seneca praises Lucilius for his control of language,
for not seeking the "alluring phrase" and being carried beyond his subject,
and for choosing always the briefest and most appropriate phrasing:

You say all that you wish, and you mean still more than you say. This
is a proof of the importance of your subject matter, showing that your
mind, as well as your words, contains nothing superfluous or bombastic
(*nihil habere supervacui, nihil tumidi*).

He praises Lucilius for his metaphors and similes and points out that the
ancient writers, "whose eloquence was simple and directed only toward
proving their case," and hence were concerned with dialectic or argument,
used comparisons freely in order "to bring both speaker and listener face to
face with the subject under discussion." (*Ep.* LIX. 4–7)

FORMS OF ATTICISM: VERSE

The main Latin writers of comedy, satire, and epigram shared in their
verse the intentions of the Attic prose style and its epistolary extensions in
the reaction to Asiatic floridness. These genres aimed to reveal with the

greatest possible candidness and accuracy what men actually do, so that when they saw themselves objectively reflected, as if in a mirror, they would be inclined to reform.[12] Comedy tried, as well, to reproduce their daily conversation. In the prologue to *Heautontimorumenos*, Terence says *in hac est pura oratio*, and he becomes for future generations the standard of Latin purity and simplicity.[13] The plain style was adopted for satire by Horace from the style of comedy. M. A. Grant and G. C. Fiske write, "The *sermo* . . . aims at relaxing emotional tension—at least the *sermo apta ad docendum et delectandum*, such as a Platonic dialogue or an Horatian satire—by an exhibition of character, whether in the orator himself, in the personages he depicts, especially in his *narratio*, or in the characters produced by poets on the comic stage."[14] The stylistic relationship between the two genres is clearly stated by Horace himself. His position is important because he extends the terms of the Attic position from prose to verse.[15]

Horace regarded Lucilius, the first Roman satirist, as his master in the type of subject matter, the attitudes toward it, and the general type of style, though he objects to his frequent roughness, obscurity, and carelessness. In the fourth satire of the first book, he describes Lucilius' dependence upon Eupolis, Cratinus, and Aristophanes, the "true poets" of the Old Comedy, who, "if there was anyone deserving to be drawn as a rogue and thief, as a rake or cut-throat, or as scandalous in any other way, set their mark upon him with great freedom."[16] To social criticism and the free expression of opinion, which were characteristic of comedy, Lucilian satire added the epistolary discipline of candid self-revelation. In a satiric dialogue with his friend Trebatius, Horace takes Lucilius as his model and praises him for entrusting "his secrets to his books, as if to faithful friends . . . so it comes that the old poet's whole life is open to view, as if printed on a votive tablet" (*Serm.* II.i.30–34). To express these attitudes toward his subject matter Horace adopted the *genus humile*, and he describes it as closely related to the plain style of comedy. First, it is not a "poetic" style in the conventional sense; neither he nor the writer of comedy should be considered poets, since they write "lines more akin to prose (*sermoni propiora*)," lines which, if it were not for "their regular beat and rhythm," would be "mere prose (*sermo merus*)." Second, he will treat abuses and situations similar to those found in comedy, such as the father raging at a drunken, spendthrift son who refuses a wife with a large dower, and will treat them in a style similar to that of comedy, whose lines, if you broke them up, would be identical in their conversational idiom to, say, a father's in actual life (*Serm.* I.iv.39–62).

The exact representation of life demands a knowledge of men and their activities, and the *Ars Poetica* re-emphasizes concern for the expression of truth stripped of cant, and for a style stripped of ornament for its own sake:

> Of good writing the source and fount is wisdom (*Scribendi recte sapere est et principium et fons*). Your matter the Socratic pages can set forth, and when matter is in hand words will not be loath to follow. He who has learned what he owes his country and his friends, what love is due a parent, a brother, and a guest, what is imposed on senator and judge, what is the function of a general sent to war, he surely knows how to give each character his fitting part. I would advise one who has learned the imitative art to look to life and manners for a model, and draw from thence living words. At times a play marked by attractive passages and characters fitly sketched, though lacking in charm, though without force and art, gives people more delight and holds them better than verses void of thought, and sonorous trifles. (*Ars Poetica* 309–22)

Again in his epistle to Florus (*Ep.* II.ii.141–44) he advises the poet "to master the rhythms and measures of a genuine life (*verae numerosque modosque ediscere vitae*)." These attitudes toward style and subject matter recur constantly in connection with the epigram, the satire, and the epistle, which Horace seemed to regard as stylistically the same as the *sermones*, for he appears to have included them under *sermones* in listing his works (*Ep.* II.ii.58–60). In any case, the sixteenth century regarded them as a single genre. Horace, in renouncing the title of "poet," is simply rejecting certain poetic conventions, especially those associated with the high and middle style, which Persius, Martial, and Juvenal, were to do after him. He was certainly completely aware of his own abilities and knew that in his own style he was unsurpassed, quietly asserting, as Cicero had commented on the style of the "Attic" orator, "My aim shall be poetry, so moulded from the familiar that anybody may hope for the same success, may sweat much and yet toil in vain when attempting the same: such is the power of order and connection, such the beauty that may crown the commonplace" (*Ars Poetica* 240–43).[17]

It is Persius who states the attitudes behind the literary revolt of the satirists most explicitly. Although he rhetorically heightens his style more than Horace, he too is not a poet in the conventional sense and leaves the solicitation of the muses "to the gentlemen round whose busts the clinging ivy twines" (*Prol.* 5–6).[18] The first satire opens with the recognition of the satirist's unlimited subject matter, *O curas hominum, o quantum est in rebus inane*, and Persius goes on, in the form of a dialogue with a friend, to criticize the fashionably bombastic poet and the love poet who "lisps out with a snuffle some insipid trash about a Phyllis or a Hypsipyle or some other dolorous poetic theme, mincing his words, and letting them trip daintily over his palate" (I.33–35). His friend answers that this is what the audience wants and that at least "we have verses flowing smoothly along, so that the critical nail glides unjarred over the joinings"; indeed, "whatever be his [the poet's] theme: whether it be the morals and luxury of the times, or the banquets of the great, the Muse furnishes him with the lofty style" (I.63–68) and the epithets and rhythmical units of epic verse. Persius responds that such rhetorical echoes of Virgil simply cover up fatuity, *arma virum! nonne hoc spumosum et cortice pingui* (I.96), and that he prefers, when asked for the truth, to say nothing rather than to "paint everything white." Better, he says, that "Lucilius flayed our city" and "Horace, sly dog, worming his way playfully into the vitals of his laughing friend, touches up his every fault" (I.110, 114–17).

Persius' most important statement for our purpose is in the first thirty lines of Satire V, in which he sums up the attitudes expressed by Horace and Juvenal: the exact representation in everyday language of what men actually do and the utterly candid representation of the author's thoughts and feelings. The satire is epistolary, addressed to Cornutus, and its stylistic prescriptions are identical to those concerning the epistle as given by Seneca and Demetrius. It is the custom, Persius says, for poets to want the grandiloquence of a hundred voices, no matter what the theme, in order to declaim such "big lumps of solid poetry." Let those "who meditate lofty themes gather vapours on Mount Helicon, if there be any who propose to set a-boiling the pot of Procne or of Thyestes." But you, Cornutus, are not one of these who croak out solemn nonsense or swell out your cheeks with rhetoric. Your language, on the contrary, "is that of everyday life (*verba togae*); skilled in clever phrasing (*iunctura callidus acri*), rounded but not full-mouthed, you know well how to chide vicious ways." And it is in this way that you and I may talk, telling each other the truth about what we feel, for, indeed,

> it is no aim of mine that my page should swell with pretentious trifles, fit only to give solidity to smoke. To yourself alone, Cornutus, do I speak; I now shake out my heart to you at the bidding of the Muse; it is a joy to me to show you, beloved friend, how large a portion of my soul is yours. Strike it and note carefully what part of it rings true, what is but paint and plaster of the tongue (*pictae tectoria linguae*). It is for this that I would ask for a hundred voices: that I may with clear voice proclaim how deeply I have planted you in the recesses of my heart, and that my words may render up all the love that lies deep and unutterable in my inmost soul. (*Sat.*V.19–29)

Here, and in the statements of the other satirists, the connections between the intention of satire, reflecting certain attitudes toward experience, and the plain style, developed centuries before for the expression of these attitudes, are clearly drawn. As the syllogism, in Bacon's phrase, is no match for the subtlety of natural phenomena, so the rhetorical schemes and tropes which make up the grandiloquence of the high style and the mellifluence of the middle, are not flexible enough to reproduce the variety of individual experience. Their inflexibility in denotative representation impairs most severely the connotative precision in the definition of feeling. A rhetorical scheme or phrase, especially one that has become a conventional figure in the treatment of a particular subject, carries with it a commitment to past connotation, which will become a burden in the definition of a new feeling or insight. The corrosion of past associations, which are immediately evoked when the figure is used, must be stripped away by separating the words and returning them, as if to a solvent, to their original referents. Then they can be recombined to take hold of a new experience and will have regained their original, unspecialized flexibility, which is necessary to explain such an experience. Just as Socrates could not conduct the new ethical investigations into the nature of goodness in the terms of sophistic rhetoric, the satirists could not describe human action by rhetorical schemes of poetic convention: both claimed the total range of human feeling and thought for their subject, and both employed the plain style to examine it.

Influenced perhaps by his early training in the schools of declamation, Juvenal developed a far more elevated style than Horace. As such, it does not really belong in a discussion of the plain style except that, like the "forcible style" described by Demetrius and "austere composition" by Dionysius of Halicarnassus, both discussed in the following section, it combines certain characteristics of the *genus humile* and the *genus grande*. In a sense, Juvenal may be said to carry out in satire certain extensions of Atticism that are parallel to the deviations from Attic prose among his contemporaries. His attitudes toward experience, however, remain the same as Horace's, and it is to him that we owe the most explicit assertion of the writer's freedom to treat all subject matter:

> quidquid agunt homines, votum timor ira voluptas
> gaudia discursus, nostri farrago libelli est.
>
> (I.85–86)

This demand for an unlimited range of subject matter, and the Socratic intention to analyze and relate it to actual human experience in the hope

that men may better understand themselves and, hence, each other, make
the satirist impatient with the rhetorical fulfillment of conventional poetic
schemes. A conventional poetic subject, such as the narration of a myth,
by its very nature limits its material to what men do not do, and the
satirist would say with Socrates that, "It appears to me to be ridiculous,
while I am still ignorant of this [self-knowledge], to busy myself about
matters that do not concern me" (*Phaedrus* 229E).[19] It is with this attitude
that Juvenal objects so strongly in his first satire to the "after dinner"
poetic recitations. Why should he be made to listen to "the Theseid of the
ranting Cordus" or to spend "the whole day with an interminable Telephus,
or with an Orestes, which, after filling the margin at the top of the roll and
back as well, hasn't even yet come to an end"? No one, he continues,

> knows his own house so well as I know the groves of Mars, and the
> cave of Vulcan near the cliffs of Aeolus. What the winds are brewing;
> whose souls Aeacus has on the rack; from what country another
> worthy is carrying off that stolen golden fleece; how big are the ash
> trees which Monychus tosses about: these are the themes with which
> Fronto's plane trees and marble halls are for ever ringing until the
> pillars quiver and quake under the continual recitations; such is the
> kind of stuff you may look for from every poet, greatest or least. (*Sat.*
> I.1-14)

Choosing, like Horace, to follow Lucilius (I.20), to attack the corruption
of the time with "that freedom (*simplicitas*) of our forefathers to write
whatever the burning soul desired," and to say with him " 'What man is
there that I dare not name?' " (I.151-53), Juvenal asks ironically, "Should
I do better to tell tales about Hercules, or Diomede, or the bellowing in
the Labyrinth, or about the flying carpenter and the lad who splashed into
the sea," than to follow in Horace's steps and write about what men actually
do (I.51-54)? You can write about such subjects without giving offense,
to be sure, but it is better, with Lucilius, to make the guilty ashamed enough
to reform (I.162-67).

Martial continues the tradition of the Horatian *sermo* in his re-emphasis
of the stylistic attitudes of the satirists and seeks the syntactical flexibility
and idiomatic purity of the epigrams of Catullus. In his first introduction
to his epigrams he defends the candidness of his language as being proper
to the genre (*lascivam verborum veritatem, id est epigrammaton linguam,
excusarem*) and advises anyone who cannot hear the truth spoken urbanely
and directly in good Latin (*si quis tamen tam ambitiose tristis est ut apud
illum in nulla pagina Latine loqui fas sit*) to read no farther. Later, in an

epigram (XI.xx), he says that Augustus had justified the frankness of his poems by his own Roman candor (*Romana simplicitate*). In both cases, Martial is defending himself against possible charges of indecency, but the attitudes behind the defense are more far-reaching; like the satirists, he is claiming for poetic subject matter anything men do, think, or feel, and the right to treat that subject matter as directly as possible. His intention, like theirs, is to correct vices. As the hearer of Lucilius' criticisms "grows red . . . [and] sweats with secret consciousness of sin" (Juvenal *Sat.* I.167), so Martial describes the reader of his book: "See, yonder fellow turns red, turns pale, is dazed, yawns, curses! This is what I want; now my verses please me!" (VI.60).[20] And, most of all, Martial follows the satirists in rejecting lofty mythological themes and the grandiloquent style in which they were written. Thalia, the muse of epigram, asks him:

> Wish you to adapt your comic shoe to the tragic buskin, or in even-footed measures [hexameters] to thunder of rough wars, that a pompous pedagogue may dictate you in hoarse tones, and tall girl and honest boy hate you? Let those themes be written by men grave overmuch, and overmuch austere, whom at midnight their lamp marks at their wretched toil. But do you dip your little Roman books in sprightly wit (*lepido sale*); let Life recognize and read of her own manners (*adgno-scat mores vita legatque suos*). (VIII.iii.13–20)

He restates his position even more explicitly in the tenth book:

> You, who read of Oedipus and Thyestes neath a darkened sun, of Colchian witches and Scyllas—of what do you read but monsters? What will the rape of Hylas avail you, . . . what the sleeper Endymion? or the boy stript of his gliding wings? or Hermaphroditus who hates the amorous waters? Why does the vain twaddle of a wretched sheet attract you? Read this of which Life can say: ' 'tis my own,' (*hoc lege, quod possit dicere vita 'Meum est'*). Not here will you find Centaurs, not Gorgons and Harpies: 'tis of man my page smacks (*hominem pagina nostra sapit*). But you do not wish, Mamurra, to recognize your own manners, or to know yourself (*sed non vis, Mamurra, tuos cognoscere mores/nec te scire*). Read the *Origins* of Callimachus. (X.4)

This epigram could serve as a manifesto for the plain style; Jonson could have taken it as an epigraph for his works rather than just for *Sejanus*.

Developed by Socrates as a method of achieving self-knowledge, the style is to treat life truthfully, with the intention of making a man see himself as he really is. One who writes about mythological subject matter, such as "the meal of savage Tereus, or of . . . dyspeptic Thyestes, or of Daedalus fitting to his son melting wings, or of Polyphemus pasturing

Sicilian sheep" (IV.49),[21] matter unrelated to immediate human problems, is more frivolous than the writer of the lightest epigrams. Martial's language, by virtue of its precision, will bring the least pretentious subjects to life, because it states the truth about them:

> You prove to me, Gaurus, that my genius is in this way a puny one, because I make poems that please by their brevity. I confess it. But you, who in twice six books write of Priam's wars in grand style (*grandia*), are you a great man? I make Brutus' boy,[22] I make Langon live: you, great man as you are, Gaurus, make a giant of clay. (IX.50)

Despite brevity, his epigrams will not be obscure, nor will they require an interpreter, a need which was also discouraged by the treatises on letter writing. "Let my poems," he comments, "please commentators—so as to do without commentators" (X.21).[23] The insistence upon lucidity as well as brevity in the accurate representation of real actions and things is characteristic of the original intention of the plain style, a principle not always observed by the later Senecan stylists.

As in the other genres employing the plain style, the epigram will reveal accurately the character and personality of the writer. Martial, addressing some of his poems that he is about to send to Rome from Spain, asks, "Why do you require a title? Let two or three verses be read: all will cry that you, O book, are mine" (XII.3.17–18). The intention stated in the following poem is very similar to that of self-revelation advocated by Seneca and the treatises on letter writing:

> While my likeness is taking form for Caecilius Secundus, and the canvas breathes, painted by a cunning hand, go, book, to Getic Peuce and prostrate Hister—these regions with their conquered peoples he rules. Small, but welcome, shall be the gift you will make to my dear comrade: more truly in my song will my face be seen (*certior in nostro carmine vultus erit*); this my song, which no chances, no lapse of years, can efface, shall live when the work of Apelles shall perish. (VII.84)

The book, or poem, is sent as a gift in which the mind of the author himself is more clearly revealed than in a portrait; Demetrius says a letter is "utterance . . . committed to writing and . . . (in a way) sent as a gift" (*On Style*, 224). Martial himself makes the connection between the epigram and the letter in the introductory epistle to his second book of epigrams in which he addresses his friend: " 'What have I to do,' you say, 'with a letter? Why, am I not bountiful enough if I read epigrams? What further are you going to say here that you cannot say in verse? I see why tragedy and comedy admit of a prefatory epistle, for they cannot speak for themselves.

Epigrams need no crier, but are content with their own tongue: in what-ever page they choose they constitute an epistle.' "[24]

JONSON AND THE FIRST-CENTURY CRITICS

These classical theorists and poets describe forms which the Attic style took and the attitudes toward experience which were developed in order to express that style in prose and verse. These attitudes, however, did not necessarily ensure the Attic qualities of style, and during the first century A.D. one characteristic or another was often heightened and repeated until it became a mannerism more easily associated with Asianism.[25] Such deviations from the plain style, which were criticized by the two Senecas, Quintilian, Tacitus, and Martial in Latin, and by Demetrius and Dionysius of Halicarnassus in Greek, may be partly accounted for by the motivations behind its original emergence. It was not merely the subordination of expression to its subject matter that Seneca, following Socrates, was advocating, but subordination to a particular kind of subject matter. Morris Croll says that the objective of the Stoics, who adapted the Attic style to their own purposes at an early date, was a kind of truth that was moral and inward, invisible to the eye, "hidden in a shrine toward which one might win his way, through a jostling, noisy mob of illusory appearances, by a series of partial initiations." Though they aimed at a passionless objectivity and professed to strive for clearness, they achieved "a highly imaginative portrayal of their relations with truth," often subverting their primary devotion to perspicuity by their brevity and contortions of style. They attempted to render their "encounter with reality as exactly, as vividly, as possible," and reality does not declare itself "in the same unmistakable uniform terms to all inquiring minds."

The secrets of nature are made known only to attentive and collected minds, prepared by a long preliminary training in the habits of exclusion and rejection; and even to them but partially, and in moments of rare and peculiar illumination. A style appropriate to the mind of the speaker, therefore, is one that portrays the process of acquiring the truth rather than the secure possession of it, and expresses ideas not only with clearness and brevity, but also with the ardor in which they were first conceived. It is no more a bare, unadorned, unimaginative style than the oratorical style is; it aims, just as oratory does, to move and please, as well as to teach, but is distinguished from oratory by the fact that it owes its persuasive power to a vivid and acute portrayal of individual experience rather than to the histrionic and sensuous expression of general ideas.[26]

Croll's description applies not only to Seneca's epistles but also to Persius' address to Cornutus in his fifth satire, and, so far as general aims are concerned, to the Socratic investigation of moral experience. Certain characteristics of Cicero's Attic orator, however, are emphasized at the expense of others for the reasons Croll gives. If one aims at psychological truth, one will describe a mental process peculiar to the individual writer; if the style is accurate, it will record the idiosyncrasies peculiar to his personality. Stylistic mannerisms of all kinds are given apparent license, and whereas Seneca stated truths about experience in a clear and compressed style which continued to be verifiable, his imitators exploited his sententious brevity for the sake of ornament.

Certain deviations in Latin from the "Attic" norm emerged rapidly during the first century A.D., and their historical development, therefore, could be traced by writers such as Quintilian living near the end of it. An Englishman in 1625, looking back over the previous seventy-five years of stylistic change, might share Quintilian's historical perspective or, at least, find in it certain similarities to his own. A sense of history comparable to that in the *Institutio Oratoria* or in the *Dialogus* of Tacitus and an explicit concern with the authority of ancients and of moderns as models would not be likely to occur in England much before the early seventeenth century. To be sure, archaisms, neologisms, and inkhorn terms had been debated from the beginning, but these early debates were concerned with building a modern English language, not with selecting from already established English styles the best to be imitated. It is this sense of history, and therefore of choice, that Jonson transfers to an English context in his adaptation of the Quintilian passage with which this chapter began and to which we return at this point.

Corresponding to the ancient Cato and the Gracchi are Chaucer and Gower, whose diction Spenser was ill-advised to imitate. By the "modern euphuists" (*recentis huius lasciviae*), who are particularly attractive to the young, Quintilian means the decadent orators and the preciously ornate imitators of Seneca among others,[27] who cultivated the epigrammatic conceit as well as those who Tacitus says affected the sensuous rhythms of theatrical dancing with *lascivia verborum et levitate sententiarum et licentia compositionis* (*Dial.* 26). To these correspond the Elizabethan Euphuists and those Senecans who continued to exploit the *sententia,* parallel syntactical structure, and balanced antithetical comparisons. That Jonson included both Euphuistic and Senecan mannerisms in his "new flowers, and sweetnesse" is implied slightly later in the *Discoveries.* Translating Quintilian again, he answers the original question about diction by saying "the eldest of the present, and newest of the past Language is the best." Then he restates the same problem by criticizing Lucretius for being "scabrous and rough" in diction in the same way that English writers are who affect Chaucerisms. He continues:

> Some words are to be cull'd out for ornament and colour, as wee gather flowers to straw houses, or make Garlands; but they are better when they grow to our style; as in a Meadow, where though the meere grasse and greennesse delights, yet the variety of flowers doth heighten and beautifie. Marry, we must not play, or riot too much with them, as in *Paranomasies*: Nor use too swelling, or ill-sounding words; *Quæ per salebras, altaq saxa cadunt.* (VIII, 622-23)

John Hoskyns's *Direccõns for Speech and Style,* which Jonson uses so extensively, discusses *paranomasia* as a favorite figure of Lyly, and indeed it becomes the most marked "flower" of the Euphuistic style. The "flower" right next to it, however, is clearly of the Senecan variety; the line cited from Martial, which I shall discuss in the following chapter, is used several times in the *Discoveries* to correct a disregard for composition and the choice of words.[28]

The first passage, then, which I have compared with its original, takes on historical depth in which one can perceive Sidney in some relation to Donne. The ways in which Livy and Sallust were regarded as models in the first century A.D. and in the Renaissance will clarify the reasons why Sallust and Donne are considered harder to understand, and these reasons are relatable to the controversies over imitation and to the rising Senecanism in both the earlier and the later periods.

The second passage in the *Discoveries* that I wish to discuss in relation to the original source occurs in a list of types of degenerate style of Jonson's own day (VIII, 584-88). Jonson adopts a passage in Seneca as a criticism both of broken composition, for which Seneca suggests Sallust as a precedent, and the easy fluency of the sonneteers, whose stylistic precedent in prose is Cicero:

> *Others,* that in composition are nothing, but what is rough, and broken: *Quæ per salebras, altaq saxa cadunt.* And if it would come gently, they trouble it of purpose. They would not have it run without rubs, as if that stile were more strong and manly, that stroke the eare with a kind of uneven[n]esse. These men erre not by chance, but knowingly, and willingly; . . . And this vice, one that is in authority with the rest, loving, delivers over to them to bee imitated: so that oft-times the faults

which he fell into, the others seeke for: This is the danger, when vice becomes a *Precedent.*

Others there are, that have no composition at all; but a kind of tune-ing, and riming fall, in what they write. It runs and slides, and onely makes a sound. Womens-*Poets* they are called: as you have womens-*Taylors.*

> *They write a verse, as smooth, as soft, as creame;*
> *In which there is no torrent, nor scarce streame.*

You may sound these wits, and find the depth of them with your middle finger. They are *Cream-bowle,* or but puddle deepe. (VIII, 585)

Jonson has added the line from Martial (XI.90) to reinforce Seneca's word *salebra* in the following passage from his epistle:

> Some are all for abruptness and unevenness of style, purposely disar-ranging anything which seems to have a smooth flow of language. They would have jolts in all their transitions (*Nolunt sine salebra esse iunctu-ram*); they regard as strong and manly whatever makes an uneven im-pression on the ear. With some others it is not so much an "arrange-ment" (*compositio*) of words as it is a setting to music; so wheedling and soft is their gliding style. . . . Or again of that softly-concluding style, Cicero-fashion, with gradual and gently poised descent, always the same and always with the customary arrangement of the rhythm! Nor is the fault only in the style of the sentences, if they are either petty and childish, or debasing, with more daring than modesty should allow, or if they are flowery and cloying, or if they end in emptiness, accomp-lishing mere sound and nothing more.
>
> Some individual makes these vices fashionable—some person who controls the eloquence of the day; the rest follow his lead and communi-cate the habit to each other. Thus when Sallust was in his glory, phrases were lopped off, words came to a close unexpectedly, and obscure con-ciseness was equivalent to elegance. (*Ep.* CXIV.15–17)

Seneca goes on to criticize L. Arruntius for imitating the mannerisms of Sallust. Jonson's second passage, taken in conjunction with Donne's as-sociation with Sallust in the first, seems to confirm Swinburne's suggestion that Donne may be the "one that is in authority."[29] Jonson's association of Sidney with Livy is also further defined. His description of the poor Pe-trarchan poet combines two types mentioned in the Senecan passage: those who have no arrangement but a slack, gliding style and those who, like the imitators of Cicero, have a repetitious arrangement in their softly concluded periods. The danger in both cases is that the style will be empty, mere sound and nothing more: "It runs and slides, and onely makes a sound." The imitators of Cicero may be associated with the imitators of Livy, at least in so far as Cicero and Livy were associated as stylistic models, particularly in contrast to Caesar and Sallust.[30] This passage in the *Discoveries* may be interpreted as a criticism of the imitators of Sidney and Donne for the mannerisms of style which the imitators of Livy and Sallust were likely to be cautioned about.[31]

A further comparison of Sallust with Livy in Quintilian is relevant to Donne and Sidney. Quintilian comments that the narrative of history has certain affinities with poetry in their mutual inadaptability to forensic debate. In some ways, indeed, history may be considered a poem written in prose (*carmen solutum*), and to avoid monotony it may use more unusual words (*verbis remotioribus*) and freer figures (*liberioribus figuris*) than oratory:

> Therefore, as I have already said, the famous brevity of Sallust, than which nothing can be more pleasing to the leisured ear of the scholar, is a style to be avoided by the orator in view of the fact that his words are addressed to a judge who has his mind occupied by a number of thoughts and is also frequently uneducated, while, on the other hand, the milky fullness of Livy is hardly of a kind to instruct a listener who looks not for beauty of exposition, but for truth and credibility (*illa Livii lactea ubertas satis docebit eum, qui non speciem expositionis, sed fidem quaerit*). We must also remember that Cicero thinks that not even Thucydides or Xenophon will be of much service to an orator, although he regards the style of the former as a veritable call to arms and considers that the latter was the mouthpiece of the Muses. (X.i.31–33)

Cicero had described the philosophical *sermo* as *umbratilis* (*Orat.* 64), meant to be read not heard, complicated, academic; and with such a style Sallust is to be read by the erudite. Donne's audience, as well, had to be an educated one. He cultivated remote words from technical terminologies, and Jonson, along with Hoskyns, whom he is quoting, may well have this characteristic of their mutual friend in mind when he says, "The next property of *Epistolarie* style is *Perspicuity,* and is often-times indangered by the former quality (brevity), often-times by affectation of some wit ill angled for, or ostentation of some hidden termes of Art" (VIII, 631). Donne's freedom with figurative comparisons, also, became notorious and was eventually regarded as the distinguishing mannerism of his imitators. Quintilian of course, does not refer to the particular kinds of brevity, diction, and figures which Donne later practiced; he is simply distinguishing between a case argued in practical court life and something read, or listened to, at leisure by a select group of people.

Jonson makes the same point when he translates M. Seneca's distinction between the schools of declamation and the actual pleading of cases in the forum:

> For it is one thing to be *eloquent* in the *Schooles,* or in the *Hall;* another at the *Barre,* or in the *Pulpit.* There is a difference betweene *Mooting,* and *Pleading;* betweene *Fencing,* and *Fighting.* To make Arguments in my Study, and confute them, is easie; where I answer my selfe, not an Adversary. So, I can see whole *volumes* dispatch'd by the *umbraticall* Doctors on all sides: But draw these forth into the just lists; . . . they scarce can find themselves, they that were wont to domineere so among their Auditors: but indeed I would no more chuse a *Rhetorician,* for reigning in a *Schoole;* then I would a *Pilot,* for rowing in a Pond. (VIII, 576–77)

Declamation is associated with recitation in its greater license of figurative language and has been frequently cited as one of the causes of the literary mannerism of the Silver Age. Livy's milky fullness is useful to the orator, Sallustian brevity to the scholar, and it is the "umbraticall Doctors" whom Seneca and Jonson associate with the declaimers. We shall find Cheke telling Ascham that Sallust wrote his histories shut up in his study in a labored style owing more to art than to natural talent. These comments are illuminating when one considers that the characteristic for which Donne and the Metaphysical School were most criticized was their labored erudition which did not take hold of real situations.[32] The suggested association of them with the schools of declamation would be particularly interesting to pursue with particular attention to style and to their method of presentation. Donne's *Paradoxes and Problems* shows how he delighted "To make arguments . . . and confute them." Quite as suggestive as these similarities between Sallust and Donne is the similarity between the *lactea ubertas* of Livy and the Petrarchan verse, which Jonson describes as smooth as cream and slack in the way that Seneca describes the imitators of Cicero. Sallust was distinguished for his rapidity (X.i.102).

In the passage introducing that to which Quintilian refers in his remarks on the style ill-suited to the forum, Cicero objects to those who "think that the only one who attains the Attic norm is he who speaks in rough and unpolished style, provided only that he is precise and discriminating in thought." Among these are those who try to imitate Thucydides, whose style is totally unfit for the forum. No one, furthermore, "succeeds in imitating his dignity of thought and diction, but when they have spoken a few choppy, disconnected phrases, which they could have formed well enough without a teacher, each one thinks himself a regular Thucydides"

(*Orator* 28–32). Cicero may have had Sallust in mind. His style had clearly been modeled on that of Thucydides, and for this reason the descriptions of the latter's style are relevant to the comparison of Sallust with Donne. These descriptions, furthermore, are far more detailed than those of Sallust. Dionysius of Halicarnassus wrote a treatise on Thucydides, part of which he quotes in his second Epistle to Ammaeus, from which I cite the following details. In his choice of words Thucydides "often adopts a figurative, obscure, archaic and strange diction, in place of that which was in common use and familiar to the men of his day."[33] His various deviations from normal usage in a highly inflected language are described, as well as a parenthetical tortuousness in the working out of his enthymemes and sentences. He also employs "showy figures" such as *parisoses, paromoeoses, paronomasiae,* and *antitheses*:

> The most obvious of his characteristics is the attempt to indicate as many things as possible in as few words as possible, to combine many ideas in one, and to leave the listener expecting to hear something more. The consequence is that brevity becomes obscurity.[34]

In *On Literary Composition* Dionysius has a chapter called "Austere Composition," in which he quotes a passage from Thucydides and comments on how inappropriate the style would be for an oration. It is marked by a "sort of antique and self-willed beauty"; it is not smooth and polished, or "euphonious and soft, and does not glide imperceptibly through the ear, but shows many features that are discordant and rough and harsh." He remarks how Thucydides "roughens and dislocates" a clause "by sundering its joints" and cultivates "a great lack of symmetry in the clauses, great unevenness in the periods, much innovation in the figures, disregard of sequence, and all the other marks . . . of the unadorned and austere style."[35] Demetrius relates these characteristics to the line Jonson uses from Martial to criticize rough composition. He says Thucydides, instead of seeking smoothness and evenness of composition, "has rather the constant air of a man who is stumbling, like travellers on rough roads" (*On Style,* 48).[36]

These descriptions, then, of obscurity and its causes lie behind Jonson's citation of Sallust. The fact that he translated some of them and made their terms part of his critical vocabulary makes their application to Donne more valid. They help as well to establish Jonson's own idea of the proper style and to clarify the position of his major Renaissance authorities discussed in the next chapter.

Although there are considerably fewer explicit associations in style be-

tween Livy and Sidney, the *Arcadia* was recommended for many of the
same reasons as Livy's *Histories*. Quintilian comments that Livy "has a
wonderful charm and transparency in narrative, while his speeches are
eloquent beyond description; so admirably adapted is all that is said both to
the circumstances and the speaker; and as regards the emotions, especially
the more pleasing of them, I may sum him up by saying that no historian has
ever depicted them to greater perfection" (X.i.101). Despite Livy's tendency to treat legend as fact, his descriptions of heroic virtues and actions,
of famous persons and historical scenes were adapted by later historians to
enliven their narratives and to illustrate the moral significance of their
own detail.[37] It was precisely for these reasons that the *Arcadia* was celebrated. John Hoskyns, for instance, dividing his *Direccōns for Speech and
Style* into the three main headings of varying, amplifying, and illustrating,
exemplifies the general nature of the last of these by a discussion of the
Arcadia. "This," he says, "haue I written of illustracōn in conveyance &
well gayning of the substance of a treatise where evident & liuely discripcōns
are in *Arcadia*. Yoᵂ haue this noate des: where the pson is aptly fitted with
speech & accōn." What he praises the *Arcadia* for is its illustration, that is,
description, of types of men "in a figured storie" who exemplify different
virtues, passions, and humors in their words and actions. What words
and actions are appropriate to these different types, Hoskyns says, Sidney
learned from reading Aristotle and Theophrastus' *Characters*. The emotions are depicted by various "psonages & affeccons" throughout the narrative: "idle retirednes in kinge *Basillius*," "vnfortunate valloʳ in *Plangus*,"
"courteous valoʳ in Amphialus," "proud valloʳ in *Anaxius*," and so with
friendship, love, anger, fear, envy, and "sluttish simplicity in *Mopsa*." Besides these, general actions are "rarely discribed," such as "a mutinye & fire
in a shipp," "causes of an vprore," a "garboile" and "armed skirmish,"
"pollicie & preparacōn," which "genᵉʳally in all pticuler accōns is noted in
yoʳ booke." Horsemanship, tilting, and other accomplishments are represented, "& wise Sʳ *Phillip Sidney's* course was (besides reading *Arle*
[Aristotle] and *Theophrastus*) to imagine the thinge pnte [present] in
his owne brayne, that [h]is pen might the better pnte it to yoᵂ whose example I would yoᵂ durst followe till I pulld yoᵂ backe."[38]

It is difficult to arrive at Jonson's estimate of Sidney. Both the sonnet
and the prose pastoral romance were literary forms which not only had
passed out of fashion but which Jonson had rejected on strong convictions
about the kind of experience worth a writer's serious attention. Yet Sidney
remained for him and his contemporaries a symbol of the cultured English-

man, soldier, and man of letters. The humanistic defense of literature in his *An Apologie for Poetrie,* with its shrewd evaluation of the dangers which threatened his literary contemporaries, many of which Jonson found still applicable years later, served most to make Sidney represent the best ideals of the preceding generation. And it is in this historical sense that Jonson's comparison of him with Livy is suggestive. What Livy and Virgil represented to Tacitus and Quintilian, Sidney might well have represented to Jonson. The epic form with its legendary material had passed out of fashion by the second century, as Persius, Juvenal, Martial, and Petronius testify, and so had the long, leisurely historical celebration of nationalism, which, Martial comments slyly, did not quite fit into his library (XIV.cxc). Yet Livy and Virgil continued to represent the great age of Augustan civilization and literature, and in the same way Sidney continued to represent, for Jacobean England, the Elizabethan political, social, and literary accomplishment.[39]

Donne, on the other hand, represented to Jonson what the later writers of the first century A.D. represented to Quintilian. Many of these strove for the stylistic qualities of Sallust, and the best of them, such as Tacitus and Seneca, became models which replaced Cicero and Livy. The imitators of these models, however, both in antiquity and in the Renaissance, fell into mannerisms for which the imitators of Thucydides and Sallust had already been blamed. Sidney and Donne came to represent two stylistic traditions and, as models, offered dangers to their imitators which had been defined centuries ago. The reasons for the mature writer's passing from the tradition of Sidney to that of Donne may be described in much the same way as a modern historian, Sir Ronald Syme, describes the ancient historians to which Jonson compares them:

> Livy was endowed with style and honesty. The style was eloquent, ornate, and flowing, well suited to serve up anew the fairy stories about the Kings of Rome or renovate the edifying narrations that exploited heroes of the early Republic—and veracity was barely relevant there. But was the style tough and tense enough for an authentic record? Honesty was poor protection against the inaccuracy of other historians, whether ingenuous, romantic, or mendacious. Nor did candour, innocence, and ethical aspirations equip a man to unmask the guile of political managers and unravel the complexities of human nature. Modern or recent history required the maturity, the penetration, and the ferocity of Sallust.[40]

These differences of intention lay behind the stylistic controversies of the sixteenth century as they had behind those of the first.

THE CONTROVERSY IN THE RENAISSANCE

In the Renaissance Livy would be regarded as a Ciceronian model, Sallust as an early example of the Senecan stylistic virtues, and the extensive critical commentary of the Ciceronian-Senecan controversy is relevant to the investigation of what opinions a writer might have of the styles of the historians. But first it must be said that if Cicero's features and attitudes are reflected in Ciceronianism, they are barely recognizable, and the same thing may be said of Seneca in the anti-Ciceronian reaction. Originally a Ciceronian was simply an advocate of Cicero as the only model to be imitated in the development of a prose style; he was concerned more with the safest method of learning to write good Latin than with the achievement of this or that particular quality. In fact, the whole point of choosing Cicero as a model was that, since he was a master of all the different styles as they were described in the rhetorical treatises, his works would illustrate the best examples of all particular qualities of style. In theory, this position was perfectly sensible, but in practice it led to pedantry and formalism, which Erasmus burlesqued in his *Ciceronianus*.[41] In order to encourage a style that would be adaptable to the individual talent of the writer and to his particular subject matter, Erasmus advocated the imitation of a variety of models. One should imitate not Cicero, which would be mere copying, but the way Cicero himself imitated his own models, and, in insisting on the imitation of the way in which something was composed rather than of the actual composition itself, Erasmus returns to the position of Quintilian.

Gradually the term became associated with the more florid, or Asian, qualities of Cicero's style and became a label for those who seemed more concerned with words than with subject matter. Those who reacted most irresponsibly against the Ciceronians, on the other hand, often affected a disregard for the formal matters of expression and justified their stylistic idiosyncrasies on the basis of an idealistic allegiance to truth, which demanded a total concentration upon content. "Ciceronian" and "Senecan" as stylistic labels had as little to do with Cicero and Seneca as they did when they referred simply to the controversy over models, for Cicero continually stressed the complete command of the subject matter as the first prerequisite for a writer, and Seneca was constantly preoccupied with the corruptions of style and with himself as a stylist. Throughout the Renaissance the terms developed an autonomous history of their own which was, for the most part, unrelatable to antiquity. Their ambiguous reference to a

pedagogic method, to particular qualities of style, or simply to literary opponents makes them extremely difficult to use precisely to describe a particular writer. In 1580 Sidney refers explicitly to "Ciceronianisme the
cheife abuse of Oxford, *Qui dum verba sectantur, res ipsas negligunt.*"[42]
By restricting the term to a controversy, he removes it from a critical vocabulary based on the doctrine of imitation and makes it a label for the
neglect of content. Ciceronians, who are poor imitators of Cicero (since
they neglect content), may be comparable, however, to poor imitators of
Sidney, who fill their love poems and prose romances with ornamental
digressions instead of matter. Considered in this way, Jonson's association
of Sidney with Livy, and hence with Cicero, as models proper for young
students, may apply to a greater variety of stylistic matters than lucidity.
In applying comments that are referable to the Senecan controversy, it is
best to set aside the labels themselves, which Jonson does not use, and to
refer strictly to the qualities of syntax and diction that Jonson probably
thought distinguished Sidney from Donne. The terms that he borrowed
from the first century A.D. continue to be used in the sixteenth century.

The most detailed discussion of Sallust is that of John Cheke, which is
reported by Ascham. A wise and worthy writer, Sallust "requireth a
learned Reader, and a right considerer of him," and for this reason he "was
not verie fitte for yong men to learne out of him the puritie of the Latin
tong, because he was not the purest in proprietie of wordes, nor choisest in
aptnes of phrases, nor the best in framing of sentences; and therefore is
his writing, . . . neyther plaine for the matter, nor sensible for mens
vnderstanding." He does not express "matter liuely and naturally with
common speach," but "it is caried and driuen forth artificiallie, after to
learned a sorte, as *Thucydides* doth in his orations." Why, Ascham asks, is
it that "*Caesar* and *Ciceroes* talke is so naturall and plaine, and *Salust* writing so artificiall and darke, whan all they three liued in one tyme?"[43] Cheke
explains that Caesar and Cicero were orators and had to make themselves
clear to even the least educated. Sallust, on the other hand, wrote his
histories "shut vp in his studie," where he read Thucydides and Cato, who
was distinguished more for matter than for style. For this reason Sallust
"smelleth moch of the roughnes of his style." Sallust's "roughness and
darknesse" are not primarily the result of his use of old words or of his
coining new ones. What distinguishes him from Cicero are his "strange
phrases made of good Latin wordes but framed after the Greeke tonge"
and "a hard composition and crooked framing of his wordes and sentences,
as a man would say, English talke placed and framed outlandish like." As

a result, "in whole sentences, where the matter is good, the wordes proper and plaine, yet the sense is hard and darke, and namely in his prefaces and orations, wherein he vsed most labor, which fault is likewise in *Thucydides* in Greeke, of whom *Salust* hath taken the greates part of his darkenesse." Thucydides did not rely so much upon his natural talent as upon art and was "caried forth by desire, studie, labor, toyle, and ouer great curiositie." Cheke gives an example of Sallust's imitation, *Multis sibi quisque imperium petentibus*, and comments that "the best Grammarien in England can scarse giue a good reule why *quisque*, the nominatiue case, without any verbe, is so thrust vp amongst so many oblique cases."[44]

These comments are remarkably accurate summaries of the classical texts cited above and contain descriptive phrases that are directly applicable to Donne. Sir Thomas Elyot, along with Jonson's two most important Renaissance authorities on style, Luis Vives and Justus Lipsius, also maintained with Quintilian that Livy was for beginners and Sallust for the mature reader.[45] Donne himself criticized the *lactea ubertas* of Livy, and his verse, which so often seems a parody of Sidney, offers countless examples of difficult syntax comparable to the one Cheke cites from Sallust.[46]

The reappearance in the Renaissance of these comments on Livy and Sallust suggests how Sidney and Donne may be distinguished by the relation of the structure of their periods to their respective subject matter and to what they wish to say about it. They are both among the best writers to learn from, even though Donne is dangerous for the beginner, and their styles represent two different types of period, both of which Jonson thought might be successfully imitated. If one were to cultivate the rounded, periodic structure in which the members were causally and temporally connected and disposed toward rhythmical balance, Sidney should be his model.[47] If one sought the broken period, which avoided concinnity and parallel structure with similar endings, at the same time omitting temporal connectives to gain an elliptical, asyndectic brevity, he might imitate Donne. The unskilled imitator, however, was vulnerable to the same faults for which Livy and Cicero, on the one hand, and Thucydides, Sallust, and Seneca on the other, had been criticized. The florid ornament of Petrarchanism was associated with Ciceronianism, and the abruptness and exaggerated conceit of "strong lines" contributed to the obscurity of Senecanism.[48]

Although Jonson thought of both Sidney and Donne as good models, his own rhetorical position, his attitudes toward experience, and the subject matter he thought proper for a serious writer, as well as his own style in the vast majority of his poems, all indicate a preference for Donne, as

Quintilian had preferred Sallust to Livy. Jonson avoided the rounded period for the same reason that Sir Ronald Syme says Sallust rejected it.

> Sallust demonstrated, once and for all, that the periodic sentence will not do, either for narration or for picture. It has balance, subordination, amplitude, and a conclusion all too often inevitable; it is persuasive, hence smooth and deceptive. History aims at verisimilitude by stating facts, not in a hierarchy, but one by one, as they present themselves to the observer. The order in which they occur will have the variety and paradox of life itself.[49]

This description is applicable to the Socratic rejection of rhetorical methods of dealing with experience, to the Stoic adaptation of the Socratic stylistic ideal, and to the intention of Horace and Martial to describe accurately what they observed around them. The *sermo* with its informal flexibility served all these purposes; the Attic style became the most sensitive recorder of both psychological and external events. For Jonson, the most Attic writer in Latin was Tacitus, who, we shall see, he associates with Lysias and who, he told Drummond, is among those who "speke best Latine" (I, 136). Syme's comment is interesting: "Tacitus moves from eloquence to concentrated vigour—in brief, Livy to Sallust" in his stylistic development.[50]

A writer's subject matter is not objective reality, that which he assumes to be both antecedent to and independent of his perception of it, but his and other men's relation to that reality, their experience of it. To describe the experience, however, the reality must be perceived with accuracy, for to distinguish the nature and extent of qualification one must first know as much as is humanly possible about the nature of what is being qualified. In a written work, the reality, for the same reason, must be represented or recorded with a certain degree of accuracy if the writer's response to it is to be understood, since it is impossible to understand an evaluation without knowing what is being evaluated. The great variety of ways of perceiving reality and then recording it has complicated both the philosophical discipline of epistemology and the literary discipline of representation or *mimesis*. In the same way that the syllogism no longer could take a philosophical hold of objective reality for Bacon, the periodic structure of oratory could not record events accurately for Sallust and Tacitus. The Arcadian style of Sidney did not record the objectively real world in sufficient verisimilitude for Donne and Jonson.[51]

Each way of representing reality, however, must, in itself, be only an approximation because of the complexity of phenomena and the limitations of the human faculties. A distinct attitude derived from a series of experiences can influence the reconstruction of the events which we assume to lie permanently fixed behind the experiences. A proper representation would have the greatest allegiance to the true event for the historian, to its probable approximation in a "fiction" for the poet; the ideal style would have the greatest fidelity to the experience of the event in the process of its representation. The style would, at its best, continually adjust the emotional response to the event. This ideal lies behind the Socratic rejection of the rhetorical styles. The chief "Attic" stylistic intention is to subserve the closest approximation to the truth achievable in the representation of reality.

Although, like Sallust and, theoretically, like Donne, Jonson wanted a style to describe the real world, it was necessary for it to acquiesce to some extent in the ordered period of Sidney to ensure lucidity. Periodic structure, in an effort to elicit a particular attitude from the audience, assumes an ordered reality in which one event is subservient to another. It is persuasive, not descriptive; it holds the reader at some distance from the things themselves. To reject the periodic structure is in part to reject the assumption of order. A contempt for matters of elocution and disposition was even occasionally suspected of being a contempt for authority. In giving up a periodic structure, a writer, to a certain extent, is refusing to impose order upon his material, and, placing the reader down in the midst of the things themselves, holds him responsible for whatever order he can make out of them. Carried to an extreme, either intention is destructive; both sacrifice the matter to the words. In the former, matter is sacrificed to the rhetorical formulae which attempt to elicit predictable emotional responses. In the latter, the material, through the exclusion of order, is lost in fragmentary detail, which often encourages a preoccupation with figurative elaboration of the individual fragments. To veer too sharply toward either of these stylistic extremes is to distort the representation of reality and thereby to blur the experience of it.

In accord with their disbelief in the possibility of discovering or imposing order, skeptics have usually rejected the periodic style. Pascal relates the style and method of the *Pensées* to their tradition for reasons that are worth citing here:

> *Pyrrhonisme.*—J'écrirai ici mes pensées sans ordre, et non pas peut-être dans une confusion sans dessein: c'est le véritable ordre, et qui marquera toujours mon objet par le désordre même.
>
> Je ferais trop d'honneur à mon sujet si je le traitais avec ordre, puisque je veux montrer qu'il en est incapable.[52]

Order in expression is to be sacrificed to the more exact representation of a disordered world. It is to the skepticism behind this intention that Ascham, a hundred years earlier, objected in criticizing those "that care not for words, but for matter":

> For Stoics, Anabaptists, and friars, with epicures, libertines, and monks, being most like in learning and life, are no fonder and pernicious in their opinions, than they be rude and barbarous in their writings. They be not wise therefore, that say, 'What care I for man's words and utterance, if his matter and reasons be good? . . . Ye know not what hurt ye do to learning, that care not for words, but for matter; and so make a divorce betwixt the tongue and the heart.[53]

Ascham is not objecting to "matter" as such, but to matter that he considered subversive to the established church, and to those who were merely concerned with justifying their own positions by whatever arguments they could. By "libertines" he means "freethinkers."[54] Intellectually, he would be hostile to the Senecan movement, a movement arising out of a faith in the dialectical means of persuasion and dedicated to the cultivation, the analysis, the expression, and even to the dramatization of the individual mind and personality. It is interesting that his argument is based directly on Cicero's criticism of the Socratic dialectic for causing philosophical schisms.[55] In the next century John Earle describes "A selfe-conceited Man" as "an Heretique, and in these days made the first Arminian," who "prefers *Ramus* before *Aristotle,* and *Paracelsus* before *Galen,* and whosoever with most Paradox is commended." As in Ascham, intellectual nonconformity is accompanied by stylistic nonconformity, for this man prefers "*Lipsius* his hopping stile, before either *Tully* or *Quintilian*."[56] He, furthermore, "is now become to [*sic*] his own booke, which he poares on continually," which suggests Montaigne, who says in the preface to his *Essays,* "I am myself the subject of my book," the central maxim of Libertinism. Montaigne and Lipsius, however, broke up the periodic structure in two different ways in their effort to come into closer contact with the actual world, and both men were associated with Sallust.

Morris Croll describes the Senecan style as tending toward two extremes: the curt and the loose period.[57] The curt period was characterized mainly by a lack of connectives and order of progression and by a deliberate asymmetry of its members, each being a complete unit in itself. More purely Senecan than the loose period, it always tended toward aphorism.[58] Croll describes its lack of logical progression, its progress depending on a series of metaphors and paradoxes to restate the writer's apprehension with more and more vivid imaginative realization.[59] If the curt period strove to break the mental process and reduce it to the "points" of aphorism and *sententia,* the loose period attempted to reproduce with the least alteration the thought process itself. The effect upon the periodic structure would, of course, be the same. Croll describes Montaigne as always looking for the natural man, "the free individual self" who would be the final eclectic judge of all philosophical schools, and as attempting to develop the most flexible style possible for the expression of individual differences of character, a style whose naturalness was restricted as little as possible by the artificial limits of literary composition.[60]

> The loose period does not try for this form [the *circuitus* or *periodes* or "round composition" of traditional oratory], but rather seeks to avoid it. Its purpose is to express, as far as may be, the order in which an idea presents itself when it is first experienced. It begins, therefore, without premeditation, stating its idea in the first form that occurs; the second member is determined by the situation in which the mind finds itself after the first has been spoken; and so on throughout the period, each member being an emergency of the situation. The period—in theory, at least—is not made; it becomes. It completes itself and takes on form in the course of the motion of mind which it expresses. Montaigne, in short, exactly described the theory of the loose style when he said: "J'écris volontiers sans project; le premier trait produit le second."[61]

The natural extension of such a style is the freely associative stream-of-consciousness technique of James Joyce and the late work of Ezra Pound, for only here can the mental process, theoretically, be reproduced with the least interference from the conscious discipline of art. It is a paradox that the style developed by Seneca for philosophical self-analysis and a direct, and fundamentally dialectical, approach to truth should gradually exclude the rationally discursive coherence of dialectic in favor of a method of communication which would depend, in its ultimate form, on purely associative connotation.

Echoing the short preface to his essays, Montaigne insists again that "These are but my humors and opinions, and I deliver them but to show what my conceit is, and not what ought to be beleeved. Wherin I ayme at nothing but to display my selfe, who peradventure (if a new prentiship change me) shall be another tomorrow."[62] He is bound to no particular authorities nor is he responsible for the accuracy of what he writes; the man, he says, "that shall make search after knowledge, let him seeke it where it is." Like Socrates, he excuses himself by saying, "The acknowledgement of ignorance, is one of the best and surest testimonies of judgement" that he can find; and he continues, "I have no other Sergeant of band to marshall my rapsodies, than fortune. . . . I will have my naturall and ordinarie pace seene as loose, and as shuffling as it is." And, he concludes, "As I am, so I goe on plodding."[63] This concern with candid self-revelation carries with it the corresponding attitudes toward style: the disgust that just as those "that have leane and thin bodies stuffe them up with bumbasting . . . [so those who] have but poore matter, will puffe it up with loftie words,"[64] and the distaste for rhetoric in general, for "all this garish painting is easilie defaced, by the lustre of an in-bred, and simple truth."[65] Montaigne's detailed descriptions of his own style are most interesting in connection with the epistolary style. Seneca's epistles make us not only eloquent but wise and teach us "not to say well, but to do well," in contrast to that "eloquence, which leaves us with a desire of it, and not of things."[66] It is "for words to serve and wait upon the matter" in such a way that they are not even noticed:

> It is a naturall, simple, and unaffected speech that I love, so written as it is spoken, . . . a pithie, sinnowie, full, strong, compendious and materiall speech, not so delicate and affected, as vehement and piercing. . . . Rather difficult than tedious, void of affection, free, loose and bold, that every member of it seeme to make a bodie; not Pedanticall, nor Frier-like, nor Lawier-like, but rather downe right, Souldier-like.[67]

The rhetorical "outward garments and cloakes may be borrowed, but never the sinews and strength of the bodie."[68] In a later essay he remarks that in conversation we "speake like unto these Essayes" with "a comical and familier stile . . . altogether close, broken, and particular." It is not a style for public negotiations or ceremonious letters, which must contain complimentary phrases and courteous words; it is no style for a flatterer. Those who consider its tone disdainful, says Montaigne, should read my esteem "in my heart," for "the expression of my words, wrongeth my conception."[69]

It is not surprising to find Montaigne remarking that "the cadences, and breakings (*coupures*) of Salust, doe best agree with my humour," and that "if I should undertake to follow this other smoothe, even and regular stile, I should never attaine unto it."[70] The avoidance of the periodic structure in the revelation of the individual personality had been implied in Erasmus' caution to imitate other models as well as Cicero, since "Each mind has an individuality of its own reflecting in speech as in a mirror and to fashion it in a different shape is nothing else than going out in masquerade."[71] As the Stoic ideal of self-examination gradually became self-preoccupation, however, even solipsism, the disregard for formal composition after Montaigne became a cultivated mannerism. The attitudes toward experience and style are expressed by Robert Burton in his preface to *The Anatomy of Melancholy*: "As I do not arrogate, I will not derogate." Burton's purpose is to reveal himself, since *"stilus virum arguit,* our style bewrays us . . . I have laid myself open (I know it) in this treatise, turned mine inside outward." He describes his style as Jonson might have described Montaigne's:

> And for those other faults of barbarism, Doric dialect, extemporanean style, tautologies, apish imitation, a rhapsody of rags gathered together from several dung-hills, excrements of authors, toys and fopperies confusedly tumbled out, without art, invention, judgment, wit, learning, harsh, raw, rude, phantastical, absurd, insolent, indiscreet, ill-composed, indigested, vain, scurrile, idle, dull, and dry; I confess all ('tis partly affected), thou canst not think worse of me than I do of myself.[72]

The satirists whom we shall see Jonson criticizing later described their style in similar terms and boasted of their lack of composition. Tacitus and Quintilian had criticized a similar lack of composition in the imitators of Seneca, and Seneca had said similar things about the imitators of Sallust. In an investigation of Jonson's comparison of Donne with Sallust on the basis of lucidity of style, the implications of such extreme rejections of the periodic structure may, I think, be taken into account. These rejections imply a distrust of how much can be represented at all, lucidly or otherwise.

In the portrayal of the personality, the consciousness, or the "heart," which Persius wishes to reveal to Cornutus and Seneca to Lucilius, the observer becomes the observed. The object, however, does not hold still long enough to be described, and in order to catch more sustained glimpses of it the writer tries to move closer. The glimpses become more intense, but no less fragmentary; the fragments simply flash more dramatically, as when another train passes within a few feet of our own. From a distance the artist can sketch the form of a mountain range, but, as he approaches it to sketch it in more detail, the range breaks up into individual mountains, the gradual slope becomes broken foothills. The closer he comes to it, the more he learns about its fragmentary canyons, but, at the same time, the more difficult it becomes to put them together on his sketch pad, or in his mind when he wishes to find his way out of them. It is precisely these glimpses that Montaigne developed his style to record. The skeptic has always maintained that one can know things only as fragments. Jonson shared neither Montaigne's skepticism nor its extension in literary theory, which assumed that an ordered representation was impossible. To be sure, he would say that the flat outline of the distant mountain range is worthless, but he would also say that there is a point at which the artist must stop approaching it in order for sufficient perspective for composition to remain. To advance closer is to lose the perspective and, so far as the composition is concerned, the subject. This difference in attitude toward the period is made clear in a passage that Jonson transcribes from Hoskyns. In the simplest terms, the choice is between an intention to portray the object or one's own personality. The first alternative, of course, takes into account that it is dealing with the experience of the object and that this experience greatly qualifies the object's appearance. But its allegiance is still to the object, and its effort is directed to refining the experience toward the accurate delineation of the object. The alternative intention is the reverse. It is concerned not with the object as object but with the sensation provoked by the object. The allegiance is not to the object but to one's own sensibilities.

> The conceits of the mind are Pictures of things, and the tongue is the Interpreter of those Pictures. . . . Then he who could apprehend the consequence of things in their truth, and utter his apprehensions as truly, were the best Writer, or Speaker. Therefore *Cicero* said much, when hee said, *Dicere recte nemo potest, nisi qui prudenter intelligit.* The shame of speaking unskilfully were small, if the tongue onely thereby were disgrac'd: But as the Image of a *King,* in his Seale ill-represented, is not so much a blemish to the waxe, or the Signet that seal'd it, as to the Prince it representeth; so disordered speech is not so much injury to the lips that give it forth, as to the disproportion, and incoherence of things in themselves, so negligently expressed. Neither can his mind be thought to be in tune, whose words doe jarre, nor his reason in frame, whose sentence is preposterous; nor his Elocution cleare and perfect, whose utterance breakes it selfe into fragments and uncertainties. (VIII, 628)

"Negligent speech doth not onely discredit the person of the Speaker," Jonson continues, "but it discrediteth the opinion of his reason and judgement; it discrediteth the force and uniformity of the matter, and substance" (VIII, 629). It was an "utterance which breakes it selfe" up in Sallust that Montaigne felt was compatible with a skepticism about the uniformity of matter. Donne's skepticism, as it is stated in *Biathanatos,* in the first and second *Anniversaries,* and in the satirical "The Progresse of the Soule," may be as sharply contrasted as Montaigne's with Jonson's attitude toward reason and nature discussed later in relation to Bacon and Vives.[73]

In Jonson's list of degenerate styles, cited in the second section of this chapter, the criticism of those who write verses as soft as cream is directly followed by a criticism of the negligent compilation of the essayist:

> *Some,* that turne over all bookes, and are equally searching in all papers, that write out of what they presently find or meet, without choice; by which meanes it happens, that what they have discredited, and impugned in one worke, they have before, or after, extolled the same in another. Such are all the *Essayists,* even their Master *Mountaigne.* These, in all they write, confesse still what bookes they have read last; and therein their owne folly, so much, that they bring it to the *Stake* raw, and un-digested: not that the place did need it neither; but that they thought themselves furnished, and would vent it. (VIII, 585–86)

Jonson is criticizing the essayist for offering as a formal composition what would normally be considered disparate material out of which a common-place book might be compiled.[74] For an epigraph to the *Discoveries* (VIII, 562) he borrows a description of the classical *silva* from a seventeenth-century edition of Statius, which may be translated:

> For just as we ordinarily are accustomed to call an indefinite and un-divided number of growing trees a forest, so the Ancients called those books, in which small works of various and separate material were brought together at random, forests or *Tymber-trees.*

The *silva* was a collection of material, brought together without any par-ticular organizational principle, or a piece of writing characterized by a lack of any artfully organized composition in its total structure, despite the excellence of individual parts. Since that subject matter is presumably selected which appeals to the individual tastes of the author, and since it is written down without a conscious concern for orderly composition, but, so to speak, as it comes into the mind, the method of compiling a *silva,* or writing a spontaneous first draft, as Quintilian uses the word, is similar to the method that Montaigne and Burton describe themselves as using in the composition of the essays.[75] Jonson's criticism of Montaigne may stand as a further comment on the necessity of submitting subject matter to the rhetorical disciplines of composition, and on the extremes to which imita-tors within the Sallustian, as opposed to Ciceronian, tradition went.

In this introductory chapter the texts I have cited are familiar, and many of the matters I have brought up have been discussed by distinguished scholars. This review has been in the interest of clarifying Jonson's rhe-torical position in the subsequent chapters and of seeing its relation to his attitudes toward contemporary poetic conventions. In organizing my ma-terial as an explanation of his comparisons of Sidney with Livy and Donne with Sallust, I have tried to indicate the particularity with which the com-parative method, based on the doctrine of imitation, may be interpreted when it is applied by a man as erudite and responsibly consistent as Jonson. Actually, the best gloss on the comparisons is a history of classical literature such as the volumes of J. W. Duff, W. C. Summers, J. W. H. Atkins, or H. J. Rose. I have been concerned chiefly with how Jonson may have thought of Sidney and Donne rather than with the justification of an implied criticism of their styles. In their best work, they represented for him the best of two periods, of two subject matters, of two styles. Although Donne represented the new way, which Jonson himself did most to define and perpetuate, he was a victim of his particular kinds of faults as often as Sidney was of his. Either style was deficient when it failed to subserve a subject matter of sufficient importance with clarity and distinction and, at the same time, to enable the intelligent reader to relate the experience described in some way to his own.

Donne is still being celebrated for his faults. His syntactical involvement and esoteric "termes of Art," which have traditionally led to obscurity, his metrical roughness, and his extreme hyperbolic extensions of conventional Ovidian, Petrarchan, and Neoplatonic conceits, which would be called "frigid" in classical terminology, "occult" in Samuel Johnson's, have been explained and often praised for many years.[76] They ruin a high percentage of his poems as complete compositions and seriously damage many of the rest. The best poems are excellent, and, in the poorer ones, individual fragments, so often cited in his defense, may haunt one for years—such as the lines beginning "Dost thou love/Beauty?" (*Second Anniversary,* 389–400), in which he rewrites the Shakespearean figure of transience (*Sonnets,* civ. 9–12) in terms of the skeptical tradition. To be sure, Donne criticizes and ridicules the Neoplatonic representation of love as unrealistic in many poems, but in a far greater number he adopts, as a structure, a Neoplatonic argument, which the reader is asked to take seriously, and his complimentary poems constantly depart to Neoplatonic hyperbole of the most arid sort. Donne's characteristic form of parody of Petrarchanism is hyperbole, as well, and the cleverness which strikes one at first often remains simply cleverness.

Hyperbole brings up the problem of realism in the presentation of experience, for which Donne has been repeatedly praised. Except in the satires, the experience is often distorted by the same mannerisms as those criticized in the first century A.D. One might question how far the intellectual distinctions and the gymnastics of the logical structure take hold of the human experience in a poem such as "Aire and Angels," and the same thing may be said for the Neoplatonic complexities in the epistles to the Countess of Bedford. Of the first, a recent writer has commented that the terms from angelology and the intricate logic "are used to add dignity and importance to the human situation."[77] I have often arrived at a plausible paraphrase of the poem, but, I confess, I have never met the experience it describes. It is more removed from human relationships than the simplest of Sidney's poems, and, if it is answered that it is describing something more philosophically or psychologically complicated or remote, I should still ask exactly what this is that is being described and on what basis the poem is demanding an emotional response or participation. Once the poem is explained, the obscurity may not be intellectual so much as emotional, or rather it lies in the difficulty of knowing in what direction to be moved or whether to be moved at all. One must obtain the answers to these questions from one's experience, but this is difficult with an argument so abstruse. The same may be said of Donne's Neoplatonic terminology. Even though, in some poems, he criticized Neoplatonism by stressing physical love, he demands that the reader take it with intellectual seriousness in far more poems than Sidney does. If one is willing to accept that system of ideas for a moment, one will find it stated with as fine a logic and far less verbal extravagance in Sidney's "Who hath his fancy pleased," where the paradoxes of Ficino (*Commentary on Plato's Symposium,* II.viii) are succinctly stated. Sidney's poem is difficult but not obscure; granted one is willing to take the ideas seriously, there is no difficulty in perceiving the emotional response demanded. For the evaluation of Neoplatonic ideals in their relation to actual experience in the real world, Jonson surpasses either poet in his sequence "The Celebration of Charis" in complexity of attitude and the subtle definition of feeling.

I do not intend these remarks on Donne to be a general evaluation of him as a poet. I have not discussed his good poems. By relating his more persistent mannerisms to the criticism in the history of a stylistic tradition as it bears on a single phrase in the *Discoveries,* I have tried to suggest more precisely what Jonson's attitude toward him might have been. The discussion of deviations from the original intention and stylistic qualities of the plain style and from its epistolary extension should elucidate the following chapters, which analyze Jonson's rhetorical position in detail. The observations on such deviations within this tradition appear more and more consistent as one compares Jonson's statements with those made both in antiquity and by modern classical scholars on the stylistic extremes of the Silver Age and their causes.[78]

2

VIVES, BACON, AND JONSON:
THE LIMITATIONS OF
THE DOCTRINE OF IMITATION

THE RHETORICAL POSITION developed by Juan Luis Vives and adopted by Ben Jonson can be described in the terms of the sixteenth-century controversy over the proper classical models for imitation. The controversy, in practical terms, was one between those who held up Cicero as the only model and those who encouraged a variety of models, particularly Seneca. The two poles of Ciceronianism and Senecanism supplied convenient categories to which to assign qualities of style. The whole system of imitation offered a way of talking about style as well as a way of learning to write. At the very center of Vives' position, however, lay certain stylistic principles that inherently opposed the practices which the doctrine of imitation imposed on the imitator.[1]

Vives, of course, discussed style by comparing one classical model with another, automatically assuming the universality of this method of description. But the style he describes is, in a sense, a rejection of all styles that can be characterized by this or that particular set of qualities. It is a style that is unspecialized, completely flexible, and nearest to that of the urbane conversation of educated men. In the formal descriptions of antiquity it is most closely approximated by that style described by Cicero in his account of the Attic orator (*Orator* 75–90) and by the philosophical *sermo*, which traces its origins to the Socratic dialogues. The classical plain style, or *genus humile*, was dedicated to the investigation of individual experience and avoided forms of language which had accumulated the emotional commitments of the rhetorical *schemata* of public oratory. In order to define an individual experience, language had to be free of the corrosive burden of established connotative associations; in order to take hold of new things the words had to be returned to their original referents.

The plain style arose originally out of the ancient controversy between rhetoric and dialectic; its intention, or *officium*, had always been to discover and to teach the truth, whereas that of the more rhetorical high and middle styles had been to persuade. In the most general terms, then, Vives was advocating a style developed in the interest of the most efficient presentation of content as opposed to the cultivation of expression for its own sake. Any emphasis upon *res*, in contrast to *verba*, would tend, so far as style was concerned, to weaken any doctrine of imitation, which must be, in the long run, concerned with words. And for models, the anti-Ciceronian would, of course, simply choose writers who treated more complicated matter in a more succinct way, thus substituting Senecan models for Ciceronian ones. But even here, one is, at least in theory, mainly concerned with content, which, though it may be repeated, cannot be imitated.

When Ascham comments that "Ye know not what hurt ye do to learning, that care not for wordes but for matter; and so make a divorce betwixt the tongue and the heart," he is primarily afraid that too much concern with matter will lead to the weakening of authority through schism, as Cicero said had happened as a result of the Socratic dialectic. But Ascham is also concerned with an emerging language and how to teach it, and his program for its improvement through imitation is as clearly defined as any in the century. Senecanism not only encouraged intellectual and political independence, it gradually threatened to destroy any program for stylistic improvement, as can be seen in the later stylistic intentions of Montaigne and Burton.

The second general cause for the devitalization of the doctrine of imitation was the eclecticism displayed in the choice of models by the anti-Ciceronians. Throughout his *Ciceronianus* Erasmus implies that many models may be imitated, depending on the subject matter, and he maintains that any imitation may be crippling if it constricts rather than fosters a particular individual's talent. This eclecticism gradually tended to justify peculiarities of styles; any author could cite particular passages among the many ancient writers as precedents. Lipsius and those who cultivated the Senecan extremes of the "libertine" manner, furthermore, began to seek an authority in particular objects and experiences and in the processes of the mind itself.[2] This led to the cultivation of certain idiosyncrasies of style, which are describable, and to mannerisms which could be associated with particular ancient models. Vives, however, rejects the individual idiosyncrasies peculiar not only to Ciceronianism but to Senecanism as well. He is looking for a "styleless" style, whose virtue is the avoidance of all that might be imitated. The return to the classical plain style of the *sermo* is a criticism, in principle, of the very concept of a style developed by means of the doctrine of imitation.

THE CRITICISM OF CICERONIANISM

The anti-Ciceronians were motivated not only by the fear that stylistic extremists would enforce their idiosyncrasies as literary laws but also by a desire to find a method of discourse that could relate the meditations of private speech to the public matters of forensic persuasion. They were seeking, in other words, a workable relationship between dialectical and rhetorical disciplines.[3] The usefulness of such a prose style would extend, of course, to all branches of humanistic learning, and one can find impatience with an empty rhetoric, which prevents such a style from developing, in intelligent men writing on education, law, philosophy, history, the refinements of a gentleman, and poetry. Their statements agree with those of Vives, Bacon, and Jonson, who were among the most influential men to apply their principles to literary criticism. In adapting a passage from the *Noctes Atticae* of Aulus Gellius, Jonson writes:

> Of the two (if either were to bee wisht) I would rather have a plaine downe-right wisdome, then a foolish and affected eloquence. For what is so furious, and *Bethl'em*-like, as a vaine sound of chosen and excellent words, without any subject of *sentence,* or *science* mix'd? (VIII, 574)[4]

Later, Jonson criticizes those "that labour onely to ostentation; and are ever more busie about the colours, and surface of a worke, then in the matter, and foundation: For that is hid, the other is seene" (VIII, 585). Although Jonson's editors cite only the Euphuists in their note, Jonson could have been referring to any extreme group of writers who, in cultivating stylistic idiosyncrasy, paid more attention to words than to matter.[5]

The Euphuists were not the only ones to neglect content for "colours." Bishop Jewel in his famous "Oration against Rhetoric" criticizes lawyers for pursuing verbal graces, obscurities, and pedantries. What do they want with tropes and *schemata* and "what they call 'colors' (to me they seem rather *shades*)." There is nothing, Jewel complains, so frivolous that it is not sought out as an ornament once the writer focuses his entire attention on refinements of speech: "Shameful, beyond question, that one who has a soul, who has a mind, who has a heart, should cultivate only the tongue."

> If in speaking we seek this (as we certainly do), that we may be understood by others with whom we deal, who can discover a better mode of speech than to speak intelligibly, simply, and clearly? What need of art? What need of childish ornament?[6]

After a warning against long allegories, "lest either wee make our selves obscure, or fall into affectation, which is childish," Jonson, translating Vives, restates the question: "But why doe men depart at all from the right, and naturall wayes of speaking?" (VIII, 625). They depart, he answers, in order to avoid offending their audience, as by obsceneness, and to gain variety.[7] His translation of a passage from M. Seneca, which seems to have been Vives' source, makes it clear that he thinks this departure should be taken as seldom as possible. Jonson describes a man he obviously admires:

> Hee never forc'd his language, nor went out of the high-way of *speaking*; but for some great necessity, or apparent profit. For hee denied *Figures* to be invented for ornament, but for ayde; and still thought it an extreme madnesse to bend, or wrest that which ought to be right. (VIII, 589)

It is not surprising that the rhetorical sophistry of law was repeatedly criticized, but it is interesting that some critics recommended, as had Socrates, the pursuit of philosophical truth. Antonius Muretus, for example, complains that law students study rhetoric to the exclusion of philosophy and asks in the sixth oration of his second book of orations how a man could make judicial decisions if he had not drawn a knowledge of justice from the philosophers:

> Would I improve your eloquence more if I recommended examples of tropes and schemes and chanted those dictations of the schoolmasters everyday . . . than when I explain the books of Plato's *Republic* or of Cicero's philosophy? True and substantial eloquence is posited not only in words but in subject matter. Moreover, Horace declares: Scribendi recte sapere est et principium et fons./rem tibi Socraticae poterunt ostendere chartae,/verbaque provisam rem non invita sequentur.[8]

Muretus, in asking the same questions that Socrates might have asked, is reiterating the philosophical origins of the attitudes expressed by the plain style, for which the lines quoted from Horace's *Ars Poetica* became practically a maxim.

In his *De Ratione Dicendi*, using a remark of Cicero as a starting point (*De Orat.* III.142–43), Vives states an anti-Ciceronian position on philosophy and language:

> If an author expresses his subject matter sufficiently clearly, he has done his job well no matter what words he uses. If one should bring eloquence as an addition to a philosopher, Cicero said, I should not reject it; if one should not bring it, I should not require it, for in all philosophy the art is concerned with meaning and not with expression, and it is better that a philosopher err in words than in truth. Much better and truer is that philosopher who expresses elegant and beautiful things in

a vulgar style than one who expresses either trifles or false things splendidly. Who does not retain a good saying spoken in Gallic, Spanish, German, or even Scythian dialect; if in these languages, why not in clumsy Latin also?[9]

Bacon is in agreement when he says, "as substance of matter is better than beauty of words, so contrariwise vain matter is worse than vain words."[10] Jonson, in a passage beginning, "It was well noted by the late L. St. *Alban,* that the study of words is the first distemper of Learning . . ." (VIII, 627–28) gives an epitome of the fourth chapter of the first book of Bacon's *Advancement of Learning.* Since he incorporated it in his *Discoveries,* it is worth giving a summary of the famous anti-Ciceronian passage. Bacon says that admiration of ancient authors, hatred for the Scholastics, study of languages, and preaching brought in an "affectionate study of eloquence and copie of speech" which grew quickly to an excess when "men began to hunt more after words than matter; more after the choiceness of the phrase, and the round and clean composition of the sentence, and the sweet falling of the clauses, and the varying and illustration of their works with tropes and figures, than after the weight of matter, worth of subject, soundness of argument, life of invention, or depth of judgment." Then the "watery vein of Osorius" became famous, Sturmius spent "such infinite and curious pains" on Cicero and Hermogenes, "besides his own books of Periods and Imitation," and Carr and Ascham tried to "almost deify Cicero and Demosthenes" and taught young men "that delicate and polished kind of learning." Then did Erasmus in his *Colloquies* "make the scoffing echo, *Decem annos consumpsi in legendo Cicerone*; and the echo answered . . . *One, Asine.*" And, he concludes, "the whole inclination and bent of those times was rather towards copie than weight."[11] Jonson praises Bacon's own style for avoiding the characteristics just criticized:

> Yet there hapn'd, in my time, one noble *Speaker,* who was full of gravity in his speaking. His language, (where hee could spare, or passe by a jest) was nobly *censorious.* No man ever spake more neatly, more presly, more weightily, or suffer'd lesse emptinesse, lesse idlenesse, in what hee utter'd. (VIII, 590–91)[12]

Morris Croll remarks that it was because Aristotle's purpose was "to establish rhetoric in an intimate, insoluble connection with dialectic . . . that his treatise was taken as the foundation of anti-Ciceronian theory in the seventeenth century."[13] In the same way that Aristotle tried to free prose from epideictic oratory in order to handle particular philosophical and scientific concerns of human experience, Horace tried to free poetry from the rhetorical poetic conventions in order to handle the problems arising from what men actually do and think. Bacon, who constantly depends, Croll believes,[14] upon Aristotle's *Rhetoric*, commends Aristotle for treating ethics well in a work on rhetoric.[15] The assumption is that the ethical material of the *Socraticae . . . chartae* is the proper subject matter for rhetoric, and the gradual preference for Aristotle over Cicero as a rhetorical authority was a result to a great extent of the renewed emphasis upon matter rather than words.[16]

When Jonson characterizes the education of a good poet, he indicates the indissoluble relation between poetry and the concerns of philosophy, and how that relationship was recognized by Horace and Aristotle:

> Hee must read many; but, ever the best, and choisest: those, that can teach him any thing, hee must ever account his masters, and reverence: among whom *Horace*, and (hee that taught him) *Aristotle*, deserve to bee the first in estimation. *Aristotle* was the first accurate *Criticke*, and truest Judge; nay, the greatest *Philosopher*, the world ever had: for, hee noted the vices of all knowledges, in all creatures, and out of many mens perfections in a science, hee formed still one Art. So hee taught us two Offices together, how we ought to judge rightly of others, and what wee ought to imitate specially in our selves. (VIII, 639–40)

Jonson, borrowing Bacon's remarks, says they are wrong who "make an Author a *Dictator*, as the schooles have done *Aristotle*," but, he goes on, "Let Aristotle, and others have their dues; but if wee can make farther Discoveries of truth and fitnesse then they, why are we envied?" Let us "gently stirre the mould about the root of the Question" (VIII, 627). This is perfectly in accord with the liberal classicism Jonson expresses in translating a passage from Vives' *In Libros de Disciplinis Praefatio*. He knows nothing, he writes, more profitable to literature than the study of the ancient writers, but one is "not to rest in their sole Authority . . . For to all the observations of the *Ancients*, wee have our owne experience." It is true they "open'd the gates, and made the way, that went before us; but as Guides, not Commanders," for "Truth lyes open to all; it is no mans *severall*" (VIII, 567). It is Vives himself, in his *De Ratione Dicendi*, who summarizes most aptly the reasons for returning to Aristotle:

> But those of us against whom we are arguing are wrong in this because they think the whole art of speaking is included in that part which concerns words or schemes, tropes, periods, and harmony of diction, which make up not so much the body itself of speaking, as if they were the substance, as the decoration and ornament of speaking. For how great a part of this art is the ornament and form of a speech? Therefore,

Aristotle, a great and ingenious man, among the first who wrote of what arts ought to be recommended, sent the reader back often in his treatment of this discipline to dialectical and philosophical works, never to rhetorical ones, because it was necessary to have an understanding of them before one of how to speak.[17]

It is not surprising that Vives, Bacon, and Jonson should share anti-Ciceronian attitudes. It is surprising, however, that they should agree in their criticisms of the Senecan reaction once the revitalizing qualities of that reaction had been made clear. A literary fashion is often composed of the superficial and self-perpetuating characteristics of a literary movement which remain after the corrective purposes that initiated the movement have been accomplished. When Senecanism had become a fashion and the superficial idiosyncrasies of style were being imitated, when the roughness and conscious carelessness, encouraged in reaction to the circular smoothness of Ciceronian periods, were used as excuses for bad writing, especially in verse, Jonson criticized it and those "who thinke those things the stronger, that have no Art" (VIII, 587) as severely as he had the Ciceronians. Vives, Bacon, and John Hoskyns did the same.

THE CRITICISM OF SENECANISM

The faults that Jonson found in the extreme Senecan styles can best be explained by a close analysis of parts of the longest passage he borrowed from Vives (VIII, 623–27), interpolating within it relevant passages from other parts of the *Discoveries* and *De Ratione Dicendi*. The Latin passages from which Jonson translates are given by Herford and Simpson (XI, 268–72).[18] I shall quote the editors' citation from the Latin only when it can clarify Jonson's meaning. Jonson lists the different types of Attic and Senecan styles:

A strict and succinct style is that, where you can take away nothing without losse, and that losse to be manifest.[a] [*Est astricta, et succincta oratio, quum nihil omnino est, quod possis demere sine iactura, qualem fuisse Lysiae Attici structuram memoriae proditum est.*]

The briefe style is that which expresseth much in little.[b] [*Est alia oratio breuis, quae dedita opera magnas sententias in pauca verba confert, & tanquam infarcit ac constipat, qualia sunt quae a Graecis nominantur*

[a] *Disc.*, ll. 1970–72. In the margin Jonson has "*De stylo*. Tacitus." Vives' Latin continues where the editors' commentary ceases to quote it: *sed omnes Attici fuerunt astricti, etsi alii plus aliis . . . Aristoteles parsimonia hac omnes superat . . .*, lib., I, cap., vi; *Opera Omnia*, II, 113.

[b] *Disc.*, ll. 1972–73. In the margin: "*The Laconicke.*"

Apophthegmata, responsa philosophorum, et prudentium vivorum et dicta illa Laconica.]

The concise style, which expresseth not enough, but leaves somewhat to bee understood.[c] [*Est alia concisa, quae minus exprimit quam intellegentia requirat, sed usus ita loquendi adiuvat sensum & supplet, quod deest.*]

The abrupt style, which hath many breaches, and doth not seeme to end, but fall.[d] [*Est diminuta, cui vitiose aliquid deest necessarium . . . In diminutis quaedam sunt abrupta, in quibus uelut destitutam se cursu suo auris deprehendit . . .*]

This short passage and those slightly longer from Vives, which serve as glosses, place Jonson fairly accurately in the Ciceronian-Senecan controversy. In the margin beside "A strict and succinct style," which Vives describes as "Attic," Jonson has written "Tacitus" who, he said to Drummond, speaks "best Latine." His preference, then, is for the "Attic" style rather than for the more "concise," "abrupt," or Senecan "Laconicke," style, which Vives describes later in his *De Ratione Dicendi*:

The most brief and clipped of all were the Lacedemonians, who used, for instance, certain very abrupt clauses (*punctis*) rather than steady discourse (*sermone*). This is not called speech, nor is there any disposition for oratory in the Spartans who prided themselves on being held to be military men, more prepared to act than to speak, and who even would have preferred to use gestures rather than words if in that way they could have been understood.[19]

The difference between the Spartan and Attic speaker, as Cicero describes him (*Orator* 75-90), indicates how far Jonson and Vives are, in general attitude, from the extreme Senecans of the sixteenth and seventeenth centuries.

Jonson, continuing to translate Vives, says that "Periods are beautifull when they are not too long," so long as one does not grow obscure in his efforts to be brief:

[c] *Disc.,* ll. 1973-75. In the margin: "Suetonius."

[d] *Ibid.,* ll. 1975-76. In the margin: "Seneca & Fabianus." Jonson probably meant "Seneca de Fabiano." Compare Heinsius' treatment of the followers of Lipsius quoted below: "Sentences hopped along; a lean and jejune speech . . . broken by some short phrases and plays on words, or by abrupt clauses and short questions . . . You would have said it was stage players, or an unfortunate train of the halt, who . . . when sometimes . . . they attempt to jump, are more likely to fall than to go." Vives' original Latin, *destitutam se cursu suo auris deprehendit,* recalls the third characteristic in Croll's description of the Lipsian style: "Il cherche plutôt à rompre le rythme en arrêtant brusquement ses phrases, manquant ainsi, comme des critiques hostiles l'ont dit, à ce que l'oreille attendait de lui." "Juste Lipse," p. 224.

For Order helpes much to Perspicuity, as Confusion hurts. *Rectitudo lucem adfert; obliquitas et circumductio offuscat.* We should therefore speake what wee can, the neerest way, so as wee keepe our gate, not leape; for too short may as well be not let into the memory, as too long not kept in. Whatsoever looseth the grace, and clearenesse, converts into a Riddle; the obscurity is mark'd, but not the valew. (VIII, 624).

Jonson's phrase "keepe our gate, not leape" is very near to a criticism of Lipsius' style made in an epigram by Joseph Scaliger:

> The uniform plainness, which Caesar and Cicero once cultivated, offends others who are pleased by "points" bound tight in the joints, which leap, rather than walk, through rough places (*Quae per salebras saltitant, non ambulant*) and, while the expectation of the reader hangs, need more to be understood than read.[20]

Daniel Heinsius gives a more extensive criticism of Lipsius' followers. In a funeral oration on Joseph Scaliger, he tells of the chaotic state in which Lipsius had left the University of Leyden when Scaliger succeeded him. The literary crisis arose from the students' attempt to imitate the style of their master, Lipsius, despite the fact that he had warned them not to imitate either himself or his own models. As a result, instead of his eloquence they achieved only a mannered roughness and awkward archaisms:

> If anyone wished to write in Latin, dead words were fetched from as far back as Pacuvius and Ennius; sentences hopped along; a lean and jejune speech, juiceless and meagre, broken by some short phrases and plays on words, or by abrupt clauses and short questions, occasioned nausea and disgust. You would have said it was stage players, or an unfortunate train of the halt, who, while the choregus is busy within, entertain the spectators to the accompaniment of a flutist, and when sometimes, with the greatest effort, they attempt to jump, are more likely to fall than to go.[21]

These criticisms of Lipsius are especially applicable to Jonson's discussions, in the *Discoveries*, of Senecan mannerisms that tended to obscurity, for he used similar statements of Scaliger and Heinsius to characterize the literary situation at the turn of the seventeenth century.

In his epigram Scaliger alludes to the following poem of Martial, which was one of Jonson's favorite critical statements:

> No poems win your favour that speed on a gentle path, only those that fall over rough places and high cliffs [*Carmina nulla probas molli quae limite currunt,/sed quae per salebras altaque saxa cadunt*], and this appears to you finer even than Homer's song:
>   "Pillar of Lucilius' house, here lieth Metrophanes."

And in amazed wonder you read of the "frugiferous terrene," and whatever phrase Accius and Pacuvius spew. Do you want *me,* Chrestillus, to
copy the old poets, your poets? May I die, but you appreciate the flavour
of virility. (XI.90)

Jonson cites the line *sed quae per salebras* three times in the *Discoveries*
(VIII, 585, 623, 649), in two of which he combines the criticism of roughness, as Martial does, with that of archaic language. In passages translated
from Quintilian (II.v.11, xi.1–3, xii.1–3) and Seneca (*Ep.* cxiv), he repeatedly expresses his dislike for intentional roughness and poor composition, which was growing fashionable, lamenting that "Right and naturall
language seeme[s] to have least of the wit in it; that which is writh'd and
tortur'd, is counted the more exquisite" (VIII, 581). Some there are who
prefer only rough composition which falls over broken and high places and
which "if it would come gently, they trouble it of purpose," not wanting it to
"run without rubs, as if that stile were more strong and manly, that stroke
the eare with a kind of uneven[n]esse." These men "erre not by chance,
but knowingly, and willingly," and, since they are admired, the great danger
is that their "vice becomes a *Precedent*" (VIII, 585). This is possible because,

> the multitude commend Writers, as they doe Fencers, or Wrastlers;
> who if they come in robustiously, and put for it, with a deale of violence,
> are received for the *braver-fellowes*: when many times their owne rude-
> nesse is a cause of their disgrace; and a slight touch of their Adversary,
> gives all that boisterous force the foyle.

It is not unnatural that the unskilled should be misled, who "judging
wholly by the bulke, thinke rude things greater then polish'd; and scatter'd
more numerous, then compos'd: Nor thinke this only to be true in the
sordid multitude, but the neater sort of our *Gallants*" (VIII, 583). These
comments of Jonson are especially interesting in relation to the satirists of
the 1590's, most of whom were rough from lack of skill but all of whom
claimed to be avoiding "art," who, one might say, "utter all they can thinke,
with a kind of violence, and *indisposition*; . . . who thinke those things
the stronger, that have no Art: as if to breake, were better then to open;
or to rent asunder, gentler then to loose" (VIII, 586–87). Jonson ends the
Discoveries with a parting shot of contempt: "You admire no *Poems*, but
such as run like a Brewers-cart upon the stones, hobling, *Et, quæ per salebras*
. . ." (VIII, 649).[22]

Jonson transcribes, word for word, a passage from Hoskyns's *Direccōns
For Speech and Style* that gives a criticism of broken composition which
might very well refer to Lipsius:

But, as *Quintilian* saith, there is a briefnesse of the parts sometimes, that makes the whole long, as, *I came to the staires, I tooke a paire of oares, they launch'd out, rowed a pace, I landed at the Court-gate, I paid my fayre, went up to the Presence, ask'd for my Lord, I was admitted*. All this is but, *I went to the Court, and spake with my Lord*. This is the fault of some Latine Writers, within these last hundred years, of my reading, and perhaps *Seneca* may be appeacht of it; I accuse him not. (VIII, 631)[23]

Hoskyns could well say that Lipsius was "of my reading," for he transcribed some passages from his *Institutio Epistolica*, which Jonson copied in turn into the *Discoveries*; Jonson owned a copy of the Antwerp edition (1606–23) of Lipsius' *Opera Omnia* (XI, 601).

In the *Direccōns*, written around 1599 or 1600, Hoskyns has some interesting remarks on the sententious style and on fashions in style generally:

> *Sententia* (if it be well vsed) is a figure (if ill & too much) it is a style, whereof none that writes humorously or factiously nowe adayes can bee cleare, for nowe there are such schismes of eloquence, that it is enough for any io yeares that all the bravest witts doe imitate Some one figure wch a criticke hath taught some great psonage, soe it maye bee wthin this 200 yeares, wee shall goe through the whole bodie of *Rhethorick*.

> It is true that we studie accordinge to the p^{re}dominancie of courtly inclynacōns, whilest mathematiques were in requests all o^r simillitudes came from lynes, circles, & Angles, whilest morall philosophie is nowe a while spoken of, it is rudenesse, not to be sententious, & for my pte, I'le make one, I haue vsed & outworne 6 severall styles, since I was first fellowe of newe Colledge, & am yet able to beare the fashion of writing companie, let o^r age therefore onlie speake morally, & let the next age liue morrally.[24]

Hoskyns says that a figure if used "ill & too much" becomes a "style"; he implies that perfect writing would be "styleless" in his sense of the word. Such a "styleless" style would be extraordinarily hard to describe as well as to write, for "as every man may hope the same;/Yet he that offers at it, may sweat much,/And toile in vaine . . ."[25] Such a style would be without mannerism and eccentricity; it would be simply the plain style, and though it shares many of its qualities and attitudes, the sententious style is something quite different. When Hoskyns says that "whilest morall philosophie is nowe a while spoken of, it is rudenesse, not to be sententious" he is talking about what Vives calls the laconic style, which Jonson marks as "The Laconicke" in the margin: *quae . . . magnas sententias in pauca verba confert . . . qualia sunt quae a Graecis niminantur Apophthegmata, re-*

sponsa philosophorum, et prudentium virorum et dicta illa Laconica. Vives himself criticizes the use of too many *sententiae*, in which "Anneus Seneca was at fault, who because of such a steady stream of sententiae left no place for shadows, which is customarily found in a picture, with the result that he overwhelmed the high lights (*obruebat lumina*) and was less pleasing."[26]

Then Hoskyns asks:

Why would the writers of these daies, imprison themselues in the straightnes of these maximes . . . It makes there stile like *Arena sine calce*, (as one saith) of such a writer, & doth not he vouchsafe to vse them that . . . [called] them poesies for ringes; If it be matter of short dirreccon for life & accōn, or notes for memorie, I intend not to discreditt this newe tricke, But otherwise hee that hath a longe Journey to walke in that pace, is like a horse that overreacheth & yet goes slowe . . .[27]

Such a person as Hoskyns describes would appear, as Heinsius said of the followers of Lipsius, to be one of "an unfortunate train of the halt" who is "more likely to fall than go."

In 1623 Bacon added a criticism of the Senecan style to his Latin translation of the *Advancement of Learning*.[28] After the "watery vein" of the Ciceronians the new fashion brought in a style which also, it might be said, grew speedily to an excess.

Litle better is that kind of stile (yet neither is that altogether exempt from vanity) which neer about the same time succeeded this *Copy* and *superfluity of speech.* The labour here is altogether, *That words may be aculeate, sentences concise, and the whole contexture of the speech and discourse, rather rounding into it selfe, than spread and dilated*: So that it comes to passe by this Artifice, that every passage seemes more witty and waighty than indeed it is. Such a stile as this we finde more excessively in *Seneca*; more moderately in *Tacitus* and *Plinius Secundus*; and of late it hath bin very pleasing unto the eares of our time. And this kind of expression hath found such acceptance with meaner capacites, as to be a dignity and ornament to Learning; neverthelesse, by the more exact judgements, it hath bin deservedly dispised, and may be set down *as a distemper of Learning*, seeing it is nothing else but a hunting after words, and fine placing of them.[29]

The Senecan style becomes corrupt in the same ways as the Ciceronian had by causing men "to hunt more after words"; and the reform of it, one may expect, will degenerate in the same way, as Bacon so shrewdly observed in speaking of the imitators of Cicero:

Here therefore is the first distemper of learning, when men study words and not matter; wherof, though I have represented an example of late times, yet it hath been and will be *secundum majus et minus* in all time.[30]

The Socratic and Stoic attitudes toward experience and the literary analysis and expression of personal experience in the *sermo* remain the same for Jonson and Vives as for the Senecans. But whereas the Senecans, especially those of the Libertine movement, tended more and more to use the *sermo* to reveal personal idiosyncrasy until the plain style itself became eccentrically mannered, Vives and Jonson retained, as an ideal, the *sermo* as described by Cicero in his discussion of the Attic orator (*Orator* 75–90). Each of the following passages should be compared with Cicero's description of the *genus tenue*. Though many of the following quotations, which are principally from Vives, illustrate an anti-Ciceronian position in general, they are cited here to show the writers' preferences for an Attic style in particular.

The last part of Jonson's long translation from Vives, discussed in the preceding section, begins with a Senecan generalization:

> *Language* most shewes a man: speake that I may see thee. It springs out of the most retired, and inmost parts of us, and is the Image of the Parent of it, the mind. No glasse renders a mans forme, or likenesse, so true as his speech. (VIII, 625)[31]

The passage goes on to work out a comparison between a human body and the various stylistic categories that make up a style. The following part of the comparison is the most pertinent to Vives' longer treatments of the Attic style:

> Wee say it is a fleshy style, when there is much *Periphrasis*, and circuit of words; and when with more then enough, it growes fat and corpulent; *Arvina orationis*, full of suet and tallow. It hath blood, and juyce, when the words are proper and apt, their sound sweet, and the *Phrase* neat and pick'd. *Oratio uncta, & bene pasta.* But where there is Redundancy, both the blood and juyce are faulty, and vitious. *Redundat sanguine, quæ multo plus dicit, quam necesse est . . .* There be some styles, againe, that have not lesse blood, but lesse flesh, and corpulence. These are bony, and sinnewy: *Ossa habent, et nervos.* (VIII, 626–27)

Vives' Latin for the next to the last sentence is *Est alia astricta & pressa, minus habens carnis & sanguinis*; it is nearly identical with his description of the Attic style, *Est astricta, et succincta oratio*, which Jonson translated "A strict and succinct style is that . . ." and beside which he wrote "Tacitus" (VIII, 623). He translates *nervos* as sinews, a word which was widely used as a critical term after Sidney.

Vives, returning later in his *De Ratione Dicendi* to corporeal terminology, says sinews are necessary for a strong style:

> The nerves are often buried by flesh and fat, so that they are weakened and are less able to perform their functions. It happens in the same way in style, that the luxuriance of words and the redundancy of flesh and that diffuse and wandering composition become responsible for a weak style, which happened to Cicero who, while he diluted his subject matter too much with words, lost strength, as a river that flows out widely. For this reason Calvus said he was without nerves and Brutus he was weak.[32]

He then goes on to distinguish Cicero's Asiatic style from the Attic:

> The Asiatic style is weak and nerveless from too great abundance of words, dilution of subject matter, and refined composition, showing many leaves, yielding little fruit. Cicero considered the philosophical style supple (*mollem*) and academic, furnished neither with words or feelings of the common people, nor bound by rhythm, but freely loose, deserving to be called conversation rather than oratory (*sermo potius quam oratio*). For, although all speech is oratory, nevertheless speech of this one type of oratory is designated by this proper name; such was the oratory of Demetrius of Phalerus whom Theophrastus the Philosopher taught.[33]

This description of the style and those that follow are either taken from or are in accord with Cicero's description of the Attic orator.

> The men of Attica, as they usually were acute and effective in speaking, did not permit their oratory to digress into unnecessary matters; it was enough for the orator to explain clearly what he wished in proper words chosen with the greatest care. They, nevertheless, admitted oratorical ornament and figures of every type as if they were certain stars and lights. Attic oratory, therefore, because of the keen judgment and refined and scrupulous ears of the people of that state, admitted nothing inept, nothing affectedly ornate or offensive, nothing redundant and faulty, to such an extent that Aeschines dared to reproach Demosthenes for not being Attic because he had sought for an allegory in a longer and harder way than necessary in which he wished the state to be understood by "the vineyard" and those who plundered it by "the vinedressers." Therefore the Attic sentence has nothing redundant and faulty, not much flesh, just enough blood and sap, and is pure, natural, brief, and clipped (*puri, et sani, brevis, astrictaque*).[34]

Considerably later in the treatise Vives supplements this description, clearly implying his preference for the Attic style:

> A speech begins to please by sharp wit which relies greatly on the intelligence of the audience, by its austere metaphors far from obscurity of diction, its sharpness of argument, and its subtlety, exciting purpose and exercising the mind. There are those among whom a strict and compressed (*astrictum et collectum*) way of speaking, concluding particular points at once, gains more credit, and among these the dialectical mode of disputing of the Stoics is permitted. Others are taken with phrases indeed wonderfully brief, but sharp, and enforced with a certain charm; there are many of this kind in Seneca, Lucian, M. Fabius, Pliny, and Tacitus. Other men, born and educated to communal participation in affairs of state, require a diffuse and ornate speech.[35]

The fact that neither Vives, Jonson, nor Bacon seemed to find Tacitus' elliptical brevity too obscure is partly explained by Henry Peacham's discussion of brevity in 1622. He praises Tacitus for being "so copious in pleasing brevity" and says that Sallust is "commended most for brevity . . . but wherein his brevity consisteth, the most are ignorant." Our grammarians, he continues, err in that they think Sallust's brevity consists "onely of the matter and persons barely and nakedly described, without circumstance and preparation, counsels and deliberations had before, effects and euents after." Actually, his brevity, "worthy your observation and imitation, consisteth in shutting up whole and weightie Sentences in three words, fetching nothing afarre, or putting in more than needs; but in quicke and stirring *Asyndeta's* after his manner."[36]

Jonson, translating Quintilian, describes "the true Artificer" as one whose art is such that "none but Artificers perceive it." As a result he is apt to be called "barren, dull, leane" by men "who without labour, judgement, knowledge, or almost sense, are received, or preferr'd before him." But, he says:

> An other age, or juster men will acknowledge the vertues of his studies: his wisdom, in dividing; his subtilty, in arguing: with what strength hee doth inspire his Readers; with what sweetnesse hee strokes them: in inveighing, what sharpenesse; in Jest, what urbanity hee uses. How he doth raigne in mens affections; how invade, and breake in upon them; and makes their minds like the things he writes.

Men will then see his propriety in diction and figures "which gentle, which strong to shew the composition *Manly*," and how he has avoided the "faint, obscure, obscene, sordid, humble, improper, or effeminate *Phrase*" (VIII,

587–88). Barrenness, dullness, and leanness are the faults that the plain
style is most likely to fall into, according to nearly every rhetorical treatise,
and in the following two passages Jonson describes how they may be
avoided:

> To speake, and to speake well, are two things. A foole may talke, but
> a wise man speakes, and out of the observation, knowledge, and use of
> things. Many Writers perplexe their Readers, and Hearers with meere
> *Non-sense*. Their writings need sunshine. Pure and neat Language I
> love, yet plaine and customary. A barbarous Phrase hath often made mee
> out of love with a good sense; and doubtfull writing hath wrackt mee
> beyond my patience. (VIII, 620)

If it is the business of the critic to describe a style which does not grow old
as the fashions turn, which does not soften from the decay of affectation, and
which, though it appear easy to define and master, is in the end the most
difficult, the *Discoveries*, as a handbook of the new authorities on style, is
the major critical work of the period.[37] Although the two passages just
quoted, as well as the one just below, are translated from Quintilian, Jonson
has made them his own, and he abides by them.

> *Custome* is the most certaine Mistresse of Language, as the publicke
> stampe makes the current money. But wee must not be too frequent
> with the mint, every day coyning. Nor fetch words from the extreme
> and utmost ages; since the chiefe vertue of a style is perspicuitie, and
> nothing so vitious in it, as to need an Interpreter.[38] . . . The eldest of the
> present, and newest of the past Language is the best. For what was the
> ancient Language, which some men so doate upon, but the ancient Cus-
> tome? Yet when I name Custome, I understand not the vulgar Custome:
> For that were a precept no lesse dangerous to Language, then life . . .
> But that I call Custome of speech, which is the consent of the Learned;
> as Custome of life, which is the consent of the good. (VIII, 622)[39]

These three passages describe not only what Jonson thought the best
style should be but what his own was considered to be by many of his
contemporaries. In an elegy on Jonson, John Beaumont, the son of Sir John
Beaumont, describes Jonson's style, and his description bears a close relation to the three preceding quotations:

> Since then, he made our Language pure and good,
> To teach us speake, but what we understood,
> We owe this praise to him, that should we joyne
> To pay him, he were payd but with the coyne
> Himselfe hath minted, which we know by this
> That no words passe for currant now, but his;

> And though He in a blinder age could change
> Faults to perfections, yet 'twas farre more strange
> To see (how ever times, and fashions frame)
> His wit and language still remaine the same
> In all mens mouths . . .[40]
>
> (ll. 41–51)

To use that language and style which remain current in every age was Jonson's aim, for it is only in such a style that the content, which a style is properly developed to express, can continue to be understood. Vives again gives the description of the style closest to Jonson's:

> There is therefore speech devoid of "colors" as that of Aristotle and Tranquillius, *naked and without ornaments,* as Cicero says the Commentaries of Caesar are, bare, direct, pleasing, stripped of all decorations of oratory as if of clothes. There is a *certain natural "color,"* and, as Cicero says *full of blood, not smeared with paint:* it consists of proper words, clear speech, moderate figures which are truthful, neat, and not farfetched but, as it were, arising from the thing itself. Such it was in the age of Demosthenes, in which, as Cicero writes, *there was that juice and uncorrupted blood in which there was a natural, not murky, brilliance.* Contrary to it is the *foreign-borrowed, the obscure, and the painted,* in which art appears and decoration imported from elsewhere. When natural speech is joined with accuracy, it is called refined, smoothed, clean, terse, belonging to those who use speech chosen from custom and observation, as a distinguished form wiped clean of sordid things and filth. Opposed to this is the obese, squalid, tumid, sordid when words are dug up from the shadows of antiquity, or taken from the refuse of the vulgar—either in their own sense or as metaphor—and obscure composition as the speech of Apuleius and Capella. The "color" is *pure* which has no blemishes and foulness . . . There are these genuine gradations of this "color": the *neat,* which is pure and natural; the *fair* to which more grace and care is added, as do Herodotus and Livy; and the *most fair* which is distinguished, perspicuous, brilliant, lucid, with chosen and clear words in which there must seem to be something sonorous, dignified, and particularly appropriate to the speaker and subject (*proprium, aptumque inesse videatur*).[41]

The use of "seems" in the subjunctive implies, as in Hoskyns, that even at its most elegant, a pure style should be "styleless," one about which it is difficult to predicate anything, whose source of power we do not completely understand because we cannot attribute it to any outstanding literary characteristics. Jonson's "pure and neat Language . . . yet plaine and customary" is that gradation of style which Vives calls "the neat, which is pure and natural." Both descriptions are identical to Cicero's of the Attic orator (*Orator* 76, 79), who "is restrained and plain (*summissus est et humilis*)" and "follows the ordinary usage (*consuetudinem imitans*)," whose "language will be pure Latin, plain and clear (*sermo purus erit et Latinus, dilucide planeque*)."

It is in just such a stylistic program that the doctrine of imitation would be the most difficult to apply. The unspecialized, styleless style, whose models are the familiar letter and urbane conversation, is by definition incapable of predication. It is characterized mainly by what it should avoid. Consequently, Cicero remarks, the audience will be sure they can speak in this way, for "that plainness of style seems easy to imitate at first thought, but when attempted nothing is more difficult" (*Orator* 76). Such a speaker must avoid a pronounced rhythm and smooth connections (77), periodic structure (78), and noticeable ornament (79). He should beware of embellishment, either in single words or in phrases (80), of symmetry, coining of words, bold and far-fetched metaphors (81). He must be sparing in the use of figures (83), of "clauses of equal length, with similar endings, or identical cadences, and the studied charm produced by the change of a letter" (84). He must avoid repetitions of word or phrase, long or glutted periods that require "stronger lungs" (85), certain types of ridicule (88), and far-fetched jests (89). Indeed, nothing is less imitable (*imitabilis . . . minus*) than the subtle simplicity of this type of speech (*orationis subtilitas*). The style that Vives, Bacon, and Jonson attempt to establish is one which remains the same as the fashions change, one to which each new period must return to break off the encrustation of mannerism of the preceding period. It cannot be imitated; each time it must be achieved anew in the terms of the subject matter to which it is subservient. This cycle, as Bacon says, "hath been and will be *secundum majus et minus* in all time."

The more important this style becomes as a remedy, the less force the doctrine of imitation can be expected to have. To be sure, men continued in the seventeenth and eighteenth centuries to describe their own styles as having characteristics of this and that model, but this is different from the way Ascham speaks of the total process of learning. The method continues in its older form mainly as applied to particular problems, such as whether to imitate Homer or Virgil in the epic, Horace or Juvenal in satire. But the terminology, for the most part, is directed by the social and intellectual critics to the practical or theoretical disciplines. For instance, Senecanism in preaching is wrong not so much on aesthetic grounds as on those of the practical expediency of the congregation's understanding what is said. Ornamental styles of every variety were impractical in the description of physical phenomena. Jonson and Bacon, although committed to the doctrine of imitation as everyone in the century was, returned to a classical style, as Vives and others had already done—a style that was, quite by accident perhaps, similar to the English prose that had been in existence long before the "stylizing" effects of the doctrine had begun to be apparent.[42] And in curing as many of these effects as possible, they established a norm of English prose that both removed many of the stylizations produced by the doctrine, and, since it was inimitable itself, greatly restricted the future possibilities of imitation.

3

THE EPISTOLARY TRADITION

*Letters ... such as are written from wise men are
of all the words of man, in my judgement, the best.*
BACON, *Advancement of Learning*, II.iii.4

DEMETRIUS DESCRIBES the epistolary as the plainest of plain styles, and so far as the familiar letter was concerned, the sixteenth and seventeenth centuries repeated his recommendations, as well as those of other ancient writers, for simplicity in diction, phrasing, and organization. Epistolary treatises in both English and Latin followed the classical definition of a letter as "the familiar and mutuall talke of one absent friend to another," as Angel Day wrote of it in his *The English Secretorie*, whose "Character" should "be simple, plaine, and of the lowest and meanest stile, utterly deuoid of any shadow of hie and loftie speaches."[1] Day refers to the style directly as "*Humile,* the lowest comicall, and most simple of all others" and characterizes it, as Horace does that of the *sermones*, as one which "sweepeth euen the very ground itselfe" and "in which neuertheless is *sua faceties et elegantia quaedam,* his certaine kind of elegancie, pleasant and neat conveyance."[2] William Fullwood also remarks that the best language for a letter "is the common and familiar speech and not [that] of rare and diffused phrases, or inckhorne termes, skummed from the Latine, nor of too base termes and barbarous, or termes unknowne except in certaine places."[3] The descriptions of the style by Vives, Lipsius, John Hoskyns, and Jonson are identical to these and to one another and offer the most accurate statement of Jonson's rhetorical position.

The necessity for a certain kind of elegance to keep the *genus humile* in a letter from becoming too low had been stated by Demetrius, and, in a sense, the epistolary tradition offers an analogue within its restricted context to the attempt in the first century A.D. to maintain a periodic composition sufficient for perspicuity. Since the letter was one side of a conversation, there were tendencies, to judge by precautionary remarks which have come down, for its prose to dissolve into the formlessness and looseness of conversation or to tighten to the brief, and perhaps sententious, force of highly emotional speech. These extremes are analogous to the loose and curt styles, discussed in the first chapter; Montaigne was criticized for the first, Lipsius for the second. "The letter," Demetrius says, "should be a little more studied than the dialogue, since the latter reproduces an extemporary utterance, while the former is committed to writing and is (in a way) sent as a gift" (*On Style*, 224). But not only should the letter avoid the formlessness of chitchat; it must also avoid the other extreme of cultivated brevity, for "the man who utters sententious maxims (γνωμολογῶν) and exhortations seems to be no longer talking familiarly in a letter but to be speaking *ex cathedra*" (232). By the third century the term Attic seems to have acquired a stronger connotation of formal, and probably sententious, elegance. Philostrato comments that "it is necessary for the form of letters to seem more Attic (ἀττικωτέραν) than common speech but, nevertheless, to come nearer to common speech than to an Attic (ἀττικίσεως) style."[4] Proclus, in the fifth century, says that one should not only embellish but "Atticize" (ἀττικίζειν) the style of a letter moderately, for the testimony of the ancients reveals that both tumid magniloquence and excessively "Attic" speech are foreign to a letter. He goes on to cite the passage above from Philostrato and comments that brevity and perspicuity are epistolary virtues. One should not, however, "be permitted to impair perspicuity by brevity nor in the interests of perspicuity to prattle on without restraint" as one might do in ordinary conversation. The eloquent man, he says, should neither "ramble on too much nor catch at brevity because he has little to tell and darken the meaning of his *sententia*."[5] Montaigne's conversational style, as he himself describes it, rambles without restraint; Lipsius, we shall see, insists on perspicuity in his curt period, as well as graceful expression (*venustas*), and so returns, at least in his theoretical statements, to the central position of the plain style.

The description of the epistolary style in Vives' treatise *De Conscribendis Epistolis* is almost identical to the one he makes of the Attic style, and both are derived from Cicero's discussion of the Attic orator.[6] Such an orator will use plain words from ordinary usage, but these will, nevertheless, differ from those that are not elegant at all and, hence, will be the usage of the educated man. He will avoid periodic structure and cultivate the pleasing informality of a careful negligence, as a handsome woman pleases more when not meticulously adorned; he must follow no rules of symmetry, but gain variation by breaking and dividing the period. His words must be of the purest native idiom, his metaphors modest, and he must avoid the affectation of eloquence, coined words, and overrefinement. So Vives says of the style of letters in a passage that may serve as a definitive description to which others may be compared:

It ought to be most effective when it expresses, as nearly as possible, conversation and familiar discourse . . . of prudent and learned men,

for everything that is best ought to be imitated by art, by which means
one, at least, attains middling results, for thus it is that any perfect art
approaches its true nature. Our daily speech, moreover, ought to be
simple, straightforward, and natural, while pure and chaste, in as much
as smutty and sordid speech belongs to ignorant men and rambling to
the negligent; further, refined speech, elegant and brilliant with ornament, smacks either of insolence or arrogance or is affected with childish
ostentation. . . . Therefore, most of the ancients considered that a letter
should be graced by simplicity and be very refined without adornment,
except meanness was to be absent, *as more pleasing is that simple and
readily available adornment in a wife than the splendid and luxurious.*
Likewise, *in men whom* we hold *to be effeminate* with manners little
worthy of a man if we see them given up to preening, who, rotting in
filthiness and licentiousness, ought to avoid *those detestable things.* The
ancients, therefore, thought the one rule for writing letters was that
no rule should be applied, provided first that stupid and muddled sense
and a too confusing order be absent, and second that the words of the
language be pure in which it was written, for grandiose, finicky, tumid,
and affected words they thought did not make a letter graceful but
ridiculous, *as peacock plumes on a military helmet.*[7]

Again this is a perfect description of the style Jonson admired; it is "pure
and neat . . . yet plaine and customary," where custom "is the consent of
the Learned."

One of the two longest descriptions of style in the *Discoveries* was borrowed by Jonson from the epistolary tradition—sections of John Hoskyns's
Direccōns for Speech and Style, which had originally been adapted from
Justus Lipsius' *Institutio Epistolica.*[8] Jonson seems to have regarded the
advice about letters as a statement about style in general, since in his tran-
scription he altered Hoskyns's "In writing of letters there is" to "In writing
there is."[9] Appended to the *Institutio Epistolica* is Lipsius' Latin translation of the section on letter writing in Demetrius' *On Style* (223–35). Para-
graph 227 reads:

Fere enim animi sui simulacrum quisque & imaginem, epistolam scribit.
Et est quidem ex alia omni oratione videre ac noscere mores scriptoris:
ex nulla tamen aeque atque ex epistola.[10]

Lipsius introduces the selection of his letters, to which his treatise is appended, with a short preface, derived from this passage of Demetrius, which
expresses attitudes identical to those expressed by the satirists. He says he
should be careful not to calumniate, especially in this genre,

which, simple in expression, warm, and candid, sets forth clearly myself
and those things which concern me (*me & mea*), even those which are

deeper and closed off by walls. *Speculum animi liber* is the old saying:
but it is spoken most truly about letters in which our feelings and almost
our very thoughts

> *Are exposed as if engraved on a votive tablet.*

How does that affect me? This way. I remember how Livius Drusus
once with great spirit told an architect who had promised to build a
house which could not be seen from either side from above or below:
*"Why do you not, if you have any skill, build it in such a way that the
eyes of all may be cast upon it and permitted to enter."* In a similar spirit
may my familiar conversations and opinions reveal myself and my
concerns.[11]

The line Lipsius quotes is from Horace's satires: *votiva pateat veluti
descripta tabella* (II.i.33). In the satire Horace is responding to Trebatius'
admonition that he be less openly critical and treat more conventional
subjects in his poems; Horace replies that he intends to follow Lucilius,
who not only treated all he saw with great frankness but candidly revealed
his own thoughts and feelings.[12] As Pliny later praised Martial's candidness
(III.xxi), Horace praises that of Lucilius, and Lipsius, using the satirist's
own words, makes candidness the ideal of his letters.

Lipsius says, "That type of style and elocution most fitting for the letter
I call conversational," and he goes on to discuss its main characteristics:

> Concerning the characteristics, therefore, of epistolary discourse, I advise
> that you observe these five: brevity, perspicuity, simplicity, graceful
> charm (*venustatem*), and appropriateness (*decentiam*).[13] That first
> characteristic is to me the first virtue of conversational style . . . those
> who usually talk the most are the least eloquent. As those who are thin
> in body, fill themselves out in clothes, so those who are deficient in talent
> or knowledge, spread themselves out in words.[14]

Brevity lies in the observation of three things, content, composition, and
diction; the qualities that make each of these brief are fundamental qualities of the plain style:

> Concerning *subject matter*, that you mix in nothing superfluous, nor
> repeat anything. . . . Concerning *composition*, that you avoid all long
> sentence structures and periods: use clauses and asyndeton often. Con-
> cerning *words*, that all copious phrases, allegories, and images be refused:
> let the style be spare and pure (*parca & pura oratio sit*), content with
> only the necessary furniture of words.[15]

Jonson, translating Vives, *De Ratione Dicendi*, warns against long allegories and, transcribing Hoskyns, says, "You are not to cast a Ring for the
perfumed terms of the time, as *Accommodation, Complement, Spirit, &c*"

(VIII, 632). A letter, according to Vives, should "not contain numerous tropes or varied metaphors, or frequent and long allegories, or other figures of speech, or grand and high-flown words, or elegant and rhythmical structure."[16]

The second main virtue is perspicuity, which, Lipsius warns, may be much endangered by brevity:

> The worst fault in a conversational style is, not only not to be under-stood, but also to be understood with difficulty. Some fall short in this by their very nature, who, themselves obscure and recondite, express themselves accordingly; more err on purpose who think nothing learned or praiseworthy unless it is abstruse and eludes ordinary minds. Stupid souls! Little skill has he whom skill is necessary to understand—espe-cially in a letter, which requires no arbitrator or interpreter. Therefore, write clearly, if you can, and briefly, but in such a way that you know the latter to be praiseworthy, the former necessary.[17]

In a verse epistle Jonson, alluding to a line in Horace's *Ars Poetica* (25–26), which he translates "My selfe for shortnesse labour; and I grow/Obscure" (VIII, 307), strikes the balance between brevity and obscurity by keeping in mind the intelligence of his reader, John Selden:

> I know to whom I write. Here, I am sure,
> Though I am short, I cannot be obscure:
> Lesse shall I for the Art or dressing care,
> Truth, and the Graces best, when naked are.[18]

In these four lines the other three characteristics of the epistolary style, simplicity, grace, and appropriateness (which Hoskyns and Jonson call "respect"), are associated with the two main characteristics, brevity and perspicuity.

The third virtue, Lipsius says, is simplicity, which he requires in the style and in the candor of the mind:

> Concerning style: certainly . . . it ought to be simple, without careful refinement, and similar to daily speech. Thus Demetrius wished a letter to be written as if it were a dialogue, & Cicero himself says, *I have con-cealed it in daily words.* Seneca appropriately says *as my conversation is unlabored and casual, as if we were sitting together or strolling, so do I wish my letters to be.* That which is said to adorn women is not to be adorned ornately: so the letter.[19]

Like Cicero in his description of the Attic style, Vives and Lipsius use the comparison of a woman simply dressed in describing the style of letters. Jonson and Hoskyns apply the comparison to the simple ordering of the material:

Vnder this vertue may come Plainenesse, which is not to be curious in
the order, as to answer a letter, as if you were to answer to Intergatories:
As to the first, first; and to the second, secondly, &c. But both in method
[and wordes] to use (as Ladies doe in their attyre) a diligent kind of
negligence . . . (VIII, 632)

So Lipsius remarks of the order that "spontaneity is the entire embellishment," for, "as in conversations we love the spontaneous and the artless: so
here . . . as it is seen, indeed as this or that comes into the mind or to the
pen."[20] Vives, too, says that there should be no certain order in the organization of a letter other than that demanded by the circumstances and
the agreeableness of an unlabored simplicity, as, for example, "Cicero, when
he has to narrate many things, is not greatly concerned what he does first,
what second; he reports things freely and tells them as they first come to
mind."[21] All rhetoric books recommended the plain style for the *narratio*
of an oration. Simplicity, furthermore, is necessary for candor, since, as
Lipsius points out,

> Whatever is simple and natural should shine forth throughout the whole
> piece of writing and reveal a certain candor of a free mind, whose nature
> and specific disposition shine out through no other thing more (as
> Demetrius has so truly written) than through a letter.[22]

Most true in a letter is the Senecan maxim, which Jonson echoes in translating Vives, "Language most shewes a man: speake that I may see thee."

To achieve grace, Lipsius says in discussing the fourth characteristic of
the style of letters, it is necessary sometimes to include allusions to the
writings and actions of the ancients, quotations of short verses, and moral
reflections from every language. But more important, one must season
freely with urbane witticisms, which are "the life and soul of letters."[23] The
iocis salibusque were traditionally associated with the plain style; Cicero
says of Attic oratory that it should be sprinkled with the salt of wit, *facetia*
and *dicacitas*.[24]

The great source of the *pura oratio*, as Terence indicated, was comedy.
Jonson thought that "in *Plautus*, wee shall see the Oeconomy, and disposition of *Poems*, better observed then in *Terence*" (VIII, 618), and more important, he agreed with the "Testimonie given by *Lucius Aelius Stilo* upon
Plautus; who affirmed, *Musas, si latine loqui voluissent, Plautino sermone
fuisse loquuturas*," and with M. Varro, "who pronounced him the *Prince*
of *Letters*, and *Elegancie*, in the *Roman* Language" (VIII, 641). Stilo's
comment that the Muses, had they wished to speak Latin, would have
spoken in the language of Plautus, was applied to Jonson himself by John

Selden (XI, 627). It is in the matter of imitation that Lipsius relates the diction of comedy so closely with that of the epistle. Although it is good, he says, that young boys should imitate Cicero, the adult should try all the ancient writers, "but especially Sallust, Seneca, Tacitus, and that type of brief and subtle writer whose luxuriousness may be quickly trimmed as if by a pruning-hook; let a style become clipped, strong, and truly manly (*oratio stricta, fortis, & vere virilis*)."[25] Plautus and Terence, he says, may be models for the refinement of any type of writing, for "from whom is the propriety of words better to be sought, from whom that Attic brilliance of phrasing, from whom is to be more often drawn first grace, then wit and civility, than from my writer of comedy?"

> For here I mean Plautus alone, and I put him before all others . . . who have attempted this paper sea in Italy or Greece. These writers of comedy are especially suitable models for letters and familiar writing . . . for what in truth is a letter if not everyday discourse (*cottidiana dissertatio*), as Artemo did not mistake, according to Demetrius, who thought the dialogue and the epistle should be written in the same way. And Pliny for the same reason praised the letters of a certain matron because she wrote in the same fashion as Terence and Plautus would have written if they had not been confined by meter. Why should I not place Pliny himself rightly in this second class, terse, pointed, bright, though somewhat effeminate at times—not without charm—and not manly enough.[26]

Despite this praise, Lipsius, like Martial and Jonson, warns against harshness and archaism, which the unwary may imitate in the writers of comedy, while missing their virtues.[27] One of their greatest virtues is as a possible corrective of affected grandiloquence or overrefinement. Jonson has Virgil in *Poetaster* advise Crispinus to read Cato "And taste a piece of Terence, sucke his phrase" (V.iii.540). After describing the source of propriety of words and Attic phrasing, Lipsius concludes his treatise with a sensible warning, one which would have appealed to Jonson:

> There must be one caution, that when the piece of writing is ready to be completed and the final touches put on it, let affectation be avoided, an unhappy fault to be sure and one which steals in imperceptibly in the guise of a virtue. It results from too much zeal without restraint in refinement (*cultus*). It is most difficult to see and avoid by yourself; happy is he who has some teacher or admonishing friend.[28]

The attitudes best expressed by the epistolary style are clearly stated also in the letters of Jonson's friend James Howell. Martial claims that his epigrams will represent his likeness more accurately than a portrait, and so, sending his book, he says to it (VII, 84), "Small, but welcome, shall be the gift you will make to my dear comrade: more truly in my song will my face be seen." Howell says of his letters that they are "the Keys of the Mind, they open all the Boxes of one's Breast, all the cells of the Brain, and truly set forth the inward Man; nor can the Pencil so lively represent the Face, as the Pen can do the Fancy."[29] Reflecting the attitudes of Seneca's epistles in phrasing nearly identical to that in which Persius addresses Cornutus in his fifth satire, Howell tells his correspondent that his letters represent him better than an "*Echo* or *Chrystal*" could do and "clearly set forth the notions" of his mind and "the motions" of his soul. His own letters fall short, but still are candid testimonies of "real and inbred Affection," and, he says, should be supplemented by "a *Crystal-casement* in my Breast, thro' which you might behold the motions of my Heart."[30] His first letter, which was added to the second edition of the collection, discusses the epistolary style. It should be simple, for, as Montaigne says of his essays, "we should write as we speak; and that's a true familiar Letter which expresses one's Mind, as if he were discoursing with the Party to whom he writes, in succinct and short Terms." Howell objects to those who write homilies rather than letters and preach rather than converse. In an interesting passage he criticizes contemporary letter writers in very Senecan terms:

Most . . . among your Latin Epistolizers, go freighted with mere *Bartholomew* Ware, with trite and trivial Phrases only, listed with pedantic Shreds of School-boy Verses. Others there are among our next transmarine Neighbours Eastward, who write in their own Language, but their Style is soft and easy, that their Letters may be said to be like Bodies of loose Flesh without Sinews, they have neither Joints of *Art* nor *Arteries* in them; they have a kind of simpering and lank hectic Expressions made up of a Bombast of Words, and finical affected Compliments only: I cannot well away with such sleazy Stuff, with such Cobweb-compositions, where there is no Strength of Matter, nothing for the Reader to carry away with him,[31] that may enlarge the Notions of his Soul. One shall hardly find an Apothegm, Example, Simile, or anything of Philosophy, History, or solid Knowledge, or as much as one new *created* Phrase, in a hundred of them: . . . it may be said of them, what was said of the *Echo, That she is a mere Sound and nothing else.*

Howell is criticizing these correspondents for not writing in the style recommended by Vives and Lipsius, for they, as Vives says of Cicero,[32] lose their stylistic sinews, arteries, and "joints of *Art*" in the loose luxuriant flesh of words "where there is no strength of Matter." In a verse letter to Jonson, Francis Beaumont describes the extreme intimacy with which he writes, which is characteristic of the easy familiarity of Howell's own letters to Jonson. Wishing only "to showe/the Loue" he carries, he will "invoake none, but the post" and will write in a style similar to that "which men/ send cheese to towne with," since "I write not," he says, "to please Ben: Johnson but to please my frend" (XI, 378).

Although the classical descriptions of the epistolary style remained virtually unchanged in the Renaissance, the sixteenth-century treatises added one extremely important prerogative to the familiar epistle: freedom of subject matter. Despite the fact that Cicero, Pliny, and others in their own familiar letters practiced the freedom later claimed by the specialized treatises of the Renaissance, the principles of decorum in subject matter for the three ancient styles were fairly strictly observed in the theoretical statements about epistolary style. These principles maintained that the grand style treated high subjects such as matters of divinity and state, the plain or low style treated matters of farce and comedy on the stage and communicated simple matters of daily life in conversation or in letters, and the middle style ranged in between and usually settled on love. Demetrius says explicitly that "we must also remember that there are epistolary topics, as well as an epistolary style," and if anybody "should write of logical subtleties or questions of natural history in a letter, he writes indeed, but not a letter. A letter is designed to be the heart's good wishes in brief; it is the exposition of a simple subject in simple terms."[33] Even when letters are not involved, Demetrius says that "in the case of the plain style, we can no doubt point to subject matter which is homely and appropriate to the style itself,"[34] and his conventional position was shared by most of the rhetoricians. Matters in which strong emotions were involved were usually treated in the grand, or perhaps the middle, style. Conversation—and the letter was a "written conversation"—ought, Cicero says, to be free from such emotions as anger, inordinate desire, indolence, and indifference.[35] Horace, including the verse epistles among his *sermones,* did most to extend the boundaries of what could be decorously treated in a letter by claiming the subject matter of the *Socraticae . . . chartae.* Though Seneca's epistolary meditations were powerfully emotional and consciously formal compositions, which were even referred to slightingly as school declamations (Suetonius *Cali.* liii), they contributed to the freedom of the epistle by using its convention of intimacy with its appearance of spontaneity as a device for persuasion. It was not until the Renaissance, however, that complete liberty was granted in the theoretical discussions of the genre, and the arguments for its liberation are essentially those of the ancient satirists and epigrammatists.

The epistolary manuals of the Middle Ages were not concerned with the familiar letter but with *dictamen*, the art of the professional letter writer, or secretary, whose business it was to compose official or ceremonious epistles to important men. Such letters imitated the formal organization of the oration, as prescribed by the classical rhetorical treatises, and in subject matter were usually divided into three categories: the Demonstrative, the Deliberative, and the Judicial. It was to these categories and to the formal and pretentious inflexibility of the official letter that Erasmus objected in his treatise *De Ratione Conscribendi Epistolas,* and he objected mainly on the grounds of its unrealistic limitations upon subject matter. Different kinds of matter, he says in his first chapter, are not less numerous than the worlds of Democritus; and in a later chapter, he asks what there is in the nature of things that is not committed to letters.[36] To accommodate the multiplicity of subjects he added a fourth category, the *genus familiare,* or familiar letter, which came to represent all letters by the end of the sixteenth century, as the plain style as described by Demetrius came to represent all epistolary styles. It is interesting to see how Erasmus' request for the complete freedom of epistolary subject matter is virtually identical, even in phrasing, to that which had been made by the satirists and the epigrammatists in classical literature.

In his first satire Juvenal describes the subject matter of satire:

> quidquid agunt homines, votum timor ira voluptas
> gaudia discursus, nostri farrago libelli est. (ll. 85–86)

Whatever men do, their vows, their fears, angers, pleasures, joys, comings and goings, is the motley subject of my book. Pliny the younger says that his epigrams treat love, hate, anger, pity, urbane wit, everything whatever which happens in life, even the concerns of the forum (*Ep.* VII.ix). In another letter (*Ep.* IV.xiv) he describes their subject matter more intimately:

> His iocamur, ludimus, amamus, dolemus, querimur, irascimur, describimus aliquid . . .

In these, he says, I joke, play, love, sorrow, complain, get angry, describe anything whatever, and Erasmus, as if he had the passage in mind, defends the unlimited subject matter of the familiar letter:

> In his gaudemus, dolemus, speramus, metuimus. In his . . . querimur, jurgamur, bellum denunciamus, in gratiam redimus, consolamur, consulimus . . . narramus, describimus, laudamus, vituperamus. In his odimus, amamus, miramur, deliberamus, . . . denique, ecquid tandem non? His tanquam certissimis ministris, omnes animi affectus, his publica, his privata, his domestica, credimus.[37]

Erasmus concludes his list of activities, which is considerably longer, by asking what finally is not contained in letters, to which one entrusts, as if to the most dependable servants, all of one's feelings, all public, private, and domestic concerns. In one letter to a friend, which was used as a preface to early collections of his letters, he writes that if letters lack honest feeling, *veris affectibus,* and do not represent a man's real life, *vitam ipsam hominis,* they are not genuine.[38] So Martial, who had claimed that each epigram could be considered a brief epistle, had written that Life itself could say in reading his epigrams " 'tis my own." Erasmus goes on to say to the same friend that the true letter should represent as in a picture, *velut in tabula,* the character, fortune, and feelings of the writer. In the preface to his selection of letters Lipsius wrote that he intended to reveal with complete candor his own mind and his own concerns; his inmost thoughts, echoing Horace, were to be exposed as if engraved on a votive tablet. The epistle, then, is given the freedom of subject matter of the other genres and is described in terms formerly applied to satire and epigram. The extent of Horace's rebellion against the conventions of style and subject is tacitly recognized by Isaac Casaubon when he says in his *De Satyrica Poesi* that they are wrong who say that Horace's *Epistulae* should not be included in the name and canon of the *Sermones.*[39]

The implications of this epistolary prerogative are extensive for the stylistic controversies of the late sixteenth century when one considers that the treatises, which gradually came to be regarded by the anti-Ciceronians as important statements about their general rhetorical position, sanctioned the treatment of any subject, human or divine, in a plain style. The gradual extension of the range of subject matter which could be decorously treated by the plain style reflects the general breakdown of the ancient characters of style in the Renaissance, and it permitted poets like Jonson and Donne to treat matters of religion and love, subjects traditionally limited to the high and middle styles, in a plain style, which had been associated with satire and comedy. The restrictions on what the other styles could treat were also breaking down, but that was comparatively less important. For, although important subjects could be treated seriously and effectively in the style of Cicero's Attic orator, which had been developed originally with a philosophic intention, trivial subjects, if treated in a high style, could only produce bombast or burlesque. The versatility of the Attic style, which Socrates and the satirists had taken advantage of, was utilized again by the poets of the late sixteenth and early seventeenth centuries.

The descriptive distinctions between the three characters of style in the

Greek and Latin rhetorical treatises were phrased in the most general terms; instead of categorizing particular pieces of writing as entirely this or that, they distinguished certain general qualities of diction and organization, which, of course, reflected certain attitudes of the speaker toward his subject and his audience.[40] The "typical" examples of each style given in the *Ad Herennium* would illustrate the style of very few entire works. Vives, in the passage quoted in the Preface, complains of the confusion resulting from the attempt to claim that a particular piece of writing is in this style or that. He says, however, that one can say that one style predominates, as a "humor" does; a man who is "bilious" is not so all the time, for he has other humors, but he is bilious most of the time. The most intelligent scholars of the sixteenth century were careful not to restrict too narrowly, in an effort to possess and apply more quickly and securely their classical learning, the terminology that they adopted from the ancient writers, but attempted instead to retain the flexibility of the original terms. Vives, for instance, is careful to distinguish in his treatise *On the Causes of the Corruptions of the Arts* three different uses of the plain style: "the letter," he says, "demands one kind of the plainest style, rural subjects another, and books on philosophy another."[41] The more popular literary writers, however, often oversimplified and obscured the problem.

The following passage from George Puttenham's *The Arte of English Poesie* may serve both as a Renaissance statement of the subject matter conventionally treated by each style and as an example of the confusions that resulted from not regarding such distinctions as that of Vives cited above:

> The matters therefore that concerne the Gods and diuine things are highest of all other to be couched in writing, next to them the noble gests and great fortunes of Princes, and the notable accidēts of time, as the greatest affaires of war & peace, these be all high subjectes, and therefore are deliuered ouer to the Poets *Hymnick* & historicall who be occupied either in diuine laudes, or in *heroicall* reports: the meane matters be those that cōcerne meane men, their life and business, as lawyers, gentlemen, and marchants, good housholders and honest Citizens, and which sound neither to matters of state nor of warre, nor leagues, nor great alliances, but smatch all the common conuersation, as of the ciuiller and better sort of men: the base and low matters be the doings of the commō artificer, seruingman, yeoman, groome, husbandman, day-labourer, sailer, shepheard, swynard, and such like of homely calling, degree and bringing up.[42]

This splitting of the subject matter of the classical plain style into two categories, the "meane" and the "base," is an error that Vives had cautioned

against. The "meane" subjects which Puttenham mentions were those traditionally treated by comedy in the plain style that Terence describes as
pura oratio; the conversation "of the ciuiller and better sort of men" is a
perfect description of the style of the Attic orator, the philosopher, and the
letter writer, all of whom employed the *genus tenue,* not the *genus floridum*.

The boundaries between the styles became more obscure the more one
tried to establish them rigidly, and one of the reasons for the breakdown
of these boundaries was the attempt to measure exactly the height of a
style in order to put certain poems or lines into "separate boxes." This is
why J. C. Scaliger may be one of the "many good clerkes" who, Puttenham
admits, "say that the loftie style may be decently used in a meane and base
subiect & contrariwise,"[43] and why Scaliger is forced continually to distinguish gradations within the three basic categories: the whole fourth
book of his *Poetices* is an attempt to classify dozens of passages of verse
according to qualities associated with one or the other of the three styles.
When a passage does not fit into the categories, he supplies a "gradation"
and even a chapter called "Gradus in Characteribus," for, he says,

> What pertains to the nature of the character is not necessarily that great
> things themselves be treated in a grand style, nor small things in a plain
> style, but it is enough if the high style maintain its dignity by well chosen
> words, sonorous and eloquent, and by rhythmical composition, and if
> the plain style keep a plain harmony by concise words besides a pure,
> strict speech, taken from customary usage (*orationem puram, pressam,
> de medio sumptam*).[44]

Gradations tend to become categories in their own right; as they increase,
they may become easier to apply to particular passages but they obscure
the intentions behind the original divisions. Scaliger says elsewhere that
"the high style is not always elevated, for it is compelled sometimes to descend to those things which are held to be more humble subjects, nor does
the plain style always lie low or crawl, but sometimes rises."[45] Vives agrees
with Scaliger that there are gradations, but he does not attempt to measure
them in the various styles; he simply comments, in Jonson's translation,
that "there is a certaine latitude in these things, by which wee find the degrees" (VIII, 626). The extent of this latitude is stated explicitly in connection with letters.

One gains a clear idea of how much freedom of subject matter the
epistolary tradition after Erasmus offered to the plain style—a freedom that
was seldom taken advantage of by the English poets before Jonson and
Donne—when one recalls the position of the conventional rhetoric book.[46]

Puttenham had stated that the middle, to say nothing of the plain, style must not treat matters of state or war, leagues, or alliances. Erasmus said explicitly, in the passage quoted above, that wars could be declared in letters (*bellum denunciamus*), and Antonius Muretus, with Lipsius the most important spokesman of the anti-Ciceronian movement, echoed him in saying that, among the great variety of subjects in letters, wars are declared and waged, peace compacted, and treaties established.[47] In describing the range of epistolary material, Francis Bacon writes that "letters are according to all the variety of occasions, advertisements, advices, directions, propositions, petitions, commendatory, expostulatory, satisfactory, of compliment, of pleasure, of discourse, and all other passages of action."[48] The new attitude is startlingly clear if one compares Puttenham's statement that matters which concern "diuine things" must be treated in a high style by "Poets *Hymnick*" with this passage from Lipsius' *Institutio Epistolica*:

> Moreover, I call the subject matter, which is different in every letter, variable: the occasion itself and reason for writing. It is many sided, nor does it extend less widely than life itself. For what is there of matters either human or divine (*rei divinae aut humanae*) which we do not communicate in conversation? Therefore, what in letters, which is another conversation (*alter sermo*).[49]

Vives explicitly states that a familiar letter can contain any subject matter whatever (*epistola quascumque res potest continere*),[50] and Melanchthon observes that the greatest subjects are often treated in letters.[51] Etienne Pasquier warns the reader that he will find a large "meslee" of subjects in his letters, some serious, some gay,[52] and Jonson's friend James Howell says that letters are "capable of any Subject."[53] The *sermo,* the style of the Socratic dialogues, the *pura oratio* of Latin comedy, the "speech more appropriate to prose" of Horace's *sermones* and Martial's epigrams, which in each case had been developed for the more flexible examination of actual experience, had always been used in familiar letters. Erasmus, however, claimed that the familiar letter should treat all emotions, *omnes affectus*; Lipsius that the *alter sermo* could treat all things human or divine; and the reasons were identical to those of Terence, Horace, Martial, and Pliny.

Pliny, Martial, and Horace, along with Tacitus and Petronius, were recommended by Jonson to Drummond as those, among the ancients, who "speke best Latine." These writers were among the main stylistic models held up by the anti-Ciceronians, and in their avoidance of the Ciceronian period they came to be associated with the Atticists, whose position Jonson defines and defends in his *Discoveries*. Vives, Lipsius, and Bacon are Jonson's main contemporary authorities. Of these, Vives describes a rhetorical position in his *De Ratione Dicendi* and his *De Conscribendis Epistolis* which is essentially that of the Attic orator. Justus Lipsius advocates a style for letters in his *Institutio Epistolica* which is similar to the ideal Stoic style described in Diogenes Laertius' *Life of Zeno*, and, since he himself was the chief reviver of Stoicism in the sixteenth century, it is likely that he considered it the best style for most purposes. Francis Bacon remarks that letters "such as are written from wise men are of all the words of man, in my judgement, the best; for they are more natural than orations, and public speeches, and more advised than conferences or present speeches."[54] There was, then, a tendency among those interested in reviving the Attic, or plain, style to consider the familiar letter as the ideal stylistic model.

It is not strange, therefore, that Jonson should apply to style in general a passage on letter writing from John Hoskyns's *Direccõns for Speech and Style*. This passage, which Hoskyns took from Lipsius' *Institutio Episto-lica* and which Lipsius derived originally from Demetrius, defines Jonson's basic rhetorical position. Since he regarded the epistolary treatise as a gen-eral rhetorical statement, he found ample contemporary justification for using the plain style to treat any subject, either human or divine. The Renaissance treatises gave explicit rhetorical sanction to the practice and stylistic assumptions of the ancient satirist, epigrammatist, and writer of comedy, who, as Terence remarks, since he is a man, considers no human thing foreign to him.[55] Though the extended subject matter of the familiar letter was more a result than a cause of the breakdown of the ancient char-acters of style in the Renaissance, the epistolary treatises stated most ex-plicitly, in terms clearly derived from the ancient revolt against conven-tional decorum, the later sixteenth-century conviction that the classical plain style could treat any subject. In its intention to analyze actual experience, it could, in verse as well as prose, define, without isolating them in ecstatic address, particular religious feelings and relate them to the general context of the writer's experience. It could in the love poem define and convey an intensity of feeling derived from the writer's effort to understand his re-lationship to his lover as one of many relationships in a real world, without addressing her as if her love were an unrelated and unique beatitude.[56]

In conclusion, one of Lipsius' descriptions of his own letters reveals his conscious association of the qualities of Atticism with both the epistolary freedom of subject matter and the *sermo* of comedy:

> Moreover, what else are familiar letters, if you look at the words and the jests, other than a reproduction of the dialogue of comedy. Among the writers of comedy who is better than Plautus? . . . He is a writer

who abounds in the purity and aptness of speech and who offers urbanity, jests, wit, and that Attic grace which you seek for in vain in the
rest of Latium. Do they regard me as one of those who write all their
letters in one way? Whether they are gay or sad, treat serious or trivial
matters, address the learned or ignorant, is their course and slow pace
everywhere the same? I do not follow them. Truly, may my letters
have wit and learning and something out of the ordinary, which may
please however often it is repeated.[57]

The influence of comedy upon the stylistic theory of the other three genres
of the plain style was discussed and applied in detail during the Renaissance.
In his own comedies Jonson continually reasserts the attitudes behind the
classical *sermo,* but some of his most explicit comments on the relation of
comedy to satire, epistle, and epigram are adapted in the *Discoveries* from
contemporary Neo-Latin scholarship.

4

THE AUTHORITY OF NEO-LATIN
SCHOLARSHIP

In mentem subijt Stolonis illud,
Lingua Pieridas fuisse Plauti
Vsuras, Ciceronis atq dictum,
Saturno genitum phrasi Platonis,
Musae si Latio, Iouisq Athenis
Dixissent.

SELDEN ON JONSON's Workes, 1616

PROBABLY AT NO POINT during the English Renaissance did neo-Latin writers have so exclusive an influence upon the English vernacular as during the emergence of the rhetorical principles and practice of the plain style. The comprehensive descriptive treatises of classical poetic theory, such as those of Minturno and J. C. Scaliger, which were extensively used by George Puttenham, Henry Peacham the elder, and other writers of English rhetoric books did not recommend and defend so much as enumerate specific principles. Since the English rhetoric books were primarily concerned with methods of amplification and the more ornate stylistic conventions of the Continental literary movements, they were directed mainly to the courtly Petrarchan imitators and borrowed little from discussions of the plain style. This meant, of course, that one had to return to the Latin text of such general reference works as Scaliger's *Poetices* for information about the *genus tenue* or the genres that employed it, and even then such works often did little more than transpose their classical sources. The neo-Latin influence upon anti-Ciceronianism in prose and anti-Petrarchanism in verse became considerably more significant, therefore, when Jonson, in reacting against the poetic attitudes and practice of the Petrarchans, looked for rhetorical corroboration for his position and found it, not only in the ancient writers, but in such men as Erasmus, Vives, Lipsius, and Bacon, who advocated various applications of the Attic style and argued their case with power and precision. Jonson also found accurate descriptions of the *sermo* and its intentions in the famous works on the four classical genres by such scholars as Daniel Heinsius and Isaac Casaubon. Jonson's *Discoveries*, which borrows largely from the men just mentioned, can best be described as a handbook of the new authorities on matters of style. These were primarily neo-Latin authorities, who exerted their formative influence on Jonson's stylistic ideas and practice and, through such books as the *Discoveries* where they were translated, on other writers of the first half of the seventeenth century.

The *Discoveries* itself, published in 1640, would not have influenced the early part of the century, but it is a succinct statement of the principles that had guided Jonson's work from the 1590's on and that he, no doubt, constantly reiterated in his conversation as well as in his poems and plays. His enormous personal influence on men both older and younger than himself is itself a testimony to the growing influence of neo-Latin commentary upon English writers. Part of Jonson's energetic originality lies in his ability to find and recognize workable stylistic principles in one linguistic tradition and to carry them over and apply them to another, to be intimate with and to learn from the greatest scholars of his day, such as Camden and Selden, and to bring that knowledge to the popular stage, to the Court, and to the readers of his poems. He was, in this sense, one of the great intellectual ambassadors of the Renaissance, an *explorator*, as his motto says, from whom no mind was safe. With this in mind, it is interesting to see that the tradition of the plain style, beginning in antiquity and reviving in the Humanists, is carried on in the neo-Latin scholarship of Jonson's own day, that in many ways a man like Isaac Casaubon is closer to the main critical center of literary activity than countless contemporary poets, and that it is men like John Selden who often appreciated Jonson most and in their occasional comments revealed their insight into an entire tradition.

Selden, "the bravest man jn all Languages" (I, 149), contributed a complimentary poem to the first collected edition of Jonson's works in 1616. He praises Jonson's understanding, art of versification, critical judgment, wit, clean style (*sermonem . . . nitidum*), and his "new pronouncements on old customs," as well as his principles, which will always remain as he has stated them, "since neither shall Lemnos be more known by its figurine, nor the consecrated bull by its spot, nor Venus by her girdle, nor Apollo by his hair," than he shall be known by his knowing Muse. When reading his works, Selden says, "there came into my mind that saying of Stilo, that the Muses would have used the language of Plautus, and the saying of Cicero, that the son of Saturn would have used the language of Plato if the Muses of Jove had spoken in Latium and at Athens."[1] Stilo's remark had often been applied to the plain style, and Selden associates Jonson's diction not only with that of Plautus but with that of Socrates, reaffirming the close relationship between the plain style and the philosophical discourse from which it was originally derived. In the *Discoveries* Jonson quotes Stilo's remark along with an epitaph on the comic poet, Naevius, in an extremely interesting passage on comedy which summarizes the general attitudes expressed by the *sermo*:

> What figure of a Body was *Lysippus* ever able to forme with his Graver, or *Apelles* to paint with his Pencill, as the Comedy to life expresseth so many, and various affections of the minde? There shall the Spectator see some, insulting with Joy; others, fretting with Melancholy; raging with Anger; mad with Love; boiling with Avarice; undone with Riot; tortur'd with expectation; consum'd with feare: no perturbation in common life, but the Orator findes an example of it in the Scene. And then, for the Elegancy of Language, read but this Inscription on the *Grave* of a *Comicke Poet*:
>
> > *Immortales mortales, si fas esset, flere,*
> > *Flerent divæ Camœnæ Nævium Poetam;*
> > *Itaque postquam est Orcino traditus thesauro,*
> > *Obliti sunt Romæ, lingua loqui Latina.*
>
> Or, that modester Testimonie given by *Lucius Aelius Stilo* upon *Plautus*; who affirmed, *Musas, si latine loqui voluissent, Plautino sermone fuisse loquuturas.* (VIII, 640–41)[2]

Jonson's "various affections of the minde" could be almost an exact translation of *omnes animi affectus,* which Erasmus applies to letters, and the passage in general is identical to the statements Martial and Horace make about their epigrams and satires.

Terence, whom Julius Caesar called *puri sermonis amator,* was praised along with Plautus for his communication of intimate feelings. In his *Ad Horatii de Plauto & Terentio judicium, Dissertatio,* included in his edition of Terence, Daniel Heinsius, whom Jonson often quoted with admiration, remarks that Terence surpassed everyone in the adaptation of dialogue to character:

> We can neither read nor remember his verbal characterizations (*moratum . . . sermonem*) without the greatest pleasure . . . from whose elegance, grace, wit, and charm the further you are removed, the less contact you have with urbanity. . . . You see speeches, which, because they are elegantly characterized, catch the innermost feelings.[3]

The recognition of the *sermo*'s ability to express emotion accurately emphasizes the implications of Selden's comparison of the intimate style of Jonson's poems with that of Plautus. The feelings will be easily understood because they arise from the familiar activities of daily life, since comedy is an *imitatio vitae, speculum consuetudinis, et imago veritatis.*[4] Ascham associates the purity of diction in comedy with the unlimited range of private feelings and actions. If Plautus and Terence are properly expurgated, each "is such a plentiful storehouse for common eloquence in mean matters, and all private men's affairs, as the Latin tongue, for that respect, hath not the like again."[5] When one treats all private men's affairs, one will, as Bacon said of letters, treat "all . . . passages of action," and the range of subject matter is infinite.[6] Vives remarks on the representation of life on the stage, borrowing a comparison from Horace, which had been used to illustrate the candidness of the epistle and of satire: "In the theatres the life of men was shown for public enjoyment, as if on a votive tablet or in a mirror."[7]

Following Horace, the scholars of the sixteenth and seventeenth centuries regarded the style and subject of satire as closely connected with those of comedy. Heinsius says in his *De Satyra Horatiana* they are virtually the same: "For if you take away the action and the story from the old comedy, since from these its scope and constitution derive, it plainly matches Horatian satire, which certainly represents things in the same ways (in a conversational style, at least, and in meter)."[8] Jonson's friend Isaac Casaubon, in his *De Satyrica Graecorum Poesi et Romanorum Satira,* which is perhaps the most distinguished contemporary work on the subject, relates the *sermones* to the style of Lucilius and of comedy:

> Lucilius' style is not different from comedy. It is low, I mean, loose, and fitted to the crowds, for which reason Horace, who imitated Lucilius, called his satires *the prosaic muse (pedestrem Musam).* . . . In another place he calls them conversations (*sermones*): *Albius, candid judge of our conversations.* The same reason holds for each appellation. For, as we noted elsewhere, in any genre of speaking which is free and without care, like that accustomed to be used in daily conversation, they call speech loose . . . and prosaic expression.[9]

It was the adherence to this natural way of speaking which led Heinsius to prefer Horace to Juvenal and Persius. Declamation, affectation, and artistry, he says, depart as far as possible from nature and such a conversational style, because they actually take away the first virtue of the speaker, namely truth and honest candor (*simplicitatem*). Juvenal little guards against this loss, partly because his verses do not keep their feet on the ground (*repunt humi*), as do those of the comic poets and of Horace, but are ornate like those of the epic poet. Persius' satires are even more elevated; his audacious metaphors exceed not only plain speech but a poetical style, which Cicero says ought to be carefully avoided by the plain orator (*summisso oratori*).[10] This preference for Horace, and the reasons for it, are behind Heinsius' famous definition of satire, to which John Dryden so strongly objected:

> Satire is a kind of poetry, without a series of action, invented for the purging of our minds; in which human vices, ignorance, and errors, and all things besides, which are produced from them in every man, are severely reprehended;[11] partly dramatically, partly simply, and sometimes in both kinds of speaking; but, for the most part, figuratively, and occultly; consisting in a low familiar way, chiefly in a sharp and pungent manner of speech; but partly, also, in a facetious and civil way of jesting; by which either hatred, or laughter, or indignation is moved.[12]

Heinsius adds that since this expresses the complete nature of satire, it is taken almost entirely from the precepts of Horace.[13] Dryden objects to Horace's having followed Lucilius' "low familiar way of speech" and prefers Juvenal's more elevated language. "Horace," he says, "is according to his subject, that is, generally grovelling." "This," he continues, "I imagine, was the chief reason why he minded only the clearness of satire, and the cleanness of expression, without ascending to those heights to which his own vigour might have carried him."[14]

Jonson probably would have sided with Heinsius because of his own admiration for Horace. In the *Discoveries* he pays many tributes, but none so extravagant as those to Horace, some of which have previously been cited (VIII, 639-40, 642). He also translates Heinsius' praise of the "wittie *Manling*" of Augustus, who, "being a man so conversant, and inwardly familiar with the censures of great men, that did discourse" on poetry and language, must have been well acquainted with the critical judgments of the highest period of Roman literary achievement (VIII, 642-43). He uses Horace as his critical spokesman in *Poetaster*, building into the play many passages from the *sermones,* and he translated the *Ars Poetica,* several odes, and "A speech according to Horace" (VIII, 213-16); his incidental borrowings are too numerous to count. Whether or not this demonstrates that he would have disagreed with Dryden's judgment is not so significant as the probable reason why he might have, which is based on a remark in the *Essay on Satire*. Dryden comments that Horace's "urbanity, that is, his good manners, are to be commended, but his wit is faint."[15] If urbanity had become simply good manners, the most vital quality of the *sermones* was lost, and it is not surprising that they should have seemed flat to Dryden. To see how differently Jonson probably regarded this quality, one should turn to Quintilian, who observes that *urbanitas* "denotes language with a smack of the city in its words, accent and idiom, and further suggests a certain tincture of learning derived from associating with well educated men; in a word, it represents the opposite of rusticity" (VI.iii.17). Drawing upon a treatise on *Urbanity* of Domitius Marsus, he points out that such language consists of "elegant sayings with a certain charm and attraction of their own, which are suitable even to speeches of the most serious kind: they are characterised by a certain urbane wit, but not of a kind to raise a laugh . . . peculiar to this city, though it was not till a late period that it was understood in this sense, after the word *Urbs* had come to be accepted as indicating Rome without the addition of any proper noun" (VI.iii.102–3).

"Urbane" meant simply Roman, and to a good Latinist like Jonson it would mean that which was characteristic of London. Urbanity, furthermore, is the distinguishing characteristic between the two main types of plain style: the language of conversation between educated men on any subject and the "low" rural speech of shepherds, whose range of subject matter would be considerably more limited. Marsus defines urbanity as "a certain quality of language compressed into the limits of a brief saying and adapted to delight and move men to every kind of emotion" (104), and, thinking this too general, since it could apply to any type of good writing, Quintilian says that for him "*urbanity* involves the total absence of all that is incongruous, coarse, unpolished and exotic whether in thought, language, voice or gesture, and resides not so much in isolated sayings as in the whole complexion of our language, just as for the Greeks *Atticism* means that elegance of taste which was peculiar to Athens" (107). Though the speech of an urbane man will be polished, familiar, and appropriate to the social context, it will display far more than good manners, and the wit that is clever but does not necessarily cause laughter may be far from polite. To reduce urbanity to good manners is to miss the intellectual sophistication of which they reveal only a part; to object to the plainness of Horace's style is to be unresponsive to the intimate familiarity with which he offers to share that sophistication. Jonson offered this familiarity as freely as Horace to a great number of people whom he knew and to everyone who read his poems. Drummond, for one, seemed unable to share his sophistication despite the intimacy of a personal visit; not to be able to participate in some way in the intimate context of the author's experience is to miss the principal quality of the plain style.

The best way to achieve urbanity in style is to avoid the affectations and mannerisms that Jonson criticizes in his development and definition of the plain, or Attic, style. In his commentary on the satires of Persius, which Jonson considered *doctissimus* (I, 52 n.), Isaac Casaubon glosses the line *verba togae sequeris, junctura callidus acri* (V.14) in terms nearly identical to those against archaism and arbitrary roughening in the *Discoveries*. The phrase *verba togae* implies the speech of urban Roman citizens, and the toga was worn in comedy, representing the dress of ordinary life. Casaubon expands Persius' praise of Cornutus: you, the satirist says:

> Use words based upon ordinary usage, not sought out of distant antiquity, as the unskilled, indeed, did, as we said at first, and certainly not bombastic and overly long words. . . . The other virtue . . . is that the right composition of the words follow the selection of them. . . . Seneca also reprehends, in letter CXIV, those who err in the effort to roughen the style on purpose: they do not want, he says, a joining to be without a jolt and think that manly and strong which hits the ear unevenly.[16]

Casaubon, like Jonson, is drawing on Seneca, and the gloss is a fairly accurate summary of Martial's epigram XI.90, discussed in connection with Jonson's criticism of those "who thinke those things the stronger, that have no Art" (VIII, 587). Casaubon's similarity to Jonson illustrates the closeness of neo-Latin scholarship to the new conventions of vernacular literature. Casaubon's is one of the great editions of Persius, and his description of the satirist's stylistic recommendations, derived from experience and understanding, is virtually identical to Jonson's description of stylistic excellence in English. In a sense, such passages as this of Casaubon could have made up a rhetorical handbook for the seventeenth century, which would have collected and defined the principles that "literary" writers were to follow.

In his gloss on the passage in Persius which connects the attitudes of the satirist most closely to those of the letter writer (V.19–29), Casaubon clearly echoes Senecan passages on style which Jonson admired and sometimes quoted. Of the phrase *secreti loquimur* (V.21) he comments that Persius wishes to speak to Cornutus as honestly and with as little pretense in their letters as friends would when they talk freely together in a private place. I do not, Casaubon writes, interpreting the satirist, "desire to chat with you in any way but as if we, when separated, were together and opened the secrets of our breasts to one another."[17] Although Casaubon considers at length the origin of the word *satire*, he is impatient with those who treat Horatian epistles separately from the satires. "Those people," he writes in his *De Satyrica*, "are not to be borne who say that the books of Epistles should not be included in the name and canon of the Satires." Lucilius, he says, and Persius, the greatest imitator of Horace, wrote satires in the form of letters, and even Horace applied the name of conversation to his letters in calling Albius *nostrorum sermonum candide iudex* (*Ep.* I.iv.1). Furthermore, since these *sermones* "were sent to absent friends, they have the appropriate name for the matter, namely, epistles."[18] The fact that the satire and the epistle were considered to be essentially the same genre and that the term satire had become associated with the "petulant paper, or scoffing verses" (VIII, 571), of those writers who avoided art explains why Jonson could use the term epistle almost exclusively, even for poems that were largely satirical.

The sixteenth-century scholars described the style of Horace's epistles in the same terms as those used by the treatises on letter writing. To justify the use of the *sermo*, Minturno says that when Horace admonishes someone in an epistle, "just as he would have a conversation with those whom he addresses, or give the appearance of doing so," he reveals indirectly by things which happen either to himself or to another person what the listener ought to beware of or to correct.[19] One of the most interesting and extensive statements on Horace's epistles and the plain style itself occurs, reasonably enough, in the edition of Horace that Jonson owned, and it affirms again the relationship between the satire and epistle. If one takes into account the number of times he must have seen the passage, his admiration of Horace as a critic and a poet, and his sympathy with the attitudes influencing the style of the *sermones*, it is difficult to imagine such a statement's not helping to form Jonson's stylistic ideas. In one of two short prefaces prefixed to the satires and epistles, "Aristarcus, nephew of Parthenius," says to the reader:

Letters indeed demand a continued and appropriate tone and an order suited to themselves; namely, they require a familiarity and a propriety of words more than they lay claim to poetical ornaments. Therefore, without any fault or blame, this genre can avoid them. In fact, if anything with respect to luxuriance and more artfully chosen figures of speech or composition, or of more refined harmony in a piece of writing be courted, it is a fault, for the nearer it approaches casual speech (*orationem solutam*) the more it retains its true nature. The style of the satires (*sermonibus*) should be considered in the same way, in which, since it has sharpness and harshness, which, nevertheless, Horace used more temperately and Juvenal and Persius more freely, no one would desire any pleasing show (*voluptatem*) or sweetness (*suavi-*

tatem) of speech. This genre is plain (*humile*), and because of its familiarity Horace used the name conversations (*sermones*).[20]

J. C. Scaliger's general treatment of the *genus tenue* is an interesting commentary on this passage. He attributes two qualities, *tenuitas* and *simplicitas*, to the plain style; *suavitas* and *voluptas* were associated with the middle and were, according to "Aristarcus," to be avoided by satirists. *Tenuitas*, Scaliger says, is purity of diction derived from custom, *puritas ex communi consuetudine loquendi; simplicitas* is purity without figures of speech, *puritas non figurata*. He adds a third quality, *securitas*, the informality necessary to the consistent allegiance to idiomatic purity, *firmitas propositi ad tenuitatem*. Such speech will avoid figures and, in words similar to Jonson's caution not to go "out of the high-way of *speaking*," *neque enim vllo modo curat aliquid figurarum, sed communi via deducitur oratio*.[21]

The scholars of the sixteenth and seventeenth centuries repeated or expanded what Martial and Pliny had said of the epigram. As an introduction to an anthology of epigrams, the *Epigrammatum delectus* (1659), Pierre Nicole wrote an "Essay on True and Apparent Beauty in Which from Settled Principles is Rendered the Grounds for Choosing and Rejecting Epigrams."[22] His definition of an epigram is as general as Pliny's was of his *poemata*: "The epigram is defined, then, as a short poem directly pointing out some thing, person, or deed" (p. 26). The emphasis is on actual people and happenings, and those literary devices which encourage poets to depart from the subject matter of actual life and therefore from truth should be avoided. If, in fact, one deals primarily in fictions which are not true, he will lose his subject matter; if he has none to begin with, he may well resort to "the use of mythological propositions, the common vehicle of poets when they have nothing to say" (p. 14).[23] In the category of things which are not true, Nicole says, "must be reckoned the hyperbolical," which "are not false in a given word, . . . but false in the whole train of thought" (p. 16). Hyperbole, in suggesting something impossible, as Demetrius remarked, was the most frigid of all figures (*On Style,* 124–25), since frigidity "overshoots the expression appropriate to the thought" (114) and bears the mark of imposture (119). Not only does hyperbole falsify the subject matter, but also it demands too great a concern with pleasing the ear, which results in "tuneful trifles and verses empty of substance." Such poets "abound in choice phrases and so are in effect content to smooth over the commonplace with a not indecorous make-up" (p. 5). Tropes, circumlocutions, and "the piling up of a single point with varying phrase" (p. 24) should all be avoided, since "there is ever an especial ornament to be derived from simplicity."

> Consequently those writers stray pretty far from beauty for whom, as it were, all nature plays the ham to the point that they say nothing in an ordinary way, imagine nothing in the way in which it is perceived outside of poems, but instead elevate, debase, alter, and clothe everything in a theatrical mask. (p. 11)

In accord with the general attitudes of the plain style, nearly all of Nicole's recommendations and criticisms are made in the interest of content, for in an epigram nothing is more difficult to achieve than "the adroit handling, the suitable and easy unfolding, of the subject so that nothing is redundant, nothing wanting, nothing out of order, obscure, or tangled up in verbiage, and yet at the same time nothing too unexpected, nothing not adequately prepared for" (p. 31). Such language Jonson described as "pure and neat."[24]

Complete freedom of subject matter continued to be given to the epigram, and the statements about it were very similar to those of Erasmus and Lipsius about the epistle. Nicole says simply: "The material of epigrams comprises any subject and anything that can be said on it—in fact, there are as many kinds of epigrams as there are kinds of things that can be said" (p. 29).[25] Thomas Bastard marks off his subject matter in his introductory poem to his epigrams, *de subiecto operis sui*:

> I speake of wants, of frauds, of policies,
> Of manners, and of vertues and of times,
> Of vnthrifts and of friends, and enemies,
> Poets, Physitions, Lawyers, and Diuines,
> Of vsurers, buyers, borowers, ritch and poore,
> Of theeues, and murtherers, by sea and land,
> Of pickthankes, lyers, flatterers, lesse and more,
> Of good and bad, and all that comes to hand;
> I speake of hidden and of open things:
> Of strange euents, of countries farre and wide,
> Of warres, of captaynes, Nobles, Princes, kings,
> *Asia, Europe,* and all the world beside
>   This is my subiect, reader, I confesse,
>   From which I thinke seldom I doe disgresse.[26]

Such conventions, which were the same for the comic poet and the satirist, were perhaps partly responsible for the increasing emphasis that the theory of the plain style placed upon particularity. The greater the range of subject matter, the greater the necessity to distinguish and to deal individually with particulars in order to arrive at valid generalizations. The emphasis of the comic poet, the satirist, and the epigrammatist upon the accurate observation of any subject is simply a concern with the particularity of individual experience, from which moral truths can then be derived. It is interesting to see how Horace's method of teaching morality by citing particulars was regarded as aesthetically pleasing and emotionally persuasive by the anti-rhetorical tradition and to what extent it is responsible for the power of Jonson's poems. It is an important part of the resolution of the conflict between content and expression which the plain style was attempting to achieve.

With the exception of Bacon's English writings, the return to the use of particulars in rhetorical matters was mentioned most explicitly by the neo-Latin humanists and scholars. Under the influence of Bacon and the Horatian tradition in general, Jonson exploited the literary possibilities of particular observation and in this way extended the use and versatility of the plain style in English. In the "Parnassus Plays," which were "academic" and sophisticated in various neo-Latin critical conventions, Jonson is called "A meere Empyrick, one that getts what he hath by obseruation."[27] The passage as a whole does not flatter him, but Jonson would have been happy to reply that "a wise man speakes, and out of the observation, knowledge, and use of things," for "sense," which is the "life and soule of Language, without which all words are dead, . . . is wrought out of experience, the knowledge of humane life, and actions" (VIII, 620f.). Whereas the Senecan stylistic attitudes tended toward the exploration of the individual personality, the conservative rhetorical methods of organizing experience worked from precept to generalization, or, as Croll remarks, "tended toward the study of the *forms* of their various sciences rather than toward the direct observation of the facts."[28] In this aspect as in others Jonson is "anti-rhetorical" and places great emphasis upon individual experience and factual observation, which were to modify even "the observations of the *Ancients*." As Croll has pointed out, the Senecan eclecticism in the choice of the proper models for imitation also encourged an empirical attitude toward men and their actions, since it sought its authority "dans la simple réalité des choses et dans les lois naturelles de la pensée."[29] The critical faculty, when it begins to evaluate individual passages of the classical authors, places greater emphasis upon the observation of particular details and upon the continual necessity to distinguish between them where once, perhaps, a precept or generalization had hidden the possibility of a distinction.

For Jonson, Bacon would have shared with Horace the distinction of being an exemplary critic and a "true judge upon cause, and reason; not because he thought so; but because he knew so, out of use and experience" (VIII, 642). He shared with him a faith in intelligent observation, which he defined as "noting the coherence of causes and effects, counsels and successes, and the proportion and likeness between nature and nature, force and force, action and action, state and state, time past and time present."[30] Both men distrusted the intellectual authority of precept. General propositions or commonplaces are not wrong in themselves, but, concerning their acquisition, Bacon writes, "of the *methods* of commonplaces that I have seen, there is none of any sufficient worth; all of them carrying merely the face of a *school*, and not of a *world*."[31] Such a method for arriving at, illustrating, and teaching general moral truths would be equally unsatisfactory for the satirist. In stating the literary principles behind the *sermones,* Horace describes how his father educated him by pointing to a particular man who had been ridiculed or punished for a particular fault or to a particularly honorable man worthy of imitation (*Serm.* I.iv.105–26), and he advises the poet similarly to look "On life, and manners, and make those his booke" (*Ars Poet.* 317–18).

In too great a reliance on one's own observations, however, there is a danger of superficiality and self-deception, since, as Jonson remarks, "very few men are wise by their owne counsell; or learned by their owne teaching. For hee that was onely taught by himselfe, had a foole to his Master" (VIII, 563). Because of his eclecticism Horace was occasionally criticized for this. Casaubon comments that the satirist himself realized that things were more complicated than he represented them; that he did not hold the same intellectual position for long but passed indiscriminately through foreign camps, not like an explorer but like a deserter (*non tanquam explorator, sed tanquam transfuga*), now a Stoic, now an Epicurean, often ridiculing both; and, not being always the magistrate of virtue, he lived as inconsistently as he wrote.[32] The passage is particularly interesting, because it varies Jonson's motto, *tanquam explorator,*[33] to make a distinction about Horace, who is described somewhat as Jonson might describe Montaigne. Jonson's skepticism was not so great as that described above, nor could he have considered Horace's to be great if he held the satirist to be the first in estimation among those best authors whom a poet should read to avoid having a fool for his master. Horace's moral generalizations were persuasive just because they were derived from observation, because they were drawn out of use and experience. Jonson, too, however, had many of the characteristics that Casaubon found in Horace. He was of mean birth, he was not always the magistrate of virtue, he changed religions (though not indiscriminately), and he made fun of the Puritans much as the Latin satirists did of the extreme Stoics; but he wrote with more consistency than he lived. Neither he nor Horace was deficient in precepts, no matter how they came by them, and what Jonson says of teaching applies to both of them:

> I take this labour in teaching others, that they should not be alwayes to bee taught; and I would bring my Precepts into practise. For rules are ever of lesse force, and valew, then experiments. (VIII, 617)[34]

The inductive process of moving from the observation of particulars to generalization was more adaptable to the understanding of physical phenomena than of human actions. Horace's method of teaching, however, presupposed such a process and assumed, when it was applied to human affairs, that the particular example would move men to good action more effectively than general statement. Bacon describes most explicitly the application of the method to the understanding and treatment of human emotions and, in a sense, gives epistemological sanction to anti-rhetorical stylistic principles. His description fits Jonson's method of writing from personal experience, of defining observations so clearly that he may move to the appropriate generalization without losing the specific subject of his observations. He avoids the fault which Bacon finds in the syllogism that "commands assent . . . to the proposition, but does not take hold of the thing."[35] In Aphorism cxxvii of the *Novum Organum*, which Jonson said "openeth all defects of Learning, whatsoever; and is a Booke, *Qui longum noto scriptori porriget ævum*" (VIII, 592), Bacon recommends the inductive method for all intellectual disciplines:

> It may also be asked (in the way of doubt rather than objection) whether I speak of natural philosophy only, or whether I mean that the other sciences, logic, ethics, and politics, should be carried on by this method. Now I certainly mean what I have said to be understood of them all; and as the common logic, which governs by the syllogism, extends not only to natural but to all sciences; so does mine also, which proceeds by induction, embrace everything. For I form a history and tables of discovery for anger, fear, shame, and the like; for matters political; and again for the mental operations of memory, composition and division, judgment and the rest; not less than for heat and cold, or light, or vegetation, or the like. But nevertheless since my method of interpretation, after the history has been prepared and duly arranged, regards not the working and discourse of the mind only (as the common logic does) but the nature of things also, I supply the mind with such rules and guidance that it may in every case apply itself aptly to the nature of things.

And therefore I deliver many and diverse precepts in the doctrine of Interpretation, which in some measure modify the method of invention according to the quality and condition of the subject of the inquiry.[36]

Bacon's "history and tables of discovery" in the matter of human emotions are analogous to the records of data from experiments in "natural philosophy." They are the same type of observed evidence that supports the generalizations on human conduct which constitute the *Essays*.

The aesthetic corollary to Bacon's aphorism is that the particular can be more pleasing and emotionally persuasive than the abstract generalization, an idea that became a fundamental artistic principle by the end of the eighteenth century. In his chapter *De movendis affectibus* Vives explicitly states why the particular is more moving than the universal:

> Although feelings are the media between the mind and the senses, they are, nevertheless, more closely connected to the senses than to the mind, so that men are incited more quickly by those which are aroused by the senses than by those which are motivated by the understanding alone, and therefore more quickly by particular individuals than by universals. For it affects the feelings more strongly if you say: *To this man I have given clothes and money, I have instructed him with erudition, endowed him with dignity, but now he returns that kindness in such a fashion that he wishes to take away my home and life,* than if you say as a generalization: *Grievous it is to be despoiled of life and property by that man to whom you have given clothes,* etc.[37]

The intimacy between the writer and the reader, the concern with specific actions and persons, and the detailed analysis of individual, personal experience all reflect this emphasis on particularity, and all are characteristic of the plain style. Dryden says of Jonson's comedies: "The description of these humours, drawn from the knowledge and observation of particular persons was the peculiar genius and talent of *Ben Johnson*."[38] And William Cartwright, a son of Ben, comments on the extent and precision of Jonson's insight into human motives and summarizes many of the attitudes and qualities of style that have been discussed in the preceding chapters:

> Where shall we find a Muse like *thine,* that can
> So well present and shew *man* unto *man,*
> That each one finds his *twin,* and thinkes *thy Art*
> Extends not to the *gestures,* but the *heart?*
> Where one so shewing *life* to *life,* that *we*
> Think *thou* taughtst *Custome,* and not *Custome thee?* . . .
> Things *common* thou speakst *proper,* which though known
> For *publique,* stampt by *thee* grow thence *thine owne*:

Thy thoughts so *order'd,* so *expres'd,* that *we*
Conclude that *thou* didst not *discourse,* but *see*:
Language so *master'd,* that *thy* numerous *feet,*
Laden with *genuine words,* doe alwaies meet
Each in his *art; nothing* unfit doth fall,
Shewing the *Poet,* like the *wiseman,* All:[39]

By way of a conclusion to these chapters on the *Discoveries* I should mention briefly the essential differences, especially in attitude, between the classical plain style, as I have discussed it, and that plainness of language advocated by religious and scientific treatises and later by the Royal Society. The religious anti-rhetorical attitudes were essentially those borrowed from the general distrust of the intellectual faculties of the obscurantist tradition. The accusations against rhetoric in such religious tracts as Walter Haddon's *Against Jerome Osorius* might well have been borrowed from Cornelius Agrippa's *De Incertitudine et Vanitate Scientiarum et Artium atque Excellentia Verbi Dei.* Their emphasis on plain language is motivated by an anti-philosophical distrust of speculative thinking and is addressed to the unlatined layman. The difference is essentially that between Horace's emphasis upon human wisdom in human affairs, derived from the *Socraticae . . . chartae* and addressed to sophisticated men, and St. Paul's intention to reach the uneducated, not by speaking *in persuasoriis humanae sapientiae verbis* but by speaking *in demonstratione spirituali et potente* (*Cor.* I.ii.4).[40]

In his essay "The Moral Sense of Simplicity"[41] R. F. Jones quotes from a large number of religious tracts of all sects which assert their own simplicity of language in contrast to their rhetorical and hence sophistic and hypocritical opponents. Eloquence is simply a synonym for deceit. Jones gives a well-documented practical reason for this: the tracts were addressed to the unlatined laymen, and "It was clearly understood that eloquence appealed to the learned, and plainness was necessary for the ignorant" (p. 274). The two audiences were frequently contrasted for scientific as well as religious writing, and such treatises as Humphrey Lloyd's *The Treasuri of Helth* (1558) were addressed to the ordinary reader. Primarily for these reasons, Jones writes, there is a great difference in the styles:

> The upholders of plainness are far removed from classical models or classical authorities, and they do not develop any suggestion of the particular stylistic ideal demanded by the anti-Ciceronians. Furthermore their ascetic and utilitarian spirit possessed little in common with the literary spirit animating anti-Ciceronianism. (p. 286)

The difference between the plainness sought by the Royal Society and that of the classical plain style is that the former was a style in which the writer himself intruded as little as possible in the description of the physical world, a language as near to mathematics as possible.[42] The classical plain style was developed to reveal the writer himself, to analyze and to portray the individual personality. The difference is not simply between philosophy and "natural philosophy," but between the methods of analysis that each subject matter imposes. The conscious exclusion of the writer's personality—even his mind, if that were possible—in the language of mathematics is directly opposed to the cultivation of the individual and psychological search for philosophic truth.

Part II: POEMS

It is almost the same, too, in the art of painting: if a man daubed with the finest colors at random, he would not as much please as by drawing a likeness on white.

ARISTOTLE, *Poetics*

But, you are he can paint; I can but write:
A Poet hath no more but black and white,
Ne knowes he flatt'ring Colours, or false light.

JONSON'S ANSWER TO *Burlase*

5

JONSON AND THE
CONTEMPORARY REJECTIONS
OF THE HIGH AND MIDDLE STYLES

METAPHOR. *Let not the mouse of my good meaning, Lady,*
Be snap'd up in the trap of your suspition,
To loose the taile there, either of her truth,
Or swallow'd by the Cat of misconstruction.
AWDREY. *You are too finicall for me; speake plaine Sir.*

A Tale of a Tub

JONSON'S ATTIC POSITION in the rhetorical controversies corresponds in the terms of the conventions of his day to anti-Petrarchanism.[1] Both movements rejected, to a greater or less extent, the attitudes of the high and middle styles and adopted those of the plain style as they are described by the classical treatises and the Latin satirists. The return to the plain style in the reactions against Ciceronianism and Petrarchanism was an attempt to revitalize language by replacing the emphasis firmly on content rather than on expression. Such a return is characteristic of the beginning of most important literary movements, and its purpose is not simply to correct stylistic excesses of the preceding generation. The plain style, as I tried to describe it in the Preface, is that style in which the distinction between the denotative and connotative qualities of language is least apparent, in which content and the feelings expressed about the content qualify one another to the exclusion of all irrelevant material, in which the division between the conceptual statement and the feelings properly associated with the statement is most nearly healed. The return to the plain style is not an attempt to isolate and to secure the didactic content against the artistic manipulations of connotative feelings, but rather an attempt to return to a workable relationship between them.

The attitudes and stylistic devices of the high and middle styles tend to cultivate and increase such a division. The device of allegory, for instance, which Vives and Lipsius disapproved of in the plain style and which Jonson said must not be drawn out "too long, lest either wee make our selves obscure, or fall into affectation, which is childish" (VIII, 625), was used more often than not to give overt didactic statement an attractive dress, thus emphasizing the dichotomy of teaching and delighting. "The Courtly

figure *Allegoria*," Puttenham says, "which is when we speake one thing
and thinke another, and that our wordes and our meanings meete not," is
used to dissemble "vnder couert and darke termes" what we think, which
"is a kinde of dissimulation, because the wordes beare contrary counte-
naunce to th'intent."[2] Spenser, whose "Allegorie," Jonson remarked to
Drummond, "he had delivered jn Papers to Sir Walter Raughlie" (I, 132),
comments first "how doubtfully all allegories may be construed" and particularly the *Faerie Queene*, "being a continued allegory, or darke conceit."
His reason for using allegory reveals how much "the Courtly figure" cultivates the division between content and expression:

> To some, I know, this methode will seeme displeasaunt, which had
> rather have good discipline delivered plainly in way of precepts, or ser-
> moned at large, as they use, then thus clowdily enwrapped in allegoricall
> devises. But such, me seeme, should be satisfide with the use of these
> dayes, seeing all things accounted by their showes, and nothing esteemed
> of, that is not delightfull and pleasing to commune sence.[3]

Allegory is the bridge suspended between a poetry of pure entertainment
and a sermon. It does not permit one to forget he is crossing, or ought to
be, from a "showe" to a "precept." The return to the plain style is an
attempt to solve the problem of how the didactic gets into a work of literature by removing the most obvious divisions between expression and intention and by using a style that avoids rhetorical figures that emphasize
those divisions.[4]

THE REJECTIONS OF THE HIGH STYLE

That sublime dicendi genus, *which walkes abroad for wast
paper in each seruing mans pocket.*

NASHE'S PREFACE TO GREENE'S *Menaphon*

Drummond reported that Jonson "had ane jntention to perfect ane
Epick Poeme jntitled Heroologia of the Worthies of his Country"
(I, 132). It is interesting to conjecture how Jonson would have written
a poem that had traditionally been written in a high style. There are
two passages that indicate that even in an epic his stylistic attitudes would
have been more Attic than one would normally expect to find in this
genre. The first is Horace's description of Virgil in *Poetaster*:

> His learning labours not the schoole-like glosse,
> That most consists in *ecchoing* wordes, and termes,
> And soonest wins a man an empty name:
> Nor any long, or far-fetcht circumstance,

Wrapt in the curious generalities of artes:
But a direct, and *analyticke* summe
Of all the worth and first effects of artes.
And for his *poesie*, 'tis so ramm'd with life,
That it shall gather strength of life, with being,
And liue hereafter, more admir'd, then now.

(V.i.129–38)

What Horace, the "true judge upon cause, and reason" (VIII, 642), says of
Virgil agrees with the general critical position stated in the *Discoveries*.
Not only is the *Aeneid* "ramm'd with life" but it accurately reveals the
writer's mind and shows the reader "A humane soule made visible in life"
(V.ii.18). The second passage is in *The Speeches at Prince Henries Bar-
riers* (VII, 328). Merlin interprets the deeds of English heroes depicted
on a shield to the young prince:

> Not the deedes
> Of antique knights, to catch their fellowes steedes,
> Or ladies palfreyes rescue from the force
> Of a fell gyant, or some score to vn-horse.
> These were bold stories of our ARTHVRS age;
> But here are other acts; another *stage*
> And *scene* appeares; it is not since as then:
> No gyants, dwarfes, or monsters here, but men.
> His arts must be to gouerne, and giue lawes
> To peace no lesse then armes.

(ll. 167–76)

Jonson's epic would deal with human beings and the problems of human
life.[5] Knighthood and its accoutrement of giants and dwarfs, the medieval
counterpart of classical mythology, are rejected in words very similar to
Martial's *non hic Centauros, non Gorgonas Harpyiasque/invenies: hominem pagina nostra sapit* (X.4).

The epic was never written, but the deeds of a knight, worthy to be
"of King Arthurs table," and his "squire, of faire degree" were celebrated.
In "The Famous Voyage" (VIII, 84), Jonson, by describing a trip through
Shoreditch in a rowboat as if it were an allegorical descent into Hell, effectively burlesques the standard mythological and chivalric machinery,
which was employed by poets not simply as a device but, as Nicole says
in his treatise on epigrams, as the subject matter itself. In the poem Jonson
makes fun of the invocation of the muses for the same reason that the
Latin satirists rejected it altogether: it usually committed the poet to a
bombastic style:[6]

                    but, me thinkes 'tis od,
That all this while I haue forgot some *god*,
Or *goddesse* to inuoke, to stuffe my verse;
And with both bombard-stile, and phrase, rehearse
The many perills of this *Port*, and how
Sans helpe of SYBIL, or a golden bough,
Or magick sacrifice, they past along!

                                        (ll. 43–49)

By mixing in archaic and pretentious diction, he parodies the "heroic" tone
of infernal descents such as Sackville's "Induction" and later imitations
which tended to retain the diction of the 1560's and earlier:[7]

    In the first iawes appear'd that vgly monster,
    Ycleped *Mud*, which, when their oares did once stirre,
    Belch'd forth an ayre, as hot, as at the muster
    Of all your night-tubs, when the carts doe cluster,
    Who shall discharge first his merd-vrinous load:
    Thorough her wombe they make their famous road,
    Betweene two walls; where, on one side, to scar men,
    Were seene your vgly *Centaures*, yee call Car-men,
    Gorgonian scolds, and *Harpyes*: on the other
    Hung stench, diseases, and old filth, their mother,
    With famine, wants, and sorrowes many a dosen.

                                        (ll. 61–71)

    A more likely target for Jonson's parody, in tone and descriptive details,
is Joshua Sylvester's translation "The Furies," which constitutes the third
part of the "First Day of the II Week" of du Bartas's *La Seconde Sepmaine
ou Enfance du Monde* (1584). Jonson thought "that Silvesters translation
of Du Bartas was not well done" and that du Bartas was not "a Poet but
a Verser" (I, 133). Sylvester's verse is pretentious, and his description of
Hell a ridiculous compilation of one grotesque detail after another. He
borrows the conventional descriptive details of Hell from the epic tradition:[8]

    And th'ugly *Gorgons*, and the *Sphinxes* fell,
    Hydras, and *Harpies* 'gan to yawn and yell.
    As the heat, hidden in a vapoury cloud,
    Striving for issue with strange murmurs loud,
    Like guns astuns, wth round, round-rumbling thunder,
    Filling the Air with noyse, the Earth wth wonder:
    So the three Sisters, the three hideous *Rages*,
    Raise thousand storms, leaving th'infernall stages.[9]

                                        (ll. 260–67)

These lines are especially similar to those of Jonson quoted above in that they make a good deal of use of feminine endings, which become for Jonson a satirical device. This section of du Bartas's poem was popular. King James himself selected it for a royal translation of over fifteen hundred fourteeners.[10] Jonson, who told Drummond that the King never saw "any verses jn England to ye Scullors" (I, 142), may have based his judgment of James on his taste for du Bartas as well as on the King's estimation of Taylor. Du Bartas describes the ravages of disease in terms often as scatologic as Jonson's, and more offensive, since one is, according to James's short preface, supposed to regard this picture of Hell as a serious moral lesson. Scatological descriptions of Satan and his devils were frequent in the Middle Ages; even Dante ends a canto with a devil's departure, *"ed elli avea del cul fatto trombetta"* (*Inferno*, xxi, 139). It is not surprising that Jonson would have made use of the convention in satirizing a descent to Hell.[11]

In "The Famous Voyage" Jonson rejects such conventions of the high style as the invocation to one or more muses, the machinery of classical mythology and medieval legend, pretentious diction, and rhetorical devices like that of seriously didactic allegory. Although he criticizes grandiloquent diction and rhetorical figures most explicitly in the *Discoveries* and in his plays, he deals directly with the muses and the mythological machinery in his poems.

> And must I sing? what subiect shall I chuse?
> Or whose great name in *Poets* heauen vse,
> For the more countenance to my actiue *Muse?*
>
> (ll. 1-3)

After ironically asking this question—and it is one with which he might have introduced any of his poems addressed to particular individuals— he continues, in a poem to Sir John and Lady Salisbury (VIII, 107), by enumerating and rejecting various mythological heroes who have been conventionally invoked as muses. The bones of Hercules are still too sore for a poet to expect much from his "dull god-head." Phoebus should tend his cart, not founder his hot team to tune his lay. Nor will he call on Bacchus or Pallas, the "mankinde maide." He then dismisses summarily the heroes dearest to the Petrarchan conventions:

> Goe, crampe dull MARS, light VENVS, when he snorts,
> Or, with thy *Tribade* trine, inuent new sports,
> Thou, nor thy loosenesse with my making sorts.

> Let the *old boy*, your sonne, ply his old taske,
> Turne the stale prologue to some painted maske,
> His absence in my verse, is all I aske. . . .
>
> Nor all the ladies of the *Thespian lake*,
> (Though they were crusht into one forme) could make
> A beautie of that merit, that should take
>
> My *Muse* vp by *commission*: No, I bring
> My owne true fire. Now my thought takes wing,
> And now an *Epode* to deepe eares I sing.
>   (ll. 16–21, 25–30)

The questions in the first line are those likely to be asked by a poet whose muse is taken "vp by *commission*," and the mythological figures of the succeeding lines might be subjects not only for invocation but for the commissioned poem itself. Jonson's "owne true fire" refers to his intention of saying precisely what he thinks about the subject he chooses. If he is careless, the muse will betray him, as he accuses her of doing in his epigram "To my Mvse" (VIII, 48):

> Away, and leaue me, thou thing most abhord,
>   That hast betray'd me to a worthlesse lord;
> Made me commit most fierce idolatrie
>   To a great image through thy luxurie.

Usually the term muse represents that person who stimulates Jonson to say something about him. It refers to the subject described in the poem and sometimes to the mind that describes it, rather than to an impersonal and independent power which is to supply inspiration, whatever that may be.

The mythology of high romance Jonson gladly gives to other fires than his own. In "An Execration upon Vulcan" (VIII, 202) for having burned his library, Jonson complains:

> Had I compil'd from *Amadis de Gaule*,
>   Th'*Esplandians, Arthurs, Palmerins*, and all
> The learned Librarie of *Don Quixote*;
>   And so some goodlier monster had begot: . . .
>   Thou then hadst had some colour for thy flames, . . .
> The *Talmud*, and the *Alcoran* had come,
>   With pieces of the *Legend*; The whole summe
> Of errant Knight-hood, with the[ir] Dames, and Dwarfes,
>   The[ir] charmed Boates, and the[ir] inchanted Wharfes;

The *Tristrams, Lanc'lots, Turpins,* and the *Peers,*
    All the madde *Rolands,* and sweet *Oliveers;*
To *Merlins* Marvailes, and his *Caballs* losse,
    With the Chimæra of the *Rosie-Crosse,*
Their Seales, their Characters, Hermetique rings,
    Their Jemme of Riches, and bright Stone, that brings
Invisibilitie, and strength, and tongues.[12]

(ll. 29-32, 40, 65-75)

Such high subjects invited a digressive and rhetorical style which must be purged, according to Don Quixote's learned librarian, by plain speech and common sense. In his preface Cervantes says that since his purpose "doth aim at no more than to diminish the authority and acceptance that books of chivalry have in the world," there is no need to "go begging of sentences from philosophers, fables from poets, orations from rhetoricians, or miracles from the saints, but only endeavour to deliver with significant, plain, honest, and well-ordered words" his subjects as clearly as possible, making his "conceits clear, and not intricate or dark."

> In conclusion, let thy project be to overthrow the ill-compiled *machina* and bulk of those knightly books, abhorred by many, but applauded by more; for, if thou bring this to pass, thou hast not achieved a small matter.[18]

The passage is interesting for its explicit statement of purpose and its specific recommendation of a style by which to accomplish it. Jonson rejected any poems that showed a preoccupation with things that did not exist. Monsters and miraculous births were returned to the darksome vale with other enchantments.[14]

I have treated Jonson's criticism of the inflated and bombastic style at some length in dealing with the *Discoveries.* Vives says:

> In general, moreover, the inflated and tumid style gives the appearance not only of complete health but of a fortunate and strong constitution: inside, however, it is corrupt. This condition is easily caused by the grandiloquence of words, the audacious and hazardous metaphors and *sententiis,* and a certain height and amplitude of style.[15]

Tumidity was called fustian and often, metaphorically, "tuftaffeta" oratory.[16] Much of Jonson's criticism of grandiloquence was directed against the dramatists, "the *Tamerlanes,* and *Tamer-Chams* of the late Age, which had nothing in them but the *scenicall* strutting, and furious vociferation, to warrant them to the ignorant gapers (VIII, 587).[17] The most strutting

and vociferation came from John Marston, "a Ruffian in his stile" who
"Brings the great battering ram of tearms to towne."[18] Jonson gives the
most skillful criticism of Marston's style in *Poetaster*, where in the person
of Crispinus, Marston is forced to spit up his affected vocabulary. Virgil
advises him to read Cato,

> And taste a piece of TERENCE, sucke his phrase
> In stead of lycorice; and, at any hand,
> Shun PLAVTVS, and old ENNIVS, they are meates
> Too harsh for a weake stomacke. . . .
> You must not hunt for wild, out-landish termes,
> To stuffe out a peculiar *dialect*;
> But let your *matter* runne before your *words*:[19]
> And if, at any time, you chaunce to meet
> Some *Gallo-belgick* phrase, you shall not straight
> Racke your poore verse to giue it entertainement;
> But let it passe: and doe not thinke your selfe
> Much damnified, if you doe leaue it out;
> When, nor your vnderstanding, nor the sense
> Could well receiue it. This faire abstinence,
> In time, will render you more sound, and cleere.
>   (V.iii.540–59)

Virgil's recommendations agree with the principles of the plain style as it
is defined by the writers whom Jonson quotes and paraphrases in the
Discoveries. The way to correct stylistic excesses is to re-emphasize content. Crispinus must gather matter in reading Cato—Jonson's equivalent
of Horace's *socraticae chartae*—and express it cleanly in the phrase of
Terence in order to return to a meaningful relationship between the statement about a human experience and the feelings associated with that
experience.

The odes come closer to being written in a high style than any other
group of Jonson's poems, but they, too, owe their power to qualities of
the plain style. The only exceptions are the ode to "Sir Lvcivs Cary and
Sir H. Morison" (VIII, 242) and the "Ode to Iames Earle of Desmond"
(VIII, 176), the failure of which, as I shall show later, results from attempted grandiloquence. There is, however, an incomplete poem in *terza
rima*, in an intended series of ten poems on Venetia Digby, which un-
mistakably attempts the high style. It is the second poem in "Eupheme"
(VIII, 272–89):

The Song of her DESCENT
I sing the just, and uncontrol'd Descent
Of Dame VENETIA DIGBY, styl'd The Faire:

For Mind, and Body, the most excellent
    That ever Nature, or the later Ayre
Gave two such Houses as NORTHUMBERLAND,
    And STANLEY, to the which shee was Co-heire.
Speake it, you bold PENATES, you that stand
    At either Stemme, and know the veines of good
Run from your rootes; Tell, testifie the grand
    Meeting of Graces, that so swell'd the flood
Of vertues in her, as, in short, shee grew
    The wonder of her Sexe, and of your Blood.
And tell thou, ALDE-LEGH, None can tell more true
    Thy Neeces line, then thou that gav'st thy Name
Into the Kindred, whence thy *Adam* drew
    Meschines honour with the *Cestrian* fame
Of the first *Lupus*, to the Familie
    By *Ranulph*——

The rest of this Song is lost.

(VIII, 274)

Perhaps, indeed, the rest of the poem was lost, but it is more likely that Jonson became bored with it. It has not only an inflated style, which he scorned, but genealogical subject matter, which he explicitly rejected in several poems, as in the following epigram:

To all, to whom I write.

May none, whose scatter'd names honor my booke,
    For strict degrees of ranke, or title looke:
'Tis 'gainst the manners of an *Epigram*:
    And, I a *Poet* here, no *Herald* am.

(VIII, 29)

Nor was it just against the manners of an epigram, for Jonson in his elegy "On the Lady Jane Pawlet" (VIII, 268) catches himself when he starts to give her genealogy:

Shee was the Lady *Jane,* the *Marchionisse*
    Of *Winchester*; the Heralds can tell this:
Earle *Rivers* Grand-Child—serve not formes, good Fame,
    Sound thou her Vertues, give her soule a Name.

(ll. 19–22)

The business of the plain style is not with pedigree but with a definition of the soul, reached by a description of the moral virtues. The heralds, on the other hand, sometimes even found justification for the immorality of the wealthy nobility in the "learned Librarie" of Don Quixote. In "A speach according to Horace" (VIII, 213) Jonson writes:

Let poore Nobilitie be vertuous: Wee,
  Descended in a rope of Titles, be
From *Guy,* or *Bevis, Arthur,* or from whom
  The Herald will. Our blood is now become
Past any need of vertue. . . .

(ll.79–83)

Jonson's projected epic was to treat the actions of English heroes, not their ancestry, and it is fairly safe to say that he would not have treated them as he started here to treat Venetia Digby.

THE REJECTIONS OF THE MIDDLE STYLE

Besides these, I doo not remember to have seene but fewe (to speake boldly) printed, that have poetical sinnewes in them. For proofe whereof, let but moste of the Verses bee put in prose, and then aske the meaning, and it will bee founde, that one Verse did but beget an other, without ordering at the first, what should bee at the last, which becomes a confused masse of words, with a tingling sound of ryme, barely accompanied with reasons.

SIDNEY, *The Defence of Poesie*

It is strange that one of the earliest and finest criticisms of Petrarchan excesses should have been made by the man whom all courtly poets tried to imitate. In the fifteenth sonnet of the *Astrophel and Stella,* Sidney makes his comments even more specific:

You that doe search for every purling spring,
Which from the rybs of old *Pernassus* flowes,
And every flower (not sweete perhaps) which growes
Neere there about, into your Poems wring.
You that doe dictionary method bring
  Into your rymes, running in ratling rowes,
  You that old *Petrarchs* long deceased woes
With new borne sighes, and wit disguised sing;
You take wrong wayes, those far-fet helps be such,
As doe bewray a want of inward tutch,
And sure at length stolne goods doe come to light.[20]

(ll.1–11)

The satirists of the 1590's did little more than repeat these criticisms in cruder terms and at greater length, and they usually missed what was most important—the attitude toward experience which lay behind them. This was essentially a Senecan attitude,[21] and Sidney's criticisms gathered from it the power generated by the entire anti-Ciceronian movement: "You take wrong wayes; those far-fet helps . . . bewray a want of inward tutch." Persius and Seneca said the same thing. It was Jonson, however, not the satirists, who returned to the classical contexts of these criticisms and adopted the attitudes toward human experience as well as those toward literary conventions. The satirists introduced a new fashion, Jonson a new style.

The term "sinnewes," which Sidney uses above, was usually selected by those who followed him to translate the Latin *nervi*.[22] The lack of *nervi* was the most characteristic defect of the middle style, which Richard Sherry says is close to that style "called dissolute, because it waveth hyther and thyther, as it were without synewes, and jointes, standing surely in no point."[23] Actually, the term *nervi*, as Quintilian uses it (VIII, Pr. 18), means content, and it became a key word in the Senecan-Ciceronian controversy. Ciceronian rhetoric, as well as a loose, florid style, lacked *nervi*, for, as Vives comments, as the sinews are often buried by flesh and fat, thus becoming weakened and less suitable for their functions, so it happens in style, as in Cicero, that the luxuriance of words and the redundancy of flesh and that full and undefined composition result in a weak style.[24] In a Senecan or Attic conception of style the "poeticall sinnewes" become the most important part of the poem, for, as Jonson paraphrases Vives, "The sense is as the life and soule of Language, without which all words are dead" (VIII, 621). The vitality of the poem will depend on the truth and complexity of what you have to say about your subject, on the *"Life, and Quicknesse*, which is the strength and sinnewes (as it were) of your penning" (VIII, 632-33).

Drummond reports Jonson's saying "That Verses stood by sense without either Colour's or accent, which," he adds, "yett other tymes he denied" (I, 143). Drummond's qualification may be based on random technical comments Jonson may have made concerning "Colour's or accent," which he no doubt did consider important, but such comments do not contradict his general opinion that "sense" is the life of a poem as it is "the life and soule of Language."[25] To check the sense or "poeticall sinnewes" Sidney suggests letting "moste of the Verses bee put in prose" and then asking the meaning. Jonson's concern for sense led him to the same thing, for, as he said to Drummond, "He wrott all his first jn prose, for so his master Cambden had Learned him" (I, 143). If a poet's chief concern is with content, he will choose the form that is most flexible and most adaptable to his subject matter. This is the most important single reason why Jonson adopted the couplet and rejected the sonnet.

Jonson told Drummond that "He had written a discourse of Poesie both against Campion & Daniel especially this Last, wher he proves couplets to be the bravest sort of Verses, especially when they are broken, like Hexameters and that crosse Rimes and Stanzaes (becaus the purpose would lead him beyond 8 lines to conclude) were all forced" (I, 132). The couplet does not commit him to any more lines than his subject demands, and in stanzas the form rather than the subject matter in many cases determines how long a given statement must be. Puttenham remarks:

> For to an historicall poeme no certain number [of stanzas] is limited, but as the matter fals out: also a *distick* or couple of verses is not to be accompted a staffe, but serues for a continuance as we see in Elegie, Epitaph, Epigramme or such meetres, of plaine concord not harmonically entertangled, as some other songs of more delicate musick be.[26]

The poet, then, will be able to add couplets "as the matter fals out."

Jonson told Drummond that "He cursed petrarch for redacting Verses to Sonnets, which he said were like that Tirrants bed, wher some who were too short were racked, others too long cut short" (I, 133–34).[27] Puttenham with some delight explains how Petrarch actually does it. In discussing the figure of amplification by distribution, he cites a translation of one of Petrarch's sonnets by Surrey (wrongfully attributing it to Wyatt):

> Set me whereas the sunne doth parch the greene,
> Or where his beames do not dissolue the yce:
> In temperate heate where he is felt and seene,
> In presence prest of people mad or wise:
> Set me in hye or yet in low degree,
> In longest night or in the shortest day:
> In clearest skie, or where clouds thickest bee,
> In lustie youth or when my heares are gray:
> Set me in heauen, in earth or els in hell,
> In hill or dale or in the foming flood:
> Thrall or at large, aliue where so I dwell,
> Sicke or in health, in euill fame or good:
> Hers will I be, and onely with this thought,
> Content my selfe, although my chaunce be naught.

With some triumph Puttenham comments:

> All which might haue bene said in these two verses.
>
> > Set me wheresoeuer ye will,
> > I am and wilbe yours still.[28]

Jonson's fundamental objection to the sonnet, then, is that it leads one to say more than one has to say in order to satisfy the form. The poet is obliged to use rhetorical figures, and his intention becomes contradictory to that of the plain style. As the rhetorical figures and the form become more important, the range of subject matter decreases. The poet who seeks the grace and charm of the middle style will do well to utilize that grace which, according to Demetrius, "may reside in the subject matter, if it is the gardens of the Nymphs, marriage-lays, love-stories" (*On Style,* 132), or "Petrarch's long-deceased woes." The freedom of the plain style to treat any subject depends on its primary purpose, which is to tell the truth. Since the *officium* of the middle style is to delight (*delectare*), many subjects must be excluded, and the emphasis is no longer on content but on expression.

The conventional adjectives for rhetorical ornateness in poetry were "sugred" or "honied," and each could be used as an equivalent for Ciceronian rhetoric itself.[29] The term "sugred" was most often applied to sonnets, such as in the famous comment of Francis Meres on "the mellifluous and hony-tongued Shakespeare, witnes his *Venus and Adonis,* his *Lucrece,* his sugred *Sonnets* among his priuate friends."[30] Among the literary genres the epigram was often regarded as a corrective for the trite diffuseness of the sonnet. The salt of incisive wit was needed to preserve the poem, which otherwise might cloy and dissolve like candy. Sir John Harington contrasts the two sets of conventions in his epigram called "Comparison of the Sonnet, and the Epigram":

> Once, by mishap, two Poets fell a-squaring,
> The Sonnet, and our Epigram comparing;
> And *Faustus,* hauing long demurd vpon it,
> Yet, at the last, gaue sentence for the Sonnet.
> Now, for such censure, this his chiefe defence is,
> Their sugred taste best likes his likresse senses.
>   Well, though I grant Sugar may please the taste,
>   Yet let my verse haue salt to make it last.[31]

In terms of the poetic conventions the rhetorical controversy between Ciceronianism and Senecanism became one between a mellifluous and a sinuous style.

In his epistle to Sidney's daughter, the Countess of Rutland (VIII, 113), Jonson praises the Countess of Bedford:

> Who, though shee haue a better verser got,
> (Or *Poet,* in the court account) then I,
>   And, who doth me (though I not him) enuy,
> Yet, for the timely fauours shee hath done,
>   To my lesse sanguine *Muse,* wherein she'hath wonne
> My gratefull soule, the subiect of her powers,
>   I haue already vs'd some happy houres,
> To her remembrance; . . .
>   (ll.68–75)

When time has brought attention to his poems and the people praised in them,

> Then all, that haue but done my *Muse* least grace,
> Shall thronging come, and boast the happy place
> They hold in my strange *poems,* which, as yet,
> Had not their forme touch'd by an English wit.
>
> (ll.79–82)

For, in them, the poet may represent the ladies so they may see, as he says,

> how, to the life, my soule presents
> Your forme imprest there: not with tinkling rimes,
> Or common places, filch'd, that take these times
> But high, and noble matter . . .[32]
>
> (ll.86–89)

Jonson's "tinkling rimes" echoes Sidney's "tingling sound of ryme, barely accompanied with reasons," and his poem "A Fit of Rime against Rime" (VIII, 183) expresses again his distrust of stanza forms:

> Rime, the rack of finest wits,
> That expresseth but by fits,
>   True Conceipt,
> Spoyling Senses of their Treasure,
> Cosening Judgement with a measure,
>   But false weight.
> Wresting words, from their true calling;
> Propping Verse, for feare of falling
>   To the ground.
>
> (ll.1-9)

Rhyme, like Petrarch's sonnets, racks the poet's true conceit, or idea, and by "wresting words, from their true calling"—and the phrase clearly expresses the idea—spoils the sense of the verses to the extent that they are propped up and held together by rhyme alone. Rhyme schemes, a figure of diction rather than a figure of thought, tend to draw the emphasis from content to expression, until the court poet, as Jonson says of the Court-Pucell, when "lip-thirstie, in each words expence,/Doth labour with the Phrase more then the sense" (VIII, 222, ll.13–14).

Jonson calls his poems "strange" because they were unconventional and had not yet been "touch't by an English wit." Although this is an overstatement, it was still unconventional in 1599 to reject genres such as the sonnet and the elegy, and it was completely original to reject them for the reasons Jonson did. How these reasons affected the poems themselves will be the subject of later chapters, but it should be pointed out here that even when Jonson shared unconventional attitudes with the satirists he drew upon authorities who, as a rule, had not been consulted by English poets about poetry. Jonson's rejection of the love elegy as a form, for example, is derived from the criticisms in the classical treatises of the defective middle style, or "the Drifting, since it drifts to and fro, and cannot get under way with resolution and virility" (*Ad Here.* IV.16). As preface to his epode "Not to know Vice at all, . . ." which does get under way with resolution, he wrote a "Proludium," which was appended with the epode to Chester's *Love's Martyr* (1601). The "Proludium" (VIII, 108), apparently a revision of the lines quoted in the first section of this chapter, "And must I sing?" completes *Forest* 10:

> An elegie? no, muse; yt askes a straine
> to loose, and Cap'ring, for thy stricter veyne.
> Thy thoughts did neuer melt in amorous fire,
> like glasse, blowne vp, and fashion'd by desire.
> The skilfull mischife of a rovinge Eye
> Could ne'er make prize of thy white Chastetye.
> Then, leaue these lighter numbers, to light braines
> in whom the flame of euery beauty raignes,
> Such, as in lustes wilde forrest loue to rainge,
> only pursewinge Constancy, in Chainge;
> Let these in wanton feete daunce out their soules.
>
> (ll. 1–11)

The elegies of Jonson and Donne took quite a different turn and often included satire on love poetry itself, such as that on the courtier who "chanc'd the lace, laid on a Smock, to see,/And straight-way spent a Sonnet" (VIII, 201).

Jonson's most explicit rejection of the high and middle styles is a passage occurring in the quarto version (1601) of *Every Man in His Humour* which was shortened in the folio (1616) edition of the works (III, 283–84).[33] Doctor Clement and Prospero are examining Matheo's poetry:

> CLEM. *Dic mihi musa virum*: are you an Author sir, giue me leaue a little, come on sir, ile make verses with you now in honor of the Gods, and the Goddesses for what you dare *extempore*; and now I beginne.
>> *Mount thee my Phlegon muse, and testifie,*
>> *How* Saturne *sitting in an Ebon cloud,*
>> *Disrobd his podex, white as iuorie,*
>> *And through the welkin thundred all aloud.*
> Theres for you sir.

PROS. Oh he writes not in that height of stile.
CLEM. No: weele come a steppe or two lower then.
> *From Catadupa and the bankes of Nile,*
> *Where onely breedes your monstrous Crocodile:*
> *Now are we purposd for to fetch our stile.*

PROS. Oh too farre fetcht for him still maister Doctor.
CLEM. I, say you so? lets intreat a sight of his vaine then. . . . What, al this verse? body of me he carries a whole realme; a common wealth of paper in his hose, lets see some of his subiects.
> *Vnto the boundless ocean of thy bewtie,*
> *Runnes this poor riuer, chargd with streames of zeale,*
> *Returning thee the tribute of my dutie:*
> *Which here my youth, my plaints, my loue reueale.*

Good! is this your owne inuention?
MAT. No sir, I translated that out of a book, called *Delia.*
> (V.iii.263–89)

Invocation of the gods and goddesses, mythological subject matter, slightly archaic diction ("welkin"), all belong to "that height of stile." On a step or two lower one may still reach for "farre fetcht" terms and monstrous subjects on the exotic Nile. But the style most suited to a prospective courtier is that of the first four lines of Daniel's first sonnet to Delia, which Matheo has "translated." Daniel, who, Jonson commented to Drummond, was "no poet" (I, 132), represented the typical sonneteer and was more severely treated than any of his contemporaries. He was criticized in the first place for excessive ornament and sweetness, in the second for plagiarism,[34] and in the third for prosiness.[35] Jonson may have thought Daniel no poet on any of these grounds, but his chief complaint with poets of the middle style was that, like the slackness of the imitators of Cicero,

> *They write a verse, as smooth, as soft, as creame;*
> *In which there is no torrent, nor scarce streame.*

You may sound these wits, and find the depth of them, with your middle finger. They are *Creame-bowle,* or but puddle deepe. (VIII, 585)

Later in the *Discoveries* he continues the criticism:

> The common Rymers powre forth Verses, such as they are, (*ex tempore*) but there never come[s] from them one Sense, worth the life of a Day. A Rymer, and a *Poet,* are two things. . . . here is the difference; Thy verses will not last those three daies; mine will to all time. Which was, as to tell him, he could not write a verse. I have met many of these Rattles, that made a noyse, and buz'de. They had their humme; and, no more. Indeed, things, wrote with labour, deserve to be so read, and will last their Age. (VIII, 638)

Though Jonson shared many of the attitudes of the contemporary satirists, their style itself had something in common with "the strong lines, that so the time doe catch," which Jonson offers to Vulcan in his "Execration" (VIII, 202). He addresses the god:

> But, on thy malice, tell me, didst thou spie
> Any, least loose, or s[c]urrile paper, lie
> Conceal'd, or kept there, that was fit to be,
> By thy owne vote, a sacrifice to thee?
> Did I there wound the honour of the Crowne?
> Or taxe the Glories of the Church, and Gowne?
> Itch to defame the State? or brand the Times?
> And my selfe most, in some selfe-boasting Rimes?
>
> (ll. 19–26)

"Nothing," Jonson says, translating Joseph Scaliger, "is of more credit, or request now, then a petulant paper, or scoffing verses" (VIII, 571). The style of the "scoffing verses" affected the Senecan lack of concern with composition, and it is, perhaps, more than coincidence that Scaliger should have been one of the most severe critics of the imitators of Lipsius.

Morris Croll, in commenting on the followers of Lipsius, says that "l'évêque Joseph Hall est un excellent example de ces hommes qui furent ses disciples littéraires."[36] Hall—whom Milton describes as "hopping short in the measure of convulsion-fits"[37]—in "A Post-script to the Reader" appended to his second volume of satires, writes:

> It is not for euery one to rellish a true and naturall Satyre, being of it selfe besides the natiue and in-bred bitternes and tartnes of particulers, both hard of conceipt, and harsh of stile, and therefore cannot but be vnpleasing both to the vnskilfull, and ouer Musicall eare, the one being affected with onely a shallow and easie matter, the other with a smoth and currant disposition. . . .[38]

The distinctions are interesting. The ignorant will object to Hall's satires because the matter is difficult, the too sensitive ear because the satires are "harsh of stile" and lack "currant disposition." Disposition, or the arrangement of parts, becomes almost the equivalent of composition when the parts are periods, phrases, and words. The Horatian *sermo* derives its greatest power from order and connection (*series iuncturaque, Ars Poet.* 242); and Casaubon's gloss on Persius' echo (*iunctura callidus acri,* V.14), cited in Chapter 4, draws, with Jonson, upon Seneca's criticism of those who roughen their style on purpose. The avoidance of trivial subject matter did not necessitate the rejection of composition "with a kind of violence, and

indisposition . . . as if to breake, were better then to open; or to rent asunder, gentler then to loose" (VIII, 586–87). The disjunctive abruptness that
the satirists affected in their cultivation of "in-bred bitternes and tartnes
of particulers" has its counterpart in the deviations from the plain style in
the first century A.D. Jonson's critical attitudes toward such verse satire can
best be understood in the terms of Seneca, Quintilian, and Tacitus, discussed in Chapter 1. In his search for particularity Sallust broke up the
rounded period of Cicero, which Livy employed, and the satirists, perhaps
in imitation of Donne, were conscious of doing the same thing to the
Petrarchans.

As in the overlaconic styles, obscurity as well as roughness resulted from
the satirists' disregard for composition. Hall states his intention to be clear,
but he describes his poems more accurately in a short conclusion appended
to the first three books of satires:

> Thus haue I writ in smother Cedar tree,
> So gentle Satyrs, pend so easily.
> Henceforth I write in crabbed oke-tree rinde:
> Search they that meane the secret meaning finde.

The elliptical syntax of the fourth line is consistent with Hall's literary
theory and practice, which bears a resemblance to the "forcible style" as
described by Demetrius. In such a style "obscurity often produces force,
since what is distantly hinted is more forcible, while what is plainly stated
is held cheap" (*On Style*, 254).

Jonson's comments in the *Discoveries* on the "furious vociferation" of
"the *Tamerlanes*" may easily apply to the satirists as well as to the dramatists. Edward Guilpin refers to satire as "the *Tamberlaine* of vice,"[39] and
the vocabulary of Crispinus, which Jonson burlesques in *Poetaster*, is drawn
mostly from Marston's satires rather than his plays. There could be no more
explicit criticism than he has given in this ranting fragment of satirical
commonplaces:

> Rampe vp, my *genius*; be not retrograde:
> But boldly nominate a spade, a spade.
> What, shall thy lubricall and glibberie *Muse*
> Liue, as shee were defunct, like punke in stewes? . . .
> Alas! That were no moderne consequence,
> To haue cothurnall buskins frighted hence.
> No; teach thy *incubus* to poetize;
> And throw abroad thy spurious snotteries,
> Vpon that puft-vp lumpe of barmy froth. . . .
> Or clumsie chil-blain'd iudgement; that, with oath,

Magnificates his merit; and bespawles
The conscious time, with humorous fome, and brawles,
As if his *organons* of sense would crack
The sinewes of my patience. Breake his back,
O *Poets* all, and some: For now we list
Of strenuous venge-ance to clutch the fist.

(V.iii.275–92)

This is the writer of the "selfe-boasting Rimes" offered to Vulcan, whom Jonson excludes from the "Tribe of Ben" (VIII, 218).

The satirists' irresponsibility toward style was similar to the stylistic libertinism of Montaigne and Burton. Marston says "To those that seem judicial Perusers" of *The Scourge of Villanie,* "He that thinks worse of my rhymes than myself, I scorn him, for he cannot: he that thinks better, is a fool."[40] So Burton had described his "rhapsody of rags gathered together . . . without art, invention, judgment, wit, learning . . . I confess all ('tis partly affected), thou canst not think worse of me than I do of myself."[41]

One of the assumptions behind cultivated negligence is that the satiric genres were topical and ephemeral. What John Weever says of epigrams would be true for satire as well: "Epigramms are much like vnto Almanacks seruing especially for the yeare for the which they are made, then these . . . being for one yeare pend, and in another printed: are past date before they come from the Presse."[42] Jonson's intention was completely different. The epigram, like any other form that he touched, was written to last, and he was conscious of this difference, as well as others which I shall take up later, when he wrote "To my meere English Censvrer" (VIII, 32):

To thee, my way in *Epigrammes* seemes new,
    When both it is the old way, and the true.
Thou saist, that cannot be: for thou hast seene
    DAVIS, and WEEVER, and the best haue beene,
And mine come nothing like. I hope so. . . .

(ll. 1–5)

A mere English censurer would be a man who was not acquainted with either the classical or the contemporary tradition of the Latin epigram and the attitudes and the principles of style that went with it. The "old way" can be achieved by study and must be estimated in the light of considered judgment. In a note accompanying an epitaph on Cecilia Bulstrode, Jonson writes (VIII, 372):

See what the obedience of friendship is, and the hazard it runnes. This I haue done, streightned wᵗʰ time (as yoʳ Man knowes) to let you know yoʳ power in mee. If it be well, as I thinke it is, for my invention hath not cooled so much to iudge, show it, though the greater Witts haue gone before. It hath somwhat in it *moris antiqui,* and suggesting the sodaynesse of it may passe.

Jonson criticized the essayists for using a method suitable for the random arrangement of the *silva* in a formal genre. And it was even worse to carry, as the satirists did, the conscious unconcern for art and composition into the still more formal structure of a poem. Spontaneity and informality do not necessarily reveal the truth, in the interest of which the Latin satirists had rejected rhetorical ornament, and may show the emptiness of a mind as well as its sincerity. The attempt to escape the responsibility to language for the conceptual and formal control of statement by pleading the ephemeral nature of the genres would be plain dishonesty.

In this chapter I have tried to show, with the least possible duplication of quotation, how closely the rejection of the high and middle styles in the poetic conventions followed the rejection of the Ciceronian and Senecan mannerisms in favor of an Attic style. The attitudes behind the reactions against Ciceronianism and Petrarchanism were similar, and the Attic position stated in the *Discoveries* applies to poetry as well as to prose. In the following chapter I shall distinguish between Jonson's style and the plain style of the native English tradition. The problem is complicated by the fact that Jonson not only shared similar attitudes with such men as Wyatt, Gascoigne, Ralegh, and Greville, but that their style often conforms to the majority of the principles of the classical plain style.

6

JONSON AND THE NATIVE TRADITION
OF THE PLAIN STYLE

The English *Poems of Sr* Walter Raleigh, *of* John Donn, *of* Hugh Holland, *but especially of Sr* Foulk Grevile *in his matchless* Mustapha, *are not easily to be mended. . . . But if I should declare mine own Rudeness rudely, I should then confess, that I never tasted* English *more to my liking, nor more smart, and put to the height of Use in Poetry, then in that vital judicious, and most practicable Language of* Benjamin Jonson's *Poems.*

EDMUND BOLTON

In HIS TREATISE on history, *Hypercritica* (*c.* 1618), Bolton associates with perceptive accuracy four poets—Ralegh, Donne, Greville, and Jonson—who wrote in a plain style.[1] For an accurate description of the changing conventions in the 1590's, however, the styles of Jonson and Donne must be distinguished from Ralegh's and in part from Greville's. Despite the fact that Ralegh shared Jonson's stylistic attitudes, Ralegh's verse is closer to an older tradition of English verse, which might be more accurately called the native English plain style, the most distinguished early representatives of which were Wyatt and Gascoigne. Before distinguishing these poets from those who followed, it is worth calling attention to the similarity of their stylistic attitudes to those of Jonson, who occasionally wrote in the native style with great power.

In his *Certayne Notes of Instruction* Gascoigne says that "it is not inough to roll in pleasant woordes, nor yet to thunder in *Rym, Ram, Ruff* . . . nor yet to abounde in apt vocables or epythetes," and he warns against writing *tanquam in oratione perpetua* without anything to say. He cautions writers, in using figures and tropes, to "remember this old adage, *Ne quid nimis* . . . Also, asmuche as may be, eschew straunge words, or *obsoleta et inusitata*," and "to place all wordes in their naturall or most common and vsuall pronunciation, so would I wishe you to frame all sentences in their mother phrase and proper *Idioma*." Your object should be to "frame your stile to *perspicuity* and to be sensible, for the haughty obscure verse doth not much delight."[2] These principles apply to much of Wyatt's poetry as well as to the best poems written by such men as Thomas Lord Vaux, Grimald, Jasper Heywood, Googe, Turberville, and Edward de Vere, who may be said to be of the school of Gascoigne.[3]

In his own satire "The Steele Glass," Gascoigne's account of how he received the ancient *speculum* shows how clearly he was aware of the origins of satire and the *sermo*.[4] It came to me, he says

> by wil and testament
> Of one that was, a Glassemaker in deede.
> *Lucylius,* this worthy man was namde,
> Who at his death, bequeathed the christal glasse,
> To such as love, to seme but not to be,
> And unto those, that love to see themselves,
> How foule or fayre, soever that they are,
> He gan bequeath, a glasse of trustie Steele,
> Wherin they may be bolde always to looke,
> Bycause it shewes, all things in their degree.[5]

Gascoigne, like Horace, makes his moral observations most subtly in the more flexible structure of an epistolary form, which he describes in his poem "Councell given to master *Bartholmew Withipoll* a little before his latter journey to Geane." Gascoigne begins by expressing the attitudes that were traditional in the letter-writing treatises, and he justifies his candid, conversational tone by professing his friendship:

> Mine owne good *Bat*, before thou hoyse up saile,
> To make a furrowe in the foming seas,
> Content thy selfe to heare for thine availe,
> Such harmelesse words, as ought thee not displease.
> First in thy journey, jape not over much,
> What? laughest thou *Batte,* bicause I write so plaine?
> Beleeve me now it is a friendly touch,
> To use fewe words where friendship doth remaine.[6]

Gascoigne achieves this tone of informal intimacy with greater concentration in one of the most powerful poems of the century, "Gascoigne's Woodmanship." In the poem, as he explains to his host, Lord Grey of Wilton, his poor marksmanship in deer hunting, missing the mark becomes a metaphor for his continual failure to succeed in a corrupt world. He uses the third person in describing himself, and in this way he is able to give a general definition of an honest man that serves the purpose of direct precept without its didactic awkwardness, and at the same time achieves the persuasive candor of particular experience.[7]

Equally reminiscent of the tone and intention of the classical plain style in their intimacy and colloquial ease of diction are Wyatt's three epistolary satires, which show a curious mixture of the traditions of Horace and Chaucer. The first of them, "Myne owne John Poynz,"[8] gives Wyatt's reasons for fleeing "the presse of courtes wher soo they goo." The poet explains "My Poynz, I cannot frame me tune to fayne," and he lists a series of vicious actions in which he cannot participate. The syntactical structure for some lines is repetitive, giving detail by detail a picture of worldly corruption, a rhetorical device that is closely echoed in "Gascoigne's Woodmanship." The poem, which is written in an extraordinarily flexible *terza rima,* concludes with the finest ease of the epistolary tradition:

> But here I ame in Kent and Christendome
> Emong the muses where I rede and ryme;
> Where if thou list, my Poynz, for to come,
> Thou shalt be judge how I do spend my tyme.

Wyatt's second satire,[9] also addressed to John Poins, puts Chaucerian speech in the mouth of Horatian mice and by means of the old fable demonstrates that it would have been better for the country mouse to have stayed where he was, for "Eche kynd of lyff hath with hym his disease." The third satire is a poem of friendly admonition, addressed to Sir Francis Bryan, warning against prodigality and giving ironic advice on how to replenish wealth.[10]

The poets of the native plain style often dealt with love with the same simplicity and directness that Jonson later extended to subject matter that was usually, by convention, treated in the more ornate styles. Gascoigne says in his *Certayne Notes of Instruction,* "If I should vndertake to wryte in prayse of a gentlewoman, I would neither praise hir christal eye, nor hir cherrie lippe, . . . these things are *trita et obuia.*"[11] Such clichés "as come under the banner of unresistable love," Sidney remarks a few years later in his *Defence of Poesie,* "if I were a mistresse, would never perswade mee they were in love: so coldly they applie firie speeches, as men that had rather redde lovers writings, and so caught up certaine swelling Phrases . . . then that in truth they feele those passions."[12] Gascoigne's own love poetry is often without ornament, and Wyatt's most interesting love poems completely abandon the stereotypes of his Petrarchan models. In his songs to his lute, where the genre might lead the reader to expect an ornate lament, his sophistication in the plainly stated argument is emphasized by the contrast. In "Blame not my lute for he must sownde," for example, Wyatt excuses his lute by explaining that it sounds what he plays:

> Blame but the selffe that hast mysdown
> And well desaruid to haue blame;
> Change thou thy way, so evyll bygown,
> And then my lute shall sownde that same:

> But if tyll then my fyngeres play
>   By thy desartt their wontyd way,
>   Blame not my lutte.[18]

With the exception of the device of the lute, the language and tone of these
lines are similar to most of the poems of moralistic admonishment in the
middle decades of the sixteenth century.

In his few poems of which the style suggests the native tradition Jonson
is perhaps closest to Ralegh in subject and tone. The following lines are
from Jonson's "To the World" (VIII, 100):

> My tender, first, and simple yeeres
>   Thou did'st abuse, and then betray;
> Since stird'st vp iealousies and feares,
>   When all the causes were away.
> Then, in a soile hast planted me,
>   Where breathe the basest of thy fooles;
> Where enuious arts professed be,
>   And pride, and ignorance the schooles,
> Where nothing is examin'd, weigh'd,
>   But, as 'tis rumor'd, so beleeu'd:
> Where euery freedome is betray'd,
>   And euery goodnesse tax'd, or grieu'd.
>   (ll. 41–52)

These lines echo the more conservative didactic tradition of the native plain
style in several ways. First, the poem, which is subtitled "A farewell for a
Gentle-woman, vertuous and noble," is in the form of the medieval complaint to fortune, or in this case the world. The poem, then, is addressed
to everybody, not just to particular people in a particular context, and its
critical observations are stated in the form of universal precepts. The structure of the poem is that of accumulated aphoristic comment, which does
not develop so much as restate familiar attitudes in various commonplaces.
Second, the diction itself of the poem is reminiscent of earlier statement
of these commonplaces. Such formulations as "My part is ended on the
stage" (l. 4), to live free "From all the nets that thou canst spread" (l. 8),
"thy gifts are baits" (l. 12), "Yet art thou falser then thy wares" (l. 20),
"Enamor'd of their golden gyues" (l. 24), and "I must not grutch" (l. 56)
all carry associations of the aphoristic school and certain commitments t
emotional attitudes from which, in the interests of flexibility, the classica
plain style would prefer to remain free. Third, the syntactical structure o
the lines is fairly uniform. In the passage quoted, the syntactical unit

completed every second line, and, except for two, each single line completes a fairly important member of the periodic unit. Gnomic verse, in which each line is a complete unit, was cultivated by the native tradition, as in Ralegh's "The Lie," and consciously avoided by the classical tradition of the plain style.[14]

In describing the similarities between the attitudes of the native and the classical traditions of the plain style I am in no sense suggesting that the ancient writers were the direct and formative influence on the attitudes of English poets. The qualities of language are characteristic of most didactic intentions, and the medieval poetic tradition was overwhelmingly didactic. Despite the structural elaborations of the allegorical method, which the sixteenth-century plain stylists were to abandon, the diction and syntax of the greatest medieval poets remained remarkably plain and beguilingly intimate. Chaucer's simplicity of statement offers a model of purity to the English language that is comparable to the one Terence gave to Latin, and their intention to represent the real concerns of ordinary people was the same. Dante writes Can Grande that one of the reasons he is calling his intricate allegory a comedy is that it is written in the *genus humile* appropriate to comedy, in a vernacular style in which even women converse. The attitudes toward experience and the stylistic qualities appropriate to them, therefore, were quite as available in the medieval tradition as they were in the classical. Jonson, then, in the late 1590's is not reacting against the native plain style in the sense that he was against the high and middle styles. He is simply returning to the classical statement of his position and adapting certain techniques of prose rhythm, derived from the very origins of the *sermo* itself, to the rhythmical structure of English verse. Once adapted, these techniques of variation gradually become principles of good prosody in general and are no longer restricted to the plain style. Although the most precise formulations of the emerging principles are contained in the classical and contemporary descriptions of the *sermo,* if one traces the changes in prosody between Gascoigne and Milton, it will appear that the most elevated style in English poetry owes perhaps its most fundamental characteristics to the innovations of the plainest.[15]

As described by Cicero and Horace, the *sermo* exploits the conversational flexibility of the informal and idiomatic speech of educated men. The most frequently observed characteristic of the masters of the plain style, therefore, is their "idiomatic purity," a quality so difficult to describe that the phrase is usually left to stand by itself as a sufficient description. In dealing with the influence of the rhythmical principles of the *sermo* on

the verse line, however, one must relate idiom to prosody, since it becomes
in that style as important a structural principle as the number of syllables
in the line. The comparison of the following passages will illustrate the
differences between the classical and native plain styles and at the same
time offer several distinctions which might be made toward a definition
of idiomatic purity in poetry.

The first passage is the second stanza of Tichborne's "My prime of youth
is but a frost of care":

> My tale was heard and yet it was not told,
> My fruit is fallen and yet my leaves are green,
> My youth is spent and yet I am not old,
> I saw the world and yet I was not seen;
> My thread is cut and yet it is not spun,
> And now I live, and now my life is done.[16]

Each line is end-stopped and has a caesura, either indicated or implied, after
the fourth syllable. The accents are relatively equal in the stressed and unstressed positions. An identical caesural pattern occurs in the other stanzas
and becomes a rhythmical scheme, a metrical equivalent of a *schema,* or
figure of diction, in rhetoric. Such a scheme makes its demands on the ear,
and the demands are formal in the sense that the pattern remains in the
mind and is easily imposed on different words to make up different poems.
Puttenham describes this process by his rules on caesura, to which I shall
refer later. Tichborne's poem is so finely executed and its simplicity of
syntax so uncompromised that it is difficult to say whether the syntactical
balance and parallelism were adopted to complement the rhythmical
scheme or vice versa. So far as idiom is concerned, however, the syntax is
secondary to the pattern; one would express oneself in this way only to
fulfill the formal demands of the ear. The importance of these demands
is more evident in less skillful poems. Even in this poem we are aware not
so much of the syntax as of the caesural pattern and the rhetorical balancing
of one line against another.

The second passage consists of eight lines from Jonson's epigram "Inviting a friend to svpper" (VIII, 64):

> Ile tell you of more, and lye, so you will come:
>   Of partrich, pheasant, wood-cock, of which some
> May yet be there; and godwit, if we can:
>   Knat, raile, and ruffe too. How so ere, my man
> Shall reade a piece of Virgil, Tacitvs,
>   Livie, or of some better booke to vs,

Of which wee'll speake our minds, amidst our meate;
And Ile professe no verses to repeate:

(ll. 17-24)

In these lines the idiomatic purity is as much a matter of rhythm as of elegance and currency of diction and syntax. The more the caesural movement of the rhythm coincides with the normal syntactical pauses, within the limitations set by the meter, the greater the idiomatic flexibility. Here the hypothetical metrical limitation, or norm, is a unit of two rhymed lines of ten syllables each, five stressed alternating with five unstressed. Jonson permits the syntax to disrupt the couplet slightly by running over and making the metrical unit give in, somewhat at least, to the syntactical demands. He avoids frequent runovers, however, since they weaken the reader's perception of the norm and hence of any variation from that norm, and carefully limits each one to only a few syllables. The fact that the trisyllabic substitution in the second position of the first of these lines is such a marked variation shows how closely Jonson has adhered to the metrical norm, for more frequent substitutions would have made this one less striking. Within the restrictions of the norm the rhythmical variations, however, are continual. The chief variation is that of the caesura, which may be indicated numerically. Each of the following numbers refers to the number of syllables between caesuras; the mark of punctuation following it refers to the type of pause expressed; and the end of each line is indicated by a bar: 5,2,4:/3,2,2,3/4;3,3:/1,1,3.3,2/7,3,/2,8,/6,4;/10:/. Of the eight lines only two are run over, the second and the fourth, but the numbers of syllables in the overlapping caesural units are only seven and nine, respectively; the largest in the poem is twelve, and it occurs but once. If one disregards the line endings and the types of pauses, the caesural movement can be expressed: 5,2,4,3,2,2,7,3,3,1,1,3,3,9,3,2,8,6,4,10. Besides the variation in degree of stress in accented and unaccented positions alike, two major principles emerge which are not implicit in the first passage cited. First, no recurring pattern of caesural placement occurs as it does in the Tichborne stanza: 4,6,4,6,4,6,4,6,4,6,4,6. Second, the caesura falls indiscriminately in odd and even positions in the line.

In prose, idiomatic purity refers generally to diction and syntax; the effects of rhythm, though important, are insufficiently restricted and measurable, except in cases of idiosyncrasy, to support the distinction between pure and impure. In verse, however, idiom must be coordinated with rhythm to meet the demands of the meter and rhyme, and hence rhythm becomes the third term in defining the concept of purity. Not much more

can be said about the diction than that it should be current, the newest of
the old and the oldest of the new, that which is ordinarily used by educated
men in normal conversation. The other two terms, however, are variables,
and their claims upon the verse line are to some extent inversely propor-
tional to each other. In their interdependence the emphasis of one over the
other, of course, will be relatively slight at any given time, but precisely
on which the emphasis falls makes the difference. The word "idiomatic"
immediately implies that the rhythmical demands are yielding to the syntactical, since idiom is more closely associated with syntax than with formal
rhythmical patterns. In Tichborne's poem one is more aware of the formal
pattern. In Jonson's the line becomes idiomatic as the emphasis shifts in
such a way that the syntax dictates the caesural placement and does not
conform to a given pattern. As will be shown, this is precisely what happens in adapting the principle of movement of the *sermo* to the verse line.
The rhythmical unit of the line is broken up by a greater number of fragmentary syntactical units, until the established caesural patterns are dispersed and the caesura floats freely to any position in the line where it is
needed to emphasize the poet's meaning. Nearly always accompanying the
increased frequency and flexibility of the caesura is constant variation in
degree of stress. This variation also has as its aim the avoidance of a too
closely defined pattern.[17] It is the authority of syntax in the rhythmical
construction of the line, curiously enough, that enables Jonson to convey
a particular feeling, for he can avoid the burden of emotional commitments
which the metrical and rhetorical schemes other than the initial metrical
norm impose. Syntax is the logical connection of words, and idiom represents the most persistent and current habits of connection. It is the most
direct reflection of the mind's linguistic operation, and what one reads in
such a reflection is the individual's personality. This is, of course, simply
a restatement of one of Jonson's favorite Senecan maxims, that the style
most shows the man.

However accurate this description may be, as an account of an historical
process it gathers meaning only when it can be reconstructed in terms of
the historical period. These terms were rhetorical, and, being derived from
classical and Renaissance treatises on rhetoric, applied almost entirely to
prose. There was, however, from classical times, a general assumption that
descriptions of prose style could be adapted to verse, and comparisons of
one with the other occurred in descriptions of the structure of syntax.
Demetrius, for instance, opens his treatise *On Style* by saying "As verse is
articulated by measures . . . so also is prose style articulated and marked

out by what are called 'members.' These members give rest, one might
say, to the speaker and his discourse; they set bounds to its various parts,
since it would otherwise extend itself without limit and would simply run
the speaker out of breath." Here the verse line is compared to a member,
or clause, which, theoretically, ought to complete a thought, since, Demetrius continues, "The proper function of such members is to indicate the
conclusion of a thought." In poetry this would be realized in a syntactical
structure such as that illustrated by the lines from Tichborne in which each
measure is a completed member. "Sometimes, however," Demetrius goes
on to say, "the member constitutes not a complete thought, but a part of it,
yet a complete part. For just as the arm, which is a whole of a certain kind,
has parts such as fingers and forearm which themselves again are wholes,
inasmuch as each of them has its own limits and its own parts; so also a
complete thought, when it is extensive, may very well comprise within
itself parts which themselves are integral." Smaller syntactical units may
break up the complete member. Extended to verse, this means that the
rhythmical unit of the line can be broken up into syntactical units. This is
brought about in both cases by the use of the *incisum* or *comma*. In prosody
comma has the technical meaning of caesura.

The difference between the older tradition of the native plain style and
the classical plain style, arising in the 1590's, can best be distinguished in
terms of the caesura. George Puttenham in "the old book yt goes about
(the art of English Poesie)," as Jonson calls it (I, 144), illustrates the earlier
attitude:

> So may you see that the vse of these pawses or distinctions is not gener-
> ally with the vulgar Poet as it is with the Prose writer because the Poetes
> cheife Musicke lying in his rime or concorde to heare the Simphonie,
> he maketh all the hast he can to be at an end of his verse, and delights
> not in many stayes by the way, and therefore giueth but one *Cesure* to
> any verse: and thus much for the sounding of a meetre.[18]

It is difficult to find a more specific rejection of this statement than the
following lines from Jonson's poem, "A Fit of Rime against Rime" (VIII,
183):

> Vulgar Languages that want
> Words, and sweetnesse, and be scant
> Of true measure,
>
> *Tyran* Rime hath so abused,
> That they long since have refused
> Other caesure.
> (ll. 43–48)

Jonson complains that caesural variation has been neglected in the interest of rhyme. Puttenham's assumption is that "euery verse is as it were a clause of it selfe," which is precisely what Demetrius implied in saying that a "measure" might be compared to a "member" which concluded a thought, and upon this assumption he hesitates to allow any more than "one *Cesure* to any verse." Furthermore, Puttenham specifies that the caesura must fall in the middle of an eight-syllable line and that a ten-syllable line "must haue his *Cesure* fall vpon the fourth sillable, and leaue sixe behinde him."[19] The lines cited from Tichborne follow these prescriptions perfectly.

Accompanying Jonson's wish to return to the classical caesura is his dislike of verses whose syntax runs from line to line without pause. Drummond writes of him, "His censure of my verses was that . . . they smelled too much of yᵉ schooles and were not after the Fancie of ye tyme. for a child sayes he may writte after the fashion of yᵉ Greeks & latine verses jn running" (I, 135). Translation of classical verse, because of the verse structure of the original and because more words were necessary in English than in the original, encouraged a loose and extended period, which tended to dissolve the structure of the English line. In 1619 Jonson criticized one of the more irresponsible reactions to the rigidity of the versification of Puttenham's time.[20] Neither extreme was satisfactory. As a result, Jonson wished to return to the principle of pausing, however lightly, at the line endings in order to keep the verses from running on in both the technical and colloquial sense. At the same time, by avoiding a fixed caesural pattern within the line he tried to reduce the monotony caused by repeated pauses at the end of each verse. Both these intentions are implicit in the stipulations about rhythm in his own rhetorical position, and in his explicit statements about versification he is merely adapting them to prosody.

Although the adaptations of certain classical relationships of syntax to the verse line led to slackness in English, which Jonson repeatedly criticized (I, 132, 133, 135), he checked this slackness by the equally classical emphasis upon caesural frequency and variation. His most valuable comment on meter to Drummond is (I, 143):

Some loved running Verses plus mihi comma placet.

The Latin phrase comes from an anonymous epitaph on Lucan, the pertinent lines of which are:

Continuo numquam direxi carmina ductu,
Quae tractim serpant, plus mihi comma placet.[21]

I have never, Lucan is made to say, written poems in an extended and continuous composition, which gradually spreads itself out by slow degrees; it has pleased me more to stop my verses abruptly. Lucan's own verse is characterized by its tense, abrupt movement and its great variation of the length of syntactical units within relatively short completed periods.

> 'Ius et fas multos faciunt, Ptolemaee, nocentes;
> Dat poenas laudata fides, cum sustinet,' inquit
> 'Quos fortuna premit. Fatis accede deisque,
> Et cole felices, miseros fuge. Sidera terra
> Ut distant et flamma mari, sic utile recto.
> (*Pharsalia* viii.484-88)[22]

Jonson translates these lines in "A speech out of Lucane" (VIII, 422).

> Just and fit actions *Ptolemey* (he saith)
> make many, hurt themselues; a praysed faith
> Is her owne scourge, when it sustaines their states
> whom fortune hath deprest; come nere the fates
> and the immortall gods; loue only those
> whom thou seest happy; wretches flee as foes:
> Looke how the starres from earth, or seas from flames
> are distant, so is proffitt from iust aymes.
> (ll. 1-8)

Jonson's lines are run over, to be sure, but they are not running verses; the number of syllables within any *comma* is tightly controlled, and the position of the caesura is continually varied. Had Jonson printed the translation himself, he probably would have expressed more of the terminal caesuras by commas, as his practice was. The lines, as they stand, not only show the influence of classical versification on the relationship of Jonson's syntax to his verse line, but indicate the possible danger of running verse in classical translations. "The translations of Homer and Virgill jn Long Alexandrines were but Prose" he told Drummond (I, 133), and the reason was probably that the caesuras did not keep the rhythm taut enough. The smallest amount of running over in a twelve-syllable line which was insufficiently broken would relax the verse into prose.

In the light of Jonson's preference for the caesura, the best commentary on his versification can be found in contemporary descriptions of the *comma*. Puttenham writes that "The shortest pause or intermissiō they called *comma* as who would say a peece of a speach cut of." The colon is the next degree of pause, and it is "not a peece but as it were a member for his larger length." A period is a full pause, "a resting place and perfection of so much former speach as had bene vttered."[23] Jonson, in *The English Grammar,* describes the comma as "a mean breathing, when the word serveth indifferently, both to the parts of the sentence going before, and following after," while "A *semicolon* is a distinction of an *imperfect* sentence, wherein with somewhat a longer breath, the sentence following is included."[24] The most helpful gloss on *plus mihi comma placet* occurs in the *Index Rhetoricus* of Jonson's friend, Thomas Farnaby:

> A period completes a sentence by divisions and members in the right proportion.
> A comma or division (*incisum*) is a thought which is not brought to conclusion by a completed rhythmical unit and is extended from two up to seven syllables, or thereabouts, of which a period not infrequently consists. . . .
> A colon or member completes a thought rounded off according to rhythmical units, but keeps the listener's attention diverted from the period, so that it can progress from the twelfth to the eighteenth and sometimes to the twenty-fourth syllable without completing the sentence.[25]

Demetrius says that a member can be either a complete thought, or an integral part, syntactically complete within itself, of a completed thought, as a clause would be a complete syntactical unit within a period. Farnaby adds the observation that the members, or cola, coincide with the rhythmical units, but that the comma, or abrupt division, does not coincide with any completed rhythmical unit. It is a *sensus non expleto numero conclusus,* a thought, or syntactical unit, not concluded by a completed rhythmical unit. What Jonson is advocating, then, is a more frequent caesural variation which is intended to counterpoint the strict rhythmical unit of the line or the couplet. It is not sufficient to say that he wanted the comma to occur more regularly at the end of the line to stop running verses. If monotony was to be avoided in writing relatively end-stopped lines and couplets, the caesural variation had to exist within the line itself.

The origin of the differences between the native and the classical plain style, whose description I have tried to reconstruct in historical terms, is implicit in Jonson's own rhetorical position. First, Cicero says, "let us release him [the Attic orator] from . . . the bonds of rhythm" (*e vinculis numerorum*). His style "should be loose but not rambling; so that it may seem to move freely but not to wander without restraint." He should avoid, like a man whose attention is more to the thought than to the words, "cementing his words together too smoothly, for the hiatus and clash of vowels has something agreeable about it." But his "freedom from periodic structure" and delicate refinement in composition makes it necessary that he handle "the short and concise clauses" with care. He should avoid the ornate schematic figures "such as clauses of equal length, with similar endings, or identical cadences, and the studied charm produced by the change of a letter, lest the elaborate symmetry and a certain grasping after a pleasant effect be too obvious." It is important that he "breaks up and divides the periodic structure" and avoids a long series of members in any single period for "this requires stronger lungs." The periodic structure would correspond roughly to the structure of the verse line, or, in the case of couplets, perhaps to a unit of two lines. The plain-stylist is released from observing the rhythmical bonds of the period and will break it up by using concise members, or syntactical units, which do not regularly coincide with the rhythmical units, or, even if they do, by introducing more syntactical units within any given rhythmical unit. This is precisely what happens within the rhythmical unit of Jonson's couplet and distinguishes it from the lines of Tichborne. The additional caesuras, which often mark off smaller syntactical units, break up the verse line or the couplet in such a way that "clauses of equal length, with similar endings, or identical cadences" are avoided.[26]

A passage by Vives indicates even more sharply how their common rhetorical position can be adapted to prosody. Vives is describing the movement of post-Ciceronian prose:

> The use of periods was greater after M. Tullius than in his age, such as in the works of Seneca, Quintilian, Pliny, and Tacitus. . . . A certain number of divisions within a sentence, completed properly within themselves, are the strength of the period. . . . The most pleasing periods are those which are made from *antitheses* . . . or from an argument sharply concluded, and, for that matter, there are certain men, like Hermogenes, who think those periods to be the only true ones which order their subject matter with a tight subtlety, shake it out in quick turns, and conclude it briefly, which do not have members but divisions in place of members, as: *Habebat vestes, et ad usum aptas, et ornatum decoras: Magnae fuit prudentiae, et in magistratu gratiam omnium, et in privata vita auctoritatem conservare.*[27]

To have divisions, or *commata*, in place of members, as Vives illustrates in breaking up his Latin *sententiae*, is to do in prose what Jonson insists on in verse. In either form the effect is to bring out the meaning sharply, but in verse the particular effect is to stress idiomatic syntax, since the rhythmical unit is being partially sacrificed to it.

Thus far I have described the changes in English prosody and the contemporary terms in which they can best be understood as revealed in the poems and comments of Jonson. I wish, now, to suggest that, since the

origin of these changes is implicit in Jonson's rhetorical position, the innovation in English verse of certain traditional characteristics of classical
prosody may be accounted for by the adaptation of the classical *sermo* to
the English verse line in the 1590's. Besides the descriptions of the *sermo*
in rhetorical treatises of the classical period and of Jonson's Renaissance
authorities, Horace offered him a model for the application of the principles
of the *sermo* to poetry. But, whereas the effects of Horace's reaction to
poetic conventions were mainly seen in subject matter and diction, Jonson's
use of the *sermo* effected, in addition to these, an essential difference in the
caesura and in the relation of syntax to the line. Horace's move toward a
style more appropriate to prose (*sermoni propriora, Serm.* 1.4.42), was a
move toward the idiomatic freedom of prose in the unrestricted treatment
of all subjects. Jonson's move toward such a language was, in addition, a
move toward the greater freedom of prose syntax from a more severely
imposed external rhythmical norm than was involved in classical prosody.
Hence the *sermo* brings into English an essentially new structure of the
line.

That this new line structure had been part of the classical tradition and
that it was relatable to prose and hence to the *sermo* is shown by Dionysius
of Halicarnassus, who gives an interesting description of how breaking up
a line and the rhythmical variation that results from it bring the movement
of the verse near to that of prose. At the beginning of his chapter on "How
Verse Can Resemble Prose" he says that it is first necessary for one to make

> the clauses begin and end at various places within the lines, not allowing
> their sense to be self-contained in separate verses, but breaking up the
> measure. He must make the clauses vary in length and form, and will
> often also reduce them to phrases which are shorter than clauses, and
> will make the periods—those at any rate which adjoin one another—
> neither equal in size nor alike in construction; for an elastic treatment
> of rhythms and metres seems to bring verse quite near to prose.

The writers of monometers, he continues, make the regularity of the meter
less obtrusive by breaking up the lines into clauses of various lengths and
construction and nearly dissolve the meter by diversifying the size and
syntax of the periods. The lyric poets not only have these means of con-
cealing a uniform rhythm, but they vary their meters as well, and "so they
produce, as by design, in lyric poems a great likeness to prose." Later in
the chapter he gives as an example some lines of Simonides and comments:

> They are written according to divisions: not into those clauses for which
> Aristophanes or some other metrist laid down his canons, but into those

which are required by prose. Please read the piece carefully by divisions: you may rest assured that the rhythmical arrangement of the ode will escape you, and you will be unable to guess which is the strophe or which the antistrophe or which the epode, but you will think it all one continuous piece of prose.[28]

The editor, Rhys Roberts, mentions Simon Bircov's illustration of this passage in his *Exempla Latina, Graecis Dionysii respondentia*. Bircov says: "The following lines of Horace's ode (III.27) can be read in this fashion, so that there are few signs left that it was in verse, for, even if there are strophes, still they fall apart when the clauses are placed together in this way, so that the ode does not seem to be so much a stanzaic poem as a piece of continuous prose." He then prints the ode as if it were prose, and comments after it: "These and many other lines of this poet seem to be similar to prose (*solutae orationi*)."[29] *Soluta oratio* was a common term for prose as opposed to verse and was applied to the *sermo,* of whose rhythm Cicero says, *Solutum quiddam sit nec vagum tamen, ut ingredi libere non ut licenter videatur errare* (*Orator* 77)—it should be loose but not rambling, free but not wandering. Extended to English versification, the description could distinguish the restricted run-over and caesural variation of the *sermo* from running verses whose syntax rambles without restraint from line to line. Cicero may well have had Simonides in mind when he writes (*Orator* 183–84) that "in poetry the presence of rhythm is more obvious [than in prose], although in certain metres, if the musical accompaniment be taken away, the words seem to lack rhythm (*cantu remoto soluta esse videatur oratio*); this is particularly true of the best of the poets whom the Greeks call 'lyric'; deprive them of the musical accompaniment and almost nothing but bare prose remains (*nuda paene remanet oratio*)." Even more important for the connections I am tracing, Cicero continues that the same thing can be true in Latin, citing a line from Ennius as an example which, along with the rest of its context, unless accompanied by the pipe, "is exactly like prose (*orationis sunt solutae simillima*)."

The application of the rhetorical principles of the classical plain style to English versification is most easily documented in the work of Jonson. These principles, however, are not restricted to English poems in the classical plain style; they become principles of good prosody in various styles, although they seem to have come into the language mainly under the sanction of Jonson and Donne in the 1590's.[30] In order to show the extent of these principles in the seventeenth century, I shall quote a poem of Jonson's in the restrained rhythm of the relatively closed couplet and then a passage of Milton's blank verse, the sources of whose rhythm have been sought for in strange places and reconstructed of strange material. The suggestion that Milton's elevated blank verse owes its most fundamental rhythmical principles to those of the plainest of styles, expanded in accord with certain conventions of diction and phrase demanded by the decorum of the high style, need not appear strange in comparison. In his poem "To Heaven" Jonson carries into the more formal statement of a religious poem the idiomatic movement of the epistolary epigram (VIII, 122):

> Good, and great GOD, can I not thinke of thee,
>   But it must, straight, my melancholy bee?
> Is it interpreted in me disease,
>   That, laden with my sinnes, I seeke for ease?
> O, be thou witnesse, that the reynes dost know,
>   And hearts of all, if I be sad for show,
> And iudge me after: if I dare pretend
>   To ought but grace, or ayme at other end.
> As thou art all, so be thou all to mee,
>   First, midst, and last, conuerted one, and three;
> My faith, my hope, my loue: and in this state,
>   My iudge, my witnesse, and my aduocate.
> Where haue I beene this while exil'd from thee?
>   And whither rap'd, now thou but stoup'st to mee?
> Dwell, dwell here still: O, being euery-where,
>   How can I doubt to finde thee euer, here?
> I know my state, both full of shame, and scorne,
>   Conceiu'd in sinne, and vnto labour borne,
> Standing with feare, and must with horror fall,
>   And destin'd vnto iudgement, after all.
> I feele my griefes too, and there scarce is ground,
>   Vpon my flesh t[o]'inflict another wound.
> Yet dare I not complaine, or wish for death
>   With holy PAVL, lest it be thought the breath
> Of discontent; or that these prayers bee
>   For wearinesse of life, not loue of thee.

The caesura falls in every position in the line, shifting throughout the poem. Its numerical tabulations for the first twelve lines are as follows: 1,3,6,/3,1,6?/10,/1,5,4?/1,4,5,/4,6,/5:5/4,6./4,6,/1,1,2,3,2;/2,2,2:4,/2,3,5./. In the entire poem there are but four syntactical units that run over into the next line, and then for only a few syllables. The largest number of syllables unbroken by a caesura is twelve, and this happens only once. Despite the extreme use of *commata,* the rhythm of the verse does not become violent, because there is a cautiously observed gradation in the weight and duration of the pauses and because the majority of the caesuras are extremely light. They slow the line down but do not stop it abruptly. This constant restraint suggests the existence of a continual, underlying movement, which requires control; it takes great skill to achieve the quietness of tone without losing the rhythmical life of the line.[31]

The following lines are from the third book of *Paradise Lost*.

> Thus with the Year
> Seasons return, but not to me returns
> Day, or the sweet approach of Ev'n or Morn,
> Or sight of vernal bloom, or Summer's Rose,
> Or flocks, or herds, or human face divine;
> But cloud instead, and ever-during dark
> Surrounds me, from the cheerful ways of men
> Cut off, and for the Book of knowledge fair
> Presented with a Universal blanc
> Of Nature's works to mee expung'd and ras'd,
> And wisdom at one entrance quite shut out.
> So much the rather thou Celestial light
> Shine inward, and the mind through all her powers
> Irradiate, there plant eyes, all mist from thence
> Purge and disperse, that I may see and tell
> Of things invisible to mortal sight.[32]

(ll. 40–55)

The caesuras in the first eleven lines may be represented as follows: 4/4,6/1,9,/6,4,/2,2,6; /4,6/3,7/2,8/10/10,/10./. As tabulated in this form, Milton has more and longer run-over lines than Jonson. The caesura appears to fall more often in even than odd positions in the line, giving it a slightly quieter tone than is characteristic. If one represents simply the *commata,* indicating neither the line-ending nor the type of pause expressed, Jonson's twelve lines give: 1,3,6,3,1,6,10,1,5,4,1,4,5,4,6,5,9,6,4,6,1,1,2, 3,2,2,2,2,4,2,3,5. Milton's sixteen lines give: 8,7,9,6,4,2,2,6,4,9,9,28,10,13,11, 3,8,16. The two rhythmical principles introduced most explicitly into English by the classical plain style are revealed in these several sequences. No recurring pattern of caesural placement appears, and the caesura is free to fall in any position in the line, odd or even. If one holds a magnifying glass, so to speak, over Jonson's lines and imagines the number of syllables greatly increased between the commas, the run-overs correspondingly more frequent, and the periods greatly lengthened, one will see the essential structure of Miltonic blank verse. The principle of the caesural unit's cutting across the rhythmical unit of the line is the same, but the unit is much larger.

I should say here that I am not suggesting that *Paradise Lost* is in the plain style or that Milton derived his blank verse from Jonson's couplet. I am suggesting that the origin of the two most fundamental variations in the rhythm of his blank verse, as in any verse after Jonson, can best be accounted for historically by the adaptation of the *sermo* to the English line. What is true of all classical versification to a greater or less extent— that the rhythmical structure is determined by syntax rather than by an arbitrarily imposed rhythmical unit of a line of given length—most logically would enter the language through a rhetorical position dedicated to idiomatic flexibility. The requirements of decorum of the high style in matters of diction, phrasing, figures, and types of statement need in no sense be incompatible with these principles of rhythm. In fact, these principles, in conjunction with the characteristics mentioned by Thomas Farnaby in a fairly typical seventeenth-century description of the *genus grande,* offer a generally accurate account of Milton's style.

> The high style, by, first, a careful selection and, then, an audacious number of words, by a fierce dignity of figures, by a grave majesty of moral sayings, by periods requiring full lungs, whose breath trembles with stronger meter, by a rapid incitement of feelings, by a driving force of crowding amplifications, not only flashes with lightning and frightens with thunder but strikes with a bolt. Nor does it creep, but rushes into the mind: as the swift torrent of the winter snows or the flash flood of a mountain river, impatient with bridge and dike, flows over the fields, rolls out rock, and where it finds no path, makes one; so it bears the listener, whether he leans with it or against it, and makes him go wherever it drags him.[33]

These details could have come from innumerable descriptions of the high style in classical and Renaissance treatises, but also, more specifically, from descriptions of Pindar's style. Quintilian refers to "*Pindarus* princeps spiritus magnificentia, sententiis, figuris, beatissima rerum verborumque copia et velut quodam eloquentiae flumine; propter quae Horatius eum merito credidit nemini imitabilem" (*Inst. Orat.* X.i.61). Horace's description of the river (*Carm.* IV.2) is very close to Farnaby's.

Abraham Cowley in his *Pindarique Odes* carries the prescriptions cited above from Dionysius beyond Milton and Jonson and dissipates his form, losing as a result his potentiality for variation. In *An Account of the Life and Writings of Mr. Abraham Cowley,* Thomas Sprat gives a description of Cowley's odes which is very near that of Dionysius:

> But that for which I think this inequality of number is chiefly to be preferr'd is its near affinity with Prose: From which all other kinds of

English Verse are so far distant that it is very seldom found that the same Man excels in both ways. But now this loose and unconfin'd measure has all the Grace and Harmony of the most Confin'd. And withal it is so large and free, that the practice of it will only exalt, not corrupt our Prose, which is certainly the most useful kind of Writing of all others, for it is the style of all business and conversation.[34]

Sprat is here referring not to Cowley's variation of *commata* but of the length of the line, which, although it is one of the things mentioned by Dionysius, is not easily adaptable to English verse, except in uniform stanzas, which Cowley consciously avoids. Jonson maintains the couplet or other stanza, Milton the ten-syllable line as a rhythmical norm against which the syntactical unit may be perceived, at any given time, to vary. In reading Cowley, one is often uncertain where the line is supposed to conclude and hence cannot be certain whether a pause is a caesura or a line-ending; the tension sustained by the syntactical check upon the rhythm is relaxed to prose, despite the grandiloquence of the Pindaric style. The effect is parallel, I think, to the slackness Jonson criticized when he told Drummond "a child . . . may writte after the fashion of y[e] Greeks & latine verses jn running" (I, 135). It is amusing that in the eighteenth century Dr. Johnson criticized Cowley's "lax and lawless versification," adding that "all the boys and girls caught the pleasing fashion, and they that could do nothing else could write like Pindar."[35]

Sprat's description indicates that the rhythm of a high style, as well as that of the *sermo,* was relatable to conversational prose. That the *sermo,* then as adapted to the verse line by Jonson, could contain within its principles the fundamental characteristics of Milton's rhythm should seem less improbable. But more convincing are the easily available examples which can be used to trace the gradual steps between Jonson's relatively closed couplet and Milton's extended blank verse period. One may trace the development, hypothetically, by considering a verse epistle by Donne, such as "To Sir Henry Wotton" ("Sir, more than kisses, letters mingle Soules"), whose metrical principles can easily be seen to be identical to Jonson's. Then one may proceed to more violent passages in his satires, or, for that matter, in one of the disputed elegies, and with these compare his seventh Holy Sonnet, which concludes in two periods, the following lines being the first:

> At the round earths imagin'd corners, blow
> Your trumpets, Angells, and arise, arise
> From death, you numberlesse infinites
> Of soules, and to your scattred bodies goe,

All whom the flood did, and fire shall o'rethrow,
All whom warre, dearth, age, agues, tyrannies,
Despaire, law, chance, hath slaine, and you whose eyes,
Shall behold God, and never tast deaths woe.[36]

Although it would be most natural to proceed to Milton's early poems, in
Latin and English, many of which were written during Jonson's lifetime,
and partly under his influence, I think one can go directly to a quieter
passage of his blank verse, such as that cited above, and then to a more
violent passage. I am not trying to establish particular rhythmical corre-
spondences but similar principles of variation.

In his prefatory note to *Paradise Lost* Milton says his meter "consists
only in apt Numbers, fit quantity of Syllables, and the sense variously
drawn out from one Verse into another, not in the jingling sound of like
endings, a fault avoided by the learned Ancients both in Poetry and all good
Oratory." Jonson had said almost exactly the same thing about rhyme in
his "Fit of Rime" quoted earlier. Rhyme has tyrannized the vulgar languages till they do not admit other caesura. For Jonson the *sermo* offered
greater caesural variation while at the same time it kept the syntax from
running on till the rhythmical unit was dissipated. Rhyme may, as Milton
says, have been avoided by all good oratory in antiquity, but in the descriptions of the three styles Cicero points out that it is the specific duty of the
Attic orator to avoid "clauses of equal length, with similar endings, or
identical cadences, and the studied charm produced by the change of a
letter" (*Orator* 84). The changing of a letter in prose may correspond to
rhyme in verse; Cicero gives the example of *nobiliorem* and *mobiliorem*
(*De Orat.* II.256). For Milton the syntactical unit, or "sense," should be
concluded within the line, not at the end. His wording corresponds with
that of Dionysius, who says "an elastic treatment of rhythms and metres
seems to bring verse quite near to prose," and to achieve this the clauses
should "begin and end at various places within the lines, not allowing their
sense to be self-contained in separate verses, but breaking up the measure."
Furthermore, the clauses should "vary in length and form," and often be
reduced "to phrases which are shorter than clauses" to make "periods—
those at any rate which adjoin one another—neither equal in size nor alike
in construction." The description not only corresponds to Milton's, it fulfills, simultaneously, the Ciceronian requirements for the *sermo*. Milton's
is not "running verse" *continuo . . . ductu,/Quae tractim serpant,* which
Lucan and Jonson reject; it is rather the expanded rhythmical structure of
Jonson's broken line. Were it running verse, there would be no sense of

movement being restrained and released; it would be slack. That Milton simply absorbed and extended a practice already established in seventeenth-century prosody by adapting certain characteristics of classical versification to English seems more probable than that he worked from isolated descriptions like that of Dionysius.

There is a close analogy between Jonson's views on composition and his views on prosody. The rounded period of Livy and Sidney in prose corresponds to the coincidence of the completed syntactical unit with the rhythmical unit of the line. Sidney's song "My true love hath my hart, and I have his," with the caesura falling evenly in the fourth or sixth position and at the end of the line, conforms to Puttenham's prescriptions. A few of Jonson's songs are in the earlier manner of Sidney, particularly "I Love, and he loves me againe" (VIII, 147) and "Oh doe not wanton with those eyes" (VIII, 144), both of which may be compared to Ralegh's "Wrong not, deare Empresse of my Heart." The broken Sallustian period, more characteristic of Donne's syntax than Sidney's, is comparable to Lucan's preference for *commata* in verse, which Jonson cites as a critical distinction. Corresponding to the conversational license of the Libertine school in its effort to avoid the rounded period is, in terms of prosody, the refusal to complete a period in a single line or uniform rhythmical unit by means of extended and continuous enjambement. Such "verses in running" resulted from yielding too much to classical conventions of prosody, a habit perhaps acquired in translation. The loss of composition in the looseness of syntactical relationships is comparable to the loss of the structure of the line in running over too extensively. The "forcible" heightening of such conversational irregularity produces the Longinian effects in prose which Cowley tried to achieve in the irregular form of his odes. Samuel Johnson's criticism of the prosody of the odes may be considered analogous in matters of form to his criticism of the composition of the metaphysical poets.

7

JONSON'S POEMS IN THE CLASSICAL
GENRES OF THE PLAIN STYLE

The learned sweat that makes a language cleane.
ZOUCH TOUNLEY *"To Mr. Jonson"*

THE CLASSICAL GENRES that employ the plain style are, leaving comedy aside, the epistle, the epigram, and the satire. The poems of Jonson that are in these genres—and they make up the largest part of his nondramatic poetry—reveal most clearly the attitudes and style described in Part I, and their power can be most easily attributed to the intentions and the qualities of language of the classical plain style.[1] Its dialectical origins and intentions are clearly implied in Jonson's first epigram, "To the Reader" (VIII, 27), which might serve as an introductory poem to his entire works.

> Pray thee, take care, that tak'st my booke in hand,
> To read it well: that is, to vnderstand.

Jonson is asking not only for a conceptual understanding of what is being said, but also for an understanding of and a participation in the emotional context of his statement. Such a participation is necessary for complete understanding, because the denotative and connotative qualities of language are nearly indistinguishable from one another; the loss of one results in the loss of the statement itself.[2]

THE INTIMATE MUSE: THE EPISTLE

No god or goddess, Jonson says, should be invoked "For the more countenance to my actiue *Muse*" nor relied upon for heroic subject matter. Nor could great patrons give such benefits,

> Nor all the ladies of the *Thespian lake*,
> (Though they were crusht into one forme) could make
> A beautie of that merit, that should take
>
> My *Muse* vp by *commission*: No, I bring
> My owne true fire. Now my thought takes wing,
> And now an *Epode* to deepe eares I sing.
>
> (ll. 25–30)

His muse burns with his own fire, and only those can warm their hands there who have qualities he admires (VIII, 108). These qualities are nearly always qualities of personal character, the moral characteristics of a man, which, since the conversations of Socrates, it had been the business of the plain style to ferret out and describe. His muse will accurately reflect the inner person, and that person by way of reflection becomes the muse itself, as the reflection in a mirror is the particular person standing in front of it. The muse, in a sense, becomes the subject itself, or that power of the subject, which draws the poet to write about it. Jonson calls one of his poems on Lady Digby "Elegie on my Muse" (VIII, 282). He begins by distinguishing her from the conventional goddesses:

> 'Twere time that I dy'd too, now shee is dead,
> Who was my *Muse,* and life of all I sey'd,
> The Spirit that I wrote with, and conceiv'd;
> All that was good, or great in me she weav'd,
> And set it forth; the rest were Cobwebs fine,
> Spun out in name of some of the old *Nine*!
> To hang a window, or make darke the roome,
> Till swept away, th[ey]'were cancell'd with a broome!
>
> (ll. 1–8)

This elegy is the ninth in the series of poems to Lady Digby called *Eupheme.* The fourth poem, "The Mind," relates Jonson's concept of the muse most closely to the intentions of his style (VIII, 277).

> Painter, yo'are come, but may be gone,
> Now I have better thought thereon,
> This worke I can performe alone;
> And give you reasons more then one.
>
> Not, that your Art I doe refuse:
> But here I may no colours use.
> Beside, your hand will never hit,
> To draw a thing that cannot sit.
>
> You could make shift to paint an Eye,
> An Eagle towring in the skye,
> The Sunne, a Sea, or soundlesse Pit;
> But these are like a Mind, not it.
>
> No, to expresse a Mind to sense,
> Would aske a Heavens Intelligence;
> Since nothing can report that flame,
> But what's of kinne to whence it came.

> Sweet Mind, then speake your selfe, and say,
>   As you goe on, by what brave way
>   Our sense you doe with knowledge fill,
>   And yet remaine our wonder still.
>
> I call you *Muse*; now make it true:
>   Hence-forth may every line be you;
>   That all may say, that see the frame,
>   This is no Picture, but the same.
>   (ll. 1–24)

It is the lady's mind itself, and by implication her moral character, that
Jonson calls his muse, and it is the job of the poet to make his lines depict
that character in his poem as a painter would be expected to depict the
body in a picture. Both poem and picture should be so accurate that each
might be taken for the person herself. But the poet has the advantage, because he can portray what is most important.

The candid and exact treatment of the moral character of the inner self,
as Persius says in his fifth satire and Lipsius writes in his *Institutio Epistolica,* is the most important intention of the epistle. This is the concern
of Jonson's muse, through whose power he gains insight into the nature of
the person and the ability to describe it. His poem "To my Mvse, the Lady
Digby, on her Husband, Sir Kenelme Digby" begins (VIII, 262):

> Tho', happy *Muse,* thou know my *Digby* well,
>   Yet read him in these lines: He doth excell
> In honour, courtesie, and all the parts
>   Court can call hers, or Man could call his Arts.
> Hee's prudent, valiant, just, and temperate;
>   In him all vertue is beheld in State:
> And he is built like some imperiall roome,
>   For that to dwell in, and be still at home.
>   (ll. 1–8)

The man is to be read in the lines, and it is the poet's business to tell the
truth about him. His muse not only will be concerned with virtue, as in
the epigram "To Sir Henry Nevil" (VIII, 70), but will, Jonson says in his
epistle "To Elizabeth Covntesse of Rvtland" (VIII, 113), commend it to
posterity:

> Beautie, I know, is good, and bloud is more;
>   Riches thought most: But, *Madame,* thinke what store
> The world hath seene, which all these had in trust,
>   And now lye lost in their forgotten dust.

> It is the *Muse,* alone, can raise to heauen,
> 　And, at her strong armes end, hold vp, and euen,
> The soules, shee loues. . . .

(ll. 37–43)

Jonson concludes the epistle from which these lines are taken by saying that the muse will "show, how, to the life, my soule presents/Your forme imprest" in his poems, as on a monument. He will write, in other words, in the way that Lipsius and Demetrius prescribe for letters. In his fine epistle "To Katherine, Lady Avbigny" (VIII, 116), Jonson explains that, just because fortune does, he does not change,

> 　Or feare to draw true lines, 'cause others paint:
> I, *Madame,* am become your praiser. Where,
> 　If it may stand with your soft blush to heare
> Your selfe but told vnto your selfe, and see
> 　In my character, what your features bee,
> You will not from the paper slightly passe:
> 　No lady, but, at some time, loues her glasse.
> And this shall be no false one, but as much
> 　Remou'd, as you from need to haue it such.
> Looke then, and see your selfe. I will not say
> 　Your beautie; for you see that euery day:
> And so doe many more. . . .
> My mirror is more subtile, cleere, refin'd,
> 　And takes, and giues the beauties of the mind.

(ll. 20–31, 43–44)

The style is as plain, intimate, and urbane as the letter-writing manuals recommend. The poem ends:

> Liue that one, still; and as long yeeres doe passe,
> 　*Madame,* be bold to vse this truest glasse:
> Wherein, your forme, you still the same shall finde;
> 　Because nor it can change, nor such a minde.

(ll. 121–24)

The glass is, of course, the glass of the satirist, which may, since friends are addressing friends, be gentler, but still must, as Demetrius says, "obey the laws of friendship, which demand that we should 'call a spade a spade'" (*On Style,* 229).

Jonson's finest and most complete statement of his attitude toward his muse is his epigram "On Lvcy Covntesse of Bedford" (VIII, 52):

> This morning, timely rapt with holy fire,
> 　I thought to forme vnto my zealous *Muse,*

What kinde of creature I could most desire,
  To honor, serue, and loue; as *Poets* vse.
I meant to make her faire, and free, and wise,
  Of greatest bloud, and yet more good then great;
I meant the day-starre should not brighter rise,
  Nor lend like influence from his lucent seat.
I meant shee should be courteous, facile, sweet,
  Hating that solemne vice of greatnesse, pride;
I meant each softest vertue, there should meet,
  Fit in that softer bosome to reside.
Onely a learned, and a manly soule
  I purpos'd her; that should, with euen powers,
The rock, the spindle, and the sheeres controule
  Of destinie, and spin her owne free houres.
Such when I meant to faine, and wish'd to see,
  My *Muse* bad, *Bedford* write, and that was shee.

He starts with the conventional situation of formulating an imaginary lady
to write love poems to, as the "Poets" were accustomed to do, but from the
beginning his attitude toward such an activity is sophisticated. He talks
objectively and without apparent embarrassment about trying to find the
lady to address without trying to hide the artificiality of the practice by addressing her as if she were real. Jonson occasionally places himself in artificial literary conventions, especially those of courtly Petrarchanism, and
treats his subject as straightforwardly as if he were taking them seriously.
Nor is there a strong satiric purpose in his seeming to accept the formula
as a general device, since his irony is usually of the gentlest kind and often
humorously directed toward his own participation in the convention. Here
he proceeds with the character sketch which the conventional poet presumably makes in his imagination before constructing the relationship described in his poems. Jonson complicates the feeling by making the sketch
itself the structure of the poem. The description also departs from the conventional details of the sonnet sequence in being far less concerned with
the physical beauty of the lady than with her character and concludes with
a beautiful statement on the power and freedom of the human mind. The
last couplet of the poem relates the formula of the hypothetical lady to
Jonson's actual subject, the particular virtues of the Countess of Bedford.
When he is about to create in his imagination, and, going beyond this,
wants to see the actual lady, his muse, acting as his judgment, insists upon
the substitution of a particular person for what would be in the convention
the imaginary lady. The relation between the muse and the lady is that
between the mind and the affections. When the muse errs, as in the epi-

gram, "To my Mvse," it is an error in judgment, usually of a person. These attitudes toward poetry are completely consistent with the tradition of the *sermo*, and the epigram to Jonson's patroness, with the exception of the first, seventh, and eighth lines—the last two punning on her name—is simple and unadorned in its diction and syntax.

In "An Epistle to a friend" Jonson uses the attitudes of the epistolary style to describe the duties of friendship (VIII, 189). The poem takes the occasion of a gift to state, like Donne's epistles to Wotton, that true friends may communicate "In letters, that mixe spirits."

> Sir, I am thankfull, first, to heaven, for you;
>   Next to your selfe, for making your love true:
>   Then to your love, and gift. And all's but due.
>
> You have unto my Store added a booke,
>   On which with profit, I shall never looke,
>   But must confesse from whom what gift I tooke.
>
> (ll. 1-6)

Jonson's epistles to his friends have always been cited as examples of his best work, and their style is derived from the genre whose purpose is, according to Vives, "to be close to someone in feeling though we are separated by distance, in which the appearance of presence will shine back among those absent, and written conversation will join those separated, in which we even mingle our soul with a friend's and pour our very thought into him."[3] In "An Epistle to Master Arth: Squib" Jonson discusses the nature of friendship in the most appropriate form and style possible (VIII, 216).

> What I am not, and what I faine would be,
>   Whilst I informe my selfe, I would teach thee,
> My gentle *Arthur*; that it might be said
>   One lesson we have both learn'd, and well read;
> I neither am, nor art thou one of those
>   That hearkens to a Jacks-pulse, when it goes.
> Nor ever trusted to that friendship yet,
>   Was issue of the Taverne, or the Spit:
> Much lesse a name would we bring up, or nurse,
>   That could but claime a kindred from the purse.
> Those are poore Ties, depend on those false ends,
>   'Tis vertue alone, or nothing, that knits friends:
> And as within your Office, you doe take
>   No piece of money, but you know, or make
> Inquirie of the worth: So must we doe,
>   First weigh a friend, then touch, and trie him too:

> For there are many slips, and Counterfeits.
>   Deceit is fruitfull. Men have Masques and nets,
> But these with wearing will themselves unfold:
>   They cannot last. No lie grew ever old.
> Turne him, and see his Threds: looke, if he be
>   Friend to himselfe, that would be friend to thee.
> For that is first requir'd, A man be his owne.
>   But he that's too-much that, is friend of none.
> Then rest, and a friends value understand,
>   It is a richer Purchase then of land.

The poem shows Jonson's style at its best. The control of general statement in a direct, unadorned, and familiar style is sinewy both in its content and, metaphorically, in its movement. Jonson's use of the abrupt period in the last nine lines is nearly as varied as his usual use of the *comma,* and the passage resembles that of Lucan quoted in the last chapter. The terse, epigrammatic statements are like the *sententiae* in Seneca's letters, in both form and content, and the generalizations are based upon particular experience. The informal context of the personal relationship and the apparently unlabored, conversational diction and phrasing give the tone an intimacy which offers the reader an emotional assurance that what is being said is the truth. The emphasis upon both the author's and the friend's knowing himself is in the Socratic and Senecan stylistic traditions and accounts for much of the power of the poem.

So far as Jonson's ideas on style are concerned, the most important of Jonson's epistles to his friends is "An Epistle to Master Iohn Selden" (VIII, 158). The poem is a summary of the ideas discussed in Part I, especially in the third chapter on the epistolary tradition, and is a condensation of much of the material in the *Discoveries* that deals with human nature in general, for Selden was "the bravest man jn all Languages" (I, 149).

> I know to whom I write. Here, I am sure,
> Though I am short, I cannot be obscure:
> Lesse shall I for the Art or dressing care,
> Truth, and the Graces best, when naked are.
>   (ll. 1–4)

Jonson begins his epistle by citing one of the traditionally accepted virtues of the plain style in answer to a traditional accusation. The lines refer to Horace's observation that the man who tries to be brief will be charged with obscurity (*brevis esse laboro,/obscurus fio, Ars Poet.* 25–26), a charge which Vives, Jonson, and others felt was justified for certain Senecan idiosyncrasies of style.[4] The accusation is mentioned, however, primarily to introduce the answer in terms of epistolary intimacy: I know to whom I write, and, therefore, I can be brief and clear.[5] The answer, formulated in terms of the ancient tradition, establishes the context of the poem. Its feeling is intensified for the reader if he understands both the historical objection and the sources of experience the poet is drawing upon to satisfy it. Jonson continues by thanking Selden for giving him his *Titles of Honour* to criticize, and says that he may praise it for itself, not simply out of friendship for the author. That would be flattery,

> Then which there is not unto Studie'a more
> Pernitious enemie; we see, before
> A many' of bookes, even good judgements wound
> Themselves through favouring what is there not found:
> But I on yours farre otherwise shall doe,
> Not flie the Crime, but the Suspition too:
> Though I confesse (as every Muse hath err'd,
> And mine not least) I have too oft preferr'd
> Men past their termes, and prais'd some names too much,
> But 'twas with purpose to have made them such.
> Since, being deceiv'd, I turne a sharper eye
> Upon my selfe, and aske to whom? and why?
> And what I write? and vexe it many dayes
> Before men get a verse: much lesse a Praise;
> So that my Reader is assur'd, I now
> Meane what I speake: and still will keepe that Vow.
>   (ll. 13–28)

These lines on the possible error of his muse, which refers here to the poet's judgment, are more complete than those of his epigram "To my Mvse," because he relates the practical difficulties of careful writing to the moral responsibility of accurate and honest evaluation. Jonson asks to be excused for overpraising some writers in commendatory verses by showing, himself, recognition and tolerance of human error: "But 'twas with purpose to have made them such."[6] Such, too, is the satirist's purpose, but seldom does the satirist express an understanding so sympathetic with failure and a didacticism so compassionate in its firmness. In order not to be deceived, Jonson intends to "vexe" what he writes for many days. The short phrase is an incisive description of writing verse, and the labor is in the interest of saying what he means and making the reader believe it.[7]

Jonson goes on to praise Selden for his knowledge of antiquity and for his energetic exploration of new ideas, and in doing so gives a remarkable definition of a humanist, which comes right out of his own resiliently versatile classicism of the *Discoveries*. Though Selden has dealt with a diversity of customs and traditions, he has been

> Ever at home: yet, have all Countries seene:
> And like a Compasse keeping one foot still
> Upon your Center, doe your Circle fill
> Of generall knowledge; watch'd men, manners too,
> Heard what times past have said, seene what ours doe:
> Which Grace shall I make love to first? your skill,
> Or faith in things? or is't your wealth and will
> T[o]'instruct and teach? or your unweary'd paine
> Of Gathering? Bountie' in pouring out againe?
> What fables have you vext! what truth redeem'd!
> Antiquities search'd! Opinions dis-esteem'd!
> Impostures branded! and Authorities urg'd!
> What blots and errours, have you watch'd and purg'd
> Records, and Authors of! how rectified
> Times, manners, customes! Innovations spide!
> Sought out the Fountains, Sources, Creekes, paths, wayes,
> And noted the beginnings and decayes!
> Where is that nominal marke, or reall rite,
> Forme, Art or Ensigne, that hath scap'd your sight?
> How are Traditions there examin'd: how
> Conjectures retriv'd! And a Storie now
> And then of times (besides the bare Conduct
> Of what it tells us) weav'd in to instruct!
> I wonder'd at the richnesse, but am lost,
> To see the workmanship so'[e]xceed the cost!
> To marke the excellent seas'ning of your Stile!
> And manly elocution, not one while
> With horrour rough, then rioting with wit!
> But to the Subject, still the Colours fit
> In sharpnesse of all Search, wisdome of Choise,
> Newnesse of Sense, Antiquitie of voyce![8]

> (ll. 30–60)

Classicism for Jonson, as for Bacon, is a habit of discovery, a constant re-evaluation of epistemological methods in the investigation of experience as well as the accumulation and mastery of ancient knowledge. The classical habit of exploration, whether in literature, philosophy, or science, is concerned with the search for the source of action—what makes a thing become what it is. The description of the source of vitality or activity of a thing is the most valuable definition of the thing itself. This attitude is reflected in the Aristotelian characterization of virtue as an activity, or of man as a rational animal, since reason appears to be his most distinctively active attribute. The mind, in its exploratory function, must ensure its own continuance of activity and hence develop powers of recovery and flexibility. In its encounter with experience it must continually recover—return to—what it can be most certain of (whether knowledge or a method). Its flexibility in recovering in order to probe again, without having lost any ground, is its power. Jonson's attitude toward the ancients themselves is classical in this sense. He admits that to study them is the most important discipline, but none should "rest in their sole Authority . . . For to all the observations of the *Ancients,* wee have our owne experience." They went before, "but as Guides, not Commanders . . . Truth lyes open to all, it is no mans *severall.*" A man may dissent from those he admires without wishing to be their equal; he need only ask that his reasons be examined with theirs and judged accordingly: no art can be a human discovery and absolute at the same time (*Disc.,* ll. 128–59). It is continually necessary to "gently stirre the mould about the root of the Question" (*Disc.,* ll. 2112–13). To do this the inquiring mind must employ a style that can itself achieve the necessary flexibility in its own structure to fulfill the purposes of such investigations.[9] Epistemologically, this is the most "classical" reason, then, for Jonson's adaptation of the Attic style: far from being a codification of terms (rules), classicism is the continual trial and selection of terms, new and old, in the effort to describe experience. "For rules are ever of lesse force, and valew, then experiments" (*Disc.,* ll. 1757–58). Such a distinction may be the crucial one between the classical and the more preceptorial neoclassical intention; in this case, Vives, Jonson, and Bacon represent the most vital recovery of classical attitudes.

In relation to this general context of ideas, the best commentary on the lines to Selden is an epitome in the *Discoveries* of the fourth chapter of the first book of Bacon's *Advancement of Learning,* which restates the intellectual intentions expressed in the epistle and describes a style adequate to fulfill them. These are discussed in the same order in the prose passage as they are in the poem. Jonson praises Selden for his "generall knowledge," presumably gathered from his studies, and his acquaintance with contemporary affairs derived from observation. Because of these he has been able to vex legendary explanations of events to find the truth, to seek and evaluate antiquities in order to expose irresponsible opinion, to point out impostures and to select the best authorities, to correct errors about former times by showing what has been added, to discover causes and the real significance of human activities, and to examine entire traditions. So Bacon is praised in the *Discoveries* for exposing the distempers of learning, one of which is deceit or the "likenesse of truth; Imposture held up by credulity." No author should be made a dictator, as the Scholastics have done with Aristotle. One may defer to an authority by "a suspension of his owne Judgement, not an absolute resignation of himselfe, or a perpetuall captivity. Let *Aristotle,* and others have their dues; but if wee can make farther Discoveries of truth and fitnesse then they, why are we envied?" We must "study the separation of opinions, find the errours have intervened, awake Antiquity, call former times into question," and "mingle no matter of doubt-full credit, with the simplicity of truth, but gently stirre the mould about the root of the Question, and avoid all digladiations, facility of credit, or superstitious simplicity." This passage, which is very close in terminology to that quoted from the poem, connects the habits of the exploring mind closely with the attitudes toward the ancients discussed above, attitudes which the ancients themselves might well have considered "classical." Jonson continues in the *Discoveries* by describing the virtues of a good style just as he does in his praise of Selden. It must thrive "in choisenesse of Phrase, round and cleane composition of sentence, sweet falling of the clause, varying an illustration by tropes and figures, weight of Matter, worth of Subject, soundnesse of Argument, life of Invention, and depth of Judgement. This is *Monte potiri,* to get the hill. For no perfect Discovery can bee made upon a flat or a levell" (*Disc.,* ll. 2090–2124). This is the style necessary to make a discovery and flexible enough to do it by relating the past experience offered by a tradition to present observation, by correcting one by the other. So in praising Selden's style Jonson falls into the same type of phrasing, which refers to the same characteristics: "excellent sea-s'ning," "manly elocution, not one while/With horrour rough, then rioting with wit!/But to the Subject," with colours (here meaning stylistic devices in general) subservient to the subject, "In sharpnesse of all Search, wisdome of Choise,/Newnesse of Sense, Antiquity of voyce!" This last couplet is a masterly summary of the intellectual qualities Jonson most admired. The newness of sense is the Baconian insistence upon the observation of particulars and all that this implies in the investigation of the real world; antiquity of voice is the use of recorded history which gives chronological and ethical coherence to the fragments of individual experience.

The type of mind that Jonson admired Selden for is the same as that of the ideal historian which he describes in his poem "To Sir Henrie Savile" (VIII, 61):

Although to write be lesser then to doo,
  It is the next deed, and a great one too.
We need a man that knowes the seuerall graces
  Of historie, and how to apt their places;
Where breuitie, where splendor, and where height,
  Where sweetnesse is requir'd, and where weight;
We need a man, can speake of the intents,
  The councells, actions, orders, and euents
Of state, and censure them: we need his pen
  Can write the things, the causes, and the men.
But most we need his faith (and all haue you)
  That dares nor write things false, nor hide things true.

(ll. 25-36)

It is the historian in particular who works in the mines of knowledge to achieve an antiquity of voice. Jonson describes the value of the ore in his poem on Ralegh's *History of the World*, called "The mind of the Frontispice to a Booke" (VIII, 175).

From Death, and darke oblivion, neere the same,
  The Mistresse of Mans life, grave Historie,
Raising the World to good or evill fame,
  Doth vindicate it to eternite.
Wise Providence would so; that nor the good
  Might be defrauded, nor the great secur'd,
But both might know their wayes were understood,
  When Vice alike in time with vertue dur'd.
Which makes that (lighted by the beamie hand
  Of Truth that searcheth the most [hidden] Springs,
And guided by Experience, whose straite wand
  Doth mete, whose lyne doth sound the depth of things:)
Shee chearfully supporteth what she reares,
  Assisted by no strengths, but are her owne,
Some note of which each varied Pillar beares,
  By which as proper titles, she is knowne
Times witnesse, herald of Antiquitie,
  The light of Truth, and life of Memorie.

The historian's duty is to state the truth, to say what happened and to explain the causes. The validity of the generalizations will depend on the knowledge and evaluation of the particular experiences, for experience is the line which sounds the depth of things. This emphasis upon continual re-evaluation is consistent with Jonson's classicism in the *Discoveries* and with Bacon's ideas discussed in Chapters 2 and 4.

The epistle to Selden was prefixed to his *Titles of Honour* in 1614. One cannot be certain that it was written as a commendatory poem, since the occasion is similar to that of other poems such as the epigram "To Iohn Donne" (*Epig.* 23), but it is likely that it was because the publication of the book must have followed closely upon Selden's sending it to Jonson for criticism. In any event the poem is helpful in understanding the far more famous eulogy, "To the memory of my beloued, The AVTHOR Mr. William Shakespeare: And what he hath left vs," which seems to have been written specifically for the publication of the First Folio edition of Shakespeare's works, although it would be difficult to establish the actual date of composition. The poem to Shakespeare is more loosely organized. It begins with an expository introduction typical of Jonson, followed by a quibble with a widely circulated elegy by William Basse, which introduces a comparison of Shakespeare first with the dramatists who immediately preceded him and then with the ancient dramatists. It continues with a general statement on the composition of poetry and concludes with a comparatively ornate passage reminiscent of Jonson's ode on Hugh Holland's *Pancharis*. It has some fine lines, a good passage on writing which is extractable, and a tone of epistolary intimacy, echoing the passage on Shakespeare in the *Discoveries* (VIII, 583–84), which makes the more formal eulogy convincing. Despite the fact, however, that certain lines such as "He was not of an age, but for all time!" encourage readers to praise the poem for an intensity of feeling derived from their own responses to Shakespeare, there seems to be a slight indecisiveness about what to praise Shakespeare for, at least in comparison with the praise of Selden. The resulting ambiguity of attitude may be overlooked by the modern reader, or it may leave him disappointed at Jonson's having given his subject nothing more perceptive than rhetorical formulae. One way to read the poem is by asking what qualities and achievements Jonson habitually thought most worthy of the highest esteem, which the eulogies in the *Discoveries* and such epistolary poems as those to Selden and Camden explicitly describe, and by trying to imagine what Jonson might praise Shakespeare for in 1623.

Nearly the entire *Discoveries* deals with the intellectual disciplines of the humanistic mind rather than with particular works we more easily regard as literary today. The passages on style relate writing to the acquisition and the use of knowledge; they are general and present a theory of style which speaks with an "antiquity of voice" about the necessity and difficulty of extending the range of human experience in the present world. For Jonson, it is Bacon who represents the most modern and vital form of humanistic exploration, and it is men like Vives, Camden, and Selden, "the bravest man jn all languages," who correct the errors about the past. One is justified in saying that Jonson thought these men worthy of the highest praise; these men were among the most vitally and comprehensively original of the Renaissance. And their virtues were the only ones, by and large, that he felt comfortable in praising in the highest terms. Our immediate reaction to the implication that Jonson may not have regarded Shakespeare's achievement as equal to theirs is that Jonson must have been either narrow, inflexible, envious, literarily imperceptive through the shrouds of his learning, or something of the kind. But Jonson was not an unsuccessful poet and dramatist turned humanist. He was one of the two greatest writers of the period, Shakespeare alone equaling him, and a master of the humanistic disciplines besides. Rather than narrowness, his admiration of Bacon and Selden shows a breadth of interest, intellectual adroitness, and learning that is astounding for a professional dramatist. It is likely that he regarded many of Shakespeare's plays as the best professional work done for the stage by another dramatist, but they were still professional work and to some extent to be taken for granted. Even in the unprecedented publication of his own plays, which I am sure he considered second to none, in his *Workes* in 1616 it is the *Epigrams* that are the ripest of his studies, and for a humanist's reasons. Work for the stage was not in the category that would be considered for the highest intellectual honors, and even in his comments on the drama itself Jonson is clear in his criticisms of Shakespeare.[10]

The first sixteen lines of the eulogy (VIII, 390) are introductory. They describe, by implication, the relationship between the two men in stating the ordinary forms of compliment which Jonson is going to avoid. Such introductions are common in his poems, but this one is long and awkwardly connected to the rest of the poem; the transition is so difficult, in fact, that he feels it necessary to say bluntly in the seventeenth line "I, therefore will begin." In the opening lines he says that it is universally agreed that no one can praise Shakespeare too much; any fool can repeat such a commonplace for a number of wrong reasons.

> 'Tis true, and all mens suffrage. But these wayes
> Were not the paths I meant vnto thy praise:
> For seeliest Ignorance on these may light,
> Which, when it sounds at best, but eccho's right;
> (ll. 5–8)

"Blinde Affection" and "crafty Malice" may injure a work by praise as well, so he will choose another way to commend the book, a way he is especially qualified to use: comparing Shakespeare favorably with the ancient dramatists. He begins with a rhetorical address,

> Soule of the Age!
> The applause! delight! the wonder of our Stage!
> My *Shakespeare,* rise;
>
> (ll. 17–19)

and refuses to compare him to Chaucer, Spenser, and Beaumont as Basse had done, concluding,

> Thou art a Moniment, without a tombe,
> And art aliue still, while thy Booke doth liue,
> And we haue wits to read, and praise to giue.
>
> (ll. 22–24)

These lines are good and in Jonson's best manner, but the following ones are syntactically obscure and reflect again the awkwardness of transitions in the poem:

> That I not mixe thee so, my braine excuses;
> I meane with great, but disproportion'd *Muses*:
> For, if I thought my iudgement were of yeeres,
> I should commit thee surely with thy peeres,
> And tell, how farre thou didst our *Lily* out-shine,
> Or sporting *Kid,* or *Marlowes* mighty line.
>
> (ll. 25–30)

The best explanation of these lines, though it does not solve all the difficulties, seems to be as follows. My reason justifies the fact that I do not compare you with these poets (since, though great, their muses are not equal to yours), because, if I had confidence in the maturity of my judgment, I would place you solely with your peers, the ancient dramatists, and declare how far superior you are to the English playwrights who preceded you. The parenthesis helps the syntax, but nothing explains the uncharacteristic and unnecessary "if my iudgement were of yeeres." Jonson seems to have had confidence in the maturity of his judgment even when he was young; for him to make such a statement after he was forty is curious. To interpret the line as meaning that he could judge if his mind could transcend the limitations of its period and evaluate the plays in the perspective of the ages seems strained, even though he praises Shakespeare for being "for all time." He continues by saying he would call the ancient tragedians, whom he mentions by name,

> To life againe, to heare thy Buskin tread,
> And shake a Stage; Or, when thy Sockes were on,
>   Leaue thee alone, for the comparison
> Of all, that insolent *Greece,* or haughtie *Rome*
>   Sent forth, or since did from their ashes come.
>   (ll. 36–40)

The ancient writers of comedy are not named individually till ten lines later in the poem, in a passage which would seem less awkward following the lines just quoted than where it actually occurs.

> The merry *Greeke,* tart *Aristophanes,*
>   Neat *Terence,* witty *Plautus,* now not please;
> But antiquated, and deserted lye
>   As they were not of Natures family.
>   (ll. 51–54)

If one inserts this passage at line 41, it forms with the lines preceding and succeeding it, a perfectly coherent unit, which ends with the section on writing, the finest in the poem:

> Triúmph, my *Britaine,* thou hast one to showe,
>   To whom all Scenes of *Europe* homage owe.
> He was not of an age, but for all time!
>   And all the *Muses* still were in their prime,
> When like *Apollo* he came forth to warme
>   Our eares, or like a *Mercury* to charme!
> Nature her selfe was proud of his designes,
>   And ioy'd to weare the dressing of his lines!
> Which were so richly spun, and wouen so fit,
>   As, since, she will vouchsafe no other Wit. . . .
> Yet must I not giue Nature all: Thy Art,
>   My gentle *Shakespeare,* must enioy a part.
> For though the *Poets* matter, Nature be,
>   His Art doth giue the fashion. And, that he,
> Who casts to write a liuing line, must sweat,
>   (Such as thine are) and strike the second heat
> Vpon the *Muses* anuile: turne the same,
>   (And himselfe with it) that he thinkes to frame;
> Or for the lawrell, he may gaine a scorne,
>   For a good *Poet's* made, as well as borne.
>   (ll. 41–50, 55–64)

The fact that lines 51–54 can be transferred (and I think a good case can be made that the change is an improvement) shows a structural looseness and, perhaps, an indecisive attitude toward the subject himself.

The last eight lines quoted above are excellent and, in a sense, extractable in the way that many Horatian passages on composition are. The lines are introduced by a compliment to Shakespeare's "Art," which seems somewhat formal in the face of Jonson's comment to Drummond in 1619 and the later passage in the *Discoveries,* criticizing Shakespeare for not revising and for not controlling his "facility." It does, however, offer Jonson as good a pretext to give some advice as a repetition of his more candid remark to Drummond. It is partly this advice and partly his remarks on the ancient writers in the poem that indicate what Jonson is trying to commend Shakespeare for in order to give him the highest kind of praise, that reserved for men like Bacon and Selden. He is simply trying to associate him as closely as he can with the humanists and to arouse the reader's sympathy by praising their virtues, since he does not feel comfortable giving to the dramatist, solely as dramatist, the amount of praise he feels Shakespeare deserves in a commendatory poem. The feeling communicated by these lines on writing, which are the most moving in the poem, is identical to that of the lines on commendatory verse in the epistle to Selden. To sweat and revise in order to write a living line is to "vexe it many dayes/Before men get a verse: much lesse a Praise;/So that my Reader is assur'd, I now/Meane what I speake"; and for a writer, while turning his subject over and over in his mind, to re-examine himself continually is similar to Jonson's saying "Since, being deceiv'd, I turne a sharper eye/Upon my selfe, and aske to whom? and why?/And what I write?" These are not merely incidental similarities; they account for the firmest and most consistent feeling in both poems. The entire effort to locate Shakespeare in the great classical tradition is humanistic and implies humanistic intellectual virtues. It is not surprising to find the line comparing Shakespeare to "all, that insolent *Greece,* or haughtie *Rome*" produced also applied to Bacon in the *Discoveries,* who "perform'd that in our tongue, which may be compar'd, or preferr'd, either to insolent *Greece,* or haughty *Rome*" (*Disc.,* ll. 916–18). The fact that Bacon's virtues were not, finally, Shakespeare's virtues accounts for a good deal of the uncertainty of intention and feeling in the eulogy.[11]

Jonson's poem to another dramatist, John Fletcher, has had less attention and yet is an example of his occasional verse at its best. The following lines on the failure of Fletcher's *The Faithful Shepheardesse* were printed in the quarto edition of the play (VIII, 370):

> The wise, and many-headed *Bench,* that sits
> Vpon the Life, and Death of *Playes,* and *Wits,*

(Compos'd of *Gamester, Captaine, Knight, Knight's man,*
  Lady, or *Pusil,* that weares maske, or fan,
Veluet, or *Taffata* cap, rank'd in the darke
  With the shops *Foreman,* or some such *braue sparke,*
That may iudge for his *six-pence*) had, before
  They saw it halfe, damd thy whole play, and more;
Their motiues were, since it had not to do
  With vices, which they look'd for, and came to.
I, that am glad, thy Innocence was thy Guilt,
  And wish that all the *Muses* blood were spilt,
In such a *Martirdome*; To vexe their eyes,
  Do crowne thy murdred *Poëme*: which shall rise
A glorified worke to Time, when Fire,
  Or moathes shall eate, what all these Fooles admire.

The poem is a good example of caesural variation, and of changing degrees
of stress in each position in the line. The four-line characterization of the
audience is a packed and individualized picture, and the feeling it conveys
of immediate experience gives power to the final generalization.

Among the most moving of Jonson's epistolary poems are those dealing
with the state of his own affairs and with his physical appearance. They
are, perhaps, the poems in which the communication between the author
and the reader is most intimate, and, hence, they fulfill most completely
the Senecan ideals of the epistolary tradition. Jonson was confined to his
bed by a paralytic stroke in 1628. The following "Epistle Mendicant" was
written "To the Right Honourable, the Lord high Treasurer of England,"
Richard, Lord Weston, in 1633 (VIII, 248).

My Lord;
Poore wretched states, prest by extremities,
Are faine to seeke for succours, and supplies
Of *Princes* aides, or *good mens* Charities.

Disease, the Enemie, and his Ingineeres,
Want, with the rest of his conceal'd compeeres,
Have cast a trench about mee, now, five yeares;

And made those strong approaches, by *False braies,*
Reduicts, Halfe-moones, Horne-workes, and such close wayes,
The *Muse* not peepes out, one of hundred dayes;

But lyes block'd up, and straightned, narrow'd in,
Fix'd to the bed, and boords, unlike to win
Health, or scarce breath, as she had never bin,

Unlesse some saving-*Honour* of the *Crowne,*
Dare thinke it, to relieve, no lesse renowne,
A *Bed-rid* Wit, then a *besieged* Towne.

The metaphor that culminates in the last line is intricately worked out from the beginning of the poem and neither exaggerates nor sentimentalizes the actual situation. One of the reasons for this is that Jonson never becomes too involved with the description of the town or the siege. His subject is his own ill health, and the metaphor simply permits him to make use of the feelings associated with the miseries of townspeople besieged to qualify and define his own feeling about his illness. The last six lines, among the finest he wrote, bring the metaphorical description to bear on his physical condition in the last line with great power. Their extraordinary caesural variation, the plainness of the diction, and the intimate accuracy of the description of himself are all reasons for the emotional power of the poem, and they, along with the controlled and often intricate use of metaphor, are all characteristic of Jonson's style at its best.

In the "Indvction" to *The Staple of Newes,* Jonson wrote a description of himself (VI, 281):

> Yonder he is within . . . rowling himselfe vp and downe like a tun, i' the midst of 'hem [the actors], and spurges, neuer did vessel of wort, or wine worke so! His sweating put me in minde of a good Shrouing dish (and I beleeue would be taken vp for a seruice of state somewhere, an't were knowne) a stew'd *Poet*! He doth sit like an vnbrac'd Drum with one of his heads beaten out: For, that you must note, a *Poet* hath two heads, as a Drum has, one for making, the other repeating, and his repeating head is all to pieces: they may gather it vp i' the tiring-house; for hee hath torne the booke in a *Poeticall* fury, and put himselfe to silence in dead *Sacke.* . . .
>
> (ll. 61–72)

He described himself in a similar fashion occasionally in his poems, with the result that they have the curious personal quality of the author's continued and unchanging presence coming through the lines no matter in what genre the poem may be. In the second love poem of "A Celebration of Charis," for instance, he is stunned by his lady (VIII, 132)

> So that, there, I stood a stone,
> Mock'd of all: and call'd of one
> (Which with griefe and wrath I heard)
> *Cupids* Statue with a Beard,
> Or else one that plaid his Ape,
> In a *Hercules*-his shape.
>
> (ll. 27–32)

And again in one of Jonson's finest love poems, "My Picture left in Scotland" (VIII, 149)—which I shall discuss later in more detail—the lady, the poet fears, has seen

> My hundred of gray haires,
>   Told seven and fortie years,
>   Read so much wast, as she cannot imbrace
>   My mountaine belly, and my rockie face,
> And all these through her eyes, have stopt her eares.
>   (ll. 14–18)

Instead of holding the glass up to someone else, as he does, say, to Lady Aubigny, he holds it up to himself and reveals with candid realism what he sees there with the personal honesty he liked being admired for. In his epistle "To my Lady Covell" he gives one of his best self-portraits (VIII, 230):

> You won not Verses, Madam, you won mee,
>   When you would play so nobly, and so free.
> A booke to a few lynes: but, it was fit
>   You won them too, your oddes did merit it.
> So have you gain'd a Servant, and a Muse:
>   The first of which, I feare, you will refuse;
> And you may justly, being a tardie, cold,
>   Unprofitable Chattell, fat and old,
> Laden with Bellie, and doth hardly approach
>   His friends, but to breake Chaires, or cracke a Coach.
> His weight is twenty Stone within two pound;
>   And that's made up as doth the purse abound.
>   (ll. 1–12)

The urbane intimacy with which he describes himself is similar to that of Horace's description of himself in his short letter to Tibullus (*Epist.* I, 4): "As for me, when you want a laugh, you will find me in fine fettle, fat and sleek, a hog from Epicurus's herd."

Jonson's most interesting self-portrait, however, is his answer to a short poem written to him by the painter, Sir William Burlase (VIII, 226–27). In the two poems the functions of the painter and the poet are compared:

> *A Poême sent me by Sir William Burlase*
> *The Painter to the Poet*

> To paint thy Worth, if rightly I did know it,
> And were but Painter halfe like thee, a Poët;
>   *Ben,* I would show it:
> But in this skill, m[y]'unskilfull pen will tire,
> Thou, and thy worth, will still be found farre higher;
>   And I a Lier.

Then, what a Painter's here! or what an eater
Of great attempts! when as his skil's no greater,
            And he a Cheater!
Then what a Poet's here! whom, by Confession
Of all with me, to paint without Digression,
            There's no Expression.

My Answer
The Poet to the Painter

Why? though I seeme of a prodigious wast,
I am not so voluminous, and vast,
But there are lines, wherewith I might b[e]'embrac'd.

'Tis true, as my wombe swells, so my backe stoupes,
And the whole lumpe growes round, deform'd, and droupes,
But yet the Tun at *Heidelberg* had houpes.

You were not tied, by any Painters Law,
To square my Circle, I confesse; but draw
My Superficies: that was all you saw.

Which if in compasse of no Art it came
To be describ'd [but] by a *Monogram,*
With one great blot, yo'had form'd me as I am.

But whilst you curious were to have it be
An *Archetype,* for all the world to see,
You made it a brave piece, but not like me.

O, had I now your manner, maistry, might,
Your Power of handling shadow, ayre, and spright,
How I would draw, and take hold and delight.

But, you are he can paint; I can but write:
A Poet hath no more but black and white,
Ne knowes he flatt'ring Colours, or false light.

Yet when of friendship I would draw the face,
A letter'd mind, and a large heart would place
To all posteritie; I will write *Burlase.*

This is Jonson's most moving poem on friendship, and one of his most
disarming. The didactic statement—and there is a good deal here—is almost indistinguishable from the statement of the situation, and the feeling
arising out of the situation makes the moral observations persuasive but

not obtrusive. The description of himself not only is accurately vivid, but, in its humorous self-depreciation, invites the reader's familiarity as well as Burlase's. The central device of comparing the functions and virtues of the painter and the poet defines by implication the qualities of a friend. The painter can draw only the external appearance of a person, whereas the poet can draw the "letter'd mind," though not necessarily by using "flatt'ring Colours, or false light." Colors, of course, is a pun on the ordinary word for a rhetorical device, which the anti-rhetorical literary traditions regarded as a false light, since it usually distorted the truth. The truth about the mind and the character of a person, upon which friendship can most safely be based, is more easily stated by the writer than by the painter for the same reason that the painter is less capable of representing the muse: his hand "will never hit,/To draw a thing that cannot sit" (VIII, 277). These devices and the attitudes behind them, however, do not completely account for the quality of the poem; another man might use them to no effect, but with Jonson they are so descriptive of his own personality and represent the stylistic expression of his habits of mind so accurately that they cease almost to be devices at all. They dissolve away as they were intended to do. The writer's image remains, acutely sensitive to circumstance and easily recognizable because of its consistency of thought and reaction, a consistency by which one can trace the relationship between the poet's admiration for the *Advancement of Learning* and his statement of his limitations as a model for his friend to paint.

The art of the painter is visual, that of the poet is intellectual; the one is fundamentally sensory, the other, conceptual. It is in this context that the sources of feeling of Jonson's short and conventional poem on Shakespeare's portrait can best be described (VIII, 390). The convention of the poem is that of the epigram which Martial expresses in saying that his face is more accurately delineated in his poems than on canvas (*certior in nostro carmine vultus erit,* VII, 84) and by wishing that a picture could depict the mind and character as well as the face, for there the finer beauty lies (*ars utinam mores animumque effingere posset!/pulchrior in terris nulla tabella foret,* X, 32). Jonson's poem is perfectly executed, and, even though its device is formal, it is as moving as the longer eulogy.

To the Reader

This Figure, that thou here seest put,
　It was for gentle Shakespeare cut;
Wherein the Grauer had a strife
　With Nature, to out-doo the life:

> O, could he but haue drawne his wit
> As well in brasse, as he hath hit
> His face; the Print would then surpasse
> All, that was euer writ in brasse.
> But, since he cannot, Reader, looke
> Not on his Picture, but his Booke.

If the intelligence could be drawn, it would surpass the face. The assertion is hyperbolic in that the condition is impossible, but the terms of the figure are perfectly conceivable and are derived from the stylistic tradition that he adopted. In asking the reader to be moved by Shakespeare's wit in reading his book, rather than by his appearance in admiring his picture, Jonson is reasserting the conviction that the truth, especially moral truth, should, when intelligibly stated, be moving in itself and capable of persuading and delighting.

"*Whosoever* loves not *Picture*," Jonson writes, "is injurious to Truth: and all the wisdome of *Poetry*," for it "is the invention of Heaven: the most ancient, and most a kinne to Nature" (VIII, 610). The long passage in the *Discoveries* from which this quotation is taken testifies to Jonson's interest in the art, and his attitudes toward painting and writing were often similar. The business of the painter was to interpret nature, not to represent things that do not exist, just as that of the poet was to write about men and what they did, not to describe monsters and to relate myths. "See where he complaines of their painting *Chimæra's*," says Jonson, translating Antonio Possevino, "by the vulgar unaptly called *Grottesque*: Saying, that men who were borne truly to study, and emulate nature, did nothing but make monsters against nature, which *Horace* so laught at" (VIII, 611). When it comes, however, to a comparison between poetry and painting, Jonson does not hesitate to make a judgment and to give his reason: "Yet of the two, the Pen is more noble, then the Pencill. For that can speake to the Understanding; the other, but to the Sense" (VIII, 610). And so with the dialectical-rhetorical controversy: the first speaks to the understanding, the second to the senses. The attitudes toward the painter and the poet in the following poem, "To the right Honourable, the Lord Treasurer of England" (VIII, 260), are the same as those expressed to Burlase and to Lady Digby in the fourth poem of "Eupheme," called "The Mind" (VIII, 277). This poem to Weston shows also how the reader of poetry will be the man most concerned with "the arts of life," the knowledge of which Jonson has admired in nearly all the poems to his friends. The rejection of painting shows a preference not only for poetry but also for the fundamental aims of the plain style, which are, in the end, simply the aims of a good poet.

> If to my mind, great Lord, I had a state,
>   I would present you now with curious plate
> Of *Noremberg,* or *Turkie*; hang your roomes
>   Not with the Arras, but the *Persian* Loomes.
> I would, if price, or prayer could them get,
>   Send in, what or *Romano, Tintoret,*
> *Titian,* or *Raphael, Michael Angelo,*
>   Have left in fame to equall, or out-goe
> The old Greek-hands in picture, or in stone.
>   This I would doe, could I thinke *Weston* one
> Catch'd with these Arts, wherein the Judge is wise
>   As farre as sense, and onely by the eyes.
> But you I know, my Lord; and know you can
>   Discerne betweene a Statue, and a Man;
> Can doe the things that Statues doe deserve,
>   And act the businesse, which they paint, or carve.
> What you have studied are the arts of life;
>   To compose men, and manners; stint the strife
> Of murmuring Subjects; make the Nations know
>   What worlds of blessings to good Kings they owe:
> And mightiest Monarchs feele what large increase
>   Of sweets, and safeties, they possesse by Peace.
> These I looke up at, with a reverent eye,
>   And strike Religion in the standers-by;
> Which, though I cannot as an Architect
>   In glorious Piles, or Pyramids erect
> Unto your honour: I can tune in song
>   Aloud; and (happ'ly) it may last as long.[12]

This poem is a political poem; at least, it is written to praise the qualities of a good statesman, and makes certain generalizations on the virtues of a monarchy dedicated to peace. Yet in the context of the *Discoveries* it is almost an *Ars Poetica*. It summarizes what Jonson thought the poet's proper subject should be, and, in distinguishing it from that of the painter, if one may interpret this poem in the light of the other poems that make similar distinctions, it says a great deal about what style that subject matter should be treated in.

SATIRE

To distinguish himself from the satirists of the 1590's, Jonson avoids calling his poems satires. In the Horatian tradition, however, the epistle was, as Casaubon testifies, included in the name and canon of the satires,[13] and Jonson includes a great deal of satire in his verse letters. In this way he could reinstate satire as an artistic literary form and return to the best classical models, not only in name, as his contemporaries were doing, but in style. The longest of the group of six poems, however, in which Inigo Jones must take his place beside Shadwell and Cibber as the most incisively treated subjects of English satire, is not written as an epistle and can, in the ordinary sense of the term, be called a satire. Jonson wrote one of the other five poems on Jones as a "corollary" to the satire, and he regarded the other four poems as epigrams. Three of these epigrams—if the editors are correct in saying that they refer to Jones[14]—Jonson put in his collection of *Epigrammes*; the other three poems are printed with his *Ungathered Verse*. Since their subject is the same and Jonson's attitude toward Jones did not change, they can be treated as a group.

The competition between Jones and Jonson was fundamentally one between painting, which spoke to the sense, and poetry, which spoke to the understanding. Their rivalry can be described, by analogy, as one between rhetoric and dialectic, between a rhetorical and a plain style. The analogy is helpful, for it explains how Jonson's passionate anger against Jones arose, in part at least, from his convictions about art in general and literature in particular. Jonson states their differences clearly in his "Expostulacõn with Inigo Iones" (VIII, 402):

> O Showes! Showes! Mighty Showes!
> The Eloquence of Masques! What need of prose
> Or Verse, or Sense t'express Immortall you?
> You are ye Spectacles of State! Tis true
> Court Hieroglyphicks! & all Artes affoord
> In ye mere perspectiue of an Inch board!
> You aske noe more then certeyne politique Eyes,
> Eyes y^t can pierce into ye Misteryes
> Of many Coulors! read them! & reueale
> Mythology there painted on slit deale!
> Oh, to make Boardes to speake! There is a taske
> Painting & Carpentry are ye Soule of Masque. . . .
> Oh wise Surueyo^r! wyser Architect!
> But wisest Inigo! who can reflect
> On ye new priming of thy old Signe postes
> Reuiuing wth fresh coulors ye pale Ghosts
> Of thy dead Standards: or (wth miracle) see
> Thy twice conceyud, thrice payd for Imagery?
> And not fall downe before it? and confess
> Allmighty Architecture? who noe less

> A Goddess is, then paynted Cloth, Deal-boards,
> Vermilion, Lake, or Cinnopar affoards
> Expression for! wth that vnbounded lyne
> Aymd at in thy omnipotent Designe!
> What Poesy ere was painted on a wall
> That might compare wth thee? what story shall
> Of all ye Worthyes hope t'outlast thy one,
> Soe ye Materialls be of Purbeck stone!
>   (ll. 39–50, 85–100)

The satire is in many ways the most loosely written of Jonson's poems.
It contains more run-over lines, violent diction, abrupt syntax, and asyndectic exclamation than most of his others and owes its power more to its
vivid description of the mechanics and the accouterments of the masque
than to any general statement about human experience. There is, however,
a magnificence in its vituperation, which makes it a kind of *tour de force,*
for supporting all of the incisively belittling details is the powerful and
characteristic assumption of Jonson:

> Your Trappings will not change you. Change yor mynd.
> Noe veluet Sheath you weare, will alter kynde.
> A wodden Dagger, is a Dagger of wood
> Though gold or Iuory haftes would make it good.
>   (ll. 25–28)

The descriptive passages and their tone are much closer to those of Juvenal
and Persius than to those of Horace, and Jonson uses the flexibility of his
rhythm to great advantage to quicken his line with a violence of contempt.

> I am too fat t'enuy him. He too leane
> To be worth Enuy. Henceforth I doe meane
> To pitty him, as smiling at his ffeat
> Of Lanterne-lerry: wth fuliginous heat
> Whirling his Whymseys, by a subtilty
> Suckt from ye Veynes of shop-philosophy.
>   (ll. 69–74)

The terminal caesuras are dropped, and the third stress is slighted in the
fourth and fifth lines; the result is a swift lilt which emphasizes the spin-
ning of his mind in its alchemic excitement.

The "Corollary" to the "Expostulaçõn" called "To Inigo Marquess
Would be" (VIII, 406), is a mild, but amusing, comparison of Jones's accomplishments with those of the architect for the Spanish court. "But
cause thou hearst ye mighty k. of Spaine/Hath made his Inigo Marquess,

wouldst thou fayne/Our Charles should make thee such?" The comparisons follow, and Jonson concedes to let him be "styld yᵉ Marquess of New-
Ditch." Far better is Jonson's close adaptation of an epigram of Martial
(XII, 61) "To a ffreind an Epigram Of him" (VIII, 407). Sir Inigo fears
a sharp epigram will depict him, but in this he is too ambitious: "The
Lybian Lion hunts noe butter flyes," and Jonson advises him to seek elsewhere for his publicity:

> If thou be soe desyrous to be read,
> Seek out some hungry painter, yᵗ for bread
> Wᵗʰ rotten chalk, or Cole vpon a wall,
> Will well designe thee, to be viewd of all
> That sit vpon yᵉ Comon Draught: or Strand!
> Thy Forehead is too narrow for my Brand.
> (ll. 9–14)

The rendering of Martial is for the most part so literal that, like the common draught, the strand may refer either to a public privy or to the place
where one was located, as well as simply to the heavily used thoroughfare,
since Martial's line is *scribit carmina quae legunt cacantes*. There are two
changes, however, worth noting. In the first place, Martial recommends
a drunken poet to celebrate his subject in verse scribbled on privy walls,
while Jonson sends his to a street painter who scrawls portraits for small
change. The variation is simply an added thrust at Jones: seek someone
like yourself to do you justice. The second change is Jonson's enormously
improved last line. Martial's is a direct statement which depends upon
the criticisms implied in the poem: this brow is not to be marked by my
brand (*Frons haec stigmate non meo notanda est*). Jonson makes the
same statement but includes in the line his reasons for making it: your
forehead is too narrow for my brand. The conclusive point is made incisively in the last line; not only is Jones too small a target for Jonson,
but it is his narrowness of mind, permitting him the "mere perspectiue of
an Inch board," that makes him so.

Jonson's "Epistle answering to one that asked to be Sealed of the Tribe
of Ben" (VIII, 218), contains some lines which he uses also in one of the
three poems on Jones included in the *Epigrammes,* "On the Townes Honest Man" (VIII, 74).[15] The epistle, which deals with Jones in so far as
he represents what a friend should not be, is more similar to Horatian
epistolary satire than the "Expostulaçon" is. The poem is about friendship
and fulfills the purpose of a letter, since in it, Jonson says, one may "read
my Character, and theirs/I would call mine" (ll. 73–74). One of the ways

he describes his character is by contrasting himself with Jones "That guides the Motions, and directs the beares" (l. 50). He will honor friends whom he need not paint, as he says to Burlase, in flattering colors or false light, those

> Such as are square, wel-tagde, and permanent,
> Not built with Canvasse, paper, and false lights,
>   As are the Glorious Scenes, at the great sights;
> And that there be no fev'ry heats, nor colds,
>   Oylie Expansions, or shrunke durtie folds, . . .
>   (ll. 64–68)

The portrait of the false friend becomes a portrait of Jones, and the terms are drawn from the pervasive antithesis between the conceptual and the visual arts, between the dialectical and rhetorical disciplines.[16] An epistle owes its flexibility of organization and transition to its tradition, whose major source of structure is Horatian satire. Such satire is addressed to particular individuals in particular situations. Once the situations are established, the poem progresses through a series of observations on life which are related generally, though in no specific order, to the themes suggested by the situations. This looseness of structure permits a freedom in the choice of subject matter and an ease of transition from subject to subject, which facilitates the satiric purpose of treating all men and their actions.[17] The danger of this flexibility is that the poem will lack coherence and gradually lose the original situation in digressive comment on related matters. Because of this danger, Horace's *sermones* are as difficult to imitate in structure as he says they are in diction.

As his epigram "Inviting a friend to svpper" (*Epig.* 101) is a description of a good host, this epistle "of the Tribe of Ben" is a description of a good drinking companion. He begins by describing types of people he does not like to drink with: those who drink too much and quarrel, who boast of their lechery or make friends only to use them, who joke about those absent and flatter those present, who pass themselves off as wits and critics of the town and "know whose ignorance is more than theirs."

> Let these men have their wayes, and take their times
>   To vent their Libels, and to issue rimes,
> I have no portion in them, nor their deale
>   Of newes they get, to strew out the long meale,
> I studie other friendships, and more one,
>   Then these can ever be; or else wish none.
>   (ll. 25–30)

There follows a fine passage on the current political gossip, which suffices for news, and Jonson's contempt for it, which is reminiscent of his epigram "The New Crie" on amateur politicians (*Epig.* 92).

> What is't to me whether the French Designe
>   Be, or be not, to get the *Val-telline*?
> Or the States Ships sent forth belike to meet
>   Some hopes of *Spaine* in their West-Indian Fleet?
> Whether the Dispensation yet be sent,
>   Or that the Match from *Spaine* was ever meant?
>   (ll. 31–36)

It will suffice, he says, that he pray and fight if necessary for the king's safety. He will be well despite the fact that Jones has been chosen to help with the reception of the Infanta and that, because of this, he might lose credit with the "animated *Porc'lane* of the Court."

> I, and for this neglect, the courser sort
> Of earthen Jarres, there may molest me too:
>   Well, with mine owne fraile Pitcher, what to doe
> I have decreed; keepe it from waves, and presse;
>   Lest it be justled, crack'd, made nought, or lesse:
> Live to that point I will, for which I am man,
>   And dwell as in my Center, as I can, . . .
>   (ll. 54–60)

From this statement of his own integrity and independence he returns to the initial situation of selecting a companion chosen from those "Such as are square, wel-tagde, and permanent." The poem ends with a directness and intimacy of address which fulfills the formal demands of the structure and relates the individual preceptorial comment to the situation:

> So short you read my Character, and theirs
>   I would call mine, to which not many Staires
> Are asked to climbe. First give me faith, who know
>   My selfe a little. I will take you so,
> As you have writ your selfe. Now stand, and then,
>   Sir, you are Sealed of the Tribe of *Ben*.
>   (ll. 73–78)

The conversational transitions from subject to subject are smoothly handled, and the individual observations on behavior arise out of the situation; the feeling conveyed by the specific detail is quite capable of making the declaration of his own integrity persuasive. The poem is, in other words, a good example of the Horatian method and does not suffer from the characteristic faults of the method as much as some of Jonson's other satirical epistles.

Of similar organization are "A speach according to Horace" (VIII, 213) and the long "Epistle to a Friend, to perswade him to the Warres" (VIII, 162). "Speach" is a direct translation of *sermo,* and the first poem is certainly a conscious imitation of Horatian satire. It sticks closely to its subject and suffers more from a preceptorial didacticism than from digression. The epistle encouraging a friend to go to join the army, however, illustrates clearly the particular danger of the method. The poem opens with the central proposition:

> Wake, friend, from forth thy Lethargie: the Drum
> Beates brave, and loude in *Europe,* and bids come
> All that dare rowse: or are not loth to quit
> Their vitious ease, and be o'rewhelm'd with it.
>
> (ll. 1–4)

The reasons that support the proposition and form the structure of the poem are a series of observations illustrating why it is dangerous for him to remain where he is, and the situation becomes an excuse to describe social evils in London.[18] If you wish to be persuaded, Jonson says, "Looke on th'ambitious man, and see him nurse/His unjust hopes" (ll. 11–12), then "Looke on the false, and cunning man, that loves/No person, nor is lov'd" (ll. 15–16), "See the grave, sower, and supercilious Sir/In outward face, but inward, light as Furre,/Or Feathers" (ll. 19–21), and you will learn

> No part or corner man can looke upon,
> But there are objects, bid him to be gone
> As farre as he can flie, or follow day,
> Rather then here so bogg'd in vices stay.
>
> (ll. 27–30)

Not only are the method of instructing and the type of precept given identical to Horace's description of his own education (*Serm.* I.iv.105–26), discussed in Chapter 4, but the actual formal structure of the poem is based on the same principles. Of necessity, in such a poem, the reader's interest must be drawn to the details of description, for they are the premises of persuasion, and gradually, since there is no logical need to clarify the relationship between the example and the general proposition, the examples tend to become more and more digressive and self-contained. Often, in this poem and others, individual descriptive passages are excellent, and thus memorable as separate units. Here, the sharply Juvenalian satire on women is a complete unit of fifty-three lines, the longest in a series of passages on social corruptions.

> How much did *Stallion* spend
> To have his Court-bred-fillie there commend
> His lace and Starch; And fall upon her back
> In admiration, stretch'd upon the rack
> Of lust, to his rich Suit and Title, Lord?
> I, that's a Charme and halfe! She must afford
> That all respect; She must lie downe: Nay more,
> 'Tis there civilitie to be a whore;
> Hee's one of blood, and fashion! and with these
> The bravery makes, she can no honour leese:
> To do't with Cloth, or Stuffes, lusts name might merit;
> With Velvet, Plush, and Tissues, it is spirit.
>
> (ll. 47–58)

The description moves from detail to detail about the ladies at court, where "the friend/Lives to the Lord, but to the Ladies end" (ll. 93–94), and then turns to other dangers, giving a fine portrait of an old man gambling.

> He that no more for Age, Cramps, Palsies, can
> Now use the bones, we see doth hire a man
> To take the box up for him; and pursues
> The Dice with glassen eyes, to the glad viewes
> Of what he throwes: Like letchers growne content
> To be beholders, when their powers are spent.
>
> (ll. 135–40)

The example is from Horace—"Volanerious, the jester, when the gout he had earned crippled his finger-joints, kept a man, hired at a daily wage, to pick up the dice for him and put them in the box" (*Serm.* II. vii.15–18) —but the description is all Jonson's. After describing as many corruptions as seem necessary, the poet finds no logical difficulty in returning to the initial situation, but the return is likely to be awkward and is always obvious. Jonson makes it by simply listing the different types of vicious men, whom his friend Colby can avoid by going to war: "O times,/Friend, flie from hence; . . . where flatterers, spies,/Informers, Masters both of Arts and lies;/Lewd slanderers, soft whisperers that let blood/. . . where the envious, proud,/Ambitious, factious, superstitious, lowd/Boasters, and perjur'd, with the infinite more/Prævaricators swarme" (ll. 161–65, 167–70). He concludes with an exhortation to virtuous action.

The looseness of the poem is not extreme, but the temptation to bring in detail in excess of the general proposition or to the extent that it is difficult to relate it unobtrusively to the situation can be seen by comparing this epistle to the one giving the qualifications for dining with Jonson and his friends. The advice to Colby has very little to do with going to war—he might just as well be planning a journey to the Continent. The subject of the poem is vice. In answering the petition to join his tribe, Jonson also criticizes faults, but the faults are those specifically concerned with the situation of the tavern table: drinking, quarreling, boasting, slandering, gossiping, newsmongering, flattering, and treacherously betraying friendships. As a result, it is easy to return to the original device of the poem and to sustain the feeling evoked by the individual detail. This is partly possible also because this epistle is much shorter than the one to Colby.[19]

EPIGRAMS: "THE OLD WAY, AND THE TRUE"

> IRONSIDE. *Who made this Epigramme, you?* COMPASSE. *No, a great*
> Clarke
> As any'is of his bulke, (BEN: IONSON) *made it.*
> *The Magnetick Lady,* I. ii. 33–34

Epigrams, Martial says in introducing his second book, need no introductory epistle, for in every page "they constitute an epistle." Not only are they directly addressed, in most cases, to particular individuals or their representative types, but they are written in the familiar, conversational tone and share the attitudes and qualities of the epistolary style. Jonson tells Lady Aubigny that she may see herself clearly reflected in his epistle to her just as Martial says that he will be more clearly seen in his epigrams than in his painted portrait (VII.84). In giving a portrait of William Herbert, he writes "an Epigramme, on all man-kind."

Jonson's criticisms of the contemporary epigram are revealing, when they are considered, either actually or hypothetically, as answers to a poem by "R. C." on Jonson's own book of *Epigrammes.*

> Iohnson, they saye, 's turned Epigramatist;
> Soe think not I, believe it they that list.
> Peruse his booke, thou shalt not find a dram
> Of witt, befitting a true Epigram.
> Perhaps some scraps of play-bookes thou maist see,
> Collected heer and there confusedlie,
> Wch piece his broken stuffe, if thou but note,
> Iust like soe many patches on a cote.
> And yet his *intret Cato* stands before
> Even at ye portall of his pamphlets dore,
> As who should say, this booke is fit for none,
> But Catoes, learned men, to looke vpon:

Or else, let Cato censure if he will,
My booke deserves the best of iudgements skill.
When every gull may see his booke's vntwitten
And Epigrams as bad as ere were written.
Iohnson this worke thy other doth distaine,
And makes the world imagine that thy vein
Is not true bred, but of some bastard race,
Then write no more, or write wth better grace,
Turn thee to plaies & therin write thy fill,
Leave Epigrams to artists of more skill.[20]

The poem is included in *The Times Whistle: or a new Daunce of seven Satires*, which was first edited by J. M. Cowper in 1871. Cowper showed that the book was composed over a period from 1614 to 1616;[21] the latter date was established because of this poem on Jonson's *Epigrammes*, which were first published, as far as it can be demonstrated, in 1616. Cowper, however, thought that R. C. had seen Jonson's manuscript before it was published, because he thought that the following lines from Jonson's forty-ninth epigram were an allusion to the third and fourth lines of the satirist's poem, and therefore must have been printed after the appearance of *The Times Whistle*:

Play-wright me reades, and still my verses damnes,
He sayes, I want the tongue of *Epigrammes*.

R. M. Alden says quite rightly that "There is nothing conclusive in the similarity."[22] There are, however, other epigrams of Jonson that seem to answer R. C.'s criticisms. If they actually do, then R. C. would have to have seen the *Epigrammes* either in manuscript or in a lost earlier edition and written his poem on them; this, in turn, to have been seen by Jonson and answered in one or more epigrams, which he added to the carefully revised 1616 edition. Although this may seem too complicated to be probable, the fact that the *Epigrammes* were entered on the Stationer's Register in 1612 and included in a manuscript note by William Drummond under "bookes red be me anno 1612" (VIII, 16) suggests, according to Jonson's editors, that an earlier edition may actually have been printed, and, if this were the case, such a sequence of events is possible.

R. C. makes fun of the "intret Cato," which concludes Jonson's dedication to the Earl of Pembroke, for being a voluntary confession that there was no licentious wit in a book fit only for learned men to look upon. So far as Jonson is concerned, nothing, of course, could be more flattering. The epigrams were written in the language of educated men, and their insight into experience was addressed to educated men. When he dedicates "the ripest of my studies" to Pembroke, he says that many will blame him because they will assume that the poems on vices are addressed to them rather than the poems on virtue:

> For, why should they remit any thing of their riot, their pride, their selfe-loue, and other inherent graces, to consider truth or vertue; but, with the trade of the world, lend their long eares against men they loue not: and hold their deare *Mountebanke*, or *Iester*, in farre better con-dition, then all the studie, or studiers of *humanitie?* For such, I would rather know them by their visards, still, then they should publish their faces, at their perill, in my *Theater*, where *Cato*, if he liu'd, might enter without scandall. (VIII, 26)

Jonson, of course, is the "studier of *humanitie*," and his style and theory of art were chosen and developed to help him be that. But such a study will only be meaningful to educated men, such as Herbert and the other men to whom he addressed his poems. He would not have asked a better audience than the one R. C. suggested, but the satirist goes on to say "thy vein/Is not true bred, but of some bastard race," and shows in this state-ment his ignorance of the classical tradition of the epigram which Jonson was following. Jonson's hypothetical reply is terse and dextrous (VIII, 32):

> ### To my meere English Censvrer
> To thee, my way in *Epigrammes* seemes new,
> When both it is the old way, and the true.
> Thou saist, that cannot be: for thou hast seene
> DAVIS, and WEEVER, and the best haue beene,
> And mine come nothing like. I hope so. Yet,
> As theirs did with thee, mine might credit get:
> If thou'ldst but vse thy faith, as thou didst then,
> When thou wert wont t[o]'admire, not censure men.
> Pr'y thee beleeue still, and not iudge so fast,
> Thy faith is all the knowledge that thou hast.

One of the reasons why R. C. thinks Jonson's vein is not true bred is that one cannot find in it "a dram/Of witt, befitting a true Epigram." Cowper sees an answer to this criticism in Jonson's epigram "To Play-wright" (VIII, 42):

> Play-wright me reades, and still my verses damnes,
> He sayes, I want the tongue of *Epigrammes*;
> I haue no salt: no bawdrie he doth meane.
> For wittie, in his language, is obscene.
> PLAY-WRIGHT, I loath to haue thy manners knowne
> In my chast booke: professe them in thine owne.

He may be right, and the following epigram covers the subject even more completely (VIII, 27):

To my Booke

It will be look'd for, booke, when some but see
   Thy title, *Epigrammes,* and nam'd of mee,
Thou should'st be bold, licentious, full of gall,
   Wormewood, and sulphure, sharpe, and tooth'd withall;
Become a petulant thing, hurle inke, and wit,
   As mad-men stones: not caring whom they hit.
Deceiue their malice, who could wish it so.
   And by thy wiser temper, let men know
Thou are not couetous of least selfe-fame,
   Made from the hazard of anothers shame:
Much lesse with lewd, prophane, and beastly phrase,
   To catch the worlds loose laughter, or vaine gaze.
He that departs with his owne honesty
   For vulgar praise, doth it too dearely buy.

Neither of these poems, however, seems to answer R. C. as directly as Jonson's epigram on his mere English censurer.

Jonson made his comments on the structure of the epigram to Drummond. "A Great many Epigrams," Drummond reports his saying, "were ill, because they expressed jn the end, what sould have been understood, by what was said," and he gives as examples those of Sir John Davies (I, 143). Jonson is referring to Davies's practice of summarizing the situation that the poem describes, and the satirical point which the situation is supposed to be illustrating, in the last two lines. Davies's twelfth epigram may be given as an example:

Quintus his wit infused into his braine,
   Mislikes the place, and fled into his feet;
And there it wandered up and downe the street,
   Dabled in the dirt, and soakèd in the raine:
     Doubtlesse his wit intends not to aspire,
     Which leaues his head, to travell in the mire.[23]

The last two lines recapitulate what has gone before without adding any new details or making any new point.[24] Jonson's comment describes the particular structural defect; we would simply call the epigram flat.

John Owen's epigrams, Jonson said, were "bare narrations," and "when Sir John Harrington desyred him to tell the Truth of his Epigrames, he answered him that he loved not the Truth, for they were Narrations and not Epigrames" (I, 138, 133). The majority of Harington's epigrams are casual anecdotes and often resemble fables without animals, which

Chaucer might have incorporated in his tales. The following epigram is one of many of its kind:

Of a Lady that sought remedy at the Bathe

A Lady that none name, nor blame none hath,
Came the last yeere with others to the Bathe:
Her person comely was, good was her feature,
In beauty, grace and speech, a louely creature.
Now as the Lady in the water staid,
A plaine man fell a talking with her maid,
That lean'd vpon the rayle, and askt the reason,
Why that faire Lady vs'd the Bathe, that season?
Whether 'twere lamenesse, or defect in hearing,
Or some more inward euill, not appearing?
No, said the Maid to him, beleeue it well,
That my faire Mistris sound is as a Bell.
But of her comming, this is true occasion,
An old Physician mou'd her by perswasion,
These Bathes haue power to strengthen that debility,
That doth in man or woman breed sterrilitie.
Tush, said the man with plaine & short discourse,
Your Mistris might haue tane a better course.
Let her to Oxford, to the Vniuersitie,
Where yong Physicians are, and such diuersitie
Of toward spirits that in all acts proceede,
Much fitter then the Bathe is for the deede.
    No, no, that will not serue, the Maid replide,
For she that Physike hath already tride.[25]

The humor consists in the anecdotal narration of circumstances, as a story-teller might relate them, rather than in a compressed series of descriptive details concluding in an antithetical generalization.

The new authorities on style and the metrical innovations, offering the diction, syntax, and sound of a language men use, help to distinguish Jonson's poems from those of his contemporaries in no genre more than in the epigram. Of his poems in the three traditional genres of the classical *sermo,* his epigrams have, as well, by far the greatest variety of subject matter. Nearly all the types of epistle and satire are represented in shorter, and in many cases superior, versions. The collection is put together with care, and the individual poems are carefully polished.

The preceding chapters may be said to have been concerned with tracing the connection between the first and last epigrams, between the serious insistence upon understanding and the scatological burlesque of mythological allegory in "The Famous Voyage." The historical relationship and the similarity of attitudes of the two poems are explicit in their literary tradition; the use of the plain style in both demonstrates that the attitudes may be consistent in the most seemingly unlike types of material. And so with the poems ranged variously between these two extremes. The epigram to Camden, praising him for the intellectual virtues described in the epistle to Selden, is followed by one "On Covrt-worme." Jonson includes without embarrassment the intimate statement on the death of his son with numerous satirical portraits of types found in his comedies, such as "On Lievtenant Shift," "On Don Surly," and "To Fine Grand." Epistolary epigrams to personal friends are mixed in with poems to personal enemies like Jones, and with masterpieces on generalized situations, such as "Inviting a friend to Svpper." Although, like Jonson, the contemporary epigrammatists treated a variety of subjects, they failed to achieve his purity of idiom because of their overcomplicated syntax,[26] their lack of structure, and their rhythmical flatness.

Both Davies and Harington, although not offending against perspicuity, exemplify in the metrical structure of their lines, the rhythmical flatness discussed in Chapter 6—a flatness that is more noticeable in the epigram than in "Nosce Teipsum," because of the tone of conversational wit or the urbane distinctions of irony which the epigrammatist tries to achieve. Davies's poem on Quintus, cited above, has the caesura falling not only in the fourth position and at the end of the line but in a precisely repeated pattern: lines of ten, four, and six; ten, four, and six; ten, four, and six syllables. A comparable rhythmical repetition can be seen in Harington's narrations. In the lines

> A Lady that none name, nor blame none hath,
> Came the last yeere with others to the Bathe:
> Her person comely was, good was her feature, . . .

or in the opening couplet of Epigram 166:

> A fine yong Clerke, of kinne to Fryer *Frappert,*
> Prompt of his tongue, of person neat and dappert: . . .

the caesural units repeat themselves and set off the adjectival epithets without much syntactical variation and with just enough syntactical inversion to give the lines a slightly stilted and archaic tone. A comparison of the rhythm with nearly any of Jonson's epigrams will reveal one of the reasons for the sense of idiomatic purity and of continual freshness of syntax that his language conveys.

In Jonson's epigram "To my Mvse" (VIII, 48) the reader moves in another world:

> Away, and leaue me, thou thing most abhord,
>   That hast betray'd me to a worthlesse lord;
> Made me commit most fierce idolatrie
>   To a great image through thy luxurie.
> Be thy next masters more vnluckie *Muse,*
>   And, as thou'hast mine, his houres, and youth abuse.
> Get him the times long grudge, the courts ill will;
>   And, reconcil'd, keepe him suspected still.
> Make him loose all his friends; and, which is worse,
>   Almost all wayes, to any better course.
> With me thou leau'st an happier *Muse* then thee,
>   And which thou brought'st me, welcome pouertie.
> Shee shall instruct my after-thoughts to write
>   Things manly, and not smelling parasite.
> But I repent me: Stay. Who e're is rais'd,
>   For worth he has not, He is tax'd, not prais'd.

In castigating his muse for dishonesty Jonson is consciously varying the old convention of a supplication in the more rhetorical styles. What is striking is how much the movement of the lines delineates the poet's personality in his reaction to the situation. It is not that Jonson avoids pauses in the fourth position, but that he avoids a pattern of pauses in any position. It is quite possible, as in lines 7–8 and 9–10, to have caesuras in the fourth position in two successive pairs of lines so long as the natural syntax demands it and there are sufficient other syntactical pauses to make it clear that it is not establishing a rhythmical scheme. Drummond's remark, incidentally, that Jonson dissuaded him "from Poetrie, for that she had beggered him, when he might have been a rich lawyer, Physitian or Marchant" (I, 149) suggests how real the situation of the epigram may have been.

Jonson's epigrams to his friends are similar in tone and statement to his epistles. Among the best are the two epigrams to Sir Henry Goodyere (VIII, 55). The first of the two, written to thank Goodyere for an invitation to the country, is reminiscent of "Gascoigne's Woodmanship," and works out with great skill an analogy between hunting with a hawk, a bird sacred to Apollo, and the pursuit of knowledge, giving by implication the humanistic function of the satirist:

> Shee doth instruct men by her gallant flight,
>   That they to knowledge so should toure vpright,
> And neuer stoupe, but to strike ignorance:
>   Which if they misse, they yet should re-aduance
> To former height, and there in circle tarrie,
>   Till they be sure to make the foole their quarrie.
>   (ll. 5–10)

The bird's movements reflect perfectly the classical ideal of exploration and the subsequent recovery of a flexible position from which new exploration can be made. The second epigram "To the same" is a beautifully written compliment to Goodyere on his choice of books and friends.

The epigram to William Roe (VIII, 50) on the shortness of life has the emotional persuasiveness of the finest statements of Horace and Martial, in which the compressed generalization arises out of varied experience:

> Delay is bad, doubt worse, depending worst;
> Each best day of our life escapes vs, first.
>   (ll. 5–6)

More complicated than this poem is the other epigram to Roe (VIII, 80):

> Roe (and my ioy to name) th'art now, to goe
>   Countries, and climes, manners, and men to know,
> T[o]'extract, and choose the best of all these knowne,
>   And those to turne to bloud, and make thine owne:
> May windes as soft as breath of kissing friends,
>   Attend thee hence; and there, may all thy ends,
> As the beginnings here, proue purely sweet,
>   And perfect in a circle alwayes meet.
> So, when we, blest with thy returne, shall see
>   Thy selfe, with thy first thoughts, brought home by thee,
> We each to other may this voyce enspire;
>   This is that good Æneas, past through fire,
> Through seas, stormes, tempests: and imbarqu'd for hell,
>   Came backe vntouch'd. This man hath trauail'd well.[27]

Jonson praised Selden for having done the same thing without leaving England, since he had acquired so much general knowledge from books and "men, manners too," that he had "all Countries seene." The epigram to Roe, however, is more complicated than the lines to Selden. Throughout the pursuit of knowledge, Jonson implies, one must be careful to retain his identity lest it be dissolved in the continuous surf of new experience. Roe must return with his first thoughts; they will, it is implied, identify him. Furthermore, knowledge is a risk; one cannot get rid of the changes its acquisition imposes, though one may forget gradually the details of sensation and lore that it brings. Knowledge, also, that is particularly rare and powerful is dangerous; men have gone to hell for it and will again. Jonson's allusion is classical, but both men were Christian, and the implications of having come back "vntouch'd" from hell are complicated in a poem encouraging a friend "To extract, and choose the best of all these knowne." The control of the rhythm and idiom in this epigram is unsurpassed. The caesura, extraordinarily sensitive to syntax, gives the line great energy and the reader the impression of great resources of speed being held in. Yet the verse is not frenetic, since the formal demands of the couplet are respected.

More famous but, finally, less interesting is Jonson's epigram "To William Camden" (VIII, 31). He praises Camden's scholarship for the same humanistic reasons as he did Selden's—the gradual clarification of error by continual research and the addition of present observation to the recorded experience of the past.

> CAMDEN, most reuerend head, to whom I owe
> All that I am in arts, all that I know,
> (How nothing's that?) to whom my countrey owes
> The great renowne, and name wherewith shee goes.
> Then thee the age sees not that thing more graue,
> More high, more holy, that shee more would craue.
> What name, what skill, what faith hast thou in things!
> What sight in searching the most antique springs!
> What weight, and what authoritie in thy speech!
> Man scarse can make that doubt, but thou canst teach.
> Pardon free truth, and let thy modestie,
> Which conquers all, be once ouer-come by thee.
> Many of thine this better could, then I,
> But for their powers, accept my pietie.

The first couplet is very fine and establishes the tone and feeling of the following lines. The parenthetical question in the third line, however, is disturbing, and the third couplet with its series of overlapping adjectives seems heavily formal. The next four lines are admirable. Although the terms are general, in Jonson's context of reference as discussed in relation to the Selden epistle, they refer to specific disciplines of the mind.

Of the epigrams addressed to friends in the arts none is as good as the epistle to Burlase. The second poem to Alphonso Ferrabosco (VIII, 82), however, is a fine statement of the necessity for the artist to judge his own work and not to be overconcerned with how it is received. Jonson's epigram to the actor Edward Allen (VIII, 56), although a fairly conventional compliment, ends with a beautiful couplet which could have stood alone:

> Weare this renowne. 'Tis iust, that who did giue
> So many *Poets* life, by one should liue.

The quality of the complimentary epigrams throughout the collection is high. Very often, being shorter, they are superior to the epistles of the same kind. On the whole, however, the most interesting epigrams are those just discussed and several discussed previously, such as the epigrams to the

Countess of Bedford and to Sir Henry Savile. The poems to Donne (*Epig.* 23, 96) are good but not among Jonson's best. The second, the better of the two, recognizes him as the authority on epigrams and restates the theme of the second poem to Ferrabosco: "A man should seeke great glorie, and not broad," and so should consult only the most discriminating critics.

Of the satirical epigrams, there are two sorts, one an amplified version of the other. The first is a short epigram of from two to six lines which moves from a descriptive character type, named in the title, directly to a witty distinction or antithesis pointing to a specific form of behavior. In the second sort Jonson describes his subject in some detail, instead of moving directly from descriptive title to concluding distinction, and concludes with a general comment on the description. The virtue of the first sort is not only the precision with which the distinction is revealed but the natural idiomatic diction and the ease of syntax with which it is stated.

To Person Gviltie

GVILTIE, be wise; and though thou know'st the crimes
    Be thine, I taxe, yet doe not owne my rimes:
'Twere madnesse in thee, to betray thy fame,
    And person to the world; ere I thy name. (VIII, 36)

The poem is over before one is aware of it. There is nothing to comment on, quarrel with, or explicate; the reader's immediate reaction is to go on to the next poem. But if he doesn't hear what is going on in these lines, he might as well close the book, for it is the perfect adaptation of the syntax to the units of the line and of the couplet which distinguish Jonson's epigrams from those of his contemporaries. The pauses emphasize the syntax and, when withheld, relax the line into the normal syntactical conclusion: "yet doe not owne my rimes." The movement must be heard, even if it is necessary to overemphasize the caesuras to do it, because the feeling is so largely conveyed by the rhythm. Furthermore, in the quietness of statement it is easy to miss the pun on "betray"; in the third line it means to violate, or treacherously subvert, the subject's reputation (which the poem is maintaining it is foolish to do), and in the fourth it means to reveal his character. The wit arises from the indication, by means of the pun, that the second betrayal automatically causes the first. Among the other epigrams of this sort are "On Gvt" (VIII, 76), which Jonson enjoyed repeating to Drummond (I, 135), and several other fine short ones. Two of them are among the most licentious of the collection. One of these is the second epigram "On Sir Volvptvovs Beast" (VIII, 35), who, even when he sleeps at home,

"He'adulters still: his thoughts lye with a whore." The second, "To Pertinax Cob" (VIII, 50), is particularly adroit:

> Cob, thou nor souldier, thiefe, nor fencer art,
>   Yet by thy weapon liu'st! Th'hast one good part.

But perhaps the best of the very short satirical epigrams is the one "On Spies" (VIII, 45), which probably comes out of Jonson's experience with informers while in prison (see I, 139):

> SPIES, you are lights in state, but of base stuffe,
>   Who, when you 'haue burnt your selues downe to the snuffe,
> Stinke, and are throwne away. End faire enough.

The meter is largely responsible for the force of the lines. The elision gives the effect of a trisyllabic substitution in the second line, which speeds it up to a kind of snap of contempt in the strongly stressed first syllable of the following line and the abrupt conclusion. The figure of spies burning down their information, as a candle burns down its wax, and guttering in the snuff stresses their expendability and indicates the contempt which even the employer has for his informer.

The second variety of Jonson's satirical epigrams seems simply an amplification of the first. The wit comes largely from the details of the description rather than from a distinction. The concluding couplet is often the weakest in the poem, as in several of the epigrams to Jones (VIII, 74, 81). The sketch, for instance, of Don Surly is wittily and sharply drawn (VIII, 35):

> H'has tympanies of businesse, in his face,
>   And, can forget mens names, with a great grace.
> He will both argue, and discourse in oathes,
>   Both which are great. And laugh at ill-made clothes;
> That's greater, yet: to crie his owne vp neate.
> He doth, at meales, alone, his pheasant eate,
> Which is maine greatnesse. And, at his still boord,
>   He drinkes to no man: that's, too, like a lord.
> He keepes anothers wife, which is a spice
>   Of solemne greatnesse. And he dares, at dice,
> Blaspheme god, greatly. Or some poore hinde beat,
>   That breathes in his dogs way: and this is great.
>   (ll. 7-18)

Despite the fact that the poem turns on the word "great," the concluding couplet is an anticlimax after the incisive description:

SVRLY, vse other arts, these only can
Stile thee a most great foole, but no great man.
(ll. 21–22)

Jonson's portraits of contemporary types in the epigrams are unsurpassed. Here is one "On Reformed Gam'ster" (VIII, 33), who has, it seems,
turned Puritan:

Lord, how is GAM'STER chang'd! his haire close cut!
His neck fenc'd round with ruffe! his eyes halfe shut!
His clothes two fashions of, and poore! his sword
Forbidd' his side! and nothing, but the word
Quick in his lips! . . .

(ll. 1–5)

This is the work of a master. Not only the details but the rhythm is used
to characterize the subject. In the fourth line the fourth stress, on "but,"
is slighted, which speeds up the line and suggests in its movement the
quickness of the word in his lips. Of similar descriptive power are two of
the epigrams on courtiers. In the first, "On Covrt-worme" (VIII, 31), he
depicts a dandy:

All men are wormes: But this no man. In silke
'Twas brought to court first wrapt, and white as milke;
Where, afterwards, it grew a butter-flye:
Which was a cater-piller. So't will dye.

The contempt expressed by the neuter pronoun is withering, and the comparison of the world of the court to the world of insects—one of Jonson's
favorite comparisons—is vivid. The same tone is used even more brutally
in the characterization of an old lord at court, "On some-thing, that walkes
some-where" (VIII, 30), a phrase referring specifically to a ghost:

At court I met it, in clothes braue enough,
To be a courtier; and lookes graue enough,
To seeme a statesman: as I neere it came,
It made me a great face, I ask'd the name.
A lord, it cryed, buried in flesh, and blood,
And such from whom let no man hope least good,
For I will doe none: and as little ill,
For I will dare none. Good Lord, walke dead still.

The short final sentence points the comparison of the lord with one of the
walking dead. His spirit, buried in flesh, shrieks from within its indifference to the living.

Many of the descriptions are more humorous than biting. One of the funniest is "To Fine Grand" (VIII, 51), which lists the things a courtly fop has had Jonson make up for him. They include a jest, some tales, a song, a charm for a ring and a picture, an *imprese,* "your mistris *anagram,* i' your hilt, " "your owne, sew'd in your mistris smock," and an epitaph on a lord's cock, many of which items were seriously discussed by Puttenham. Jonson wrote several epigrams on plagiarists, a conventional target for satire (*Epig.* 56, 81, 100, 112), but he was excellent at depicting all satirical types; and, as in his poem "On English Movnsievr" (VIII, 56), the cleanness of idiom and rhythmical variation give his lines a personal tone.

> Would you beleeue, when you this Movnsievr see,
>   That his whole body should speake *french,* not he?
> That so much skarfe of *France,* and hat, and fether,
>   And shooe, and tye, and garter should come hether,
> And land on one, whose face durst neuer bee
>   Toward the sea, farther then halfe-way tree?
>
> (ll. 1–6)

The loose style, as Morris Croll describes it in Montaigne, appears here in the repetition of the conjunction, which stresses the accumulation of detail to emphasize the ridiculousness of the portrait.

A complex treatment of a less common type than the French is the epigram "The New Crie" (VIII, 58), which satirizes young men who attempt to be amateur statesmen:

> Ere cherries ripe, and straw-berries be gone,
>   Vnto the cryes of *London* Ile adde one;
> Ripe statesmen, ripe: They grow in euery street.
>   At sixe and twentie, ripe. You shall 'hem meet,
> And haue'hem yeeld no sauour, but of state.
>   Ripe are their ruffes, their cuffes, their beards, their gate,
> And graue as ripe, like mellow as their faces. . . .
> The councels, proiects, practises they know,
>   And what each prince doth for intelligence owe,
> And vnto whom: They are the almanacks
>   For twelue yeeres yet to come, what each state lacks.
> They carry in their pockets Tacitvs,
>   And the Gazetti, or Gallo-Belgicvs:
> And talke reseru'd, lock'd vp, and full of feare,
>   Nay, aske you, how the day goes, in your eare.
> Keepe a *starre*-chamber sentence close, twelue dayes:
>   And whisper what a Proclamation sayes.
>
> (ll. 1–7, 11–20)

They meet, Jonson says, in sixes in all the market places and buy "the names of books" which are apt to have state revelations in them. They also dabble in espionage, seeking the sundry ways

> To write in cypher, and the seuerall keyes,
> To ope' the character. They'haue found the sleight
> With iuyce of limons, onions, pisse, to write,
> To breake vp seales, and close'hem. . . .
>   (ll. 26–29)

It is an extremely vivid description of the self-important secret man, who is not alone of the Renaissance but occurs in every period and in every profession. The descriptive vividness of the epigrams seems usually, as in this case, to be a result of Jonson's taking certain details from a conventional stereotype and making them so incisive that he seems to be depicting a particular and unusual individual.

Another group of epigrams that should be distinguished are the epitaphs. Jonson wrote about fifteen of them, distributed throughout the three collections of his poems. They owe their form and style to the Latin and Greek epigram, the most formal convention that Jonson adopted. There is not a great deal that can be said about them as a whole except that they are beautifully executed and perfectly realize the virtues of the style that I have been discussing. They are one of the most perfect adaptations in English of a traditional classical form. In several of them, however, Jonson has used the form to write poems of considerably more complicated feeling, and it is worth while to distinguish among them. Most representative of the tradition, in a Christian context, of course, would be such an epigram as "On my first Davghter" (VIII, 33):

> Here lyes to each her parents ruth,
> MARY, the daughter of their youth:
> Yet, all heauens gifts, being heauens due,
> It makes the father, lesse, to rue.
> At sixe moneths end, shee parted hence
> With safetie of her innocence;
> Whose soule heauens Queene, (whose name shee beares)
> In comfort of her mothers teares,
> Hath plac'd amongst her virgin-traine:
> Where, while that seuer'd doth remaine,
> This graue partakes the fleshly birth.
> Which couer lightly, gentle earth.

The feeling is not complicated; its sources are apparent and available. There is nothing in the formal statement, beyond its excellence in diction and syntax, that is particularly characteristic of Jonson, except, perhaps, his specific reference to himself as the child's father. Had the poem, in other words, not been printed by Jonson, a reattribution of its authorship would not be surprising, as in the case of the epitaph on the Countess of Pembroke, "Underneath this sable herse," now assigned to William Browne. This is true, I think, of many of the epitaphs, and might even be said of the beautiful "Epitaph on S[alomon] P[avy] a child of Q. El[izabeths] Chappel" (VIII, 77). There are, however, beyond the fact that Jonson's friendship with the boy is reported elsewhere, indications of Jonson's particular skill and tone. In the first place, the form is very intricate, with varying length of line and alternating masculine and feminine endings, and despite this intricacy the ordinary order of prose syntax is never violated. This takes the greatest skill and is characteristic of Jonson's most complicated songs. Second, the conceit is masterful, and the particular combination of the classical allusion with the actual and habitual activity of the boy to construct and resolve the poem is typical of Jonson. (The same device is used, for instance, in the beautiful lines in the epigram "On Lvcy Covntesse of Bedford" (VIII, 52), discussed earlier: "Onely a learned, and a manly soule/I purpos'd her; that should, with euen powers,/The rock, the spindle, and the sheeres controule/Of destinie, and spin her owne free houres.") It is a combination that is difficult to make without the allusion's seeming strained and gratuitous.

> Yeeres he numbred scarse thirteene
>   When *Fates* turn'd cruell,
> Yet three fill'd *Zodiackes* had he beene
>   The stages iewell;
> And did act (what now we mone)
>   Old men so duely,
> As, sooth, the *Parcæ* thought him one,
>   He plai'd so truely.
> So, by error, to his fate
>   They all consented;
> But viewing him since (alas, too late)
>   They haue repented.
> And haue sought (to giue new birth)
>   In bathes to steepe him;
> But, being so much too good for earth,
>   Heauen vowes to keepe him.
>   (ll. 9–24)

There is great beauty in the perfect conceit where the added complication of feeling helps to define the emotional attitude in the actual situation.

Not nearly so good a poem but an interesting extension of the form is "An Epitaph on Master Vincent Corbet" (VIII, 151). The poem is forty lines long and actually adopts the tone of a moral epistle. Jonson asks for the reader's sympathy by an extended description of Corbet's virtues:

> Deare *Vincent Corbet,* who so long
> Had wrestled with Diseases strong,
> That though they did possesse each limbe,
> Yet he broke them, e're they could him,
> With the just Canon of his life,
>   (ll. 7–11)

Corbet was a gardener, and his mind was "as pure, and neatly kept,/As were his Nourceries." Such references to his occupation, and the implication of how difficult it must have been in his illness to follow it, engage the reader's feelings more than the generalized didacticism. The most moving lines in the poem—as so often in Jonson—are those that express Jonson's own relationship with the man:

> Much from him I professe I wonne,
> And more, and more, I should have done,
> But that I understood him scant.
> Now I conceive him by my want,
>   (ll. 29–32)

These qualities are more characteristic of Jonson's epistles than of the traditional short epitaph, which usually tries to evoke its feeling by a sudden, sharply conceived perception of transience. Such a loss, however, Jonson was surely writing about in his finest epitaph, "On my First Sonne" (VIII, 41), but the poem goes far beyond the traditional form in its complication of statement and feeling.

> Farewell, thou child of my right hand, and ioy;
>   My sinne was too much hope of thee, lou'd boy,
> Seuen yeeres tho'wert lent to me, and I thee pay,
>   Exacted by thy fate, on the iust day.
> O, could I loose all father, now. For why
>   Will man lament the state he should enuie?
> To haue so soon scap'd worlds, and fleshes rage,
>   And, if no other miserie, yet age?
> Rest in soft peace, and, ask'd, say here doth lye
>   BEN. IONSON his best of *poetrie.*
> For whose sake, hence-forth, all his vowes be such,
>   As what he loues may neuer like too much.

Poetrie, of course, in the tenth line is a pun based on the original meaning of the word, that which is made or created. The pun, which is neither an embellishment nor a lapse in taste, contributes to the logical development of the theme, for the theme is rather the relation between father and son than the death of the child. In the third couplet Jonson says were it not for the relation, he, as a Christian, would not lament the child, now in heaven, or at least he would not feel the sorrow as sharply, and so he asks to "loose all father." This being impossible, he asks the boy to state the relation in its broadest and simplest terms: here lies the poet's greatest achievement, the most nearly perfect thing he made. Neither the relation nor the feeling of loss can be altered, but the emotional attitude can be modified in order to make the grief less painful. He states the modification by means of a distinction in the last line, an adaptation of Martial's line, *quidquid ames, cupias non placuisse nimis* (VI, 29), desire that what you love has not pleased you too much. Jonson translates the line by making a distinction between "love" and "like," which were ordinarily used redundantly in a formulaic combination.[28] The apparently casual association of the two, when a distinction is being made, increases the reader's perception of the antithesis. Jonson makes "what" (he loves) the object of both love and like, whereas Martial makes it the object of love but the subject of please. Jonson could have retained the syntax, "That what he loves may never please too much," with "him" as the understood object of please, but the power of the distinction would have been nearly lost; the parallel positions of the verb emphasize the contrast. Once the difference between love and like has been called to the reader's attention, the connotations of those words give the line its subtlety. Jonson's observation is extremely acute, and its implications are both extensive and severe. Because of the nature of the insight and the tone of its emotional acceptance in such lines as this and the eighth, "And, if no other miserie, yet age," the poem carries an authority of experience and a personal intimacy with the reader which it would be very difficult to communicate in the diction and movement of any other style.

The remaining epigrams to be noted deal with disparate situations, some highly generalized and some concerning specific incidents in Jonson's life. Of the latter kind, perhaps, are a series of epigrams on the king's household (*Underwood* 62–66, 68, 72, 76). Most of these are complimentary or purely occasional poems on births and birthdays, but two are of particular interest. "The humble Petition of poore Ben. To th'best of Monarchs, Masters, Men, King Charles" (VIII, 259) is a request for the payment of the hundred marks' annuity granted to Jonson by King James, and it specifically men-

tions the attacks by "the lesse-*Poëtique* boyes," among whom apparently
was Jones, since his name is written beside the second line of Martial's epigram (IV, 27) from which the petition is adapted. This and the following
poem concern the personal difficulties which increased as Jonson grew older.
The epigram "To the House-hold" (VIII, 241) is one of the five sonnets
Jonson wrote. It is curious largely because its diction and rhythm give it a
tone not usually associated with the form. The royal household seems not
to know him any more. He explains, however, that they should find themselves repaid were they to encourage him to write, instead of withholding
his royal grant of wine,

> And rather wish, in their expence of Sack,
>   So, the allowance from the King to use,
> As the old *Bard,* should no Canary lack.
>   'T were better spare a Butt, then spill his *Muse.*
> For in the *Genius* of a *Poëts* Verse,
>   The Kings fame lives. Go now, denie his *Teirce.*
>   (ll. 9–14)

The yearly "teirce" of wine, forty-two gallons, was granted in 1630. The
tone of cajolery, the quibble on "spill" in the sense of destroy, and the direct,
idiomatic address to such a formidable establishment are humorously emphasized by the contrasting formal structure of the sonnet.

   More general are those epigrams dealing with the proper pursuit of
certain professions, several of which Jonson repeatedly satirized. His epigram "To true Sovldiers" (VIII, 69), for instance, repudiates in part the
preceding epigram "To Captayne Hvngry," and praises their great profession, which he once tried. "An Epigram to the Councellour that pleaded,
and carried the Cause" (VIII, 186), in the manner of an epistle, was written
to Sir Anthony Benn, whose manners and virtues made Jonson "conceive
a Lawyer new," and its tone makes up somewhat for Jonson's severity on
lawyers throughout his plays and some of his poems. Although these poems
are usually directed to specific people, they are fairly general in their subject
matter and differ a bit in tone from the epigrams to close friends which
praise certain disciplines or activities. They are not of such general application, however as "An Epigram. To the small Poxe" (VIII, 188), which is
one of two poems, the other being "To Sicknesse" (VIII, 104), that angrily
address a disease for attacking specific ladies. The victim of smallpox is
not named, and incidence of the disease among well-known women was
frequently enough recorded to imagine the poem's applying to a common
hazard. Jonson begins by asking the disease if "there not be/One beautie

in an Age, and free from thee?" and goes on to say that the particular lady had no quarrel with nature and did not use unhealthy cosmetics:

> What was the cause then? Thought'st thou in disgrace
>   Of Beautie, so to nullifie a face,
> That heaven should make no more; or should amisse,
>   Make all hereafter, had'st thou ruin'd this?

> (ll. 13–16)

The lines are curiously moving in their suggestion of the finality in the loss of an individual face, whose beauty can never again be perceived or reproduced and gradually slips even from the memory.

The finest poem concerned with an unspecified occasion but with a specified situation is the epigram "Inviting a friend to svpper" (VIII, 64). It is one of Jonson's best adaptations in English of a classical convention, for without departing greatly in detail and not at all in attitude toward the subject from his classical models, he achieves an idiomatic purity of English and, in the adaptation of idiom to the demands of the verse, an unsurpassed excellence in the pentameter couplet. If the poem, quoted below, is read with a slightly greater caesural emphasis than the reader might ordinarily use, he should hear in his mind the flexible control of a potentially swift movement, which is released in larger units of syllables and restrained in smaller but never dissipated to slackness by running on through several lines without pauses.

Inviting a friend to svpper

> To night, graue sir, both my poore house, and I
>   Doe equally desire your companie:
> Not that we thinke vs worthy such a ghest,
>   But that your worth will dignifie our feast,
> With those that come; whose grace may make that seeme
>   Something, which, else, could hope for no esteeme.
> It is the faire acceptance, Sir, creates
>   The entertaynment perfect: not the cates.
> Yet shall you haue, to rectifie your palate,
>   An oliue, capers, or some better sallade
> Vshring the mutton; with a short-leg'd hen,
>   If we can get her, full of egs, and then,
> Limons, and wine for sauce: to these, a coney
>   Is not to be despair'd of, for our money;
> And, though fowle, now, be scarce, yet there are clarkes,
>   The skie not falling, thinke we may haue larkes.
> Ile tell you of more, and lye, so you will come:
>   Of partrich, pheasant, wood-cock, of which some

May yet be there; and godwit, if we can:
    Knat, raile, and ruffe too. How so ere, my man
Shall reade a piece of VIRGIL, TACITVS,
    LIVIE, or of some better booke to vs,
Of which wee'll speake our minds, amidst our meate;
    And Ile professe no verses to repeate:
To this, if ought appeare, which I not know of,
    That will the pastrie, not my paper, show of.
Digestiue cheese, and fruit there sure will bee;
    But that, which most doth take my *Muse,* and mee,
Is a pure cup of rich *Canary*-wine,
    Which is the *Mermaids,* now, but shall be mine:
Of which had HORACE, or ANACREON tasted,
    Their liues, as doe their lines, till now had lasted.
Tabacco, Nectar, or the *Thespian* spring,
    Are all but LVTHERS beere, to this I sing.
Of this we will sup free, but moderately,
    And we will haue no *Pooly*', or *Parrot* by;
Nor shall our cups make any guiltie men:
    But, at our parting, we will be, as when
We innocently met. No simple word,
    That shall be vtter'd at our mirthful boord,
Shall make vs sad next morning: or affright
    The libertie, that wee'll enioy to night.

This is the fashionless style that Vives, Lipsius, Bacon, and Hoskyns describe. It has not grown old in nearly three hundred and fifty years of changing fashions; in 1616 it had avoided the Ciceronian hunt for words and was avoiding the temptations of Senecan ingenuity, which, of course, led to the same thing. The idiomatic purity, as described earlier, is as much a matter of rhythm as of elegance and currency of diction and syntax. Here the hypothetical metrical limitation, or norm, is a unit of two rhymed lines of ten syllables each, five stressed alternating with five unstressed. Jonson demonstrates Lucan's preference, *plus mihi comma placet,* and even permits the syntax to disrupt the couplet slightly by running over and making the metrical unit give in, somewhat at least, to the syntactical demands.

Besides the classical models, from which many of the details are taken, the *Leges Convivales,* the house rules Jonson wrote for a special room set aside in the Old Devil Tavern and called the Apollo, are the best gloss on his dinner invitation (VIII, 656).[29] The rules borrow some of the same details from Horace and Martial and are written in their flexible and idiomatic Latin. Let no one, the laws begin, who will pay for nothing come, unless he be a guest of someone who has been officially invited. Let the insipid, melancholy, and frowzy fool stay away; let the learned, the urbane, the gay, and the honest be admitted; nor should well-chosen ladies be kept out. Let there be nothing in the linen to offend the noses of the guests. Let the dishes be prepared with refined taste rather than with expense; let the purveyor and the cook be well acquainted with the tastes of the guests. There must be no wrangling about the seating arrangement. Those who serve the food must be watchful and silent, and the wine waiters attentive and swift. The wine must be drawn from fountains which admit no dilute mixture, or else the host must be punished. It should be permitted that the toasters challenge one another in moderate cups, but let the competition be more in anecdotes than in wine. Let no guest talk too much or be silent, and let no one who is full of food and drink discourse on serious or sacred matters. Let no musician in who has not been summoned. It is allowed that our private mysteries be celebrated with laughter, dances, choruses, songs, jokes, and all the festivity of the Graces. All jokes must be without gall, and no flat poems may be recited; let none be compelled to write verses. There must be no clamor of argument, but let there be a free corner for the sighs and disputes of lovers. No one shall be permitted to fight with great goblets in the manner of the Lapithians, to break glassware, to knock out windows, or rip apart the furniture. Let him be let out who lets out to the world what we do or say, for the liquor must make no one a culprit. Let the fire be always burning. It is to such a dinner that Jonson is inviting his friend, although the party purports to be smaller, and with fewer *ministri.*

There is more, however, in the rules and in the epigram than a humorous description of a dinner and half-jocular instruction for convivial behavior. The sources of feeling lie in attitudes that go back to and beyond the writers Jonson most admired in the Latin tradition. The dinner party is almost a symbol for the social, moral, and aesthetic values of the host. The poems of Catullus, Horace, and Martial, which describe the modest fare and entertainment of their hospitality, are declarations of taste as well as of means. Let the food, Jonson demands in his sixth law, be prepared more with selectivity than with great expense; the guests are, in the end, the most important ingredient of a good party. It is the fair acceptance by the guests, whose grace may make that dinner something that else could hope for no esteem, that makes the entertainment perfect, the epigram states in nearly these same words. Yet, the food will be good though simple, and you may relax, Martial says in one of his invitations (V.78), *et voltu placidus tuo recumbes,* stretch out, at ease in your own face, and no one will make up gossip about you when your guard is down. The food is simple, but he says with Jonson, I'll lie about delicacies to make you come, and, though you read your poems, I'll recite nothing (XI.52). The entertainment will accord with the quality and tastes of the guests: good books and conversation in place of show girls, though Catullus offers a beautifully scented *puella* to his friend, and Jonson's laws allow for a girl in the corner. People are invited who are, as Jonson stipulates, *eruditi, urbani, hilares, honesti,* and anyone who comes may expect to enjoy and be protected by these qualities in his companions. And what makes these qualities important are the things, revealed by implication, that are *not* there: the mindless extravagance, brutal sensuality, and dishonest affectation described by Juvenal and Petronius.

The intimate supper of Horace and Martial is a rejection of such banquets as that of Trimalchio in the *Satyricon* of Petronius, which gives one of the most detailed pictures of the flagrant misuse of wealth, the body, and the mind in classical literature. The richness of the banquet becomes a symbol for the moral poverty of the host, and seems to remain such throughout the Western satirical tradition, at least down to Pope's satire on the use of riches in his description of Timon's villa and his buffet. The contrast between the supper and the banquet is given most completely in Juvenal's eleventh satire, where each is described. He invites his friend Persicus to dine on food grown on his own farm; the fare is choice but simple, and such as was enjoyed in former days. Now the rich man enjoys only what is conspicuously expensive: ivory tables with silver legs alone help the digestion, and the servant must be a graduate of a carving school. Such men live only for their palate, *in solo vivendi causa palato est.* Furthermore, Juvenal goes on, at my dinner you can ask for anything you want in Latin; I do not have the affectation of foreign slave boys. There will be no lascivious dances, but readings from Homer and Virgil. In this context, then, Jonson's invitation to supper refers to considerably more important attitudes than it might seem at first. He himself knew many of the wealthy and seems to have been forced upon occasion "to sit (as some, this day,/At great mens tables) and yet dine away" (VIII, 95). The details in the epigram do not simply reflect their classical context; they represent Jonson's own tastes, both in food and books, and what he expected in a drinking companion, described also in his epistle to one who wished to join his tribe. The epigram, by implication, is actually a definition of a friend, not of a dinner, and states the ethical and aesthetic requirements in social terms.

The sources of feeling may still elude the modern reader. The tone of the poem is difficult to describe as well as to respond to, but I think Jonson's *Leges* suggest a place to start in the adjectives describing the guests: *eruditi, urbani, hilares,* and *honesti.* By coincidence perhaps, these adjectives accurately describe the tone of the epigram. The poem is written with an honest directness which is inescapable if the epistolary style is in any way realized successfully; it is the honesty of candor, derived from the ancient concept in satire of *libertas* or *simplicitas,* for which Jonson most loved to be valued as a poet. The tone is gay in its grace and wit, and erudite not only in its evocation of classical attitudes but in its assumption of a certain sophistication in the reader that enables him to imagine a party combining Tacitus with a great deal of liquor. It is, however, the quality of urbanity that is most helpful in indicating the most available and valuable responses. The style is urbane in Quintilian's terms, for it admits no incongruity, coarseness, or exoticism in thought or language, and the urbanity lies in the whole complexion of the language, not in isolated sayings, in the same way that Atticism meant for the Greeks a pervasive and persistent elegance of taste that was peculiar to Athens (*Inst. Orat.* VI.iii.107). To achieve these stylistic qualities, however, a context of attitudes and experience which the audience shares with the speaker must be assumed. Not only must allusions be perceived, but the feelings which elicited them and the responses expected must be perceived and anticipated. An urbane statement is one that offers listeners the opportunity to participate in the speaker's observations upon shared experience and encourages them to adopt similar emotional attitudes toward it. Such an expectation seems to be fulfilled in two ways. The speaker may, on the one hand, refer to a particular incident or person; the humor or insight will depend upon the listeners' clearly and rapidly perceiving the generalization implied. Or, on the other hand, the speaker may make a general statement, counting on his listeners to make their own quick applications to particulars. The process is, of course, associative, but the necessity of a common context should prevent it from becoming too subjective. When it has no such context, a type of obscurity peculiar to the plain style results. Urbanity, then, consists in one sense of the intimate commerce between the particular and the generalization which the common context suggests or imposes. The more rapidly and flexibly the audience can move from one to the other, the more the speaker will be effectively urbane. The sources of feeling will be available to the reader of Jonson's invitation to his friend in proportion to the reader's ability to participate in the experience described; they will arise, in other words, from the reader's own experience. To the extent that he is familiar with a situation that is relatable to the context of the poem, he will be able to perceive and respond to the feeling Jonson is asking him to share.

In conclusion, it might be said that both the florid style and that higher style blown, as Farnaby says, with full lungs have always seemed to require more art and skill than the plain style, and, as a corollary, have always seemed more emotionally convincing and even more personal. That the tone of the plain style is, on the contrary, the most intimately personal is reasserted throughout the history of its literary tradition. Since it records the most sensitive adjustment between the denotative meaning and its connotative qualification, which the least defect will impair, it is perhaps the most difficult style to write. The style will become more persuasive as the reader's experience gradually verifies, in an increasing number of contexts, the accuracy of this adjustment. Whether or not the reader will at first find the style moving will depend upon his expectations, which, in turn, will depend upon his literary training and experience. Scholars who write on the epigram often apologize for what they feel is not really poetry.[30] Demetrius might answer them by responding that rhetorical ornament is inappropriate both to the expression of strong feeling and to the delineation of character, "For simplicity and naturalness is the mark alike of passion and of character-drawing" (*On Style,* 28). In the Renaissance it is Sir Henry Wotton, perhaps, who comments most explicitly on the emotional power of the plain style in a letter drawing attention to his epigram on Morton and his wife:

> He first deceas'd. She for a little tried
> To live without him: lik'd it not and died.

"If the Queen," Wotton writes, "have not heard the epitaph of Albertus Morton and his lady, it is worth her hearing for the passionate plainness."[31]

8

"THE PASSIONATE PLAINNESS":
POEMS IN OTHER THAN THE FOUR GENRES
OF THE PLAIN STYLE

THE POEMS OF JONSON other than those that are written in any of the four
genres traditionally associated with the classical *sermo* owe their excellence
to the intentions and the qualities of language of the plain style, which were
beginning to be extended to genres that had habitually employed the *genus
floridum* and the *genus grande*. The incursion by the plain style into the
subjects of the high and middle styles in the sixteenth century was not a
result of an entirely new stylistic strategy as much as it was simply a further
step in the direction that the plain style had traditionally taken. The step,
however, was an important one, and Jonson took it as decisively in poetry
as Erasmus, Vives, and Lipsius had done in rhetoric.

In his *De Augmentis Scientiarum* Bacon treats as a separate branch of
learning only the poetry that he considers "feigned history," dividing it into
"Poesy *Narrative, Dramatic,* and *Parabolical.*" Of the shorter verse forms
he says: "I dismiss from the present discourse Satires, Elegies, Epigrams,
Odes, and the like; and refer them to philosophy and the arts of speech.
And under the name of Poesy, I treat only of feigned history."[1] It is not
surprising that Bacon should refer these shorter forms to philosophy as well
as to the rhetorical arts. The *sermones* were to take their material from the
Socraticae chartae. The epigram not only was closely related to satire but
was, save for matters of musical accompaniment, indistinguishable from
short poems in general, *poemata,* to which today we inclusively give the
term lyric. The ode was merely a form of lyric, and elegies were often
simply satirical epistles dealing with love. Stylistically, the lyric, like the
sermo, had been regarded in antiquity as the poetic form nearest prose in
its word order and its rhythmical flexibility (*Orator* 183–84). Dionysius of
Halicarnassus, in a passage quoted at greater length in Chapter 6, gives two
reasons for the similarity between a lyrical and a prose rhythm. Since the
lyric poets, such as Simonides, "compose their strophes in many metres"
and make their "clauses vary from time to time in length and form," making their divisions irregular, "they hinder our apprehension of any uniform

rhythm, and so they produce, as by design, in lyric poems a great likeness to prose" (*On Lit. Comp.*, ch. XXVI). In English, of course, only one meter is normally used throughout the poem, however varied it and the stanzaic structure may be. Bacon's distinction of these shorter genres from "Poesy" and their reference to dialectical as well as rhetorical disciplines, is compatible with the return to the classical attitudes concerning lyric poetry.

To the two qualities of the lyric, rhythmical flexibility and simple word order, that, as they are described in the classical treatises, are consistent with the plain style, may be added a third: unlimited freedom of subject matter.[2] In Martial and Catullus, for instance, the lyric may claim the same prerogative as the epigram, since one cannot be distinguished from the other, as Pliny points out (*Epist.* IV.14). Despite the fact that under the Petrarchan influence the lyric became associated with the *genus floridum* and almost restricted to a poem which dealt with love, the thorough classical scholar of the Renaissance, such as J. C. Scaliger, was quite explicit about its versatility. Scaliger writes of the lyric as Erasmus writes of the epistle:

> Horace clearly shows the subject matter of lyrics. Thus it seems to me that it is right to put into lyric meters whatever can be included in a short poem: praises, loves, quarrels, insults, revelries, reproofs, vows, urgings to and against self-indulgence, desires, complaints, explanations of places and times, new advice, counsel for and against undertaking an occupation, invitations, refusals, dissuasions, execrations, and whatever else. This poem, moreover, loves a freedom of mind no less than satires or epigrams.[3]

The lyric is described in the same terms as the classical epigram. Jonson, then, in returning to the classical tradition and extending these qualities of the plain style to the lyric, is able to make use of the philosophical attitudes and the stylistic intentions of the plain style in his short poems.

THE ODES AND DIVINE POEMS

The extension of the plain style into the more intricately formal genres, which usually employed the high or middle styles, is particularly apparent in Jonson's odes. In general, Jonson did not like a strict and complicated stanzaic form, believing that if the stanza had to be repeated often, it would lead him beyond his matter. The subject matter of most of the odes is serious, and their plain and direct style shows the extended freedom of the *genus humile* to treat any type of material. It is, in fact, the flexibility of the plain style, operating within the intricate stanzaic form, that gives the odes much of their power.

Jonson's earliest ode, "An Ode to Iames Earle of Desmond, writ in Queene Elizabeths time, since lost, and recovered" (VIII, 176), attempts a higher style and fails. The rhetoric becomes grandiloquent, for most of the poem is invocation of one sort or another, and the discursive structure is confused. It begins:

> Where art thou, *Genius?* I should use
> Thy present Aide: Arise Invention,
> Wake, and put on the wings of *Pindars* Muse,
> To towre with my intention
> High, as his mind, that doth advance
> Her upright head, above the reach of Chance,
> Or the times envie:
> *Cynthius,* I applie
> My bolder numbers to thy golden *Lyre*:
> O, then inspire
> Thy Priest in this strange rapture; heat my braine
> With *Delphick* fire:
> That I may sing my thoughts, in some unvulgar straine.
>   (ll. 1–13)

The second stanza goes on: "Rich beame of honour, shed your light/On these darke rymes," that they may reveal the virtues of Desmond, held in the Tower on suspicion of treason. Within the context of the stanza the "beame of honour" most probably refers to Desmond himself, but the stanzaic transition is obscure. The third stanza consoles the Earl by pointing out that his innocence is ample protection against injustice, and ends with a labored and grotesque anatomical image, which may show an early influence of Donne:

> O vertues fall,
> When her dead essence (like the Anatomie
> In Surgeons hall)
> Is but a Statists theame, to read Phlebotomie.
>   (ll. 36–39)

The fourth stanza (ll. 40–52) uses a long image describing the Cyclopes to illustrate the point that "Gold, that is perfect, will out-live the fire," a poetic device that Jonson later criticized more than once. The last stanza expresses Jonson's hopes for Desmond's release. The poem is overextended for what it has to say, and the metaphors and diction are complicated to the point of obscurity. The word order is often confusing and the tone is pretentious. Judging by his own stylistic principles, I should think that Jonson might even have excluded the ode from *Underwood* had he put the collection together himself.

On the other hand, his ode "To Sir William Sydney, on his Birth-day," (VIII, 120) although not the most ambitious or the greatest of the odes, exhibits as clearly as any the grace of the plain style. Like an epistle, the poem is a direct address to a particular person and deals with a particular situation; however, it is written in a song stanza as complicated as any Jonson wrote. Despite the intricate stanza, the diction and the word order are as simple and as near to prose as those of a letter.

> Now that the harth is crown'd with smiling fire,
>   And some doe drinke, and some doe dance,
>   Some ring,
>   Some sing,
>   And all doe striue t[o]'aduance
> The gladnesse higher:
>   Wherefore should I
>   Stand silent by,
>   Who not the least,
>   Both loue the cause, and authors of the feast?
>   . . . .
> This day sayes, then, the number of glad yeeres
>   Are iustly summ'd, that make you man;
>   Your vow
>   Must now
>   Striue all right wayes it can,
> T[o]'out-strip your peeres:
>   Since he doth lacke
>   Of going backe
>   Little, whose will
>   Doth vrge him to runne wrong, or to stand still.
>   . . . .
> 'T will be exacted of your name, whose sonne,
>   Whose nephew, whose grand-child you are;
>   And men
>   Will, then,
>   Say you haue follow'd farre,
> When well begunne:
>   Which must be now,
>   They teach you, how.
>   And he that stayes
>   To liue vntill to morrow' hath lost two dayes.
> So may you liue in honor, as in name,
>   If with this truth you be inspir'd,

> So may
> This day
> Be more, and long desir'd:
> And with the flame
> Of loue be bright,
> As with the light
> Of bone-fires. Then
> The Birth-day shines, when logs not burne, but men.
>
> (ll. 1–10, 21–30, 41–60)

The poem is a beautiful one of its kind, but it is apt to be dismissed as a graceful piece of occasional verse. Only by reading it slowly, paying attention to the caesural pauses and not overemphasizing the rhymes, does one become aware of the quietness of tone and subtlety of movement that are achieved by the controlled variation of the syntactical unit against the rhythmical unit of the verse line. The complicated pattern of the stanza will elude one, as Dionysius says of Simonides, although one will be aware of the rhythmical variation that it is in part responsible for. If one prints this poem as prose, as Bircov did Horace's ode, one will see that the word order is that of the spoken language. Here is the first stanza:

> Now that the harth is crown'd with smiling fire, and some doe drinke, and some doe dance, some ring, some sing, and all doe striue to aduance the gladnesse higher: wherefore should I stand silent by, who not the least, both loue the cause, and authors of the feast?

The ode is beautifully organized. The initial description of the hearth and the festivities, which honor Sidney's twenty-first birthday, provide a context and an occasion for Jonson's praise and advice, from which, in the last stanza, he makes a generalization in metaphorical terms that return to the opening description: "Then/The Birth-day shines, when logs not burne, but men." The language throughout has the characteristic quiet elegance of Jonson's best epistles. It is interesting to compare it, for example, with his epistolary tribute to Bacon's birthday, written in couplets and addressed to the protective household deity of York House (VIII, 225). The language of both poems has the simple diction of specific everyday speech: "How comes it all things so about the[e] smile?/The fire, the wine, the men! and in the midst,/Thou stand'st as if some Mysterie thou did'st!" For all its stanzaic elaboration, the Sidney ode has the same quietness and ease of statement that the couplets have.

"To Penshvrst" (VIII, 93) shares many of the qualities of the two birthday poems. I have no defensible reason for treating it with the odes rather

than with the epistles or even the epigrams; the greater part of the poem,
the description of Penshurst itself, has more in common with the epistle
"To Sir Robert Wroth" than, perhaps, with any other of Jonson's poems.
It is, however, like the poem on Bacon's birthday, addressed to a place
rather than to a person, and since it was probably the hearth of Penshurst
before which William Sidney celebrated his birthday and by which Jonson
did not stand silent, it seems, perhaps only by association, to share some of
the feeling of the birthday ode. It begins by a direct address:

> Thou art not, PENSHVRST, built to enuious show,
>   Of touch, or marble; nor canst boast a row
> Of polish'd pillars, or a roofe of gold:
>   Thou hast no lantherne, whereof tales are told;
> Or stayre, or courts; but stand'st an ancient pile,
> And these grudg'd at, art reuerenc'd the while.
>   (ll. 1–6)

The poem then continues with a description of the grounds, where

> The earely cherry, with the later plum,
>   Fig, grape, and quince, each in his time doth come.
>   (ll. 41–42)

The praise of the place culminates, as one might expect, in the praise of
the moral integrity of the owners, and, as in the ode, Jonson conveys a sense
of his own participation in the great household and a feeling that it will
slight neither his talents nor his comforts. The Sidney table is one

> Where comes no guest, but is allow'd to eate,
>   Without his feare, and of thy lords owne meate:
> Where the same beere, and bread, and selfe-same wine,
>   That is his Lordships, shall be also mine.
> And I not faine to sit (as some, this day,
>   At great mens tables) and yet dine away.
> Here no man tells my cups; nor, standing by,
>   A waiter, doth my gluttony enuy:
> But giues me what I call, and lets me eate,
>   He knowes, below, he shall finde plentie of meate,
> Thy tables hoord not vp for the next day,
>   Nor, when I take my lodging, need I pray
> For fire, or lights, or liuorie: all is there;
>   As if thou, then, wert mine, or I raign'd here:
> There's nothing I can wish, for which I stay.
>   (ll. 61–75)

Jonson does not simply praise the liberality of the Sidney household, but, characteristically, describes his own experience there to show how he himself has never lacked anything.[4] The movement of the lines is completely relaxed without ever being loose, and the apparently effortless control of the continually moving caesura maintains a quiet and perpetual rhythm, which, almost without being perceived, gives life to the verse. As the Sidney ode ends with a comparison of the fire in the hearth to the love with which the tenant should live his life, so Penshurst is praised for the fullness with which its occupants have led their lives:

> Now, PENSHVRST, they that will proportion thee
>   With other edifices, when they see
> Those proud, ambitious heaps, and nothing else,
>   May say, their lords haue built, but thy lord dwells.

> (ll.99–102)

The shortest ode Jonson wrote is among the finest of his poems (VIII, 180).

> High-spirited friend,
> I send nor Balmes, nor Cor'sives to your wound,
>   Your fate hath found
> A gentler, and more agile hand, to tend
> The Cure of that, which is but corporall,
> And doubtfull Dayes (which were nam'd *Criticall,*)
>   Have made their fairest flight,
>   And now are out of sight.
> Yet doth some wholsome Physick for the mind,
>   Wrapt in this paper lie,
> Which in the taking if you mis-apply,
>   You are unkind.
>
>   Your covetous hand,
> Happy in that faire honour it hath gain'd,
>   Must now be rayn'd.
> True valour doth her owne renowne command
> In one full Action; nor have you now more
> To doe, then be a husband of that store.
>   Thinke but how deare you bought
>   This same which you have caught,
> Such thoughts wil make you more in love with truth.
>   'Tis wisdome, and that high,
> For men to use their fortune reverently,
>   Even in youth.

The person addressed has not been identified, but some circumstances of his life and a great deal of his personal character are given indirectly in the poem. He seems to have been a somewhat impetuous and ambitious young man, who sought his fortune in war or in a duel, distinguished himself in action, and was severely wounded. Jonson advises him, since it takes only one battle to prove one's courage, not to challenge fortune again, which is a dangerous practice even for a young man, but to remember how much his gaining a reputation for valor has already cost him. The character and situation of the person addressed, in the absence of any specific evidence, might fit any number of Jonson's friends, the most likely person, perhaps, being Sir John Roe.[5] Despite the complex stanza, the structure and style of the ode are essentially those of the epistle, and Jonson might have written the poem in couplets without greatly changing the quality of feeling. It is the prerogative of the epistle to send personal advice to friends, which, if offered in some other way, might be offensive, and Jonson adopts this excuse. However elegant in diction, it is the constantly changing relation between the syntactical units and the length of the lines which gives to the poem an informal flexibility consistent with its purpose of friendly admonishment. The first sentence is a fine example of the caesural variation of the *sermo*; the run-over lines obscure the demands of the complicated stanza just enough to suggest the informal address without losing the curious tone achieved by not compromising the word order of ordinary prose in working out the intricate form. The diction is current as well as elegant; we still use the word "critical" in precisely the same way both in ordinary speech and in medical jargon. And, finally, as in all the best examples of the style, the didactic content arises so naturally out of the situation that the precept is indistinguishable from the feeling.

The ode "To the immortall memorie, and friendship of that noble paire, Sir Lvcivs Cary, and Sir H. Morison" is more ambitious and less successful (VIII, 242). It is composed of twelve stanzas divided into four groups, each group consisting of three stanzas in the same sequence, called "the turne," "the counter-turne," and "the stand," which correspond to the Pindaric order of the strophe, antistrophe, and epode. The poem is written to console Cary for the death of his friend Morison. The following is an abridged paraphrase. An infant being born during Hannibal's taking of the town of Saguntum returned to the womb to die and so fortunately escaped the horrors of the pillaging; so would all infants could they but foresee the miseries of their future life (ll. 1–20). It is not the length of life but how well it is lived that counts; it is better that that man who "For three of his foure-score" years did no good should have died at twenty (ll. 21–42). Morison died young, but his brief life was an example for all men, for life is evaluated by each action's timeliness and execution, not by the accumulation of separated and trivial actions. One cannot judge how well a man has lived by how long he has lived, as one might value a tree for its size; a flower reaches a greater perfection in a few short days, and, though the tree stands longer, it will "fall a logge at last" (ll. 43–74). Cary, then, should not long lament his friend, who now has gained immortality; even though they are separated, the two friends, like two stars in a small contellation temporarily separated, must continue to shine, though one illuminate heaven and one the earth (ll. 75–96). And so they will, since their friendship was not made by chance nor for profit nor over wine, but out of a common love of goodness, which, in the similarity of what they loved, made them copies of each other, and they in turn became a model of friendship for men to emulate (ll. 97–128).

The poem as a whole is too long for what it has to say. Several of the stanzas simply repeat what has been said before, either directly or metaphorically, seemingly in order to fill out the triple stanza pattern. The ode opens in a more rhetorical style than that used in its most successful stanzas. The first two stanzas develop, in effect, an hyperbole in which the writing is "frigid." The second stanza, except for the fifth and sixth lines, simply lists the horrors of war, without any particularization from Jonson's own experience, as a kind of formula reminiscent of the early English traditions of didactic poetry:

> Did wiser Nature draw thee back,
> From out the horrour of that sack?
> Where shame, faith, honour, and regard of right
> Lay trampled on; the deeds of death, and night,
> Urg'd, hurried forth, and horld
> Upon th'affrighted world:
> Sword, fire, and famine, with fell fury met;
> And all on utmost ruine set;
> As, could they but lifes miseries fore-see,
> No doubt all Infants would returne like thee.
> (ll. 11–20)

The hyperbole of the infant's retreat before the miseries of the world is frigid here not only because, as Demetrius says, "it suggests something impossible" but because the miseries themselves are not really brought to life. The lines, "Sword, fire, and famine, with fell fury met;/And all on utmost ruine set," could have been spoken by the chorus in an old morality play. Compare lines 19 and 20 above, for instance, with two lines in Jonson's epigram "On my First Sonne": "To haue so soone scap'd worlds, and fleshes rage,/And, if no other miserie, yet age" express essentially the same thought, but they have all the weight of Jonson's personal observations behind them. They are not an exaggerated rhetorical figure, but a plain statement about the probabilities of human life.

In the third and fourth stanzas of the ode, Jonson returns to a plainer style. Here, in some of the best writing in the entire poem, he gives a satirical portrait of a nobleman, complete in itself, but only indirectly connected with the subject: by describing someone else, he shows what Morison is not. The structure of the ode is similar to that of Jonson's "An Epistle to a Friend, to perswade him to the Warres" where the advantages of being in the war are demonstrated by the reasons why it is dangerous to stay at home. In a eulogy of the length of this ode the method is useful, since there are only so many things one can praise a man for, but the danger is great that the poem will become overextended and fragmentary, and the stanza simply commits the poet to longer individual fragments than the couplet does. For this reason it is even more important for the ode to be compact and tightly organized than it is for a poem written in Jonson's favorite form.

The ode is not free from poor writing. The lines which begin the fifth stanza, "Alas, but *Morison* fell young:/Hee never fell, thou fall'st, my tongue," could not fall more flatly themselves. The comparison of the friendship to a constellation is not inappropriate, but it is awkwardly handled. The last three stanzas deal with the familiar theme of the virtues of friendship. They are well written but not up to Jonson's best treatments of the subject, and they do not lessen the feeling that the poem is too long and that it repeats ideas which are not sufficiently complicated, either in content or in feeling, to support the repetition.

Jonson's less interesting odes make little use of the qualities of his own style. The most elaborate was written in honor of the publication of *Pancharis* by his friend Hugh Holland (VIII, 366). It is a graceful allegorical description of a black swan's flight over the British Isles, enumerating geographically the places to which the author's fame will extend, but it is entirely composed of ornamental detail and makes no effort to deal with human nature. No more successful is his "Ode gratulatorie," which compares the return of Jerome Weston "from his Embassie" to the return of spring (VIII, 250). The compliment seems perfunctory, and the natural description is undistinguished.

The emotional intensity of the three odes that Jonson wrote to himself sometimes makes it difficult to see that they owe their essential power to

the qualities of the plain style. The subject itself is in accord with the
Senecan aim to understand one's own experience. It is to the application
of such an aim by the Latin satirists, however, that the odes are most indebted for their tone and their particular use of the plain style, and the
connection between them and Jonson's own satire is extraordinarily close.
This connection is most easily seen in the ode on the failure of *The New
Inne* (VI, 492). The plain diction, the prose word order, and the satirical
detail, carefully drawn from particular observations of daily life, make the
poem a satirical epistle to himself, written in stanzas rather than in
couplets.

> Come leaue the lothed stage,
> And the more lothsome age:
> Where pride, and impudence (in faction knit)
> Vsurpe the chaire of wit!
> Indicting, and arraigning euery day
> Something they call a Play.
> Let their fastidious, vaine
> Commission of the braine
> Run on, and rage, sweat, censure, and condemn:
> They were not made for thee, lesse, thou for them.
>
> (ll. 1–10)

It is foolish, Jonson goes on in the succeeding stanzas, to cater to the corrupt tastes of an audience whose "palate's with the swine." Some moldy
tale like *Pericles,* stale as an old crust, serving as a whole meal, may be
thrown into its "almes-basket of wit" to feed "Braue *plush,* and *veluet-
men."* The details of these stanzas, which form the main body of the
poem, are very similar to Jonson's other satirical descriptions of the stage,
and, in conformity with the structure of satire, he continues in the fifth
stanza by making the generalization which the preceding observations
suggest:

> Leaue things so prostitute,
> And take the *Alcaick* Lute;
> Or thine owne *Horace,* or *Anacreons* Lyre;
> Warme thee, by *Pindares* fire:
> And though thy nerues be shrunke, and blood be cold,
> Ere yeeres haue made thee old;
> Strike that disdaine-full heate
> Throughout, to their defeate:
> As curious fooles, and enuious of thy straine,
> May, blushing, sweare no palsey's in thy braine.

As is characteristic of him, the statement concerns his particular situation, in which his future position in literary warfare will be seriously restricted by his failing health, and conveys something of the feeling expressed in his epistles on his physical appearance. The subject and attitudes are so similar to those of the Latin satirists and the style to the English adaptations of the classical *sermo* that the ode is useful in showing the relation between the other odes addressed to himself and the more conventional genres of the plain style.

Although in the other two odes to himself Jonson occasionally uses a more elevated diction, the poems bear the same resemblance to satire as his "Come leaue the lothed stage." This resemblance can be seen most clearly if one compares them with "An Apologeticall Dialogue," which is appended to *Poetaster* (IV, 324). In the dialogue Jonson defends himself and the mission of satire in the same way as Horace does in the first satire of his second book. Both of these odes borrow some lines from the apology. The conversational tone carries over from the dialogue to the odes, not just because of the identical lines, but because of the directness of their address to the author and the reader. The first, "Yff Men, and tymes were nowe" (VIII, 419), deals with Jonson's literary position and his own state of mind at a time when none is regarded who "hath not Countrye impudence enough to laughe att arte," though, like a blaze of straw, "Hee dyes wᵗʰ an Ill sent." Jonson alters the arrangement of the words surprisingly little in adapting pentameter lines to a stanza whose lines are varied in length, another indication of his particular concern for idiomatic syntax. Certain details are reminiscent of his epigrams, and lines 24–27 recall his epistolary descriptions of his own person.

The most famous, and the greatest, ode to himself combines all the qualities I have been discussing with certain rhetorical devices that were permitted by the classical plain style (VIII, 174).

> Where do'st thou carelesse lie,
>   Buried in ease and sloth?
> Knowledge, that sleepes, doth die;
> And this Securitie,
>   It is the common Moath,
> That eats on wits, and Arts, and [oft] destroyes them both.
>
> Are all th'*Aonian* springs
>   Dri'd up? lyes *Thespia* wast?
> Doth *Clarius* Harp want strings,
> That not a Nymph now sings?

Or droop they as disgrac't,
To see their Seats and Bowers by chattring Pies defac't?

If hence thy silence be,
   As 'tis too just a cause;
Let this thought quicken thee,
Minds that are great and free,
   Should not on fortune pause,
'Tis crowne enough to vertue still, her owne applause.

What though the greedie Frie
   Be taken with false Baytes
Of worded Balladrie,
And thinke it Poësie?
   They die with their conceits,
And only pitious scorne, upon their folly waites.

Then take in hand thy Lyre,
   Strike in thy proper straine,
With *Japhets* lyne, aspire[6]
Sols Chariot for new fire,
   To give the world againe:
Who aided him, will thee, the issue of *Joves* braine.

And since our Daintie age,
   Cannot indure reproofe,
Make not thy selfe a Page,
To that strumpet the Stage,
   But sing high and aloofe,
Safe from the wolves black jaw, and the dull Asses hoofe.

The most obvious rhetorical device used here is the substitution of a descriptive epithet for a proper name, such as *"Japhets* lyne" for Prometheus and "the issue of *Joves* braine" for Minerva. This figure, however, usually called *antonomasia,* was included with metaphor under figures of thought, or tropes, rather than under figures of diction, or schemes. Although the plain style repudiated schemes, it encouraged a moderate use of tropes, especially metaphors, and Jonson is not violating its tenets. The figure makes these lines less direct, but it is used so sparingly that it does not alter the tone or concision of the poem as a whole. The mythological reference is used here almost as a device of brevity, and hence, like a kind of *metonymia,* which "serueth aptly to breuity,"[7] is not decorative but rather condenses and elucidates Jonson's intention to write a specific kind of poetry. The fire, which Prometheus stole with the help of Minerva, goddess of wisdom, connotes an intellectual power, for with it Prometheus, who invented the human arts, gave his human clay figures knowledge and life. When Jonson strikes his "proper straine" in verse, he will write from knowledge, a knowledge like Horace's, gained out of use and experience.

The ode is an introspective meditation on the causes and dangers of the poet's having ceased to write. He implies that the causes were unworthy of him because they were motivated by the injury that his critics had given to his self-esteem, rather than by any principle. The dangers of his inactivity are far greater than the injury to his pride, however, since knowledge must be used if it is to be kept, and minds to be truly free must not depend upon the judgments of the ignorant, who will "die with their conceits." The poet, then, in order to be free of the ignorant and at the same time to write, must turn from the stage to the smaller audience of learned men. His poems may then make the greatest possible use of his knowledge, and his poetic talent may enable others to share in that knowledge. The ode is a philosophical statement about the powers of the human mind and the powers of literature if it properly makes use of the mind. Jonson's attitudes are completely consistent with the philosophical origins of the Attic style.

Stylistically, Jonson seldom varies from a prose word order, and the diction, with the exception of the classical allusions, is that of ordinary usage. The five six-syllable lines of each stanza are nearly all end-stopped, though lightly for the most part, and the rhythmical tension is built up to the last verse, where it is released in a twelve-syllable line. It is not dispersed suddenly, however, but by degrees, for most of the hexameters are slowed down by internal caesuras. The effect is one of a strong movement kept tightly under control, and the feeling of control gives the verse a typical Jonsonian quietness of tone. The syntactical units, which end in the middle and much more often at the end of the short lines, break up the rhythmical unit of the stanza in the same way that the caesuras break up the rhythmical unit of the couplet. The principle of variation is the same in both forms. The stanza gives the impression of a certain emotional intensity—not to be mistaken for rhetorical elevation, for there are few purely rhetorical devices—because it tends to compress the accumulation of personal, introspective detail into generalization, increasing the natural elegance of the Attic style.

In his few religious poems, Jonson extends the style of the odes to "matters," as Puttenham writes, "that concerne the Gods and diuine things" which are to be treated by "Poets *Hymnick*."[8] Extending the epistolary style, the *alter sermo,* to divine matters as well as human (*rei diuinae aut humanae*),[9] Lipsius, by his Stoic stylistic principles, virtually made identical the styles appropriate to philosophical and theological subjects. The style became what amounts to a technique of contemplation, a method for defining in a short meditative poem the poet's feeling about a complicated subject. The technique itself encouraged a greater psychological analysis in secular terms of the religious experience, which has been variously accounted for in the Metaphysical poets. Vives describes the contemplative style as essentially the plain style:

> Contemplation requires learned words, appropriate to their subject, a plain composition, fitted, clear, and more concerned with truth than with expression, a style subtly sensitive to things experienced (*oratio-nem sensis subtilem*), quiet, serious, chaste, modest, and, as Cicero says, one which you would call a discourse (*sermonem*) rather than an oration (*orationem*).[10]

Later on he comments that "a poem ought not to be written about our religious mysteries and highest faith unless it is brief, spare, and reserved."[11]

If one excludes his epitaphs and such epigrams as "Of Death" and "Of Life, and Death" (VIII, 37, 53), the group of three poems entitled "The Sinners Sacrifice" (VIII, 127–30) and "To Heaven" (VIII, 122) constitute Jonson's religious poetry.[12] Of the triad the second poem, "A Hymne to God the Father," is the best. It uses the plainest possible diction and, except for one inversion in the last stanza, a word order proper to prose:

> If thou hadst not
>   Beene sterne to mee,
>   But left me free,
> I had forgot
>   My selfe and thee.
>
> For, sin's so sweet,
>   As minds ill bent
>   Rarely repent,
> Untill they meet
>   Their punishment.
>   (ll. 7–18)

The style is similar to Herbert's, which draws upon the plain styles of both the native and classical traditions.[13]

Jonson's "To Heaven" (VIII, 122) is one of the finest religious poems of the seventeenth century. The rhythm and its qualification of feeling, as discussed in Chapter 6, exhibit fully the classical conventions of prosody restrained to the formal demands of the English couplet. The poem is a religious and moral meditation, and the style, developed for this purpose, provides a method of introspection. Jonson does not attempt to isolate the religious experience in order to suggest its mystical qualities, but places it, as he does secular love, in the context of his entire personal experience:[14]

> Good, and great GOD, can I not thinke of thee,
>   But it must, straight, my melancholy bee?
> Is it interpreted in me disease,
>   That, laden with my sinnes, I seeke for ease?
>
> (ll. 1-4)

Jonson addresses God in the secular language of contemporary psychology. The disease in the third line refers to the supposed state of melancholia mentioned in the second. Starting with these questions, the poem considers the possibility and implies the temptation of despair over human imperfection and the consequent human isolation from God. It ends with the extraordinary lines that may have suggested to Herbert the conclusion of "The Pulley." Jonson's lines are finer than Herbert's, and for a significant reason. There is a very slight connotation of the specialized diction and phraseology characteristic of the hymnal or conventional religious poem in the last line of "The Pulley": ". . . yet wearinesse/May tosse him to my breast." The word "toss," which Jonson uses himself in his "Hymne to God the Father," suggests such a context more than the vocabulary he uses in "To Heaven," despite its phraseology drawn from the Bible. The last line of "The Pulley" lacks the urbanity of diction and movement which comes from the conversational idiom of a completely unspecialized language:

> lest it be thought the breath
> Of discontent; or that these prayers bee
> For wearinesse of life, not loue of thee.

The style is, as Vives says, subtly sensitive to things experienced, quiet, serious, chaste.

THE SONGS AND LOVE POEMS

Gif your purpose be of loue, to vse commoun language, with some passionate wordis.
KING JAMES VI, *Ane schort Treatise*

The plain style, with its intention to describe accurately the personal experience of real situations, brought to the English love poem, which had before been the property of the *genus floridum,* an intensity of feeling derived not only from the candid sincerity of the author's statement but also from the urbane evaluation of the position that any specific kind of love should hold in relation to the human context of his experience as a whole. In this sense, the style encouraged in the love poem that same critical awareness of human values and human situations which it had first brought to satire from its Socratic origins. Such an awareness can be felt in some of the love poems of Wyatt, Gascoigne, and Sidney, in whose *Astrophel and Stella* there is a good deal of plain writing which is concerned with a precise moral evaluation of his feelings for Stella. Sidney, however, did not use the native plain style consistently or from principles that were firmly established. It was Jonson and Donne and their followers who adopted the attitudes and the traditional stylistic qualities of the classical plain style and extended them, by the authority of certain principles of the style itself, into all genres of poetry.

In Jonson, as in Catullus and Martial, it is often difficult to distinguish between an epigram and a lyric or song; it is best to do as Pliny does and include them all under one general title (*Epist.* IV, 14). The lyric, for instance, "That Women are bvt Mens shaddowes," is called a song in the carefully edited *Forest* (VIII, 104), but Drummond refers to it as an epigram (I, 142). With their decorative ornament often stripped away, Jonson's songs primarily depend on their clear idiom and the relationship of their syntax to the length of line as it is extended through a complicated stanza to convey their feeling precisely. This can be seen in the simplest type of lyric he wrote, the graceful compliment, such as that in *Cynthias Revels* (IV, 161), "Qveene, *and* Huntresse, *chaste, and faire,*" written to Elizabeth, the "*Goddesse, excellently bright.*" The beauty of the poem comes not from the decorative details or any spectacular phrase, but from the Horatian purity of diction and from the arrangement, or *dispositio*, of the phrasing within the structure of the seven-syllable line. The phrase "excellently bright" is an example of Jonson's typical avoidance of the conventional and often redundant sensory modifier, which might have been used to emphasize the visual quality of brightness. The adverb "excellently" refers to the activity of excelling all others in brightness; Jonson implies that perfection is an activity, as virtue is an activity for Aristotle. This attitude, which can be seen throughout his poems to his friends and the men he admired, is responsible here for giving vitality to a line, upon which a simple complimentary song turns, which would have been only a formula in the conventional lyrics of the day.

Jonson's songs are often written as logical demonstrations of proposi-

tions and have the dialectical economy of a prose argument.[15] A good
example is the lyric just mentioned, "That Women are bvt Mens shaddowes" (VIII, 104):

> Follow a shaddow, it still flies you;
>   Seeme to flye it, it will pursue:
> So court a mistris, shee denyes you;
>   Let her alone, shee will court you.
> Say, are not women truely, then,
>   Stil'd but the shaddowes of vs men?
> At morne, and euen, shades are longest;
>   At noone, they are or short, or none:
> So men at weakest, they are strongest,
>   But grant vs perfect, they're not knowne.
> Say, are not women truely, then,
>   Stil'd but the shaddowes of vs men?

The poem is a close adaptation of an epigram in Barthelemi Aneau's *Picta
Poesis*, which Jonson has simplified in a characteristic way by leaving out the
supporting allusion to classical mythology. A translation of the Latin lines
*Phoebum virgo fugit Daphne inviolata sequentem./Echo Narcissum dum
fugit insequitur* would have been mere decoration in his poem.[16] Some of
the songs in *Underwood* also have a dialectical structure, similar to that
of Donne. "A Song Apologetique," which is spoken "In the person of
Woman-kind" (VIII, 145) and the poem which follows it, "In defence of
their Inconstancie," are identical in their style. Their language is terse and
bluntly idiomatic and may be easily distinguished from that of "I Love, and
he loves me againe" (VIII, 147) which is more in the style of Sidney. Here,
their conversational tone and dialectical structure are used for wit, in the
manner of Donne, but Jonson also adapted them to didactic lyrics similar
to his odes, such as "Against Iealousie" (VIII, 150), without loss of flexibility
or authority.

    The best introduction to the love poems that are most characteristically
Jonson's is his own introductory poem to the *Forest*, "Why I write not of
Love" (VIII, 93):

> Some act of *Loue's* bound to reherse,
> I thought to binde him, in my verse:
> Which when he felt, Away (quoth hee)
> Can Poets hope to fetter mee?
> It is enough, they once did get
> MARS, and my *Mother*, in their net;

I weare not these my wings in vaine.
With which he fled me: and againe,
Into my ri'mes could ne're be got
By any arte. Then wonder not,
That since, my numbers are so cold,
When *Loue* is fled, and I grow old.

The reasons Jonson gives for his rejection of the Petrarchan hero reveal the attitudes which give his love poetry its power. He places the experience of love in the context of his experience as a whole. Hence, he is not pre-occupied with isolating it in order to give it more emphasis than it would ordinarily seem to have; he does not wish to strip from it the ethical and circumstantial world in which it must take place. To do so would be to distort the truth. Real lovers exist in a real world. Hence, love is only one of their problems, and their feelings about it are greatly complicated by the others. This is why Jonson's poems seem to be less expressions of love than statements about it. They take into account his age and his appearance, both of which he may reasonably expect to give him difficulty. His first intention, however, is to tell the truth about himself and to take his chances (which, according to Drummond, seem to have been pretty good). His honesty, as he implies in one of his elegies (VIII, 199), should be as persuasive as the poeticizing of the young and the facile:

Let me be what I am, as *Virgil* cold;
    As *Horace* fat; or as *Anacreon* old;
No Poets verses yet did ever move,
    Whose Readers did not thinke he was in love.
Who shall forbid me then in Rithme to bee
    As light, and active as the youngest hee
That from the Muses fountaines doth indorse
    His lynes, and hourely sits the Poets horse?
                                    (ll. 1–8)

The variety of tone and feeling which Jonson could command in the love poems without violating his stylistic principles or greatly distorting the reader's impression of his personality can only indicate the breadth and receptiveness of that personality rather than the narrowness and violence often attributed to it.

More complicated than any single love poem is a group of short lyrics entitled "A Celebration of Charis in ten Lyrick Peeces" (VIII, 131–42). To my knowledge, the terms and their sources, which make up the general context in which the poems are written, have not been discussed in detail, nor has the immediate situation described in the poem been examined in relation to its most celebrated analogues in the literature of the Renaissance. More often than not particular poems have been detached and admired— and, to be sure, some of the individual lyrics are better than others—but the attitudes expressed in the sequence and most of the feelings associated with them disappear when the poems are separated. Furthermore, unless the context is clear, a good deal of misinterpretation can arise from impos- ing certain general attitudes of Jonson toward contemporary poetic con- ventions—attitudes that are supported by certain poems in the sequence— upon all the poems of the sequence. Such an imposition leads the inter- preter very often to see more parody than was intended, and, consequently, to miss the feeling of regret for the loss of certain Neoplatonic values, no longer applicable to real experience, that the poet was trying to define.[17] I shall go through the sequence in some detail first, in order to establish the particular ideas and conventions against which, it might be said, Jonson is setting his poems. My intention is not to establish specific sources, since the ideas involved had an enormous circulation and even verbal similarities are misleading, but to give a point of reference around which to trace Jon- son's attitudes toward the conventions he is using. Second, I shall discuss what he is actually saying about his subject and the feeling he is trying to communicate, for which the context of conventions was simply a means. And, third, I shall comment on several of the individual poems.

At first glance the "Celebration of Charis" seems to be Jonson's version of a Petrarchan sonnet sequence celebrating a lady. If he were to write one, he might describe himself, as he does here, as a hopelessly ineffectual lover in the toils and turmoils of Cupid's world, a buffoon in the ordinary exercise of courtly love. Here he can treat himself and the Petrarchan con- ventions with playful urbanity and make the sonneteer out to be quite as ridiculous as he and Donne, along with the satirists, did formerly with their direct criticisms. But there is serious statement in the poems, which is not in negative or satirical terms, and which, judging from the rest of his work, Jonson would have taken seriously. The first poem in particular states an attitude not generally associated with the sonneteer, in insisting on the effi- cacy of language and truth in making love. The fact that in the sequence this finally fails to be sufficient does not mean that Jonson did not believe that the truth ought to be effective; he is simply commenting on what one generally finds in the world. Actually, the positive statements in the poems are rather idealistic and go far beyond the anti-Petrarchan objections to the sensuality of the court and the meaningless luxury of courtly rhetoric. The terms of the idealism are Neoplatonic rather than anti-Petrarchan, and Jonson's sequence seems more a version and an evaluation of the first two of Spenser's *Fowre Hymnes* than of a conventional Petrarchan sonnet cycle.[18]

The general context of Jonson's "Celebration" is the literary convention of the *discorso* or *questione d'amore* in the court of love. The convention of discussing a general proposition about love among a group of friends, each giving his particular opinion in the effort to reach an acceptable solution or definition, goes back at least to Plato's *Symposium*. From there the Neoplatonists drew the structure and many details of their theory of love, which they tried to synthesize with the doctrines of Christianity, and the dialectical intentions of the Platonic *sermo* offered a model for the philosophical treatment of the nature of love in the candid conversations of the informal gatherings of friends. The literary conventions of such *discorsi* became flexible to the extent of offering a situation or "framework" for nearly any subject matter, from the stories of Boccaccio's *Decameron*, which treated of love but not always philosophically, to Ficino's attempt to return to the form of the *Symposium* in his commentary on its philosophy. From such commentaries the Neoplatonic ideas of love were carried into courtesy books such as Castiglione's *The Courtier*, which continued to utilize the dialogue form, each participant offering a different point of view on the subjects under discussion. It is in such a context, the conventions of which were used repeatedly throughout Europe in the Renaissance, that it is helpful to examine the structure of Jonson's sequence of lyrics, and it is in the Neoplatonic extensions of Plato's terms that the individual poems can best be understood.

Although it is not specifically indicated in the sequence that other people are present besides the speaker, from the beginning the "Celebration" conforms in subject and structure to the general discussions of love as exemplified in *The Courtier*.[19] Jonson's "Excuse for loving" is offered as a response to a hypothetical criticism of an old man's loving, the propriety of which is attacked and defended extensively in the fourth book and discussed occasionally throughout the first three books of *The Courtier*. Bembo's defense of his loving is in Neoplatonic terms, which refer back through Ficino to their origins in the *Symposium* and coincide with Jonson's reasons. There follows a whimsical narration of his encounter with Cupid, which is used partly as a device to describe Charis, a central purpose of the participants in the *discorsi* being to tell whom they would most like to love and how. Charis is then held to her promise to contribute her description of an ideal lover, and finally another lady offers her objection to such idealizations and frankly says, "'Tis one good part I'ld lie withall." One or more of such iconoclasts, holding various points of view, are conventionally included in the *discorsi* in order to enliven the dispute and to offer a supply of arguments to which the central speakers may respond.

As Signor Morello da Ortona is the plainest speaker from the sensual world in *The Courtier,* Lord Beaufort is the worldly courtier in Jonson's most detailed presentation of the courtly trial of a *questione* of love in *The New Inne* (III.ii). The scene from *The New Inne* (acted 1629) is useful as a gloss to the "Celebration" for several reasons. It gives a complete presentation of a disquisition in the court of love, so often the subject of the conventional *discorso,* which, although analogous to the total situation of the sequence of lyrics, is only fragmentarily implied in the "Celebration" itself. Also, it establishes Jonson's use of the Neoplatonic terminology and his adoption of it from Ficino in passages directly translated from his commentary on the *Symposium.* It demonstrates how seriously Jonson could apply the Neoplatonic terms, as well as the situation of the courtly discussion of love, in other genres than the masque, and it makes certain passages in Ficino's commentary available and convincing as explications for specific poems in the "Celebration."[20] In a good-humored parody of legal jargon and procedure Jonson has the Lady Frampul, the defendant, and Herbert Lovel, the appellant, sworn into the court of love, in which, upon his completing satisfactorily a description of love and later of valor, she must forfeit two kisses. In the particular details Jonson is obviously making fun of the procedure, but the general situation of making a definition of love before a group of people, and the definition itself, are to be taken perfectly seriously in terms of the play. "Tell vs," says the Lady, "what *Loue* is, that we may be sure/There's such a thing, and that it is in nature" (III.ii.59–60). Such was the convivial purpose of the *Symposium,* and in the courtesy books it takes the form of a description of the appearance, behavior, and intellectual qualifications of the ideal lover.[21] Lovel proceeds to give a Neoplatonic "definition" of love, and Lord Beaufort, the gay sensualist, breaks in with mildly erotic jokes and scoffs:

> I relish not these *philosophicall* feasts;
> Giue me a banquet o' sense, like that of *Ovid*:
> A forme, to take the eye; a voyce, mine eare;
> Pure *aromatiques,* to my sent; a soft,

> Smooth, deinty hand, to touch; and, for my taste,
> *Ambrosiack* kisses, to melt downe the palat.
> (III.ii.125–30)

Lovel praises the mind, and Beaufort responds "Gi' me the body, if it be a good one" (l. 155). Morello's observations in *The Courtier,* which will be referred to later, are parallel to Beaufort's and in the origin of the literary form they probably grow out of the urbanely witty, though enormously affectionate, spoofing of Socrates by Alcibiades in the *Symposium.* Finally, as Bembo describes his ideal lover as an older man, Lovel, with his *"Platonick* loue" (l. 238), is accepted by the Lady despite his age

> For, tho' he be somewhat strooke in yeares, and old
> Enough to be my father, he is wise,
> And onely wise men loue, the other couet.
> (III.ii.230–32)

The older man may win the lady by being wise, for it is not always youth and physical beauty that count, but, as the "Celebration" concedes, even under the best circumstances, it usually is.

In the first poem of the "Celebration" Jonson, too, is somewhat struck in years. Except for purposes of dating, it makes little difference whether he was actually fifty when he wrote the poem or whether he adopted that particular age to represent a man old enough to be at a disadvantage in a love affair, on the suggestion, perhaps, of Horace's Ode IV.i, of which he made one of his best translations (VIII, 292).[22] The sequence thus begins with "His Excuse for loving":

> Let it not your wonder move,
> Lesse your laughter; that I love.
> Though I now write fiftie yeares,
> I have had, and have my Peeres;
> Poëts, though divine, are men:
> Some have lov'd as old agen.
> And it is not alwayes face,
> Clothes, or Fortune gives the grace;
> Or the feature, or the youth:
> But the Language, and the Truth,
> With the Ardor, and the Passion,
> Gives the Lover weight, and fashion.
> If you then will read the Storie,
> First, prepare you to be sorie,
> That you never knew till now,
> Either whom to love, or how:

But be glad, as soone with me,
When you know, that this is she,
Of whose Beautie it was sung,
She shall make the old man young,
Keepe the middle age at stay,
And let nothing high decay,
Till she be the reason why,
All the world for love may die.

The assumptions against which Jonson is protesting are stated in *The Courtier,* particularly in the fourth book, and are the explicit occasion for Bembo's redefinition of love in Neoplatonic terms. A difficulty had arisen in discussing what kind of lover the ideal courtier should be, because all of his other qualities depended upon a knowledge and experience which only an older man could be expected to have, and it was generally granted that "in olde men love is a thing to bee jested at" (p. 119). "I can not see," Lord Gaspar says, "whan hee is well drawen in yeeres, howe it wyll stande well wyth hym to be a lover, considerynge (as it hath bine said the other night) Love frameth not with olde men, and the trickes that in yonge men be galauntnesse, courtesie and precisenesse so acceptable to women, in them are meere folies and fondnesse to be laughted at, and purchase him that useth them hatred of women and mockes of others. . . . I feare me, he woulde forgete to teach his Prince: and paraventure boyes would mocke him behinde his backe, and women would have none other delite in him but to make him a jesting stocke" (pp. 340–41). Bembo objects and, "somewhat settlinge hymselfe as thoughe he shoulde entreat uppon a waightie matter," begins his famous account of the stairway of love:

> My Lordes, to showe that olde menne maye love not onlie without sclaunder, but otherwhile more happilye then yonge menne, I must be enforced to make a litle discourse to declare what love is, and wherein consisteth the happinesse that lovers maye have. (p. 342)

Such a discourse on what love is should help to indicate whom to love, just as one of the purposes of Jonson's story is to teach the reader who "never knew till now,/Either whom to love, or how." Bembo is quite as methodical, for after he has shown by his discourse "that olde men may love more happelye then yonge," he goes on to show the manner in which they should love, to "show this excelent Courtier how to love contrarye to the wonted maner of the commune ignorant sort" (p. 352).[23]

In telling how to love, Bembo says the lover should lay aside "the blinde judgemente of the sense" and enjoy with the eye and ear, "the ministers of reason," the "two senses, which have litle bodelye substance in them," the foods that "feede the soul" (p. 353). Such recommendations were repeatedly formularized into idealistic commonplaces in Elizabethan love poetry, but Jonson gives them a vitality of practical application in the tone and implied circumstances of his statement. There is a sly sophistication in the word "alwayes," which suggests the ending of his "Storie," and implies his judgment on the impracticality of the idealized standards as well as on the people who cannot meet them:

> And it is not alwayes face,
> Clothes, or Fortune gives the grace;
> Or the feature, or the youth:
> But the Language, and the Truth ,
> With the Ardor, and the Passion,
> Gives the Lover weight, and fashion.

Although the wealthy and the handsome are nearly always the most successful lovers, it is worth saying that the rarer accomplishments, which take time and effort to achieve, should be appreciated, even though the chance of their being appreciated also by the person one desires is infinitesimal. The ardor and the passion refer to the intellectual energies necessary for the appreciation of the true and generalized beauty of the Neoplatonist in the same sense in which Lovel speaks of them in his definition of love.

> It is a flame, and ardor of the minde,
> Dead, in the proper corps, quick in anothers:
> Trans-ferres the Louer into the Loued.
>   (III.ii.96–98)

The ardor is the passion with which one dies in the metaphorical sense of losing one's own identity in the union with the loved one. The double meaning of the word "die" is rivaled in its frequency during the Renaissance only, perhaps, by the pun on the horns of a cuckold; whatever its ultimate source, however, and despite its popularity simply as an erotic quibble, its most detailed explication is the elaborate and philosophical explanation of the act of love in Ficino's commentary on the *Symposium*. As a gloss on the lines from *The New Inne,* Jonson's editors cite *oratio* II.viii: *Ille, inquit* [Plato], *amator animus est proprio in corpore mortuus, in alieno corpore vivens. . . . Moritur autem quisquis amat. Eius enim cogitatio, sui oblita semper in amato se versat.*[24] Jonson seems to be translating directly from Ficino, who offers here at some length the logical solution to the paradox in Neoplatonic terms, a paradox which Jonson uses to resolve his poem. Charis is the lady whose "Beautie" shall "make the old man young," or, perhaps as Bembo might put it, in the proper adoration of such a beauty "olde men may love more happelye then yonge" (p. 352). This beauty, since it transcends the physical world and leads the lover to the realm of permanent values, is able to keep everything worthwhile from degenerating, and the lady herself will become "the reason why,/All the world for love may die." The double meaning of the word "die" creates a double meaning in the word "world." Love of this lady will lead everybody ("All the world") to put aside his own identity to unite with her, and such a transcendent love will literally destroy the physical world in the minds of her lovers.

The next four poems in the series (2–5) describe Jonson's meeting and early wooing of Charis, a beautiful woman of James's court, in a jocular allegory of an adventure with Cupid. He treats Cupid humorously, but the humor is more urbane than caustic, and the urbanity permits him to see himself objectively in a ridiculous situation. He has made himself ridiculous by doing precisely what Castiglione said made old men in love appear foolish, that is, following the gallantry and devices of the young; Jonson has already lost a little of the decorum and dignity which were to be his excuse in the first place. But there is another Neoplatonic convention, originating in the *Symposium* itself, that can explain and in part justify his behavior. The greatest lover of the Platonic tradition was an old man of undignified appearance and unsavory personal habits, Socrates himself. "I shall praise Socrates in a figure which shall appear to him to be a caricature," Alcibiades declares at the end of the banquet, "and yet I do not mean to laugh at him, but only to speak the truth."

> I say then, that he is exactly like the masks of Silenus, which may be seen sitting in the statuaries' shops, having pipes and flutes in their mouths; and they are made to open in the middle, and there are images of gods inside them. I say also that he is like Marsyas the satyr. You will not deny, Socrates, that your face is like that of a satyr.[25]

In the second lyric, "How he saw her," Jonson describes how he ran to fetch Cupid when he saw Charis beautifully attired, how he removed Cupid's blindness and how Cupid was frightened by such beauty and ran away, and how he picked up the bow and arrow, intending to shoot Charis himself, when

she threw
Such a Lightning (as I drew)

At my face, that tooke my sight,
And my motion from me quite;
So that, there, I stood a stone,
Mock'd of all: and call'd of one
(Which with griefe and wrath I heard)
Cupids Statue with a Beard,
Or else one that plaid his Ape,
In a *Hercules*-his shape.[26]

(ll. 23–32)

Recalling the masks of Silenus-Socrates, Jonson sees himself as a bearded statue of Cupid or of a giant monkey, probably stooped and potbellied. Despite his undignified position, Jonson is in good company, and his similarity to Socrates does not depend solely on age or grotesque statuary which might associate Silenus with Cupid in some way beyond their usual comradeship. The Neoplatonists specifically identified Socrates with Cupid, and Jonson was apparently familiar with at least one of their treatments of the relationship. Ficino, in the second chapter of the seventh speech, entitled "Socrates was the true Lover and was like Cupid," discusses Alcibiades' humorous exchange with Socrates at the end of the *Symposium*: now that "the guests had sufficiently praised the God of lovers, it remained, naturally, for them to praise the true worshipers of this God," and it was "unanimously agreed that Socrates had loved most truly of all lovers."

> Have you not noticed, gentlemen, in what has already been said, that in describing Love Himself, Plato pictures the whole image of Socrates himself, and that he describes the appearance of that divinity from the appearance of Socrates as though true love and Socrates were exactly alike, and that therefore Socrates is the truest and most genuine lover of all? Come now, and recall to mind the picture of love. You will see pictured in it Socrates.[27]

The picture Ficino draws is that of a carelessly groomed, dirty old man, barefoot and practically naked. This is the archlover of the Neoplatonic tradition. It is not really a very great step from the dignified request in Jonson's excuse that no one laugh at his falling in love to his humorously disreputable picture of himself as an unshaven Cupid, "Mock'd of all," and described by one who, of course, is Charis herself.

Such a description, with its humorous realism and candor, is closely related to the epistolary self-portraits with their intentions to tell the truth, which are derived from the origins of the plain style. In the love poems, however, these intentions may be slightly qualified by the coincidence that one of the Platonic dialogues dealt with love with the candor and flexibility of the *sermo,* and the concepts of the *Symposium* carried with them into the later Neoplatonism the urbanely realistic and unflattering pictures of Socrates with the belly of a Silenus and the face of a satyr, along with the words of Diotima.[28] When, in "My Picture left in Scotland," Jonson describes, perhaps quite truthfully, his mountain belly and his rocky face and how they prevent his lady from listening to his words, his lines are moving, despite their grotesqueness, in the same way that Alcibiades' candid and affectionate raillery about his own failure to seduce Socrates is moving. It is with this tone of urbanity and objectivity that the "Celebration" is written, and, despite the details of simple parody which it contains, its feeling is complicated. Charis, like Molière's Célimène, has, in many way, more of the reader's sympathy than her idealistic suitor, and, despite his own predicament, Jonson accepts the situation.

In the third lyric, called "What hee suffered," after scorns like these, Jonson continues, she was content to give him back his sight and motion to torment him more. With the bow and arrows returned to Cupid, the god shoots him in the heart and leaves him helpless to revenge himself otherwise than "in either Prose, or Song,"

> Which how Dexterously I doe,
> Heare and make Example too.

The song celebrating Charis, "Her Triumph," the fourth in the sequence, follows. It is a curious mixture of classical and Renaissance sources, and, being a kind of interpolated piece in the sequence, like a song in a play, it neither advances the "storie" nor refines the terms or conventions of the sequence as a whole. The last two stanzas of the poem had already been used as a set piece, a song in *The Divell is an Asse* (II.vi.94–113), acted in 1616, and the general description in the first of Love's chariot, drawn from Ovid's *Metamorphoses* X and XV and *Amores* I.ii, had been followed in *The Haddington Masque* of 1608 (*Works,* VII, 250).

> See the Chariot at hand here of Love,
>   Wherein my Lady rideth!
> Each that drawes, is a Swan, or a Dove,
>   And well the Carre Love guideth.
> As she goes, all hearts doe duty
>   Unto her beauty;
> And enamour'd, doe wish, so they might
>   But enjoy such a sight,
> That they still were to run by her side,
> Th[o]rough Swords, th[o]rough Seas, whether she would ride.

Doe but looke on her eyes, they doe light
   All that Loves world compriseth!
Doe but looke on her Haire, it is bright
   As Loves starre when it riseth!
Doe but marke, her forehead's smoother
      Then words that sooth her!
And from her arched browes, such a grace
      Sheds it selfe through the face,
  As alone there triumphs to the life
All the Gaine, all the Good, of the Elements strife.
          (ll. 1–20)

The most detailed source of the first nine lines is Ovid's *Amores* I.ii.23–42, but the tenth line alludes to a Platonic observation, which, besides its adoption by Ovid in *Amores* I.ix, finds its way into the Neoplatonic love poetry of the Renaissance. In "An Hymne in Honovr of Love," for instance, Spenser says of Love:

Thou art his god, thou art his mightie guyde, . . .
Through seas, through flames, through thousand swords and speares.[29]
          (ll. 225, 228)

That Love will give the lover courage to follow him, in the form of the beloved, through dangers of all kinds is Phaedrus' reason for wishing in the *Symposium* that an army be made up of lovers, for they, rather than be dishonored before the eyes of their loved ones, would be ready to die a thousand deaths and, fighting at one another's sides, would overcome all men.[30] In the eyes of Alcibiades, Socrates, of course, fulfilled the ideal of the perfect soldier as well as of the perfect lover.

The last four lines of the second stanza of "Her Triumph" seem to refer more specifically to Neoplatonic commentary than to classical models. The light from the lady's eyes, which illuminates "All that Loves world compriseth," is easily associated with the divine light emanating from God, which is responsible for the harmonious proportion of parts that is called beautiful. Such proportion depends on a certain balanced combination of the four elements, *elementorum quattuor temperata complexio,* according to Ficino, so that the body will resemble the heavens in its harmony, undisturbed by any excessive humor. Beauty, then, is a certain grace, first infused into the angels by the illuminating light of God, and then into the souls of men and into the shapes of their bodies, *pulchritudinem esse gratiam quandam vivacem et spiritalem, dei radio illustrante angelo primum infusam; inde et animis hominum, corporumque figuris.*[31] This seems to be the context of Jonson's description of beauty as a grace, *gratia*, which sheds itself through the face, *infusa corporum figuris*, in such a way that the perfections, "all the Gaine, all the Good," of the proper balance of the otherwise competing elements, "the Elements strife," will be completely manifested. I shall refer later to the third stanza, which is partially adopted from Martial (V. xxxvii. 4-6).

The fifth poem of the sequence, "His discourse with Cupid," concludes his adventures with the god of love. Cupid, finding him composing verse, sees in his songs written about Charis a perfect description of his mother. Such an identification had been calculated from the beginning, since in the *Iliad* Charis is the wife of Hephaestus and therefore identified with Venus.[32] Cupid reads off the conventional physical charms listed, for which, he says, Homer and Anacreon had also praised her,[33] and concludes with some amazement, "Her very Name,/With my Mothers is the same." Jonson's reply is precisely what one would expect; he objects, and describes Charis as having the qualities that would enable her to respond to the sophisticated love he offers:

> I confesse all, I replide,
> And the Glasse hangs by her side,
> And the Girdle 'bout her waste,
> All is *Venus*: save unchaste.
> But alas, thou seest the least
> Of her good, who is the best
> Of her Sex; But could'st thou, *Love*,
> Call to mind the formes, that strove
> For the Apple, and those three
> Make in one, the same were shee.
> For this Beauty yet doth hide
> Something more then thou hast spi'd.
> Outward Grace weake love beguiles:
> Shee is *Venus*, when she smiles,
> But shee's *Juno*, when she walkes,
> And *Minerva*, when she talkes.
>
> (ll. 39-54)

Most ethical systems warn that the love beguiled by outward grace is weak, but in the context of the "Celebration" Jonson's line is a Neoplatonic formula, and Cupid, the power of sensual love, sees the least of the lady's perfections. Charis is Venus, it is true, "but" she is also Juno and Minerva. In Neoplatonic terms Minerva would be associated with the Venus Urania, or heavenly Venus, whose power is wisdom and intellection and whom

Plato, in the Symposium, and Ficino, in his commentary, distinguish from
the Venus Pandemos, or earthly Venus, the power of generation.³⁴ However hyperbolic the comparisons, Jonson is saying that Charis is a person to
be reckoned with, and, though she may be flirtatious, she is a prudent and
intelligent woman. The passage is important because it shows that, although the courtship fails, each was worthy of the other's desires, and that
Charis when she names the qualities of the lover she wants is probably
aware of the banality of some of her own requirements.

After having described the context in which the relationship takes place
and his attitude toward it, in the concluding five lyrics Jonson shows Charis
moving through the real world. In the sixth poem of the sequence, in
order to win a kiss, he writes a complimentary description of her participation in a wedding at Court. She surpasses the bride in beauty, and whether
she sits, walks, or dances, she is "more the eye, and talke/Of the Court, to
day, then all/Else that glister'd in *White-hall*." The seventh lyric is a song,
which Jonson recited to Drummond (*Conv. Dr.*, ll. 96–101), begging another kiss "on colour of mending the former"—as beautiful of its kind as
"Her Triumph." With no one around, why should she hesitate, he asks:

> I'le taste as lightly as the Bee,
> That doth but touch his flower, and flies away.

She gives in, but is too brief, since "What w'are but once to doe, we should
doe long," and Jonson, after these preliminary successes, brings her directly
to the point in the following poem, "Urging her of a promise," by insisting
that she say what kind of man she could love well, that is, take as a lover.
These last three poems explicitly adopt the conventions of the *discorsi*: the
fulfillment of a specific promise or of the conditions of a general agreement
among the participants to discuss a subject related to love, and very often,
as in the case of Lord Gaspar in *The Courtier,* to describe the most pleasing
type of lover to have. The other participants may take the liberty of inter-
rupting when they disagree, and they often do it for the sake of a pleasantry.

> *Charis* one day in discourse
> Had of Love, and of his force,
> Lightly promis'd, she would tell
> What a man she could love well:
> And that promise set on fire
> All that heard her, with desire.
> (ll. 1–6)

But she delays with excuses "spun every day," until Jonson threatens that
he will interrupt her daily habits and pleasures with his constant urging

unless she comply. There follows a humorous spoofing of the vanities of
a lady of fashion, which are characteristic not of Charis but of the trivial
sensuality of the courtly women represented by the lady who takes exception
to Charis's description. He is, of course, needling her when he lists the
activities she will be forced to give up:

> You shall neither eat, nor sleepe,
> No, nor forth your window peepe,
> With your emissarie eye,
> To fetch in the Formes goe by:
> And pronounce, which band, or lace,
> Better fits him, then his face;
> Nay, I will not let you sit
> 'Fore your Idoll Glasse a whit,
> To say over every purle
> There; or to reforme a curle;
> Or with Secretarie *Sis*
> To consult, if *Fucus* this
> Be as good, as was the last:
> All your sweet of life is past,
> Make accompt, unlesse you can,
> (And that quickly) speake your Man.
>
>   (ll. 15–30)

The "emissarie" was one who sought for sights or news, and here the word
is an amusing pun on the proper function of the Neoplatonic eye—to emit
the beams of love. A careful comparison of this feminine portrait with
the Charis pictured indirectly in the ninth lyric, "Her man described by
her owne Dictamen," will show that her requirements, however banal some
of them may be, or jocularly presented, are respectable and worth having,
even though neither Jonson nor Silenus can boast of many of them.

In many ways the "Dictamen" is the most easily misinterpreted poem
in the sequence because of Jonson's lifelong contempt for the affectations
of the Court and because the man Charis is looking for is the ideal young
courtier. The best commentary on the poem is *The Courtier* itself, along
with the list of attributes which Hoby appended to his translation as a kind
of outline (pp. 368–73). The final quality, to which the description builds
up at the end and with which most of the details accord throughout, is the
Aristotelian mean in behavior, to which the courtesy books are usually
dedicated. The charm of the poem resides in the gaiety of Charis's personality and the ease with which she describes criteria that automatically
exclude Jonson:

> Of your Trouble, *Ben,* to ease me,
> I will tell what Man would please me.
> I would have him, if I could,
> Noble; or of greater Blood:
> Titles, I confesse, doe take me;
> And a woman God did make me:
> French to boote, at least in fashion,
> And his Manners of that Nation.
>
> (ll. 1–8)

French clothes and manners must give her lover fashion, not the language and the truth, and it might as well be admitted, she likes titles. She is teasing Jonson, for she knows that no qualities could irritate him more than these. But then, although she goes on in the same spirit as if in response to his "Excuse" to specify the face, feature, and youth, now that she has mentioned the fortune, she begins to slip in details which Jonson would be forced to admit were good: "Young I'ld have him to[o], and faire,/Yet a man," despite the beauties of the Petrarchan adolescent, which she lists specifically. He must have "Eye-brows bent like *Cupids* bow," a cheek as smooth as a billiard ball, and a chin "as woolly as the Peach," for if "he cherish'd too much beard" she would be afraid. Such details, of course, are simply calculated to poke fun at Jonson—"*Cupids* Statue with a Beard," as she had described him earlier in the sequence—and, perhaps, to parody the banality of her insistence upon a young man. Then she becomes less jocular:

> 'Twere to[o] long, to speake of all:
> What we harmonie doe call
> In a body, should be there.
> Well he should his clothes to[o] weare;
> Yet no Taylor help to make him;
> Drest, you still for man should take him;
> And not thinke h'had eat a stake,
> Or were set up in a Brake.
> Valiant he should be as fire,
> Shewing danger more than ire.
> Bounteous as the clouds to earth;
> And as honest as his Birth.
> All his actions to be such,
> As to doe no thing too much.
> Nor o're-praise, nor yet condemne;
> Nor out-valew, nor contemne;
> Nor doe wrongs, nor wrongs receave;
> Nor tie knots, nor knots unweave;

And from basenesse to be free,
As he durst love Truth and me.
        Such a man, with every part,
I could give my very heart;
But of one, if short he came,
I can rest me where I am.
                (ll. 33–56)

Most of these qualities are recommended in *The Courtier* (pp. 45–61) and justified by reference to the "Aristotelian mean" of behavior, which encouraged each man in all his actions "to doe no thing too much." To achieve harmony in the body Castiglione would have the courtier "to bee of a good shape, and well proporcioned in his lymmes" (p. 52). Too much carelessness in dress can be as affected as too much care. He must wear his clothes well, Charis insists, for, in Hoby's words, the graceful ease of behavior is lost in a "reckelesnes' which lets "a mans clothes fal of his backe" as well as in "preciseness" which makes him carry his "head so like a malthorse for feare of ruffling his hear" (p. 60) that he appears to be a fop whom no one would take to be a man. Charis is specific about this gentlemanly mean in bearing as well as in dress. Her man must not flaunt an air of importance as if "h'had eat a stake," and bear himself as stiffly as if he "were set up in a Brake" (that is, in the wooden frame used to hold colts steady while being shod). Castiglione emphasizes ease of carriage and as an example points out how ill it becomes a man at arms "to goe so bolt upright setled in saddle" (p. 60). So, too, the courtier should not rush rashly into combat, but once in it he must show "a readinesse and a stomake" (p. 53) just as Charis's lover must fight with courage, not in the rashness of anger. Her lover, furthermore, must beware of all extremes in matters of judgment, so that he neither wrong anyone nor willingly suffer anyone to wrong him. He must stay out of other people's affairs[35] and avoid "basenesse," which so often means in Jonson specifically envy. The end to which all these last qualities, largely intellectual ones, are directed is the love of "Truth and me," which Charis playfully equates in value, while at the same time alluding to Jonson's praise of the language and the truth, both of which must be used in the effort not to overpraise "nor yet condemne;/ Nor out-valew, nor contemne." Whatever the tone arising from the situation of the sequence, these are good qualities in themselves, and there is no question that Jonson admired them.

Charis will accept a man with all these parts, "But of one, if short he came," she could manage without a lover. Another lady of the group picks up this line, and, by drawing attention to just what part would suffer most from being short, she makes Charis's reservation serve as a transition to the last poem of the sequence.

Another Ladyes exception present at the hearing

> For his Mind, I doe not care,
> That's a Toy, that I could spare:
> Let his Title be but great,
> His Clothes rich, and band sit neat,
> Himselfe young, and face be good,
> All I wish is understood.
> What you please, you parts may call,
> 'Tis one good part I'ld lie withall.

Although Jonson seems to be ending the sequence rather irresponsibly with a joke, this poem gives the final clarification of Charis's point of view and of Jonson's attitude toward it. The lady's objection is in the convention of the *discorso* and corresponds to Lord Beaufort's interruptions in *The New Inne* and to Morello's in *The Courtier*. In Book II, Morello says with some irritation that so far as love is concerned, old men might as well be excluded from being courtiers, since it is thought they make such fools of themselves in their courtship.[36] What should they do with women, he asks ironically, tell fables? When Bembo, in Book IV, tries to explain what he should do, Morello retorts that such a love "I for my part understande not: and (me think) the possessing of this beawtye, whiche he prayseth so muche, without the body, is a dreame" (p. 347). Bembo persists, however, in maintaining that the "sowinge of vertue in the gardein of that mind . . . be the right engendringe and imprinting of beawtye in beawtie"; to which Morello responds:

> The engendringe . . . of beawtye in beawtye aright, were the engendringe of a beawtyfull chylde in a beautifull woman, and I woulde thinke it a more manifest token a great deale that she loved her lover, if she pleased him with this, then with the sweetnesse of language that you speake of. (p. 354)

Such responses force Bembo to clarify his position, and, in a way, although the process is reversed, the lady's exception forces the reader to be aware of the distinctions that Jonson has been making, by referring him back to specific passages in the earlier lyrics.

The lady's view of love is completely sensual, and she demands precisely what Jonson excuses himself for not having in the first lyric: a title (fortune), clothes, youth, face, and by implication in the last two lines a good figure. What he offers as a substitute she regards as a toy, and she frankly admits that the qualities she requires are good mainly for making her lover's best part more attractive. What is more important, however, is how the lady distinguishes herself from Charis. In the first place, when Jonson teases Charis, in the eighth lyric, for having the conventional vanities of courtly women, he is describing the tastes and habits of the lady in the tenth. Charis's "emissarie eye" presumably fetches in the forms that go by the window to "pronounce, which band, or lace,/Better fits him, then his face," but it is the specific concern of the lady that her lover's clothes be rich "and band sit neat." Jonson's implication is that both women are completely concerned with the trivial. He is correct about the lady, for "All I wish is understood," but Charis is goaded into "speaking her man" in order to defend herself. Second, the apparent frivolity of much of Charis's description—she, too, says she wants a title, clothes, youth, face, and feature—is largely qualified by the last poem, because the exclusiveness of the lady's requirements emphasizes Charis's insistence upon those other qualities that are generally admired. The lady's opinion implies, furthermore, that Charis made up her materialistic criteria partly to retaliate on Jonson, in a peculiarly feminine way, for his picturing her as a conventional flirt. It is possible that he added the poem in the fear that some would misinterpret her "Dictamen" and think that it was inconsistent with his own description of her in the fifth lyric of the sequence:

> Shee is *Venus*, when she smiles,
> But shee's *Juno*, when she walkes,
> And *Minerva*, when she talkes.

And third, there is a quality of self-awareness in the first half of Charis's description of herself, as well as a recognition, both gentle and witty, of Jonson's failure to meet her criteria, which is absent in the last poem.

The reason for describing the context of the "Celebration" in such detail is simply that without it the subtlety of what Jonson is saying about contemporary attitudes toward love would be lost. Within the context, Jonson's comment on the terms and the situation lies in the story, for, to borrow an observation on the drama from Lily B. Campbell, if you want to know what the writer's point of view is, as distinct from those of his characters, look at the plot.[37] The qualities which he says are most valuable and which even Charis herself may admire most are not sufficient in themselves to win her as a lover in the practical world. Her rejection of him is a comment on the inapplicability of Bembo's ideals, and, it follows, on the inadequacy of the Neoplatonic theory of human love, but there is no contempt for the ideals themselves. He, as an old man, is forced to offer only what is in accordance with them, but their value does not make old age any more desirable. As far as the world is concerned, Charis represents the combination of sensory desires and intelligent discrimination that can actually be achieved, despite her idealistic reservation that she can rest as she is if no man meets her requirements. She represents the mean between Jonson's "excuse" and the lady's "exception." The poems are complicated by a feeling of regret that the ideals are insufficient, but, in contrast to the countless other Renaissance poems expressing similar attitudes, the regret is qualified and almost concealed by the author's good-humored awareness of his own physical appearance and his acceptance of the fact that appearances, though they may not always be important, nearly always are. It is the manner in which this realization is stated, without the overt cynicism of Donne or the conventional anger and self-pity of the Petrarchans, that makes the feeling of Jonson's best love poems unique. His devices are intricate. He makes use of the Petrarchan Cupid by playing upon conventions included in the Socratic origins of his stylistic attitudes and by describing himself as the god of love with the beguiling urbanity of Plato. He cautions the Neoplatonic lover against complacency, while valuing his principles, by the sly irony of his showing how (though he might have remembered that Socrates could have been successful with Alcibiades had he wished) he himself failed to persuade Charis. He comments, in other words, on conventions, often critically, by describing himself objectively as he might appear were he placed in the situations they demand, a device that he used also in his epigram "On Lvcy Covntesse of Bedford" (VIII, 52), when he sees himself as a sonneteer looking for an imaginary lady to address, "as *Poets* vse." Two of the situations of the "Celebration," one, that of an older man perfectly ready to believe in and use the Neoplatonic arguments as a means of persuasion, if they would only carry weight in the real world, and the other, the urbanely objective Silenic self-portrait, equally Platonic in origin, each offer part of the context of two other love poems as well, which are probably Jonson's best.

Drummond writes that Jonson sent him the short lyric, "My Picture left in Scotland" (VIII, 149), "which is (as he said) a picture of himselfe" (I, 150). The poem is an epitome of the plot and of the observations on love in the "Celebration," and the device by which the actual difficulties of an older lover are presented in a Neoplatonic context is, again, the figure of Silenus:

I now thinke, Love is rather deafe, then blind,
For else it could not be,
That she,
Whom I adore so much, should so slight me,
And cast my love behind:
I'm sure my language to her, was as sweet,
And every close did meet
In sentence, of as subtile feet,
As hath the youngest Hee,
That sits in shadow of *Apollo's* tree.

Oh, but my conscious feares,
That flie my thoughts betweene,
Tell me that she hath seene
My hundred of gray haires,
Told seven and fortie years,
Read so much wast, as she cannot imbrace
My mountaine belly, and my rockie face,
And all these through her eyes, have stopt her eares.

The lyric is a final summary and evaluation of the situation described in the poems addressed to Charis. It could be taken as the eleventh poem of the sequence. The older lover must persuade the lady with his language, but, even though she may listen to it and admire it, he has reason to fear that what she sees will make her forget what she hears. Qualifying the acceptance of this way of the world is the feeling of regret in the lines that his appearance should be more persuasive than what he says. The playing on the words "wast" and "cannot imbrace" to introduce the vivid details of his mountain belly and his rocky face modifies the severity of his description with the same type of urbanity that Alcibiades uses in describing Socrates' Silenic belly. One cannot forget the value of the original Socratic arguments, which Jonson is saying no longer apply; a tone almost like nostalgia for the lost Neoplatonic ideals accounts for the feeling in the poem.

Jonson's elegy "Though Beautie be the Marke of praise" (VIII, 173) states this feeling of loss more directly, although it uses a certain amount of Neoplatonic ornament. The love elegy was traditionally associated with the middle style, or *genus floridum*. J. C. Scaliger describes it as candid, "honied" (*mollem*), neat and clear, sincere, concerned with feelings, uncluttered by collected moral reflections (*exquisitiis sententiis*) and examples (*fabulis*), cleanly groomed rather than shaggy (*pexus*). Some of these qualities are those of the plain style, and to them may be added a freedom of subject matter nearly as broad as that of satire, which Scaliger describes in a manner reminiscent of Erasmus' description of the epistle and Pliny's of his epigrams. Of the possible arguments Scaliger writes, "cōmemoratio diei, a quo initium amandi factum fuit. Eiusdem laudatio aut execratio. Querela, Expostulatio, Preces, Vota, Gratulatio, Exultatio, Furti narratio, Fletus, Conuitium, Vitij aut flagitij obiectio, Recantatio, Propriae vitae explicatio."[38] Elegies can be addressed to doors, porters, handmaids, mothers, husbands, storms, or heaven itself. Because of this range of subjects and recipients, "this genre of poem," Scaliger says, "rightly includes epitaphs and letters." The elegy, of course, should be about love, but when it permits *Vitij aut flagitij obiectio,* it invites satire, especially on women, and there is an enormous amount of satirical writing in the elegies of the late sixteenth and early seventeenth centuries. As the elegy becomes satirical, its style becomes, as might be expected, less "honied," and ends up essentially as the plain style. Jonson's entire elegy "Let me be what I am" (VIII, 199), which is a satire on women at court, is as direct and incisive as his poems on Jones. The effect of the *sermo* can be seen by comparing it with the love elegies of Drayton or Marlowe.

In "Though Beautie be the Marke of praise" Jonson introduces a kind of serious moral statement which had not been characteristic of the love elegy and which Scaliger seems to discourage, by implication at least, in excluding *sententiis.* He deals with love in the entire context of human experience.

> Though Beautie be the Marke of praise,
>   And yours of whom I sing be such
>   As not the World can praise too much,
> Yet is't your vertue now I raise.
>
> A vertue, like Allay, so gone
>   Throughout your forme; as though that move,
>   And draw, and conquer all mens love,
> This subjects you to love of one.
>
> Wherein you triumph yet: because
>   'Tis of your selfe, and that you use
>   The noblest freedome, not to chuse
> Against or Faith, or honours lawes.
>
> But who should lesse expect from you,
>   In whom alone Love lives agen?
>   By whom he is restor'd to men:
> And kept, and bred, and brought up true.

His falling Temples you have rear'd,
    The withered Garlands tane away;
    His Altars kept from the Decay,
That envie wish'd, and Nature fear'd.

And on them burne so chaste a flame,
    With so much Loyalties expence,
    As Love, t[o]'aquit such excellence,
Is gone himselfe into your Name.

And you are he: the Dietie
    To whom all Lovers are design'd,
    That would their better objects find:
Among which faithful troope am I.

Who as an off'ring at your shrine,
    Have sung this Hymne, and here intreat
    One sparke of your Diviner heat
To light upon a Love of mine.

Which if it kindle not, but scant
    Appeare, and that to shortest view,
    Yet give me leave t[o]'adore in you
What I, in her, am griev'd to want.

The general situation of the poem accounts to a great extent for its strange quality of feeling. Jonson has found his love wanting in virtue, probably fidelity, and is asking another woman, whom he admires, to give to her, from her own abundant stock, the qualities he misses. If his love will not accept the gift, he will admire the qualities in his friend, since he must do without them in his beloved. Despite the figurative description in many of the stanzas, the poem states actual relationships with a good deal of realism; love is not idealized, and, though virtue is praised, the poet realizes that it does not always accompany love and that love is not necessarily less strong for its absence. These generalizations, however, are implied only at the end and with the utmost subtlety and tact; they represent the real situation. The feeling of regret that virtue is no longer a necessary condition of a love relation is intensified by the Neoplatonic figures of the temple, the altars, the deity (obviously spiritual here), chaste flame, shrine, divine heat, hymn, all of which establish the context in which Jonson is making his comparison between the two ladies.[39]

The terms of the elegy are essentially those that Lovel uses in his definition of love in *The New Inne* (III.ii.65-200). The virtue, which, like an alloy, runs through a beautiful form, strengthens the person until her love may perfectly settle upon one object and remain there. So Lovel says of love, which should reside in his lady:

> That both his nature, and his essence might
> Haue found their mighty instauration here,
> Here where the confluence of faire, and good,
> Meets to make vp all beauty. . . .
>
> (III.ii.69–72)

The deity in the elegy "To whom all Lovers are design'd,/That would their better objects find" is to be associated, since his nature is virtuous, with heavenly love, or Aphrodite Urania, rather than with sensual love, or Aphrodite Pandemos, as Plato distinguishes them in the *Symposium*.[40] The lady's capacity to enable lovers to find their better objects is attributed to Charis in Jonson's "Excuse for loving," for until his readers know who she is they will be ignorant of "Either whom to love, or how." As the sequence gradually reveals, however, Charis is not quite ready to become Urania entirely; she is still Venus when she smiles. The resemblance seems to stop after the idealistic opening lyric, and despite the fact that love, or rather Venus, has gone into Charis's name, it is a distinctly different kind of love from that which has gone into the name of the person addressed in the elegy.

The Platonic affection of Jonson's friend is defined in more general terms in a lyric in his masque *Loves Triumph through Callipolis* (VII, 735). The device of the masque is a brief Platonic allegory. Euphemus is sent down from heaven to Callipolis, or beautiful city as Plato designates it in the *Republic*, "which is vnderstood the Citty of *Beauty* or *Goodness*," and tells the queen that "*Loue*, who was wont to be respected as a speciall Deity in Court, and Tutelar God of the place," has discovered some "deprau'd Louers" on the outskirts of the city (ll. 16–49). He then instructs the court and the lovers by singing a lyric on the nature of love:

> Loue is the right affection of the minde,
> The noble appetite of what is best:
> Desire of union with the thing design'd,
> But in fruition of it cannot rest.
>
> (ll. 54–57)

The use of the word "design'd" is identical to that in the elegy. Euphemus recounts the myth of Porus and Penia concerning the birth of love as it is given in the *Symposium*. He then addresses the queen to ask her "to grace Loues triumph here":

To you that are by excellence a Queene!
The top of beauty! but, of such an ayre,
As, onely by the minds eye, may be seene
Your enter-wouen lines of good, and fayre!
(ll. 66–69)

If she will grace the triumph, the infections of the suburbs will no longer impair the proper function of love:

Then will he flow forth, like a rich perfume
Into your nostrils! or some sweeter sound
Of melting musique, that shall not consume
Within the eare, but run the mazes round.
(ll. 78–81)

These concluding descriptive lines are beautiful in themselves and show a particularly skillful transition from a highly abstract statement to its meta-phorical expression in sensory terms. The lines describing the queen's beauty, which must be seen by the eye of the mind, offer a significant gloss upon the Neoplatonic terms of the elegy. The "enter-wouen lines of good, and fayre" correspond to the alloy of virtue running through a beautiful person and to the "confluence of faire, and good" in Lovel's definition of love.

The meter of the elegy is quieter than that of many of Jonson's poems. The caesura falls most of the time after even syllables, although in different places in the line. The syntactical units, however, often begin and end in the middle of the line, as Dionysius prescribes, and this, along with the caesura's occasionally falling after the odd syllable, varies the quiet tetram-eter so subtly that it echoes the song meters.[41] The first stanza establishes a norm in which the caesura falls after even syllables and at the end of the line. The second and third stanzas vary from it, almost imperceptibly:

A vertue, like Allay, so gone
Throughout your forme; as though that move,
And draw, and conquer all mens love,
This subjects you to love of one.

Wherein you triumph yet: because
'Tis of your selfe, and that you use
The noblest freedome, not to chuse
Against or Faith, or honours lawes.

By introducing a caesura after the third syllable and by letting the syntac-tical unit run over four syllables into the next line, the subtlest rift is made across the metrical pattern. The caesura is shifted to the second and sixth positions, and by the time it returns to the fourth in the third stanza the syntactical unit goes from the middle of one line to the middle of the next, carefully avoiding any pause at the end of a line until the close of the rhythmical unit of the stanza. To bring so much life to the verse line with such minute variations shows a mastery comparable to that in the fourth song of the "Celebration of Charis."

Perhaps of all his songs the fourth lyric of the Charis sequence, "Her Triumph," best illustrates the complex delicacy of Jonson's metrical technique, which led his most talented admirers to imitate his slighter poems rather than his more original and more comprehensive didactic verse. The triumphal song owes a great deal to the metrical conventions of the Elizabethan songbooks and to the popular ballad meters, both of which seem to be echoed in the charms and many of the songs in the masques. The charms are characterized by a swift lilt repeated, often irregularly, by means of the substitution of trisyllabic feet in successive lines, usually of varying lengths. Their material is most often borrowed from folklore, and the meter is used to suggest the slightly eerie and ethereal nature of the supernatural agency operating behind the movements of the little animals associated with incantation. One of the most graceful is in the *Masqve of Qveenes* (VII, 285), beginning:

> The Owle is abroad, the Bat, and the Toade,
> And so is the Cat-à-Mountaine;
> The Ant, and the Mole sit both in a hole,
> And Frog peepes out o'the fountayne.

Equally famous is the song "The faery beame vppon you" from *The Gypsies Metamorphos'd,* whose meter Herrick apparently borrowed for his "Night-Piece for Julia." The third song in this masque (VII, 575) is curious, because it uses the meter of the charm on material that Jonson usually treated more seriously.

> To the old, longe life and treasure,
> To the young, all healthe and pleasure,
>   To the faire, theire face
>   Wᵗʰ eternall grace,
> And the foule to be lou'd at leasure.
>
> To the wittie, all cleare mirrors,
> To the foolishe, their darke errors,
>   To the lovinge sprite
>   A secure delight,
> To the iealous his owne false terrors.

Such commonplaces are often found in drinking songs, but this meter gives the statements a certain subtle irony, implying that the things mentioned will really never come to pass. In the song to Charis, Jonson uses the same trisyllabic feet but with greater restraint, much as Shakespeare does in his "Fear no more the heat o'the sun," since the song is presumably describing a stately procession. The first two stanzas are quoted earlier; the third is as follows:

> Have you seene but a bright Lillie grow,
> > Before rude hands have touch'd it?
> Have you mark'd but the fall o'the Snow
> > Before the soyle hath smutch'd it?
> Have you felt the wooll o' the Bever?
> > Or Swans Downe ever?
> Or have smelt o'the bud o'the Brier?
> > Or the Nard i' the fire?
> Or have tasted the bag o'the Bee?
> O so white! O so soft! O so sweet is she!

The return to a firm iambic meter in the second and fourth lines keeps the trisyllabic feet from running away with the poem. This restraint, combined with the extraordinary lightness of the initial syllables in those feet, which Jonson emphasizes by his elision, gives the lines the lilt of the song meters, which otherwise might have been the crudest anapestic galloping. Jonson is careful to stop the lilting rhythm, which is permitted more freedom in the charms, at the end of each line and to break up the last line by firm caesuras, as he might use the *comma* for emphasis in the *sermo,* in order to check the rapidity of the meter.[42]

There has been a genuine misunderstanding of Jonson's love poetry. It is usually called artistic, impersonal, or passionless with some condescension by those who regard the love poem solely as a form for spontaneous expression of feeling and as somehow suspect if it displays the objectivity necessary to a controlled statement. This opinion, which is widely accepted,[43] has arisen, I think, from a lack of understanding of the basic qualities of Jonson's style. The style, actually, is the most personal style, as the epistolary genre is the most personal genre. If one looks well, one will see that Gascoigne is, in reality, a far more personal poet than Spenser; that is, he usually talks in his own person about his personal experience. Jonson is, for the same reason, a more personal poet than Sidney and the sonneteers. He does not treat love in isolation but in the whole context of his experience; the increased objectivity should not be interpreted as lack of passion.[44] By using the tone and simplicity of the plain style, he can give even the worn comparisons of conventional love poetry a passionate plainness rarely equaled in English literature. The following lines, for example, are from Wittipol's speech to Mistress Fitz-dottrel in Jonson's finest love scene (*The Divell is an Asse,* I, vi), in which Fitz-dottrel permits Wittipol to woo his wife in his presence for fifteen minutes in exchange for Wittipol's expensive cloak. "Vse all the *Tropes*/And *Schemes,* that Prince *Quintilian* can afford you;/And much good do your *Rhetoriques* heart" (I.iv.100–102), Fitz-dottrel advises, but Wittipol chooses to speak in the simplest language (VI, 181):

> Let not the signe o' the husband fright you, Lady.
> But ere your spring be gone, inioy it. Flowers,
> Though faire, are oft but of one morning. Thinke,
> All beauty doth not last vntill the *autumne.*
> You grow old, while I tell you this. And such,
> As cannot vse the present, are not wise.
>
> (I.vi.127–32)

The heavy caesura blocks off the conventional comparisons in the simplest statements, giving them a tense vitality which they had long lost in their more decorative contexts. The passage culminates in a statement borrowed from Horace, "You grow old, while I tell you this," which, abandoning comparisons, uses an unexpected observation of simple fact as a kind of hyperbole to intensify the listener's awareness of transience.

The persuasiveness of these qualities of diction and meter owes a great deal to the recovery of a workable relationship between connotation and denotation, between the rhetorical and the dialectical intentions in a piece of writing, and, more generally, between expression and matter, form and content. Cicero and Quintilian attempt to remove the division between *verbum* and *res* by defining rhetoric as the art of speaking well; the word "well," in referring to both, is little more than a pun, and the solution is merely verbal. Spenser regarded allegory, and I suspect other figures of rhetoric, as a bridge between a literature of pure entertainment and a homily, between a "showe" and a "precept." But, like Horace, he does not state a relationship between them beyond their coexistence. It is to Aristotle that one must return in this matter, as in so many others, when considering the plain style.

Aristotle says that emotional pleasure is derived from learning something new, from a new perception, new insight, and his example is metaphor. "All men take a natural pleasure in learning quickly; words denote something; and so those words are pleasantest which give us *new* knowledge. Strange words have no meaning for us; common terms we know already; it is *metaphor* which gives us most of this pleasure. Thus, when the poet calls old age 'a dried stalk,' he gives us a new perception by means of the common *genus*; for both things have lost their bloom . . . A simile . . . is a metaphor with a preface; for this reason it is less pleasing because it is more lengthy; nor does it affirm that *this* is *that*; and so the mind does not even inquire into the matter." Similarly, good enthymemes are those "which give us a new and rapid perception," either those "which convey knowledge, as soon as they are uttered" or "behind which intelligence lags only a little; for here there is a sort of acquisition."[45] The theory of imitation rests upon the assumption that pleasure is caused by perceiving something new, for in any form of artistic imitation "one's joy is not in the thing itself; rather, there is a syllogism—'*this* is *that*'; and so it comes that one learns something" (*Rhet.* 1371b). Again in the *Poetics* (iv.4-5), accounting for the enjoyment that representation brings, Aristotle says that "Learning things gives great pleasure not only to philosophers but also in the same way to all other men . . . The reason why we enjoy seeing likenesses is that, as we look, we learn and infer what each is, for instance, 'that is so and so.' "[46] The emphasis in each case falls upon the acquisition, which the stylistic devices of rhetoric are supposed to facilitate; if what is acquired, or perceived, is valuable and relatable to the reader's experience, the feelings conveyed will be persuasive. And so in the plain style. Connotation ceases to be so completely a matter of expression, and hence distinguishable, on the surface, from content. It arises rather from the understanding of the writer's insight and depends upon the reader's ability to participate in the writer's experience. The divisions between what amount to the affective and intellective qualities of style are healed: denotation is the statement, and connotation is the understanding of the statement in the context of the reader's particular experience.

A poem in the plain style offers the reader the intimacy of a specific situation and its context of feeling. The generalizations, either stated or implied, arise out of particular detailed experience and are persuasive because the reader is encouraged to participate in the experience rather than simply to acquiesce in a moral precept. The emotional attitude is established and conveyed by an inductive process analogous to that suggested by Bacon. The intimacy between the poet and the reader is strengthened by the urbanity of tone that has traditionally given the plain style its vitality. It is the urbanity which claims the experience as the writer's own but which, at the same time, recognizes that it is relatable to the experiences of others and that the relationship might be valuable.

These, then, are the qualities that give Jonson's poems their power. It may be suggested that they could be achieved in a more decorative style and that the resulting poems would be more effective. It has seemed to me, however, that the qualities of the poems and the plain style itself are both dependent on the same attitudes. A different style involves different intentions and hence different attitudes toward experience. If you change the intentions to change the style, you will lose, or at least weaken, the qualities of statement and feeling that I have tried to describe in the preceding chapters.

NOTES

1. *Institutio Oratoria* II.v.19–23, Loeb ed., trans. H. E. Butler (London, 1953). All future references will be to this edition.

2. Although it is more plausible to argue that Jonson is referring to the prose of Sidney and Donne rather than to their verse, the entire context of his passage refers to writing in general and seems to apply to prose and verse indiscriminately. The application of traditional rhetorical classifications and descriptions of prose style to the poetry of the Renaissance can be more extensively explored in Jonson's case than it has been in the past in those of other poets, since his rhetorical statements are so consistent with his own practice and since he has left sufficient commentary on ancient and modern writers to enable us to apply his theoretical comments to his particular literary judgments. Once such an application proves valuable in describing Jonson's intentions, it can be assumed to be relevant to the interpretation of other writers. Although it will be necessary to find explicit evidence in dealing with their work, the type of evidence to look for and a way of applying it shall have been indicated. This introductory chapter may be said to raise again the problem of interpreting the critical method imposed by the doctrine of imitation in the application of its statements about prose to verse. The rest of the book may be said to offer one way of approaching a solution. In their discussions of poetry, the humanistic scholars of the fifteenth and sixteenth centuries more often than not used the passages cited from antiquity or their own day to establish and verify their critical method rather than the critical method to evaluate the poetry. By the early seventeenth century the terminology had become sufficiently established to have critical precision when used by a sensitive and erudite man.

3. For general treatments of this subject see G. L. Hendrickson's "The Origin and Meaning of the Ancient Characters of Style," *AJP*, XXVI (1905), 249–90, and Morris Croll, " 'Attic Prose' in the Seventeenth Century," *SP*, XVIII (1921), 79–128, hereafter cited as "Attic Prose."

4. Loeb ed., trans. E. W. Sutton (London, 1942). See also *De Orat.* III.xix.72.

5. It must be remembered, however, that despite his allegiance to the Asiatic school of oratory, Cicero's compromise is simply that the ideal orator will be a philosopher, for "no one can be a good speaker who is not a sound thinker," and, therefore, "whoever devotes himself to true eloquence, devotes himself to sound thinking" (*Brutus* vi.23, Loeb ed., trans. G. L. Hendrickson [Cambridge, Mass., 1939]). Hendrickson translates *prudentiae* as "sound thinking" and glosses it as being used with a philosophic meaning. Other statements of the necessity of knowledge and the emphasis upon meaning recur often; see especially *De Orat.* I.xi.48, III.x.38, and III.xxxv.142–43.

6. See Cicero *De Officiis*, I.134, for the Socratics as a model for daily conversation. See also G. C. Fiske, *Lucilius and Horace*, Univ. of Wisc. Studies, No. 7 (Madison, 1920), p. 86.

7. *Orator* 64, Loeb ed., trans. H. M. Hubbell (Cambridge, Mass., 1939).

8. "Attic Prose," pp. 88–89.

9. For other comments of Cicero, see *Brutus,* 201ff. and *Orator* 20ff., as well as passages dealing with the *narratio* of an oration, especially *De Orat.* II.lxxx.326ff. He discusses the plain style in passages on the Asiatic-Attic controversy and the Stoic style: *De Orat.* III.xviii.66 and *Brutus* 119, 283ff. For other general discussions of the plain style see Quintilian on the relationship between meaning and expression (*Inst. Orat.* VIII.Pr.20–26); on the subordination of ornament to content (VIII.ii. 22–23, IX.i.13ff., and IX.iv.19); on the Asiatic-Attic controversy (VIII.Pr.17ff., X.i.44., 64ff., and XII.x.16–62); on the *narratio* (IV.ii.36–47); and on various types of wit, especially *urbanitas* (VI.iii.17ff.). The author of the *Ad Herennium* divides the conversational tone into four kinds: the dignified, the explicative, the narrative, and the facetious (III.23). Later in the treatise (IV.11–16) he gives short examples of the three characters of style to accompany his descriptions of them and then gives three further examples to illustrate the type of faults peculiar to each. For the example of the proper use of the *genus tenue* he relates an anecdote that, except for its use of slang, would not be out of place in the New Comedy or in Horace's *sermones.* Much sixteenth-century critical terminology was borrowed from his description of the faulty styles. The high style slips into the swollen (*sufflata*) style, "For just as a swelling often resembles a healthy condition of the body, so, to those who are inexperienced, turgid and inflated language often seems majestic—when a thought is expressed either in new or in archaic words, or in clumsy metaphors, or in diction more impressive than the theme demands." The middle style becomes "the Slack (*dissolutum*) because it is without sinews and joints (*sine nervis et articulis*); accordingly I may call it the Drifting (*fluctuans*), since it drifts to and fro, and cannot get under way with resolution and virility." Those who miss the elegant simplicity of the plain stlye "arrive at a dry and bloodless kind of style which may be called the Meagre" (IV. 15–16). Dionysius of Halicarnassus describes the simple diction of the *Odyssey* XVI, 1–16 (*On Literary Composition,* III); the simplicity of the Platonic dialogues ("Letter to Pompeius"); and how lyrical verse may imitate the periodic structure of the *sermo* in his chapter on "How Verse Can Resemble Prose" (*On Lit. Comp.,* XXVI). The *Dialogus* of Tacitus is pertinent in that it supports a style which both avoids the periodic circumlocution of Ciceronian oratory (*Dial.* 22) and the literary preciousness of some of the imitators of Seneca, both of which Jonson criticized in his *Discoveries.* Although *On the Sublime* describes a position at the furthest extreme from the plain style, there are certain characteristics of the *sermo,* especially in its Senecan developments, such as brevity and asyndeton, which contribute to the sublime. The connection is drawn clearly by Demetrius in his discussion of the "forcible style" (*On Style,* 240ff.), where extreme brevity is used for intensity, and the accompanying obscurity and roughness of style is described as forceful (246–55). Demetrius' main passages on the plain style are *On Style,* 190–222 and 223–39, the latter being a discussion of the epistolary style. All references are to the Loeb ed., trans. W. R. Roberts (Cambridge, Mass., 1953).

10. Cicero expresses his impatience with those who equivocate with the term in his *De Opt. Gen. Orat.,* especially 11–13.

11. Seneca, *Epistulae Morales,* Loeb ed., trans. R. M. Gummere (London, 1917).

12. The *speculum* becomes a symbol for comedy and satire at an early period. Fiske cites the fragment of Lucilius, *sicuti te, qui ea quae speciem vitae esse putamus,* as an allusion to the New Comedy (*Lucilius and Horace,* p. 289). Terence jokes about the symbol in *Adelphoe* 410–31, by drawing a parallel between the moralist and the cook, who should look into his dish as into a looking glass.

13. Cicero comments that the unmannered simplicity of his mother-in-law's reading aloud reminded him of Plautus (*De Orat.* III.45), and Pliny says that hearing

some letters of the wife of Pompeius Saturnius was like hearing Plautus or Terence in prose (I, xvi). Cicero relates the iambic meter of comedy to the plain style, for it is the closest meter to the rhythm of ordinary speech (*Orator* 184–96). Aristotle made the same observation in the *Poetics* (1459a) and in the *Rhetoric* (1404a and 1408b). See also Quintilian (IX.iv.76) and Demetrius (*On Style*, 43). Quintilian cites Varro's quotation of Aelius Stilo: "If the Muses wished to speak Latin, they would use the language of Plautus" (X.i.99).

14. M. A. Grant and G. C. Fiske, "Cicero's 'Orator' and Horace's 'Ars Poetica,'" *Harvard Studies in Classical Philology*, XXXV (1924), 34.

15. Grant and Fiske summarize this agreement: "So far as the theory of diction impinges upon that of the plain style or *genus tenue*, as described by Cicero in [*Orator*] 76–90, I am still inclined to believe that as a *tenuis poeta* in his *Sermones* and *Epistulae* and even to a degree in his *Odes*, Horace followed a theory of diction which is in essential harmony with that of the *tenuis orator* as sketched by Cicero." *Ibid*, p. 26.

16. *Satires, Epistles, and Ars Poetica*, Loeb ed., trans. H. R. Fairclough (London, 1934), *Serm.* I.iv.1–8.

17. "Ex noto fictum carmen sequar, ut sibi quivis/speret idem, sudet multum frustraque laboret/ausus idem: tantum series iuncturaque pollet,/tantum de medio sumptis accedit honoris." For discussions of Horace's theory of the plain style, see G. L. Hendrickson, "Horace, *Sermones*, i.4, A Protest and a Program," *AJP*, XXI (1900), 121ff., and "Satura—the Genesis of a Literary Form," *CP*, VI (1911), 129ff., and the work of G. C. Fiske cited above. To the honor which Horace says the commonplace may achieve by skillful disposition compare the remark made in the third century A.D. by Philostrato on the epistolary style: "clare autem eloquemur, nec sordida tamen erit oratio, ubi vulgares sententias noviter, novas vulgariter proferemus." *Epistolographi Graeci*, ed. Rudolphus Hercher (Paris, 1873), p. 15.

18. *Juvenal and Persius*, Loeb ed., trans. G. G. Ramsay (London, 1924).

19. Compare Juvenal's eleventh satire: "Rightly do I despise a man who knows how much higher Atlas is than all the other mountains of Africa, and yet knows not the difference between a purse and an iron-bound money-box. The maxim 'Know thyself' comes down to us from the skies; it should be imprinted in the heart, and stored in the memory, whether you are looking for a wife, or wishing for a seat in the sacred Senate" (ll.23–30).

20. See also, VI.64. Martial, *Epigrams*, Loeb ed., trans. C. A. Ker (London, 1930).

21. See also V.16.

22. "A statuette admired by Brutus" (Ker's note).

23. See Jonson's first epigram. In a letter concerning Farnaby's edition of Martial, Jonson echoes this final clause (*Works*, I, 215).

24. The younger Pliny praises Martial for his wit and candor (III.21). In discussing his own short poems, he makes no distinction between the epigram and the lyric, calling them simply *poemata* or hendecasyllables (IV.14). As Martial and Juvenal claim all subject matter for their poems, so Pliny claims all emotions and activities as his subjects (IV.14 and VII.9). He defends his enjoyment of comedy and licentious verse by quoting the famous line from Terence, *homo sum; humani nihil a me alienum puto* (V.3), which summarizes the attitudes toward experience behind the plain style—a line which Vives uses later to criticize the insular point of view of those who object to corresponding with people in foreign countries (*De Conscribendis Epistolis*, cap., ii; *Opera Omnia*, II, 270–71). Pliny, as a man, might be considered a prototype of John Hoskyns, who was a lawyer, a member of the literary circle of the Inns of Court, a wit of the most sophisticated order, a first-rate epigrammatist, a satirist, a literary critic, and a writer of accomplished love poems and urbane and

graceful letters. It was Hoskyns's father of whom Aubrey reports Jonson's saying, "I was your father's sonne, and t'was he that polished me" (*Brief Lives*, ed. Andrew Clark, I, 418). Despite the fact that Pliny encourages an orator occasionally to practice a *pressus sermo purusque ex epistulis petitur* (VII.9), he holds the ideal of the *genus grande* of Cicero (IX.24 and II.3) or a mixture of different styles (II.5). Occasionally, however, he seems to regret the current necessity to be florid (II.19 and III.18). He gives his most detailed statement about style in his letter to Tacitus (I.20).

25. After Cicero, the terms "Attic" and "Asian" became more and more imprecise when applied to particular stylistic devices that grew to be recognizable mannerisms. The dominant feature of the Attic orator, for instance, will be "an abundance of apposite maxims dug out from every conceivable hiding place" (*acutae crebraeque sententiae . . . nescio unde ex abdito erutae, Orator* 79). Yet one of the two types of Asiatic styles, Cicero says, is "sententious and studied, less characterized by weight of thought than by charm of balance and symmetry" (*sententiosum et argutum, sententiae . . . nescio unde exabdito erutae, Orator* 79). Yet one of the two types of difference is clear in Cicero, but the precise point at which the former turns into the latter is not always easy to discriminate in subsequent writers. Whatever convictions concerning an "Attic" allegiance to subject matter the imitators of Seneca may have adopted from their master, Tacitus and Quintilian criticized them for an epigrammatic preciousness that was closer to the sententious "Asian" style.

26. Croll, "Attic Prose," pp. 112–13, 115–16.

27. After finding much to praise Seneca for, Quintilian comments that "if he had only despised all unnatural expressions and had not been so passionately fond of all that was incorrect, if he had not felt such affection for all that was his own, and had not impaired the solidity of his matter by striving after epigrammatic brevity, he would have won the approval of the learned instead of the enthusiasm of boys" (X.i.130). See also Aulus Gellius, *Noctium Atticarum*, XII.2. In certain other passages (II.v. 10ff., xi.1–7, xii.1–12) which Jonson drew upon in his criticisms of "indisposition," discussed in the following chapter, Quintilian may have been referring to Seneca or his imitators. Vives comments that in the Silver Age "the language became extravagant, and changed towards voluptuousness along with the ways of the state, so that the writings are more like counterfeits and semblances than the earlier ones, and the writers seem rather to want to please, than to teach or to express in words the thoughts of their minds." (*De Tradendis Disciplinis*, III, vi, trans. Foster Watson, *Vives: On Education* [Cambridge, 1913], p. 132). Under his heading *"Like ending, and like falling,"* Thomas Wilson echoes the criticisms of Quintilian and Tacitus: "So that for the flowing stile and full sentence, crept in Minstrels elocution, talking matters altogether in rime, and for waightinesse and grauitie of wordes, succeding nothing els but wantonnesse of inuention. *Tullie* was forsaken, with *Liuie, Caesar,* and other: *Apuleius, Ausonius,* with such Minstrell makers were altogether followed. And I thinke the Popes heretofore (seeing the peoples folie to bee such) made all our Himnes and Anthemes in rime, that with the singing of men, playing of Orgaines, ringing of Belles, and riming of Himnes and Sequences, the poore ignorant might think the harmonie to be heauenly, and verely beleue that the Angels of God made not a better noyce in heauen." *The Arte of Rhetorique,* ed. G. H. Mair (Oxford, 1909), p. 203.

28. *The Life, Letters, and Writings of John Hoskyns,* ed. L. B. Osborn (New Haven, 1937), pp. 129–30. For a discussion of the relationship between the schematic prose of the Euphuists and the pointed prose of the Senecans, see George Williamson, *The Senecan Amble* (Chicago, 1951), pp. 61–88. Williamson concludes that it "would

be no more difficult to argue that Senecan style was a development from Euphuism" than to argue that it was a reaction to it (p. 89). Hoskyns is careful not to include Sidney with Lyly and the Senecans in their use of *paranomasia* by quoting Sidney's own definition of it in the *Astrophel and Stella* as " the *Dictionary* method, & the verses soe made rymes running in ratling rowes, wch is an example of it" (*Hoskyns,* p. 129). The freedom from such mannerisms makes it still easier to connect Sidney with the open, however extended, candidness of Livy and Cicero.

29. *A Study of Ben Jonson* (London, 1889), p. 142.

30. See Sir Ronald Syme, *Tacitus* (Oxford, 1958), I, 137–38. Syme's discussions of the styles of the ancient historians are particularly helpful.

31. Quintilian points out that imitators will usually imitate the most obvious characteristics of a style and turn them to mannerism, achieving "those faults which are hardest to distinguish from virtues." As a result, "those who flaunt tasteless and insipid thoughts, couched in an uncouth and inharmonious form, think that they are the equals of the ancients; those who lack ornament and epigram, pose as Attic; those who darken their meaning by the abruptness with which they close their periods, count themselves the superiors of Sallust and Thucydides; those who are dreary and jejune, think they are serious rivals to Pollio, while those who are tame (*otiosi*) and listless (*supini*), if only they can produce long enough periods, swear that this is just the manner in which Cicero would have spoken" (X.ii.16–17). These distinctions are important in the Renaissance controversies over imitation. Thomas Wilson's list of contemporary faults in composition is very similar to Jonson's in tone and detail; it is quite probable that they were drawing upon the same classical sources. *The Arte of Rhetorique,* pp. 166–69.

32. It is sufficient to call attention at this point to the most famous observations. Drummond writes to his friend Arthur Johnston about 1630, "In vain have some men of late, transformers of everything, consulted upon her [poetry's] reformation, and endeavored to abstract her to metaphysical ideas and scholastic quiddities, denuding her of her own habits and those ornaments with which she hath amused the world some thousand years." John Dryden comments in his *Discourse concerning the Original and Progress of Satire,* 1693, that Donne "affects the metaphysics, not only in his satires, but in his amorous verse, where nature only should reign; and perplexes the minds of the fair sex with nice speculations of philosophy." Both excerpts are cited from *Poetry of the English Renaissance,* ed. J. W. Hebel and H. H. Hudson (New York, 1929), p. 906. The most complete and accurately detailed description of the metaphysical style is Samuel Johnson's in his *Life of Cowley.* This description is almost a summary of the observations in antiquity and the Renaissance mentioned in this chapter.

33. The Attic style permitted a certain amount of archaism (*Orator* 80) so long as it was used sparingly and avoided obscurity. Sallust's archaisms were often commented on (Quintilian VIII.iii.29–30; Gellius, IV.15, XVIII.4; Suetonius, *Gr.* 10, 15, *Aug.* 86.3) not so much as being bad in his own writings but as being a poor thing to imitate. In the initial passages cited in this chapter, Quintilian and Jonson discuss archaism in connection with the imitation of lucid models by the young. Jonson, however, cites Spenser; Donne's obscurity results more from the Sallustian characteristics pointed out by Cheke to Ascham.

34. *The Three Literary Letters,* ed. W. Rhys Roberts (Cambridge, 1901), pp. 133–37. For Sallust's surpassing Thucydides in brevity, see M. Seneca, *Contro.* IX. i.13–14.

35. *On Literary Composition,* ed. W. Rhys Roberts (London, 1910), pp. 229–33.

36. Demetrius uses the comparison again in his description of the "forcible" style:

"But violence, too, may in composition produce force. Yes, in many passages words hard to pronounce are forcible, just as uneven roads are forcible" (246). Like Dionysius' "austere composition," the forcible style is a kind of Longinian version of the conventional high style, with certain characteristics, however, of the plain style, especially after the latter had been qualified by Seneca's influence. The figures and diction, Demetrius says, will be those of the elevated style (271–72), but the distinguishing characteristic is intensity gained by extreme brevity, brief phrases used instead of clauses, and an abrupt, curt periodic structure, for "length paralyses intensity, while much meaning conveyed in a brief form is the more forcible" (241). Traditional rhythms should be avoided as well as exact antitheses and symmetry of words and phrases in a period (247). Violence of diction and rhythm is forceful, because "cacophony produces vigour, especially if the subject requires harshness" (255). Cicero had said that the clashes of vowels and hiatus were characteristic of the plain style of the Attic orator (*Orator* 77–78), and, in attempting to describe the charm of everyday speech, had suggested the way toward the later extremes of Senecanism, which were more nearly corruptions of characteristics of the Attic style than anything else. One such corruption is that of obscurity, which, Demetrius says, "often produces force, since what is distantly hinted is more forcible, while what is plainly stated is held cheap" (*On Style,* 254). In the Renaissance certain Senecan stylistic extremes, such as elliptical, asyndectic syntax, which often resulted in obscurity, the abrupt transitions from member to member, and the roughness of the prosody, which achieved cacophony rather than virility, fit Demetrius' description perfectly (also noted by Williamson, *The Senecan Amble,* p. 197). Jonson criticized the "strong lines" of the period (VIII, 206) and objected to the "abrupt" or Laconic style with which Demetrius associates the forcible style with regard to brevity (242). Longinus comments as well on the emotional power of asyndeton and unnatural syntax (*On the Sublime,* 19–22).

37. For Tacitus' use of Livy, see Syme, *Tacitus,* I, 200–201.

38. Osborn, *Hoskyns,* pp. 154–56. For a similar account, see Gabriel Harvey's long description beginning "Read the Countesse of Pembrookes Arcadia, a gallant Legendary, full of pleasurable accidents and proffitable discourses" (*Elizabethan Critical Essays,* ed. G. G. Smith [Oxford, 1950], II, 263–64). Greville comments that Sidney's aim in the *Arcadia* "was not vanishing pleasure alone, but morall Images, and Examples (as directing threds) to guide every man through the confused *Labyrinth* of his own desires, and life" (*Life of Sir Philip Sidney,* ed. Nowell Smith [Oxford, 1907], p. 223. See also Francis Meres, borrowing Sidney's own words, "As Xenophon, who did imitate so excellently as to giue vs *effigiem iusti imperii,* 'the portraiture of a iust empyre,' vnder the name of *Cyrus* . . . made therein an absolute heroicall poem . . . so Sir Philip Sidney writ his immortal poem, *The Countess of Pembrooke's Arcadia* in Prose" (*Eliz. Crit. Ess.,* II, 315–16). See as well Abraham Fraunce, *The Arcadian Rhetorike,* ed. E. Seaton, *Luttrell Soc. Repr.* 9 (Oxford, 1950) *passim.* These descriptions of the *Arcadia* are strikingly similar to Livy's own statement about his history in his preface: "This . . . is the most wholesome and most fruitful outcome of historical knowledge, to have before one's eyes conspicuous and authentic examples of every type of conduct, whence the student may choose models for his own imitation and that of his country, and be warned against things ill begun which have likewise ended ill" (trans. H. J. Rose, *A Handbook of Latin Literature* [New York, 1960], p. 295). Erasmus echoes Livy's preface in his advice for teaching a young prince: "Euoluendus etiam Titus Liuius, tum propter leuem et dulcem facundiam, tum propter historiam, in qua et multa sunt exempla ad virtutem et peritiam rei militaris" (*Opus Epistolarum Des. Erasmi Roterodami,* ed. P. S. Allen,

12 vols. [Oxford, 1906–58], I, 138). The connection of Livy with Sidney reveals how certain functions of history were taken over by fiction. The Sallustian historical tradition moves toward modern historical methods, the Livian toward the novel. For the persistence of the Livian tradition in the didactic use of *illustratio* and *imago,* see David Levin's detailed analysis of novelistic portraiture in the nineteenth-century American historians, *History as Romantic Art* (Stanford, 1959). Jonson blamed Lucan, Guarini, and Sidney for not keeping decorum in making their characters all speak as well as themselves (I, 132, 134, 149). This insistence upon realism, which was greater than Hoskyns demanded, was typical of Jonson, and he might well have thought the same thing about Livy. For this problem of decorum in his own pastoral drama, see his editors' comments (II, 226). His association of the *Arcadia* with a legendary history, comparable to Livy's history of Rome, is implied in Drummond's report that "for a Heroik poeme he said ther was no such Ground as King Arthurs fiction & yt S. P. Sidney had ane jntention to have transfform'd all his Arcadia to ye stories of King Arthure" (I, 136).

39. For a sense of how the successors of Livy and Virgil may have looked back upon them as representative of the best of the Augustan age, see J. W. Duff's chapter on "Augustan Prose and Livy" in *A Literary History of Rome from the Origins to the Close of the Golden Age* (London, 1953), pp. 455–82. Duff comments on Livy's narrative in a way one might speak of Sidney's. Livy uses rich, luminous phrases to reanimate figures of the past as actors on a stage. His narrative is nearer fiction than document, and "by the use of poetic and sometimes distinctly Virgilian words, Livy illustrates the hold which *poeticus color* was now obtaining upon Latin prose." Duff continues that he "marks the culmination of the periodic style in history. He holds in the evolution of prose a place analogous to that held by Virgil in the evolution of poetry. Livy's master in prose was Cicero. His general preference was for the flowing style—the Isocratean rather than the Thucydidean. Thus, although he varies his stately periods with short, lively sentences—especially in describing character—he avoids the abruptness of Thucydides's Greek and Sallust's Latin" (p. 480). A distinction that Drummond makes between Sidney and Donne is extremely pertinent to Jonson's attitude toward Sidney. "*Donne,* among the Anacreontick Lyricks, is Second to none, and far from all Second. But as *Anacreon* doth not approach *Callimachus,* tho' he excels in his own kind, nor *Horace* to *Virgil,* no more can I be brought to think him to excel either *Alexander's* or *Sidney's* Verses." (Cited from *Critical Essays of the Seventeenth Century,* ed. J. E. Spingarn [Oxford, 1908], I, 216.) The close relation between Livy and Virgil indicates how readily Jonson, in looking for a comparison for Sidney, could have accepted Livy as a substitute for Virgil when he found him cited by Quintilian in the passage quoted at the beginning of this chapter.

40. *Tacitus,* I, 202.

41. Paolo Cortesi's answer to Politian's encouraging the imitation of other models as well as Cicero is perfectly reasonable. Since it is agreed that Cicero practiced the various formally categorized styles as well as, if not better than, anyone else, why not choose him as the best model and risk as little as possible the imitation of personal mannerism in other writers? Such conservatism is understandable when the enormous temporal and cultural distance is considered between the imitators and any of the classical models. For the correspondence between Politian and Cortesi, see Izora Scott's introduction to his translation of Erasmus' *Ciceronianus,* in *Controversies over the Imitation of Cicero* (New York, 1910), pp. 14–22. For a general summary, see J. W. H. Atkins, *English Literary Criticism: The Renascence* (London, 1955), pp. 8–34. Erasmus and Vives took Politian's side, and so did Jonson, who, translating M. Seneca (*Contro.* i. prae. 6), writes that "*One,* though hee be excellent, and the chiefe, is not

to bee imitated alone. For never no Imitator, ever grew up to his *Author*; likenesse is alwayes on this side Truth" (VIII, 590).

42. *The Complete Works of Sir Philip Sidney*, ed. Albert Feuillerat (Cambridge, 1923), III, 132.

43. Cicero and Sallust were often juxtaposed to illustrate different styles in order to define style in general. See George Puttenham, *The Arte of English Poesie*, ed. G. D. Willcock and A. Walker (Cambridge, 1936), p. 148. In an epigram Joseph Scaliger contrasts the roughness and obscurity of Lipsius' style to the openness and smoothness of Cicero's and Caesar's, *Poemata Omnia* (Berlin, 1864), p. 21.

44. Cited from *Eliz. Crit. Ess.*, I, 39–43.

45. Elyot says of the student that "it is best that he begynne with Titus Liuius . . . for his elegancie of writinge, whiche floweth in him like a fountaine of swete milke," whereas those historians who deal more relentlessly with the bare narration of events "without any varietie," such as Caesar and Sallust, require "an exact and perfect iugement" of a more experienced person (*The Boke Named the Gouernour*, ed. H. H. S. Croft [London, 1883], I, 81–86). In his *De Ratione Studii Puerilis ad Carolum Montjoium Guilielmi filium*, Vives has a section on historians, in which he comments on the "delightful fluency, and, as Jerome says, a milky fountain of eloquence" of Livy. Suetonius, he continues, "has more nerves than body," and Caesar has the "chastity of style of Roman conversation," terse, polished, elaborate. Sallust is "more suited to those who have made considerable progress in the language." He is "inimitable, and, however often any reader goes back to Sallust, he never feels tedium or satiety" (*Vives and the Renascence Education of Women*, ed. Foster Watson [New York, 1912], p. 246). This description of Sallust is similar to Lipsius' of Thucydides, "Everywhere for elocution grave; short, and thick with sense; sound in his judgments. . . . Whom the oftener you read, the more you shall carry away; yet never be dismissed without appetite" (Hobbes's translation cited from Williamson, p. 215). In contrast to this is Lipsius' judgment of Livy, quoted with disapproval by J. G. Vossius, *De Historicis Latinis*, cap. xix: "Nos quoque supinum eum alibi, aut frigidum, imo & ταυτολογον agnoscimus" (cited from *Titi Livii Patavini Historiarum Libri*, ed. Joannes Dujatius [Venice, 1714], I, prae.). Quintilian described the poor imitators of Cicero as *supini*. Lipsius cautions the young against brevity, whose imitation will too easily beguile them (*Breuitatis imitatio facillime aetatem hanc decipit*) or will make their style dry and flat (*aridus plerumque & exsuccus*). It is better to start with more copiousness which later can be pruned away (*initio vbertas quaedam & luxuries sit, quam aetas paullatim depascat*) (*Institutio Epistolica*, app. to *Jvsti Lipsi Epistolarvm Selectarvm*, [Antwerp, 1605], cap. vii). Slightly later, Lipsius says that Cicero is the only model for *puerilis imitatio* and, for adolescents, those writers least differing from him among whom is Livy. To adults he gives complete freedom of choice, but he stresses Sallust, Seneca, and Tacitus: "Sed inprimis suadeam Sallustium, Senecam, Tacitum, & id genus breuium subtiliumque scriptorum iam legi, quorum acuta quasi falce luxuries illa paullisper recidatur; fiatque oratio stricta, fortis, & vere virilis." *Inst. Epist.*, cap. xi.

46. "If a Livy or a Guicciardine, or such extensive and voluminous authors, had had this story in hand; God must have made another world, to have made them a library to hold their books, of the making of this world. Into what wire would they have drawn out this earth? Into what leaf-gold would they have beat out these heavens?" (*The Works of John Donne*, ed. H. Alford [London, 1849], IV, 491). Williamson relates this remark to the Ciceronian-Senecan controversy, *The Senecan Amble*, p. 243; it is reminiscent of Martial's comment that his library was not big enough to hold Livy (XIV. cxc). Montaigne criticizes Guicciardini for too many digressions and dissertations, "for, endevouring to omit nothing that might be spoken,

having so full and large a subject, and almost infinite, he proveth somewhat languishing, and giveth a tast of a kind of scholasticall tedious babling." *The Essayes of Montaigne,* trans. John Florio, Modern Library ed. (New York, 1933), p. 370.

47. In his list of distinguished writers, Jonson says "Sir *Philip Sidney,* and Mr. *Hooker* (in different matter) grew great Masters of wit, and language; and in whom all vigour of Invention, and strength of judgement met" (VIII, 591). The remark is interesting because Hooker was famous for his rounded Ciceronian period.

48. Jonson willingly committed "strong lines" to the fire (VIII, 206). The testimony of Hobbes in his reply to Davenant (1650) may stand as an example of their association with obscurity and brevity well past the time with which I am concerned. "To this palpable darkness I may also add the ambitious obscurity of expressing more then is perfectly conceived, or perfect conception in fewer words then it requires. Which Expressions, though they have had the honor to be called strong lines, are indeed no better then Riddles, and not onely to the Reader but also after a little time to the Writer himself, dark and troublesome." Cited from *Crit. Ess. of the Seventeenth Cent.,* II, 63. See also Williamson, "Strong Lines," in *Seventeenth Century Contexts* (London, 1960), pp. 120–31, and *The Senecan Amble, passim.*

49. *Tacitus,* I, 197. See also Syme's general discussion of the earlier historical styles, pp. 132–43. Sallust's stylistic objectives were close in many ways to those of the satirists, in verse as well as in prose, and history in its later development asserted its allegiance to the objective depiction of truth in the same way as satire. Lucian in his "The Way to Write History" (38–61) summarizes the characteristics of the classical plain style and, in a portrait of the ideal historian reiterates the attitudes behind it which might have come from Horace or Martial. "There stands my model, then: fearless, incorruptible, independent, a believer in frankness and veracity; one that will call a spade a spade, . . . never heeding what this or that man may think, but setting down the thing that befell" (41). *The Works of Lucian of Samosata,* trans. H. W. Fowler and F. G. Fowler (Oxford, 1905), II, 129.

50. *Tacitus,* I, 197 n. Jonson's declared preference for Tacitean prose would indicate a preference of Donne's style to Sidney's. For Syme's account of Tacitus' later style and its derivation from Sallust's, see *Tacitus,* I, 340–63; their avoidance of the periodic structure and the cultivation of *inconcinnitas* are particularly pertinent (p. 347).

51. One of the most suggestive treatments of the problems of representing objective reality is Erich Auerbach's *Mimesis* (trans. Willard Trask [New York, 1957]). Auerbach uses the term "paratactic" for the abrupt style which omits connectives and the term "hypotactic" for the style which expresses as completely as possible the causal and temporal relationships between its members. He implies throughout that, ideally, the hypotactic style is the more sensitive to the relationships between events and thus to the depiction of their continuum. Both in the skeptical distrust of the human capacity to perceive the relationships accurately enough to make recording them worth while and in the religious lack of concern with a continuum of events *per se* in the Biblical tradition, however, the paratactic style tended to replace the hypotactic. These two types cut across the ancient characters, or levels, of style in their subject matter, but their relation to the characters is describable in each particular work. Auerbach maintains that in antiquity paratactic constructions belonged to the "low style" and matters of comedy (pp. 63, 95) and contrasts its use in high matter in the Biblical tradition. (It must be remembered, however, that the *sermo* developed from the Socratic treatment of equally serious material and was always seeking to break through the conventional restrictions set upon its subject matter. It is sufficient to cite Horace and Seneca.) In the case of Sallust, the effort to grasp events in greater

particularity sacrifices the general view of their continuum. Like the skeptics, he might suspect that the continuum, as we think we perceive it, is a fiction fit for legend. Auerbach's long analysis of the growing concern with vivid dramatization of particular events, or fragments of the continuum, is interesting in relation to the exploitation and elaboration of particular detail which coincides with the rejection of the periodic structure.

52. *Pensées,* 373, ed. Emile Faguet (Paris, 1949), p. 201.

53. *The Whole Works of Roger Ascham,* ed. J. A. Giles (London, 1864), III, 211.

54. Foxe uses the term in an almost identical context: "Euen the infidels, Turkes, Iewes, Anabaptistes, and Libertines, desire felicitie." Cited from *The Oxford English Dictionary* (1933), "Libertine" A.2.b; the same section quotes R. Cawdrey (1604): "*Table Alph., Libertine,* loose in religion, one that thinks he may doe what he listeth."

55. Cicero says that too great an emphasis on content alone is apt to cause schisms, especially in philosophy: "This [the Socratic dialogues] is the source from which has sprung the undoubtedly absurd and unprofitable and reprehensible severance between the tongue and the brain, leading to our having one set of professors to teach us to think and another to teach us to speak. For because of the plurality of schools that virtually sprang from Socrates, owing to the fact that out of his various and diverse discussions, ranging in every direction, one pupil had picked up one doctrine and another another, there were engendered families at discord with one another and widely separated and unlike, although all philosophers claimed and sincerely claimed the title of followers of Socrates." *De Orat.* III.xvi.61. Discussion was dangerous, then, to the established order when the subjects were "various and diverse," when one was not simply arguing about how a thing should be said but about what should be said. In a letter to Sturm, Ascham complains of Senecan stylistic models, "I plainly do not know what trend all those at Oxford are following, but some months ago I met someone of that university in the courtyard who seemed to me in preferring Lucian, Plutarch, Herodianus, Seneca, Aulus Gellius, and Apuleius too much to confine everybody's tongue too much to a weakened and decadent age." (Quid omnes Oxonienses sequuntur, plane nescio, sed ante aliquot menses, in Aula incidi in quendam illius Academiae, qui nimium praeferendo *Lucianum, Plutarchum* et *Herodianum, Senecam, Aulum Gellium,* et *Apuleium,* utramque linguam in nimis senescentem et effoetam aetatem compingere mihi videbatur.) *Works,* I, 190.

56. *Micro-Cosmographie,* ed. E. Arber (London, 1868), p. 32. Williamson, taking from Earle the title for his chapter on Lipsius, gives an extensive treatment of his style and its relation to Senecanism with his valuable documentation; see *The Senecan Amble,* pp. 121–49.

57. For a detailed analysis of Jonson's dramatic prose in terms related to those of Morris Croll, see Jonas A. Barish, *Ben Jonson and the Language of Prose Comedy* (Cambridge, Mass., 1960).

58. Morris Croll, "The Baroque Style in Prose," *Studies in English Philology,* ed. K. Malone and M. Rudd (Minneapolis, 1929), pp. 432–36, hereafter cited as "Baroque Style."

59. *Ibid.,* p. 440. Justus Lipsius developed the curt period more systematically than anyone else. Because of his importance for Jonson as a stylistic authority, I include here an abbreviated version of the six characteristic qualities of his style which Croll gives in his essay devoted to him, "Juste Lipse et le mouvement anti-cicéronien à la fin du XVIᵉ et au début du XVIIᵉ siècle," *Revue du Seizième Siècle,* II (Paris, 1914), 224–26, hereafter cited as "Juste Lipse." The criticism of Lipsius which Croll refers to in the third of these had been made of the followers of Thucydides and Sallust in antiquity and was applied to Lipsius by Joseph Scaliger. "(1) La concision. Par là

nous entendons ses phrases courtes, ses locutions brèves, où, constamment, il nous faut compléter les ellipses, et l'habitude qu'il a d'éviter volontairement, et avec quelque affectation, les détours polis, des préfaces, des apologues et des exordes cicéroniens. (2) L'omission, chaque fois qu'il le peut, des conjonctions et des transitions. Ce caractère est presque nécessairement celui du style haché, fait de phrases courtes, et, au contraire, ne se rencontre pas dans le style périodique. (3) Lipse évite les phrases qui se répondent, il évite le parallélisme, la similitude et tous les autres procédés de la 'concinnite' cicéronienne. Il cherche plutôt à rompre le rythme en arrêtant brusquement ses phrases, manquant ainsi, comme des critiques hostiles l'ont dit, à ce que l'oreille attendait de lui. (4) Il faut un emploi fréquent des parenthèses et des tournures concises. . . . Les parenthèses de Lipse sont fameuses, et c'est un des signes qui permettent de reconnaître les auteurs qui l'ont imité. (5) Lipse s'exerce aux pointes ou 'acumina,' c'est-à-dire aux pensées subtiles (généralement très brèves et très serrées et présentées sous forme d'antithèse), qui veulent défier la vivacité d'esprit du lecteur. (6) Il aime les métaphores. Voilà un trait caractéristique de la prose du XVIIᵉ siècle, et qui la distingue de celle du XVIᵉ, qui préférait la comparaison plus claire et plus diffuse. Ce goût a d'abord marqué le style des chefs du mouvement anticicéronien, Montaigne, Bacon, Lipse, et des concettistes espagnols, et, dans les théories de ces derniers, il a joué un rôle très important."

60. Morris Croll, "Attic Prose: Lipsius, Montaigne, Bacon," *Schelling Anniversary Papers* (New York, 1923), p. 130. Williamson adds that the "conversational style may be said to sacrifice the psychological order as little as possible to logical and grammatical requirements, not at all to rhetorical order" (*The Senecan Amble,* p. 59). Croll associates Montaigne with Balzac, Burton, Sir Thomas Browne, and Pascal, describing them as "hommes désillusionnés et mélancoliques, las du bruit de la vie, spectateurs contemplatifs, moralistes stoïciens, égoïstes qui se plaisent à étaler leur 'moi' faible et sans héroïsme" ("Juste Lipse," p. 204). See also Croll's "Muret and the History of 'Attic' Prose," *PMLA,* XXXIX (June 1924), 305–9, hereafter cited as "Muret," in which he shows in more detail how the Libertine extensions of Atticism tended to express their melancholy and unrest in raillery, satire, and paradox.

61. Croll, "Baroque Style," pp. 446–47.

62. *The Essayes of Montaigne,* p. 110.

63. *Ibid.,* pp. 359–61.

64. *Ibid.,* p. 119.

65. *Ibid.,* p. 132. Just preceding this comment, Montaigne cites three classical statements on the subservience of expression to matter. The first is Horace's *verbaque praevisam rem non invita sequentur* (words not unwillingly will follow when the matter has been well considered), *Ars Poet.* l. 311; the following two are from the elder Seneca (*Controv.* vii. Proae.): "When matter hath possest their minds, they hunt after words" and "Things themselves will catch and carry words." My quotations from Montaigne are taken mostly from I. xxv; other criticisms of rhetoric occur in I. xxxix and li. The main criticisms of Cicero are in I. xxxix and II. x. Montaigne's preference for Terence, Plutarch, Seneca, his appreciation of Catullus and Martial, and his dislike for Cicero and the Petrarchans—all expressed in II. x—show him in accord with the "Senecan" literary tastes.

66. *The Essayes of Montaigne,* p. 201.

67. *Ibid.,* p. 134.

68. *Ibid.,* p. 135.

69. *Ibid.,* p. 202.

70. *Ibid.,* p. 578.

71. Scott, *Controversies,* p. 122.

72. *The Anatomy of Melancholy,* Everyman ed. (London, 1932), I, 26–27. Like Montaigne, Burton carries certain Senecan attitudes to an extreme and holds up what might be called the slogans of the satirist. He writes whatever comes to his lips first "in an extemporean style . . . out of a confused company of notes, and writ with as small deliberation as I do ordinarily speak, without all affectation of big words, fustian phrases, jingling terms, tropes, strong lines, that like Acestes' arrows caught fire as they flew, strains of wit, brave heats, elogies, hyperbolical exornations, elegancies, etc., which many so much affect." He is "a loose, plain, rude writer, *ficum voco ficum et ligonem ligonem* [I call a fig a fig and a spade a spade]." He cites four authorities for his concentration on matter and contempt for the ear. About the last he proclaims, "I am therefore in this point a professed disciple of Apollonius, a scholar of Socrates, I neglect phrases, and labour wholly to inform my reader's understanding, not to please his ear; 'tis not my study or intent to compose neatly, which an orator requires, but to express myself readily and plainly as it happens." *Anatomy,* I, 31–32.

73. See Williamson's "The Libertine Donne," in *Seventeenth Century Contexts,* pp. 42–62. For similarities of Donne's early thought to Montaigne's, see L. I. Bredvold, "The Naturalism of Donne," *JEGP,* XXII (1923), 471–502.

74. In his forty-fifth essay Sir William Cornwallis describes himself as an essayist, "who am but newly bound Prentise to the inquisition of knowledge and vse these papers as a Painter's boy a board, that is trying to bring his hand and his fancie acquainted. It is a maner of writing wel befitting vndigested motions, or a head not knowing his strength like a circumspect runner trying for a starte, or prouidence that tastes before she buyes." *Essayes by Sir William Cornwallis,* ed. D. C. Allen (Baltimore, 1946), p. 190. This is interesting when taken in conjunction with Cornwallis's general skepticism about language. In his forty-seventh essay, "Of Wordes," he says he prefers to learn by what he sees rather than by speech or writing, for our sight brings us closer to things than words can. "Naturally we carry matter better then wordes, in which nature telles vs shee vseth words but for an interpretour because our ignorance vnderstandes not her Language, which puttes vs to a great deale of paine and makes vs go a great way about in our inquisition of knowledge; for there is lesse drosse in the letters of Nature then in wordes, the substance of Bookes" (p. 219). For his praise of his master Montaigne, see p. 42.

75. Aulus Gellius writes that he will not call his "haphazard" arrangement of "assembled notes" a *silva* as those do who have "laboriously gathered varied, manifold, and as it were indiscriminate learning" together (*Noctes Atticae,* prae. 2–6, Loeb ed., trans. J. C. Rolfe [London, 1927]). Quintilian describes the *silva* as a first draft. There are those, he says, "who insist on first making a rapid draft of their subject with the utmost speed of which their pen is capable, and write in the heat and impulse of the moment. They call this their rough copy (*hanc silvam vocant*)," X.iii.17. Bacon follows Cicero (*De Orat.* III.103) in letting the word refer to an abundance of subject matter, *Advancement of Learning,* ll, pref., 12.

76. For the obscurity and roughness in the Metaphysical style, see R. L. Sharp, "Some Light on Metaphysical Obscurity and Roughness," *SP,* XXXI (1934), 497–519; Arnold Stein, "Donne's Obscurity and the Elizabethan Tradition," *ELH,* XIII (1946), 98–118; R. Daniells, "English Baroque and Deliberate Obscurity," *Jour. of Aesthetics,* V (1948), 119ff.; A. Alvarez, "Donne and the Understander," *The School of Donne* (London, 1961), pp. 17–44. Alvarez says he does not understand Jonson's statement about Donne's perishing for not being understood, "since every Renaissance poet worth his salt was supposed to be difficult" (p. 21), and goes on to point out that Donne was attempting to separate himself from the professional writers by his wit and obscurity (p. 32). Stein goes so far as to say that "When Ben Jonson said 'that

Done himself for not being understood would perish' he did not mean this by way of disparagement" (p. 112), but was noting the fact that audiences were not likely to be able to appreciate a complex writer. Stein's interpretation is out of the general tone of the other remarks in the *Conversations,* but, more than this, it contradicts Jonson's general stylistic position as it is stated throughout his works. That poetry was going to be more difficult for the reader than prose and therefore would demand more effort to read was the caution behind most requests for "understanders," not a justification of stylistic obscurity. Difficulty was one thing and obscurity another. The first refers to poetry as an art, the second to characteristics of style. No one asked more often that his works be understood (most often as a professional dramatist) than Jonson, and yet no one criticized the stylistic qualities which led to obscurity more consistently than he. The writers of satire and strong lines, who claimed prestige for their work because its obscurity implied a restricted audience, were concerned more with advertisement than with style. Jonson made quite clear what he thought of their style, and his comments must be interpreted in terms of the critical context in which he speaks.

77. Alvarez, *The School of Donne,* pp. 19–20. In his last chapter, "The Metaphysicals and the Metaphysicians," Alvarez relates the increasing rejection of the Metaphysical style in verse to the increasing distrust of abstract language in the scientific movement of the seventeenth century. He shows the similarity between Sprat's criticism of the scholastic philosophers and Dr. Johnson's criticism of the Metaphysical poets by citing extended, though edited, passages from each. By taking all the particular points Johnson makes, however, of which Alvarez cites slightly over half, it appears that the terms of Johnson's criticism, like those of Ben Jonson, go back to the first century A.D. Johnson has restated the comments of Quintilian on Seneca (X.i. 130), and echoed those of Tacitus and Seneca himself, when he suggests that the wit and matter of the poets, if "expanded to perspicuity, and polished to elegance," could achieve distinction. It is the assumption that other virtues can replace those of composition which he is objecting to, that "the mass of material that ingenious absurdity has thrown together" can stand on its own merits, and this is what Ben Jonson said of Montaigne. Johnson's criticism is not so much of details in themselves, such as heterogeneous ideas "yoked by violence together," or nature and art (that is, technical disciplines) "ransacked for illustrations, comparisons, and allusions." He is objecting to the absence of composition in which they may be related to one another and to general experience. The reason these poets fail in their representation of reality and "cannot be said to have imitated anything" in nature or life, neither the "forms of matter" nor the "operations of the intellect," is precisely the lack of composition affected by the skeptical insistence upon the analysis of parts in their effort to break "every image into fragments" and "laboured particularities." The criticism of labored or "scholastic" erudition is not only in Sprat; it is in Drummond and Cheke, and through Ben Jonson's comment on the "Umbraticall doctors" it is taken back to M. Seneca's criticism of the schools of declamation. It is Bacon himself, however, who most clearly states the relation between the philosophical breaking up of experience into scholastic quiddities and the Senecan fragmentation of subject matter and syntax into *sententiae.* He uses a first-century critical observation on style, probably adapted from Quintilian, as an analogy for the methods of investigation and discourse of the schoolmen. Their solutions to problems were "not confutations, but distinctions: whereas indeed the strength of all sciences is, as the strength of the old man's faggot, in the bond." In syntax, the bond would correspond to the connections of composition, to the relationship between the parts. "If you take out every axiom, as the sticks of the faggot, one by one, you may quarrel with them and bend them and break them

at your pleasure: so that as was said of Seneca, *Verborum minutiis rerum frangit pondera,* so a man may truly say of the schoolmen, *Quaestionum minutiis scientiarum frangunt soliditatem.*" Such a procedure corresponds to lighting corners with a candle, one by one, while the room remains in comparative darkness. Although the "generalities of the schoolmen are for a while good and proportionable," when you "descend into their distinctions and decisions, . . . they end in monstrous altercations and barking questions." These "degladiations about subtleties" not only refer to the combats of the medieval schoolmen but also recall those of the ancient schools of declamation and the traditional criticism of their influence on style (*Advancement of Learning,* I.iv.6, ed. W. A. Wright [Oxford, 1926], pp. 32–33). Bacon employs the Latin criticism again in his twenty-sixth essay, "Of Seeming Wise," and there attributes it to Aulus Gellius, in whose work it has not been traced. Some seem wise who "by amusing men with a subtilty, blanch the matter," and Bacon cites Prodicus in Plato's *Protagoras* as a satirical portrait of such a man.

I am not chiefly, here, taking issue with Alvarez on the relevance of Sprat's statements about language to eighteenth-century criticism; rather, I am questioning his suggestion that the revitalization of poetic language might have been achieved by a return to the qualities of style that Johnson describes. Taken in the wider context of ancient and Renaissance criticism, Johnson is reiterating that any style which does not describe the intellectual and sensory experience of objective reality will be deficient. It may fail from an artificial periodicity that does not sufficiently take hold of particulars or from a lack of composition that does not permit sufficient relation to appear between the particulars. In the latter case, digressive elaboration and hyperbole will often lead the particular away from the experience, to which it initially referred, into sensory or intellectual subtleties. If it departs from the actual experience, it will, as Johnson says, not be "successful in representing or moving the affections." The fact is, I believe, that the Metaphysical style itself contributed largely to the destruction of poetic language, which Alvarez attributes to Bacon and the reforms of the Royal Society. It often simply destroyed the relationship between the particular and the general human experience of the individual reader in which it must participate to be emotionally persuasive.

78. A statement of J. B. Leishman is particularly interesting with regard to the ancient schools of declamation. He comments on Donne's ingenious analogies and his scholastic argumentation in defending preposterous paradoxes or making hyperbolic compliments. He continues that there is "Little that can be regarded as the direct expression of personal experience, or, indeed, of more than a part, a small part, of the poet's self; little that is more than half-serious; little that is what a modern reader is accustomed (perhaps too accustomed) to call 'sincere.' A pervading detachment, an impression of one playing, albeit with remarkable skill and strenuousness, a kind of elaborate game." *The Monarch of Wit* (London, 1951), p. 140. For one of the most balanced evaluations of Donne's virtues and shortcomings, see Clay Hunt, *Donne's Poetry* (New Haven, 1954), pp. 118–201.

CHAPTER TWO

1. The best general introduction to Vives in English is Foster Watson's preface to his translation of the *De Tradendis Disciplinis* (*The Transmission of Knowledge*) in *Vives: On Education.* Watson discusses in some detail the similarity between Vives and Bacon in their mutual emphasis upon experiment, observation, and a psychology based primarily upon sense perception (pp. ciii–cxxii). The criticism of the

lingering scholastic control of the liberal arts and of the stylistic extremes to which the humanists went in order to break that control is nearly identical in the two men. Jonson shared their liberal classicism, which attempted to apply the methods and knowledge of the ancients to the intellectual and social problems of the Renaissance. Each period, in a sense, became for them a criticism of the other in the avoidance of a static application of fixed precept, dogma, or method. In his chapter on imitation, Vives, like Erasmus, does his best to preserve the flexibility and practicality of the doctrine (pp. 189–200). Cicero must not be the only model, for imitation of his "words is useful and safe; but not of his style; for if anyone cannot achieve success in the attempt he will degenerate into a redundant, nerveless, vulgar and plebeian kind of writer" (p. 191). Sallust's brevity is on "the verge of the laconic," and for "a diffuse historical style there is Livy" (pp. 192–93). The greatest vitality of the doctrine during the Renaissance came through an emphasis upon the imitation of the way a given work was composed rather than of the work itself (p. 196). If this were kept firmly in mind, the student would be more likely to "treat it in accordance with his own judgment" (p. 197). Behind all of his cautions lies the awareness of the dangers and limitations of the doctrine. "The attempt to excel or at least to equal the ancients in adornment and elegance, is not so much bad and blameworthy as danger-ous, for fear lest we depart from our own strength and fall into absurdities" (p. 197). Since a style imitated for a long time gradually becomes our own, it is foolish to accustom oneself to individual mannerisms, "extravagances of expression, or a rough-ness of style in oration rather than to an easy, clear, pure, and elegant style" (p. 198). It is such a style that Vives describes in his *De Ratione Dicendi* and *De Conscribendis Epistolis.* For a clear summary of Vives' relation to English humanism, see Atkins, *English Literary Criticism: The Renascence,* pp. 35–65. Atkins gives the best general account of Jonson's critical position and its relationship to Vives and Bacon, pp. 313–35.

2. Croll writes, in "Juste Lipse," p. 235: "Nulle autre méthode, en effet, n'était possible à une époque où l'on croyait encore à l'imitation. Mais, d'un autre côté, cette doctrine de l'imitation elle-même se trouvait menacée et affaiblie par la forme nouvelle qu'elle prenait. Car, un goût qui est assez raffiné pour pouvoir distinguer les qualités et les défauts des différents modèles classiques sans qu'aucune autorité, aucune méthode le guide, affirmera bientôt son indépendance et commencera à chercher une autorité dans la simple réalité des choses et dans les lois naturelles de la pensée."

3. Croll points out the attempt of Antonius Muretus, an early leader of the Senecan movement, to combine the private wisdom derived from self-knowledge (*sapientia*) with public or worldly wisdom (*prudentia*) in the sciences of politics and jurispru-dence ("Muret," pp. 279–81). The interest of Muretus and his followers in such a method of discourse was literary as well as legal, and they derived their principles from Aristotle's *Rhetoric,* an authority equal to Cicero "to which they could appeal in their effort to divorce prose-writing from the customs of epideitic oratory and wed it to philosophy and science" (p. 286). It is not surprising, then, to find many of those interested in reforms of language primarily concerned with reforms of law, and it is interesting to note that the new poetic conventions in England during the 1590's were established by men connected with the Inns of Court.

4. Gellius is drawing upon Cicero's own statements, *De Orat.,* I.51 and III.142. Compare Montaigne, who prefers a style "Rather difficult than tedious, void of affec-tion, free, loose and bold, that every member of it seeme to make a bodie; not Pedanticall, not Frier-like, nor Lawier-like, but rather downe right, Souldier-like." *The Essayes of Montaigne,* p. 134.

5. For instance, Sir Thomas Elyot, a moderate Ciceronian, makes a similar criti-cism in his treatise on princely education when he remarks that the man "that hath

nothinge but langage only may be no more praised than a popiniay" when he speaks with too much refinement. "Wherefore they be moche abused that suppose eloquence to be only in wordes or coulours of Rhetorike, for, as Tulli saith, what is so furiouse or mad a thinge as a vaine soune of wordes of the best sort and most ornate, contayning neither connynge nor sentence? Undoubtedly very eloquence is in euery tonge where any mater or acte done or to be done is expressed in wordes clene, propise, ornate, and comely." *The Gouernour,* I, 116–17. Elyot, like Erasmus, is objecting to extreme Ciceronianism and is translating the same sentence from Cicero that Jonson, finding it quoted by Gellius, translates in the passage quoted.

6. Hoyt H. Hudson, "Jewel's Oration Against Rhetoric," *The Quarterly Journal of Speech,* XIV (1928), 383, 380f. Hudson is inclined to believe that Jewel is sincere in his anti-Ciceronianism (p. 377).

7. Translating an earlier passage in the *De Ratione Dicendi* of Vives, Jonson writes that in metaphor "wee must only serve necessity (*Nam temere nihil transfertur a prudenti*) or commodity, which is a kind of necessity; that is, when wee either absolutely want a word to expresse by, and that is necessity; or when wee have not so fit a word, and that is commodity. As when wee avoid losse by it, and escape obscenenesse, and gaine in the grace and property, which helpes significance" (VIII, 621).

8. *M. Antonii Mureti Opera Omnia,* ed. C. H. Frotsher (Leipzig, 1834), I, 339. My translation.

9. *Joannis Ludovici Vivis Valentini Opera Omnia* (Valencia, 1782) II, 227: *De Ratione Dicendi,* III, viii. (This and all subsequent translations from Vives are mine. The original Latin and references of Jonson's translations, which I cite from his *Discoveries,* are given in the notes of Jonson's editors.) Vives goes on to say that Aristotle is sparing of words and yet says more about his subjects (*rebus est densissimus*). See also Watson, *Vives: On Education,* pp. 274, 296.

10. *Advancement of Learning,* I.iv.5; Wright ed., p. 31.

11. *Ibid.,* I.iv.2, pp. 29–30. Vives summarizes these ideas of Bacon when he says, "It ought to be always observed when one's purpose is to persuade, that greater care should be taken with subject matter than with words; the subject should not be neglected for the ornament of some word." *De Rat. Dic.,* II, xiii; *Opera Omnia,* II, 163.

12. Compare the description of Bacon's style given by his first biographer, William Rawley, in *The Works of Francis Bacon,* ed. J. Spedding, R. L. Ellis, and D. D. Heath, 14 vols. (London, 1859–74), I, 11. Bacon says in his *Aphorisms on the Composition of the Primary History* (*Works,* IV, 254–55) that "in a great work it is no less necessary that what is admitted should be written succinctly than that what is superfluous should be rejected. . . . And for all that concerns ornaments of speech, similitudes, treasury of eloquence, and such like emptinesses, let it be utterly dismissed." Edmund Bolton, who says that all of Bacon's writings "have the freshest, and most savoury form and aptest utterances, that . . . our Tongue can bear" (*Hypercritica; or A Rule of Judgment for writing, or reading our History's* [Oxford, 1722], p. 234), agrees with him about the proper style for history. Continuing the Sallustian rather than Livian tradition, Bolton echoes Lucian when he says the ideal historian is "to set forth . . . things as they are" (p. 214) and "should call a Figg a Figg" (p. 216). It is interesting that he cites Sidney's *Arcadia* as an example of language which is impractical for this purpose, suggesting, as Jonson had done, the association of Sidney with the Livian tradition. Sidney's "rich Conceit and Splendour of Courtly Expressions" are "warily to be used by an Historian; whose style should have gloss and lustre, but otherwise rather Sollidity and Fluency, then Singularity of Oratorial, or Poetical Notions" (p. 232). For him, Jonson's style has the virtues of the best historian's, and, he says, "I never tasted *English* more to my liking, nor more smart, and put to the height of Use in Poetry,

then in that vital judicious, and most practicable Language of *Benjamin Jonson's Poems*" (p. 237). Earlier, Vives also had commented that the true narration of history must be dedicated to truth and in no way needs "colors" and refinements (*De Rat. Dic.*, III, iii; *Opera Omnia*, II, 206). Jonson considered Tacitus the best Latin stylist, and Bacon considered him the best ancient historian (*Letters and Life of Francis Bacon*, ed. James Spedding [London, 1861–74], II, 25). Henry Peacham's description of the best style is very similar to that of Vives, Bacon, and Jonson (*Peacham's Compleat Gentleman*, ed. G. S. Gordon [Oxford, 1906], pp. 42–43). His taste in historians is equally Senecan. He praises Bacon (p. 53), Caesar, Tacitus (p. 46), Curtius, Sallust (p. 48), Camden, Selden (p. 51), and Plutarch and Seneca (p. 52).

13. "Muret," p. 282 n.

14. "Attic Prose: Lipsius, Montaigne, Bacon," p. 143 n.

15. *De Aug.*, VII, 3; *Works*, V, 23.

16. Ralph Lever shows the controversy over the two authorities. I confess, he says, that "I onely folow Aristotle," not only because he writes "more true, and profitable things" than anyone else, but his "manner, and trade of writing, is more perfect and playner." As for "Ciceronians," he continues, "& suger tongued fellowes, which labour more for finenes of speach, then for knowledge of good matter, they oft speake much to small purpose, and shaking foorth a number of choise words, and picked sentences, they hinder good learning, wyth their fond chatte." *The Art of Reason* (London, 1573), pp. 11–12.

17. *De Rat. Dic.*, praefatio; *Opera Omnia*, II, 92. John Hoskyns says in his "Direcõns For Speech and Style" that "the vnderstanding of Aristotles *Rhetorique*, is the directest meanes of skill to discribe, to moue, to appease, or to prevent any mocõn, whatsoeuᵉʳ; whervnto, whoesoeuer can fitt his speech, shalbe truely eloquent." Osborn, *Hoskyns*, p. 155.

18. Jonson's editors cite the collected edition of 1555. The pertinent passage in the edition I have used is *De Rat. Dic.*, I, iv–viii; *Opera Omnia*, II, 110–27.

19. *De Rat. Dic.*, II, prae.; *Opera Omnia*, II, 136. Seneca, whose style is nearest the "Laconicke" of those described here by Vives and Jonson, remarks in Ep. LXXV, "If it were possible, I should prefer to show, rather than speak, my feelings" (Gummere trans.).

20. *Poemata Omnia*, No. 14 (Berlin, 1864), p. 21; my translation. Croll discusses this epigram in "Attic Prose: Lipsius, Montaigne, Bacon," p. 126. Harvey, commenting on Quintilian's discussion of perspicuity (VIII.ii), remarks: "Excellit hac laude latinè Caesar: graecè Xenophon. Ambo prudentissimi viri; ambo fortissimi duces: ambo elegantissimi scriptores, et sine vllis salebris fluentissimi." *Gabriel Harvey's Marginalia*, ed. G. C. Moore Smith (Stratford-upon-Avon, 1913), p. 115.

21. Translated in G. W. Robinson, *Autobiography of Joseph Scaliger* (Cambridge, Mass., 1927), pp. 82–83. Compare Tacitus, *Dialogus* 21, 26. Although they should probably be regarded only as literary gossip, some remarks that Iacobus and Petrus Puteanus report as Joseph Scaliger's are interesting: "Lipsius est cause qu'on ne fait guere estat de Cicéron; lors qu'on en faisoit estat, il y avoit de plus grands hommes en eloquence que maintenant. . . . *Virgilium Lipsius non magnificat & Terentium, quia Latine scribunt & eorum periodi cohaerent, non vero Lypsianae*" (*Scaligeriana, siue Excerpta ex ore Iosephi Scaligeri* [The Hague, 1669], pp. 197–98). If true, it is amusing, in view of Heinsius' funeral oration, that Scaliger should remark "*Heinsius* vient quelquefois yvre de Lipsius, quelquefois de Muret, quelquefois d'Erasme, & dit que les autres sont des Asnes," p. 146.

22. See "Horace, of the Art of Poetrie," ll. 633ff., *Works*, VIII, 335.

23. Osborn, *Hoskyns*, pp. 119–20. Demetrius makes the same criticism (*On Style*, 4).

24. *Hoskyns*, pp. 152–53.

25. Jonson's translation of Horace's *Ars Poetica* 350–52; *Works*, VIII, 321.

26. *De Rat. Dic.*, II, i; *Opera Omnia*, II, 139. Compare Quintilian II.xii.7 where he, too, may have had Seneca in mind.

27. Osborn, *Hoskyns*, p. 154. The phrase *arena sine calce* was supposed to have been applied to Seneca's style by Caligula (Suetonius *Caligula* LIII); it is strange that just before it Hoskyns should echo Seneca's own praise of Fabianus for avoiding rigid *sententiae*: *sensus honestos et magnificos habes, non coactos in sententiam* (*Ep.* C).

28. The passage has been often discussed in modern scholarship. See Croll, "Attic Prose: Lipsius, Montaigne, Bacon," p. 138, and "Juste Lipse," p. 234; Williamson, *The Senecan Amble*, pp. 82, 112; K. R. Wallace, *Francis Bacon on Communication & Rhetoric* (Chapel Hill, 1943), p. 153.

29. Translation by Gilbert Wats (Oxford, 1640), p. 29.

30. Bacon, *Advancement of Learning*, I.iv.3, p. 30.

31. Compare this with *Disc.*, ll. 954–57, and with Seneca's *Ep.* lxxv and cxiv. Compare Peacham, *Compleat Gentleman*, p. 42: "Speech is the Character of a man, and the Interpreter of his mind, and writing, the Image of that."

32. *De Rat. Dic.*, II, v; *Opera Omnia*, II, 144. *Ad Her.* IV, 14–16, seems to have been Vives' source.

33. *De Rat. Dic.*, II, v; *Opera Omnia*, II, 145.

34. *De Rat. Dic.*, II, prae.; *Opera Omnia*, II, 134.

35. *De Rat. Dic.*, II, xvi; *Opera Omnia*, II, 177–78.

36. *Compleat Gentleman*, pp. 46, 49. The last comment is J. C. Scaliger's: "Breuitas igitur Sallustiana . . . quia tribus vocibus integras explet sententias, non circunducit, non interponit: asyndetis vtitur, omittit verba." *Iulii Caesaris Scaligeri Poetices libri septem* (1607), IV, xxiv; pp. 451–52.

37. I disagree with the comments of Jonson's editors that "In criticism Jonson achieved no work worthy of his powers" and that "the finest sayings of the *Discoveries* do not relate to books or theories of art" (II, 450). Atkins's perceptive discussion of the *Discoveries* concludes by saying that in Jonson appeared "the first great English critic, one who gave to criticism a definite place in literary activities, and who did much in diffusing a critical atmosphere and in conveying his love of letters to his own and later generations" (p. 335).

38. A commonplace of the plain style. Martial says, "Your books do not require a reader, but an Apollo"; Ker glosses "Apollo" as "an interpreter." Later in the same epigram (X, xxi) he writes, "Let my poems, Sextus, please commentators—so as to do without commentators." Echoing this epigram, Jonson, writing in Thomas Farnaby's edition of Martial, praises his annotations, which are written in such a way *ut videri possit, sine commentario, commentator* (I, 216). Justus Lipsius says of the epistolary plain style: "Stulti! quia male ingeniosus ille, ad quem capiendum opus est ingenio: praesertim in Epistola, quae arbitrum aut interpretem non quaerit" (*Institutio Epistolica*, cap., viii, appended to *Jvsti Lipsi Epistolarvm Selectarvm*). Donne, in a verse letter to Wotton, says he does not ask for "labored letters" nor those "which should feare/Dishonest carriage: or a seers art." *The Poems of John Donne*, ed. H. J. C. Grierson (Oxford, 1938), I, 189.

39. See Richard Mulcaster: "For sure the writers, when theie speak of *custom*, theie mean that rule in doing; and vertewous life, wherein good men agré and their consent is that, which these men term *custom* therein: as theie call that rule in speaking and writing the *custom* thereof, wherein the skilfull and best learned do agré" (*Mulcaster's Elementarie*, ed. E. T. Campagnac [Oxford, 1925], p. 94). Thomas Wilson's discussion of plainness should be compared to these remarks of Jonson's and Mul-

caster's, *The Arte of Rhetorique,* pp. 162–65. That Spenser should affect archaisms is not surprising when one considers Wilson's remark that "The fine courtier will talke nothing but *Chaucer*" (p. 162).

40. The poem is cited in "Jonson's Literary Record," *Works,* XI, 437–39.

41. *De Rat. Dic.,* II, i; *Opera Omnia,* II, 137–38.

42. I am thinking of the native tradition of English prose, whose development R. W. Chambers traces back to Alfred in *The Continuity of English Prose,* which forms the introduction to his edition of *Harpsfield's Life of More* (E.E.T.S., 1932). The nature and origins of Bacon's and Jonson's style are different, to be sure, but the intentions and the practical consequences of their style have more similarity, within the context of classical imitation, to the native plainness of English tradition than do those of writers who attempted to imitate more specialized ancient models.

CHAPTER THREE

1. *The English Secretorie* (London, 1595), p. 8.

2. *Ibid.,* p. 10.

3. *The Enimie of Idlenesse,* ed. Paul Wolter (Potsdam, 1907), pp. 51–52.

4. *Epistolographi Graeci,* pp. 14–15. My translation is of the Latin version of the Greek text printed opposite it.

5. *Ibid.,* p. 7.

6. Compare *Orator* 84–85 with the description of the epistolary style by Gregory Nazianzen in the fourth century: Figuras admittamus quidem, sed paucas easque non immodestas. Paria paribus opposita et similiter cadentia et membra syllabarum serie sibi respondentia sophistis relinquemus, sin autem quando recipiamus, ut ludentes magis hoc faciemus quam studio persequentes. *Ibid.,* p. 16.

7. *De Conscrib. Epist.,* ix; *Opera Omnia,* II, 297–98.

8. Miss Osborn cites the most important parallel passages, which had been pointed out by Maurice Castelain; some of them are also noted by H. H. Hudson in his earlier edition of the *Direccōns* (*Directions for Speech and Style* [Princeton, 1935]). There is another parallel worth pointing out for our purposes. Hoskyns's "The next good pptie of Epistolarie style is perspicuitie & is often tymes indangered by the former quallity (*Brevity*) . . ." (Osborn, *Hoskyns,* p. 120) is a translation of Lipsius' "Virtvs altera, *Perspicuitas;* de industria a me Breuitati subtexta, quia periculum magnum huic ab illa" (*Inst. Epist.,* cap. viii, p. 11). Castelain cites this passage in printing large sections of the Latin text from the first ten chapters of the treatise (*Ben Jonson, Discoveries* [Paris, 1906], pp. 110–16). He makes no critical application of the material, nor any comment on it, and seems not to have known that Jonson was borrowing from Hoskyns. Morris Croll discusses the treatise in his general treatment of Lipsius' style ("Juste Lipse," *passim*), and Williamson has limited his discussion to "the text relevant to Hoskyns's condensation" (*The Senecan Amble,* p. 140). For a later descriptive summary, see E. C. Dunn, "Lipsius and the Art of Letter-Writing," *Studies in the Renaissance,* III (1956), 145–56. Jean Robertson's *The Art of Letter Writing* (Liverpool, 1942) and K. G. Hornbeck's *Complete Letter-Writer in English, 1568–1800* are helpful studies in the general subject of epistolography.

9. Osborn collates the *Direccōns* with the *Discoveries.* See p. 271.

10. The edition of the *Institutio* used is that appended to *Jvsti Lipsi Epistolarvm Selectarvm.* "It may be said that everybody reveals his own soul in his letters. In every other form of composition it is possible to discern the writer's character, but in none so clearly as in the epistolary" (W. Rhys Roberts trans.).

11. This and the following translations from Lipsius are mine unless otherwise indicated.

12. Jonson closely translates the whole passage, when Horace asserts in *Poetaster*:

> My pleasure is in feet, my words to close,
> As, both our better, old LVCILIVS does:
> He, as his trustie friends, his bookes did trust
> With all his secrets; nor, in things vniust,
> Or actions lawfull, ran to other men:
> So, that the old mans life, describ'd was seene
> As in a votiue table in his lines.
>
> (III.v.49–55; *Works*, IV, 259)

13. These characteristics are very nearly those which Diogenes Laertius describes as the virtues of the Stoic style in his *Life of Zeno* (VII, 59): "There are five excellences of speech—pure Greek, lucidity, conciseness, appropriateness, distinction. By good Greek is meant language faultless in point of grammar and free from careless vulgarity. Lucidity is a style which presents the thought in a way easily understood; conciseness a style that employs no more words than are necessary for setting forth the subject in hand; appropriateness lies in a style akin to the subject; distinction in the avoidance of colloquialism." *Diogenes Laertius*, Loeb ed., trans. R. D. Hicks (London, 1925).

14. *Inst. Epist.*, vii, pp. 9–10.

15. *Ibid.*, vii, p. 10. Lipsius' echo of Terence's *in hac est pura oratio* is interesting, since in this same treatise he declares again his revolutionary preference for the diction of Terence and Plautus.

16. *De Consc. Ep.*, ix; *Opera Omnia*, II, 300.

17. *Inst. Epist.*, viii, p. 11. Cf. Jonson's adaptation of Quintilian: "the chiefe vertue of a style is perspicuitie, and nothing so vitious in it, as to need an Interpreter" (VIII, 622).

18. "An Epistle to Master Iohn Selden," *Underwood* 14; *Works*, VIII, 158.

19. *Inst. Epist.*, ix, pp. 11–12.

20. *Ibid.*, vi, p. 9.

21. *De Consc. Ep.*, vii; *Opera Omnia*, II, 291. See also ix, II, 300, where he objects to a letter's being divided into the five parts of a formal oration.

22. *Inst. Epist.*, ix, p. 12.

23. *Ibid.*, x, p. 12.

24. *Orator* 87; the best extended discussion of urbane wit is Quintilian's, *Inst. Orat.* VI.iii.17ff.

25. *Inst. Epist.*, xi, p. 15.

26. *Ibid.*, pp. 14–15. Jonson included Pliny with Tacitus among those who "speke best Latine." *Conversations with Drummond*, 138; *Works*, I, 136.

27. *Inst. Epist.*, xiii, p. 17.

28. *Ibid.*, xiii, p. 18.

29. *The Familiar Letters*, ed. J. Jacobs (London, 1892), II, 395.

30. *Ibid.*, I, 224. Such descriptions persist. Sprat says of Cowley's letters: "In such Letters the Souls of Men should appear undress'd: And in that negligent habit they may be fit to be seen by one or two in a Chamber, but not to go abroad in the Streets," "An Account of the Life and Writings of Mr. Abraham Cowley," *Crit. Ess. of the Seventeenth Cent.*, II, 137.

31. Cf. Tacitus *Dialogus* 22, where he says of Cicero, "There is nothing you can

extract, nothing you can take away with you," Loeb ed., trans. W. Peterson (London, 1932).

32. *De Rat. Dic.,* II, v; *Opera Omnia,* II, 144.

33. *On Style,* 230–31. In a similarly Senecan passage Vives describes the transference of the heart's good wishes "in which the appearance of presence will shine back among those absent, and written conversation will join those separated, in which we even mingle our soul with a friend's and pour our very thought into him," *De Conscribendis Epistolis,* Intro. Ep.; *Opera Omnia,* II, 263.

34. *On Style,* 190. See Cicero *Orator* xxi.

35. *De Officiis* I, 136. See also *Orator* 64: "There is no anger in it [the *sermo*], no hatred, no ferocity, no pathos."

36. *De Ratione Conscribendi Epistolas,* i, *Opera Omnia* (Leyden, 1703), I, col. 345; xxxi, *Opera Omnia,* I, col. 379.

37. *De Rat. Conscr. Epist.,* xxxi, *Opera Omnia,* I, col. 379.

38. *The Epistles of Erasmus,* ed. F. M. Nichols (London, 1901), I. lxxx.

39. *De Satyrica Graecorvm Poesi et Romanorvm Satira,* ed. I. I. Rambach (Halle, 1774), pp. 229–30.

40. Rosemond Tuve is right in saying that "Applied to poetry as well as oratory, these three divisions marked out rather three stylistic tendencies than three separate boxes to put poems in" (*Elizabethan and Metaphysical Imagery* [Chicago, 1947], p. 232). Later she uses the word "tone" as the main thing the categories were differentiating.

41. *De Causis Corruptarum Artium,* IV, ii; *Opera Omnia,* VI, 162.

42. *The Arte of English Poesie,* p. 152.

43. *Ibid.,* p. 150.

44. *Poetices,* p. 401.

45. *Ibid.,* p. 447.

46. Douglas Bush writes that Donne "did not banish 'rhetoric,' he inaugurated a new kind; or rather, he carried into the poetry of love the colloquial, dramatic, ironic realism that decorum had reserved for satire" (*English Poetry* [New York, 1952], p. 57). Earlier, Miss Tuve had implied that there was nothing exceptional in this, for "Many appearances of rugged, homely, harsh, or violent qualities in the diction of Metaphysical poems are to be referred not to changed theories of poetry but to the conventional theories concerning the "low" style proper to poems in the satirical kinds" (*Imagery,* p. 243 n.). However available the plain style was as a recognizable convention, certain theoretical changes had been taking place regarding decorum for such a style to treat "grave and high matter." Using Puttenham as her principal authority for the three styles, Miss Tuve is occasionally imprecise, as when she assigns the verse epistle to the middle style, because it is "likely to show less rough and violent figures than satire proper" (p. 241). Not only does the classical tradition of the *sermo* assign the familiar letter to the plain style, but the principal English treatise, that of Angel Day, ascribes to it the technical adjective *humile.* The error arises from Puttenham's referring to the plain style as the "base style," which was classically only one of several plain styles, a mistake not made by Jonson or his authorities.

47. *Opera Omnia,* I, 403–4.

48. *Advancement of Learning,* II.iii.4; Wright ed., p. 100.

49. *Inst. Epist.,* v, p. 8.

50. *De Conscr. Epist.,* ii; *Opera Omnia,* II, 269.

51. *Opera Philippi Melanthonis,* ed. C. G. Bretschneider (Halle, 1834), I, fol. 5.

52. *Les Œuvres* (Amsterdam, 1723), II, fol. 4.

53. Howell, *Letters*, I, 18.
54. *Advancement of Learning*, II.iii.4.
55. *Homo sum; humani nihil a me alienum puto* (*Heaut.* 77). Vives, defending the letter from abroad against the insular point of view of those who "consider everything foreign to them outside of their own society and community of friends," cites the same line in favor of international correspondence, *De Conscr. Epist.*, ii; *Opera Omnia*, II, 270–71.
56. In his essay on Cowley, Sprat comments on the stylistic similarity of the verse and prose epistles: "I told you, Sir, that he was very happy in the way of *Horaces* Speeches. . . . I know some Men dis-approve it, because the Verse seems to be loose, and near to the plainness of common Discourse. But that which was admir'd by the court of *Augustus* never ought to be esteem'd flat or vulgar. And the same judgment should be made of Mens styles as of their behaviour and carriage: wherein that is most courtly and hardest to be imitated, which consists of a Natural easiness and unaffected Grace, where nothing seems to be studied, yet everything is extraordinary. This familiar way of Verse puts me in mind of one kind of Prose wherein Mr. *Cowley* was excellent, and that is his Letters to his private Friends" (Spingarn, *Crit. Ess. of the Seventeenth Cent.*, II, 136–37). Examples of verse letters were often cited in treatises on letter writing, and occasionally an appendix was attached, offering models for poetical correspondence. Quite as often verse epistles repeated the commonplaces of the prose treatises. Donne begins one letter to Wotton, "Sir, more then kisses, letters mingle Soules;/For, thus friends absent speake," and ends another:

> I aske not labored letters which should weare
> Long papers out: nor letters which should feare
> Dishonest carriage: or a seers art:
> Nor such as from the brayne come, but the hart.

His epistle "If, as mine is, thy life a slumber be" is practically a versification of Lipsius' *Institutio Epistolica* (*The Poems of John Donne*, ed. Grierson, I, 180, 189, 209). (These observations on extended freedom of subject matter [pp. 68–75] have appeared in slightly different form in *PMLA*, LXXVII [1962], 21–26.)
57. "At Epistolae familiares, siue verba, siue iocos spectes, quid alius sunt quam exemplar Comici sermonis? Inter Comicos autem quis melior Plauto? . . . Ille enim scriptor est qui puritatem, qui proprietatem sermonis suppeditet: ille qui vrbanitatem, iocos, sales, & eam Atticorum Venerem sufficiat, quam frustra in reliquo Latio quaeras. An vocant me at illorum exemplum, qui omnes Epistolas suas vno modo scribunt? Rideant, doleant; ioca, seria tractent, doctos, indoctos compellent: idem vbiq. tenor est, eadem lentitudo? Non sequor. Meae vero Epistolae & facetum aliquid habeant, & eruditum, & remotum a captu vulgi, & quod saepius repetitum placeat." *Epistolicarum Quaestionum Libri V*, p. 192. This work is one of two published together in *Ivsti Lipsi Opera Omnia qvae ad criticam proprie spectant* (Antwerp, 1585).

CHAPTER FOUR

1. "John Selden on the *Workes*, 1616," *Works*, XI, 326–27, ll. 6–31.
2. Compare Horace *Serm.* I.iv.25ff. In *Musae Subsecivae seu Poetica Stromata* (1676), James Duport also attributes the pure style of the comic poets to Jonson:

> Per te Scena loqui didicit: tibi candida vena,
> Et jocus innocuus; . . .

Dramate tu recto, tu linguae idiomate puro,
Exornas soccosque leves, grandesque cothurnos.
Si Lyricus, tu jam *Flaccus*; si Comicus, alter
Plautus es ingenio, tersive *Terentius* oris
Anglicus . . . (Jonson, *Works*, XI, 536).

3. *Pub. Terentii Comoediae Sex, Ex Recensione Heinsiana* (Leyden, 1635).

4. A commonplace, which Donatus attributes to Cicero, quoted from Thomas
Lodge, *The Defence of Poetry*, in *Eliz. Crit. Ess.*, ed. Smith, I, 81. Minturno cites the
same definition and then adds one which "Aristotle greatly approved, an imitation
which ought to depict in a pure and graceful style (*sermone*) some action in civil or
private affairs, not indeed of great importance, or serious, but certainly pleasing and
funny, with the intention of improving morals." *Antonii Sebastiani Minturni De
Poeta* (Venice, 1559), p. 280.

5. Ascham, *Works*, III, 246.

6. Minturno writes that "Comedy introduces . . . merchants, field laborers, sol-
diers, slaves, parasites, whores, panders, old men, youths, and others who vary in age,
sex, fortune, status, and customs, who have been accustomed to lead their private lives
in the city or in the country or in the military camps." *De Poeta*, p. 281. For a similar
list see Puttenham, *The Arte of English Poesie*, p. 32.

7. *De Rat. Dic.*, III, vii; *Opera Omnia*, II, 220.

8. *Quintus Horatius Flaccus accedunt nunc Danielis Heinsii De Satyra Horatiana
Libri duo* (Leyden, 1629), p. 76. See also Minturno on Horace: "Nec dubitandum
est quod ipse de Comedia statuit, quin de Satyra idem censeat; merum fore sermonem,
nisi a sermone pede certo differret." *De Poeta*, p. 425.

9. *De Satyrica Graecorvm Poesi et Romanorvm Satira*, ed. I. I. Rambach (Halle,
1774), p. 216.

10. "A natura enim & sermone tali quam longissime recedunt. Quare? quia,
scilicet, quae prima virtus est dicentis, eam tollunt. Veritatem & Simplicitatem nempe.
De quo parum Iuuenalis cauit. Partim propter versus: qui non repunt humi, sicut
Comicorum & Horatii, sed exquisite facti sunt, vt plurimum, & Epici. Persii autem
opus magis etiam assurgit. Cujus, vt jam caetera omittam, non sermonem modo
humilem, sed & poeticum, translationes audacissimae excedunt: quas summisso oratori,
maxime vitandas esse, Tullius inculcat." *De Satyra Horatiana*, p. 70.

11. Compare Minturno: "Satire can thus be defined as the imitation of certain
vicious and depraved actions, which is suitable for plain verses and, indeed, pure
speech (*sermone puro*), but sharply directed to the improvement of life." *De Poeta*,
p. 424.

12. Dryden's translation, *The Works of John Dryden*, ed. Walter Scott and George
Saintsbury (Edinburgh, 1887), XIII, 107.

13. "Quae vt totam Satyrae exprimit naturam, ita tota fere e praeceptis Flacci est
desumpta." *De Satyra Horatiana*, pp. 53–54.

14. Dryden, *Works*, XIII, 88, 89.

15. *Ibid.*, p. 88.

16. *Auli Persii Flacci Satirarum Liber*, ed. Isaac Casaubon (Leipzig, 1839), pp.
245–46.

17. *Ibid.*, p. 248.

18. *De Satyrica*, pp. 229–30.

19. *De Poeta*, p. 425.

20. *Bernardini Parthenii Spilimbergii in Q. Horatii Flacci Carmina atq. Epodos
Commentarii* (Venice, 1584).

21. *Poetices,* IV, xix–xx, pp. 443–44. Jonson's phrase (VIII, 589) is a translation from the elder Seneca: "Judicium autem fuit strictius; non placebat illi orationem inflectere nec umquam recta via decedere, nisi cum hoc aut necessitas coegisset aut magna suasisset utilitas" (*Controversiae* i. Prae. 23). This may have been Scaliger's source as well.

22. The text used is that translated by J. V. Cunningham, *The Augustan Reprint Society,* No. 24 (Los Angeles, 1950).

23. Compare Martial (X. 4), who complains against such "vain twaddle," claiming *hominem pagina nostra sapit.*

24. Peacham writes: "In *Martiall* you shall see a divine wit, with a flowing purity of the Latine tongue, a true Epigrammatist: his verse is cleare, full, and absolute good, some few too wanton and licentious, being winked at" (*Compleat Gentleman,* pp. 89–90). Jonson wrote in the margin of his edition of Martial "durè, durè, mi Murete, et false" (*Works,* I, 253) beside the following criticism by Muretus: "There is as much difference, moreover, between the writings of Martial and Catullus as between the trivial chatter of some rake and the expansive (*liberalis*) humor which is sprinkled with much urbane wit. I should not deny, however, that many good sayings also have been wisely discovered in Martial, but the number of worse is far greater. There is, indeed, that source of native idiom in Latin that seems to have been corrupted by affectation as little as possible; in Martial there is none, in Catullus a predominance. While I have always drawn back from the former for these reasons, . . . I have always . . . greatly loved Catullus." Jonson's edition was *M. Val. Martialis Nova editio Ex Museo Petri Scriverii* (Leyden, 1619); I am translating from a later printing of the same edition (Amsterdam, 1650), p. 10. For Lipsius' disagreement, see *Epistolicarum Quaestionum,* I, v: "Qvid censes tu? non melius de Martiale Scaliger iudicauit, qui versus eius candidos, numerosos, plenos, Epigrammata multa diuina dicit: quam ille, qui scurram de triuio appellat? Nollem excidisset viro magno hoc iudicium iudicij dissimile. Nihil ad Catullum Martialis, scio: sed & hoc scio, Epigrammata illa nec in triuio nata, nec omnia in triclinio. Multa foeda, obscaena in Martiale: & mehercle in vno Catulli libello non pudiciora, sed pauciora. Ignorat saeculum illud, qui hoc accusat. Sunt & ioci aliquot leues, vulgati, pueriles: sed meliorum maior est numerus" (p. 7).

25. Compare J. C. Scaliger: "Epigrammatum autem genera tot sunt, quot rerum. Tot versuum generibus explicantur, quot sunt versuum genera. Tot verbis generumque generibus, speciebus, formis, figuris, modis cōponuntur, quot sunt in quocunque linguae, nationis, populi, gentis ambitu, genera, species, formae, figurae, modi verborum." *Poetices,* III, cxxv. So Campion of Martial:

> Quasuis sed quasi silua Martialis
> Miscet materias suis libellis,
> Laudes, stigmata, gratulationes,
> Contemptus, ioca, seria, ima, summa.

Campion's Works, ed. Percival Vivian (Oxford, 1909), p. 275.

26. Thomas Bastard, *Chrestoleros* (1598), I, 1; *The Spenser Society Reprints* No. 47 (1888), pp. 1–2. See also I, 5 and VI, 37 and compare Herrick's introductory poem to the *Hesperides,* which is more interesting for its differences than for its similarities.

27. *The Return from Parnassus* II, I.ii.294–95; *The Three Parnassus Plays,* ed. J. B. Leishman (London, 1949), p. 244.

28. Croll, "Muret," p. 267.

29. Croll, "Juste Lipse," p. 235.

30. *Letters and Life,* ed. Spedding, II, 14.

31. Bacon, *Works*, III, 398.

32. Casaubon, *Auli Persii Flacci Satirarum Liber*, p. 2.

33. Casaubon is merely reversing Seneca's comment: "soleo enim et in aliena castra transire, non tamquam transfuga, sed tamquam explorator" (*Ep.* II.5), from which Jonson drew his motto and which he transcribed completely in his inscription to Joachim Morsius (VIII, 664).

34. The second sentence is a translation from Quintilian unnoted by the editors: "Nam in omnibus fere minus valent praecepta quam experimenta" (II.v.15).

35. Bacon, *Novum Organum*, I.xiii; *Works*, IV, 49.

36. *Novum Organum*, I.cxxvii; *Works*, IV, 112.

37. *De Rat. Dic.*, II, xiv; *Opera Omnia*, II, 166–67. For an interestingly similar observation see *The Magnetick Lady*, I.i.69–82. Compare George Herbert's advice on preaching, "particulars ever touch, and awake more than generalls," cited by Douglas Bush, *English Literature in the Earlier Seventeenth Century* (Oxford, 1945), p. 127. Vives' general position on the empirical and inductive methods in the examination of sensory experience is essentially that of Bacon. An art is a method of generalization for handling particulars. It begins with sensory impressions and must continually validate its procedure by returning to them. See Foster Watson, *Vives: On Education*, pp. cxi–cxxii, 19–22, 37–41, 166–71, 227–31.

38. Quoted from "Jonson's Literary Record," *Works*, XI, 517.

39. *Ibid.*, p. 455.

40. *Novum Testamentum, ex interpretatione Theodori Bezae* (Berlin, 1898).

41. *Studies in Honor of Frederick W. Shipley* (St. Louis, 1942), pp. 265–87.

42. For a summary of the stylistic program of the Royal Society, see Williamson's *The Senecan Amble*, pp. 275–300. For the most detailed treatment, see the studies of R. F. Jones on the influence of science on the English language.

CHAPTER FIVE

1. Douglas Bush comments that Metaphysical "poetry was indeed a chronological and ideological parallel to the anti-Ciceronian movement in prose, which grew out of sceptical, empirical, and scientific distrust of the traditional verities and traditional 'public' style." *English Poetry* (New York, 1952), p. 55.

2. Puttenham, *The Arte of English Poesie*, p. 186.

3. *Complete Poetical Works of Edmund Spenser*, ed. R. E. Neil Dodge (Boston, 1908), p. 136.

4. The satirists and epigrammatists who began writing in the 1590's criticized the grandiloquence of the high style and the ornateness of the middle style, in terms borrowed from Horace, Persius, and Martial, without achieving the balance between statement and feeling which the plain style offered them. A complete discussion of Jonson's attitudes toward contemporary poetic conventions ought to include considerable quotation from contemporary satirists. Since, however, their critical comments have been dealt with thoroughly, I shall refer only to those passages that are relevant to particular problems of style, not to general similarities of attitude concerning subject matter. See C. R. Baskervill, *English Elements in Jonson's Early Comedy*, Bulletin of the Univ. of Texas, No. 178 (Austin, 1911); R. M. Alden, *The Rise of Formal Satire in England* (Philadelphia, 1899); J. B. Leishman, *The Three Parnassus Plays;* and A. Davenport, *The Collected Poems of Joseph Hall* (Liverpool, 1949).

5. Jonson's idea of the epic is summarized in his comment to Drummond (I,

132–33) "that Michael Draytons Polyalbion (if he had performed what he promised to writte the deads of all ye Worthies) had been excellent" (*Conv. Dr.,* 25–27). The virtues of the epic poet were identical to those of the historian, which Jonson described in his epigram "To Sir Henry Savile" (VIII, 61):

> We need a man, can speake of the intents,
> The councells, actions, orders, and euents
> Of state, and censure them: we need his pen
> Can write the things, the causes, and the men.
>
> (ll. 31–34)

6. It was conventional for the English satirists to do the same. Marston in *The Scourge of Villanie* (1598) says:

> I invocate no Delian deity,
> No sacred offspring of Mnemosyne;
> I pray in aid no Castalian muse,
> No nymph, no female angel, to infuse
> A sprightly wit. . . .
> (*Proemium in Librum Tertium*)

The Works of John Marston, ed. A. H. Bullen, 3 vols. (London, 1887), III, 353. Jonson's "Famous Voyage" has been generally overlooked as an assertion of literary values. It is, nevertheless, in the historical tradition of the Socratic demand for understanding as expressed in his first epigram. Herford and Simpson find the poem neither decorous nor funny (II, 339, 341), and G. B. Johnston seems to assume that Jonson is burlesquing "his beloved and revered classics" (*Ben Jonson: Poet* [New York, 1945], p. 24).

7. Compare, for example, Jonson's lines with these from the "Induction" (*The Mirror for Magistrates,* ed. L. B. Campbell [Cambridge, 1938], p. 305):

> An hydeous hole al vaste, withouten shape,
> Of endles depth, oerwhelmde with ragged stone,
> Wyth ougly mouth, and grisly Iaws doth gape,
> And to our sight confounds it self in one. . . .
> A deadly gulf where nought but rubbishe growes,
> With fowle blacke swelth in thickned lumpes that lyes,
> Which vp in the ayer such stinking vapors throwes
> That ouer there, may flye no fowle but dyes.
> (ll. 204–7, 211–14)

8. See *Od.* xi.633; *Aen.* VI.286ff.; Tasso *Ger. Lib.* IV, 5; Milton, *Paradise Lost,* II, 628.

9. *The Complete Works of Joshuah Sylvester,* ed. A. B. Grosart (Edinburgh, 1880), I, 116.

10. *The Poems of James VI of Scotland,* ed. James Craigie (Edinburgh, 1955), I, 106–95.

11. The alimentary details, which Sylvester gives in a tone of grandiloquent seriousness, seem almost a parody in themselves:

> But see (alas!) by far more cruell foes
> The slippery bowels thrill'd with thousand throes;
> Wᵗʰ prisoned winds the wringling *Colick* pains them,
> The *Iliack* passion with more rigour strains-them;

Streightens their Conduits, and (detested) makes
Man's mouth (alas!) even like a lothsome Jakes.
Then, the *Dysentery* with fretting pains
Extorteth pure bloud from the flayéd veins.
On th' other side, the *Stone* and *Strangury,*
Tort'ring the Reins with deadly tyranny,
With heat-concreted sand-heaps strangely stop
The burning urine, strainéd drop by drop:
As opposite, the *Diabete* by melting
Our bodie's substance in our Urine swelting,
Distils us still, as long as any matter
Unto the spout can send supply of water.
(*The Furies,* ll. 460–75; *Works,* I, 118)

12. For similar criticism see *The New Inne,* I.vi.124–29, and *Every Man Out of His Humour,* II.iii.67–68. Such subjects were associated with the high style by the satirists. For example, see Joseph Hall in "His Defiance to Enuie," ll. 49–56, and *Satires,* I.iv.5–14 and VI.i.221–32. Like Erasmus and Ascham, Vives criticizes the reading of romances, especially by the young; see *Vives and the Renascence Education of Women,* ed. Foster Watson, pp. 57–59.

13. *The History of Don Quixote,* trans. Thomas Shelton, ed. A. W. Pollard (London, 1900), I, xxi.

14. When Jonson uses mythology in the masques, it usually supplies a workable structural device for the spectacle as well as a fiction flexible enough to include songs and dances. The conceptual content of the masque is slight; the device, if it fulfils the decorative and structural requirements, would not, as in a poem, be a substitute for subject matter. In some of the masques themselves, such as *A Challenge at Tilt, Mercury Vindicated,* and *Christmas His Masque,* Jonson burlesques mythological characters in the same way as he does Hero, Leander, and Cupid in *Bartholomew Fair,* V, iii–iv. In his "Introduction" to *Bartholomew Fair,* in saying "Hee is loth to make Nature afraid in his *Playes,* like those that beget *Tales, Tempests,* and such like *Drolleries,*" he seems to be alluding to Shakespeare's monstrous Caliban and fabulous plots. He criticizes Drayton for similar reasons (VIII, 398, ll. 83–88).

15. *De Rat. Dic.,* II, iv; *Opera Omnia,* II, 144. The author of *Ad Herennium* describes "the Swollen style": "For just as a swelling often resembles a healthy condition of the body, so, to those who are inexperienced, turgid and inflated language often seems majestic—when a thought is expressed either in new or in archaic words, or in clumsy metaphors, or in diction more impressive than the theme demands" (IV.x.15).

16. John Hoskyns wrote a "Tuftaffeta Speech," which was included in the *Prince d'Amour,* an entertainment put on before the young men of the Middle Temple, of which he says "yo^w shall find most of the figures of *Rhetorick* there, meaning neither harme, nor good, but as idle as yor selfe, when yo^w are most at leisure" (Osborn, *Hoskyns,* p. 165). He calls attention to his example of *symploce* in his "fustian speech about Tobacco in derision of vayne Rhetoricke" (p. 127) and later comments that "Agnominacõn" will give an opportunity to "the tuff taffata Orato^r.^s to skipp vpp & downe the neighbourhood of these wordes, that differ more in sence, then in sound, tending neerer to meeter, then to matter" (p. 130).

17. The ignorant gapers would be "the multitude [who] commend Writers, as they doe Fencers, or Wrastlers; who if they come in robustiously, and put for it, with a deale of violence, are received for the *braver-fellowes*: when many times their owne

rudenesse is a cause of their disgrace; and a slight touch of their Adversary, gives all that boisterous force the foyle" (VIII, 583). Hall remarks on "One higher pitch'd doth set his soaring thought / On crowned kings that Fortune hath low brought: / Or some vpreared, high-aspiring swaine / As it might be the Turkish *Tamberlaine*" (*Satires* I.iii.9–12).

18. *The Parnassus Plays*, pp. 241–42. Leishman feels sure that Furor Poeticus, referred to here, "was certainly intended as a vehicle for the parody of Marston's style" (p. 82). Furor proclaims in the second part of *The Return from Parnassus*:

> Hang him whose verse cannot out-belch the wind,
> That cannot beard and braue *Don Eolus*,
> That, when the cloude of his inuention breakes,
> Cannot out-cracke the scarr-crow thunderbolt.
> Hang him, I say.   (ll. 489–93)

Furor's speeches are among the funniest in the play. See ll. 1611–28, 1299–1316, and 1339–50.

19. See *Cynthias Revels*, Prol. 20: "Words, aboue action: matter, aboue words."

20. *Works*, ed. Feuillerat, II, 248–49.

21. Sidney's relationship to the Senecan movement should be studied. There is at least one letter of his to Lipsius which has survived. His criticism of poetic diction, "that hony-flowing Matrone *Eloquence,* apparrelled, or rather disguised, in a Courti-sanlike painted affectation" (*Defence*, p. 42), is analogous to the criticism of Ciceroni-anism at Oxford, made in the letter to his brother, cited earlier. Some of Sidney's own lines can be more intelligently explained in terms of Senecan conventions. The last line of the first sonnet of *Astrophel and Stella,* for example—"Foole saide My muse to mee, looke in thy heart and write"—could appear to be a recommendation for emotional self-indulgence. It is, however, a plea for introspection and intellectual honesty, much nearer in spirit to Persius's words to Cornutus, "I now shake out my heart to you at the bidding of the Muse," and to the context in which that line occurs (V.1–29), than to an emotional release of spontaneous feelings. The heart in this tradition was regarded as the intellectual faculty, and in stylistic matters what we refer to as the mind and the heart Cicero refers to as the heart and the tongue: Socrates was responsible for the "severance between the tongue and the brain (*discidium* . . . *linguae atque cordis*)," which necessitated one person to teach speaking and another thinking (*De Orat.* III.xvi.61). The ear was often substituted for the tongue, and Jonson's friend Peter Heylin provides an interesting gloss on Sidney's line: "If itching eares which commonly follow shallow iudgements expect contradictory epithites, fustian phrases or a stile which no common capacity can goe ouer, I professe no satis-faction for them. I had rather informe the minde then please the hearing, and could wish my booke were laid rather next my readers heart then hung like a Iewell in his eare. Againe the brevitie which I vse, and the subiect concerning which I write are not capable of strong lines and elegant raptures." From the Preface to *Microcosmus,* London, 1621; quoted from Williamson, *The Senecan Amble,* p. 198.

22. See Jonson's translation of "Horace, *of the Art of Poetrie*": "This, striving to run smooth, and flow, / Hath neither soule, nor sinewes (*Sectantem levia, nervi / Deficiunt animique*)," ll. 36–37. In *Poetaster* (III.v.4) he translates *sine nervis* as "wants pith." Florio translates Montaigne's "succulent et nerveux" as "pithie, sin-nowie." Henry Peacham says Horace's own style is "elegant, pure, and sinewy" (*Compleat Gentleman,* p. 89).

23. *Figures of Grammar* (London, 1555), fol. lxi. Sherry's source is *Ad Heren-nium* IV.16.

24. *De Rat. Dic.*, II, v; *Opera Omnia*, II, 144. The passage is quoted in full in Chapter 2. James Howell criticizes French letters for being "like Bodies of loose Flesh without Sinews, they have neither Joints of *Art* nor *Arteries* in them" (*Letters*, I, 18).

25. Jonson is quite clear about which he considered most important: "You have others, that labour onely to ostentation; and are ever more busie about the colours, and surface of a worke, then in the matter, and foundation: For that is hid, the other is seene" (VIII, 585).

26. *The Arte of English Poesie*, p. 66.

27. Jonson may have been remembering the following passage in Campion's *Obseruations in the Art of English Poesie*: "But there is yet another fault in Rime altogether intollerable, which is, that it inforceth a man oftentimes to abiure his matter and extend a short conceit beyond all bounds of arte; for in *Quatorzens* me thinks the Poet handles his subiect as tyrannically as *Procrustes* the thiefe his prisoners, whom, when he had taken, he vsed to cast vpon a bed, which if they were too short to fill, he would stretch them longer, if too long, he would cut them shorter." *Campion's Works*, p. 37.

28. *The Arte of English Poesie*, pp. 222–23.

29. In *The Arte of Reason* (1573) Ralph Lever refers to the Ciceronians as "suger tongued fellowes" (pp. 11–12), and the author of *The Pilgrimage to Parnassus* makes the identification equally clear (*The Three Parnassus Plays*, p. 111):

> *Studioso* Let idle tongues talke of our tedious waye,
> I neuer sawe a more delicious earth,
> A smoother pathwaye, or a sweeter ayre
> Then here is in this lande of Rhetorique.
> Hearke howe the birds delight the mouing ayre
> With prettie tunefull notes and artless lays.
> Harke shrill Don Cicero how sweete he sings,
> See how the groues wonder at his sweet note
> And listen vnto theire sweet nightingale. . . .
> *Philomusus* Indeede I like theire sugred harmonie.
>   (ll. 288–96, 302)

In his introduction Leishman gives a general account of these epithets (pp. 52ff.), and the plays themselves make much fun of the sonneteer. Petrarchan conceits (pp. 116–17), sonnets on pets (pp. 178–79), anthologies of Petrarchan poetry (pp. 230ff.), and the writing of courtly verses (p. 301) are burlesqued. Sir John Davies, the "English Martial," whose "playner verse" and "vnaffected vaine" Iudicio praises in the second part of *The Return from Parnassus* (l. 255), wrote nine "Gullinge Sonnets" which parodied certain rhetorical affectations. "Yet," Davies says in the dedicatory sonnet, "some praise those and some perhappes will praise/euen these of myne" (*Complete Poems of Sir John Davies*, ed. A. B. Grosart [London, 1876], II, 55). A. Davenport's introduction to his edition of Hall's poems, cited above, is helpful in showing the close similarities among the satirists. Hall himself wrote some of the most direct satire on the love-sick sonneteer (*Satires*, I.vii.7–16 and VI.i.245ff.). For the degree to which the other satirists imitated him and one another, see the works of Alden and Baskervill cited above.

30. *Palladis Tamia* (1598), quoted from *Eliz. Crit. Ess.*, II, 317.

31. *Letters and Epigrams of Sir John Harington*, ed. N. E. McClure (Philadelphia, 1930), pp. 162–63, Epig. 38.

32. Herford and Simpson think that the "better verser" is more likely to have been Drayton than Daniel, since by 1599, when the poem was written, Drayton had

dedicated five works to the Countess of Bedford and Daniel none. For this reason, they believe that the "sanguine *Muse*" is "apparently an allusion to the 'tragical' themes of *Piers Gaveston, Robert of Normandy,* and *Mortimeriados*" (*Works,* XI, 45). This is certainly plausible, but it is worth pointing out that Jonson could also have been referring to the love poetry of the middle style, since an amorous disposition was characteristic of a sanguine humour and, therefore, of the lighter vein of the sonneteer. Crites in *Cynthias Revels,* for example, "is neyther to phantastikely melancholy, too slowly phlegmaticke, too lightly sanguine, or too rashly cholericke" (II. iii. 126–27).

33. For a detailed discussion of the close relationship between Jonson's plays and contemporary satire see Baskervill's *English Elements in Jonson's Early Comedy.*

34. See *The Return from Parnassus,* Part II, ll. 235–40. Sir John Davies associates Daniel, colors or figures of diction, colors as in cosmetics, and Ciceronian rhetoric with one another in his forty-fifth epigram:

> Dacus with some good colour and pretence,
> Tearmes his love's beauty "silent eloquence:"
> For she doth lay more colour on her face
> Than ever Tully us'd his speech to grace.

It is a summary of anti-Petrarchan terms. Jonson makes fun of the same phrase from Daniel's *Complaint of Rosamond* in *Every Man Out of His Humour* (III. iii. 24–25) and in *The Staple of Newes* (III. ii. 271–72). The sonneteers were occasionally charged with being bombastic because of their farfetched and resounding metaphors. See Francis Beaumont's epistle to Jonson in which he complains of rural wine, "Good only for a Sonnett straine/wth fustian Metaphors to stuff the Braine" (Jonson, *Works,* XI, 375, ll. 9–10). If Daniel was, in Sidney's phrase, a "pick-purse of another's wit," it is interesting to see how the fashionable purses had changed by 1605. Lady Wouldbee is discussing Guarini:

> All our *English* writers,
> I meane such, as are happy in th'*Italian.*
> Will deigne to steale out of this author, mainely;
> Almost as much, as from MONTAGNIE:
> He has so moderne, and facile a veine,
> Fitting the time, and catching the court-eare.
> Your PETRARCH is more passionate, yet he,
> In dayes of sonetting, trusted 'hem, with much.
> (*Volpone,* III. iv. 87–94)

35. See Sir John Davies, *Complete Poems,* II, 30, Epig. 30; Michael Drayton, "To my Dearly Loved Friend, Henry Reynolds," ll. 125–28; and Edmund Bolton, *Hypercritica,* pp. 235–36.

36. Croll, "Juste Lipse," p. 202.

37. *The Student's Milton,* ed. F. A. Patterson (New York, 1933), p. 556.

38. *Collected Poems,* ed. Davenport, p. 97.

39. *Skialetheia,* "Satyre Preludium," 1.89, Shakespeare Assoc. Facsimiles No. 2 (Oxford, 1931).

40. *The Works of John Marston,* III, 305–6.

41. *Anatomy,* I, 26.

42. *Epigrammes in the Oldest Cut and Newest Fashion,* ed. R. B. McKerrow (London, 1911), p. 13.

CHAPTER SIX

1. *Hypercritica*, p. 237. Greville himself distinguishes his own style from Sidney's: "For my own part, I found my creeping Genius more fixed upon the Images of Life, than the Images of Wit, and therefore chose not to write to them on whose foot the black Oxe had not already trod, as the Proverbe is, but to those only, that are weather-beaten in the Sea of this World, such as having lost the sight of their Gardens, and groves, study to saile on a right course among Rocks, and quick-sands; And if in thus ordaining, and ordering matter, and forme together for the use of life, I have made those Tragedies, no Plaies for the Stage, be it known, it was no part of my purpose to write for them, against whom so many good, and great spirits have already written." Greville goes on to state that the didactic intention of drama is achieved by the same means as that of satire and history. "He that will behold these Acts upon their true Stage, let him look on that Stage wherein himself is an Actor, even the state he lives in, and for every part he may perchance find a Player, and for every Line (it may be) an instance of life, beyond the Authors intention, or application, the vices of former Ages being so like to these of this Age, as it will be easie to find out some affinity, or resemblance between them, which whosoever readeth with this apprehension, will not perchance thinke the Scenes too large, at least the matter not to be exceeded in ac-count of words." *Life of Sir Philip Sidney* (London, 1907), pp. 224–25. Greville's distinction between "Images of Life" and "Images of Wit" is interesting in view of the later criticism of Donne for being unable to represent the passions of actual life because of his involvement in erudite subtleties and verbal ingenuity. Petrarchan and Metaphysical wit both failed to represent objective reality, for both became more con-cerned with words than with matter, in precisely the same way that, as Bacon pointed out, Senecanism followed Ciceronianism in beginning to hunt primarily for words. Greville's use of "wit" in this way is an instance of the word's gradual loss of its mean-ing of good judgment or prudence. Morris Croll says of Greville's "Images of life," on the other hand, that the "emotional power of bare unadorned words in expressing intense convictions and deep feeling is one of the secrets of his impressiveness," and that in this way he is able to keep "his abstract truths close to the emotions of life" and alive with the experience in which they were born. *Works of Fulke Greville* (Phila-delphia, 1903), pp. 23–24.

2. *Eliz. Crit. Ess.*, I, 47–48, 52–53.

3. In an essay on the sixteenth-century lyric Yvor Winters discusses the best work of these men, which has been almost entirely overlooked by literary critics, and relates it to that of the later poets of the plain style. Their poems are characterized, he points out, by a subject that is generally broad and obvious and that often is treated in a series of aphoristic restatements of proverbial truths, in the manner of Chaucer's "Flee fro the prees"; the feeling and rhetoric are restrained to the minimum required by the subject: "The wisdom of poetry of this kind lies not in the acceptance of a truism, for anyone can accept a truism, at least formally, but in the realization of the truth of the truism: the realization resides in the feeling, the style. Only a master of style can deal successfully in a plain manner with obvious matter: we are con-cerned with the type of poetry which is perhaps the hardest to compose and the last to be recognized, a poetry not striking nor original as to subject, but merely true and universal, that is, in a sense commonplace, not striking nor original in rhetorical procedures, but direct and economical, a poetry which permits itself originality . . . only in the most restrained and refined of subtleties in diction and in cadence, but which by virtue of those subtleties inspires its universals with their full value as

experience. The best poems in the early school are among the most perfect examples of the classical virtues to be found in English poetry." "The 16th Century Lyric in England," *Poetry,* LIII, No. 5 (February 1939), 262–64; the two other parts of the essay appear in the March and April issues.

4. In an introductory poem to his works, "The opinion of the aucthor himself after all these commendations," Gascoigne says of the satirical genres:

> *Lucillius* ledde the daunce, and *Horace* made the lawe,
> That poetes by Aucthoritie, may call (A dawe) *A Dawe,*
> And eke (a hore) *A Hore,* but yet in cleanly wordes,
> So that the vice may be rebukt, as though it were in bourdes.

Complete Works of George Gascoigne, ed. J. W. Cunliffe (Cambridge, 1907), I, 33. Ralegh's poem "In commendation of the Steele Glass" (II, 139) reasserts that this freedom is the satirist's prerogative and echoes the comment that Horace makes about the plain style to justify Gascoigne's blank verse:

> As for the verse, who list like trade to trye,
> I feare me much, shal hardly reache so high.

The suggestion that Gascoigne may have chosen blank verse because it was a form of verse near prose is possible, since he was following in the footsteps of Lucilius.

5. Gascoigne, *Works,* II, 148–49.
6. *Ibid.,* I, 344.
7. *Ibid.,* I, 348–52. Winters considers this Gascoigne's best poem, and he discusses it in detail in the first part of his essay cited above.
8. *Collected Poems of Sir Thomas Wyatt,* ed. Kenneth Muir (Cambridge, Mass., 1949), pp. 185–87.
9. *Ibid.,* pp. 188–91.
10. *Ibid.,* pp. 191–93.
11. *Eliz. Crit. Ess.,* I, 48. For similar advice, see King James's *Schort Treatise* on Scottish poetry published in 1584, *Eliz. Crit. Ess.,* I, 220.
12. Sidney, *Works,* III, 41.
13. Wyatt, *Collected Poems,* pp. 122–23. Wyatt's other lute song, "My lute awake! perfourme the last" (p. 49) is a more conventional complaint, but it, too, derives its feeling from a plainly stated realism:

> Perchaunce the lye wethered and old,
> The wynter nyghtes that are so cold,
> Playnying in vain vnto the mone;
> Thy wisshes then dare not be told;
> Care then who lyst, for I have done.

This is a simple statement of a situation that Donne treats with greater severity in his poem "The Apparition." There is a greater subtlety in the definition of feeling than in the lute songs in Wyatt's "They fle from me that sometyme did me seke" (p. 28) where, despite the initial comparison, the language is perfectly plain. He writes as an older man looking back upon his former mistresses and compares them to little animals which at one time came to his hand for food but now are no longer tame. The poem is an urbane reflection upon the frailty of affection and the impermanence of passion which the aging lover can expect from women. The central comparison, however, prevents the poem from being bitter or cynical; Wyatt treats his former lovers with great gentleness and combines a realistic evaluation of physical love with an intense feeling of nostalgia for the past. The poem has three stanzas, the second being an extremely concise description of a particular incident which defines and substantiates the feeling of gentleness and regret. Wyatt's sonnet "Who so list to hount, I knowe where is an hynde" (p. 7) is similar. Although it seems to have been suggested by and partly adapted from Petrarch (CXC) or Romanello (Son. 3), its meaning is subtler than these. It uses a conventional comparison of the lady to a deer to describe a situation that is dangerous, whether one accepts the identification of the lady with Anne Boleyn or not. The sonnet expresses a persistent nostalgia, particularly in lines 5–7, which qualify in a strange way the last two lines, in which the lady's feelings are left ambiguous. The situation is not resolved, and the figurative language, "wylde for to hold, though I seme tame," suggests the feeling that might actually accompany such a state of irresolution.

14. Compare Ralegh's "Farewell to the Covrt," the first four lines of which are as follows:

> Like truthles dreames, so are my ioyes expired,
> And past returne, are all my dandled daies:
> My loue misled, and fancie quite retired,
> Of all which past, the sorow onely staies.

The Poems of Sir Walter Ralegh, ed. A. M. C. Latham (London, 1951), p. 12.

15. In his remarkable essay "Classical and Medieval: Statius 'On Sleep' " (*Tradition and Poetic Structure* [Denver, 1960], pp. 25–39), J. V. Cunningham distinguishes between the structure and poetic devices of the classical poem and those of the medieval and Renaissance poem. One of his distinctions concerns the relation of syntax to the verse line. In order to make clear the differences between the two traditions with regard to rhythm, he cites the opening four lines from Gascoigne's "The Steele Glass" and the beginning of Milton's *Paradise Lost.* Of the first selection he observes that each line conforms to an explicit norm, "a regular alternation of unaccented and accented syllables with a pause after the fourth syllable." Each line is end-stopped, and the syntactical units are alternately four and six syllables. In contrast to this, he points out, "it is the principle of Milton's prosody that the sense should be 'variously drawn out from one Verse into another,' that the thought should be apprehended in units that cut across the metrical structure." Milton's lines illustrate the rhythmical practice of the classical poets, Gascoigne's that of the poets of the Middle Ages and the Renaissance. Cunningham's observations, the extent of which my oversimplification does not indicate, are excellent, and the evidence I shall cite to show the effect of a rhetorical position on prosody will coincidentally support his descriptive terms.

16. *The Oxford Book of Sixteenth Century Verse,* ed. E. K. Chambers (Oxford, 1945), p. 230.

17. See G. P. Krapp's distinction "that prose is expression which is primarily organic, that is in which the expression responds immediately to the sinuosities of the thought, and secondarily manipulated, whereas verse is expression which is primarily manipulated and only secondarily organic." *The Rise of English Literary Prose* (New York, 1915), p. 346.

18. *The Arte of English Poesie,* p. 75.

19. *Ibid.,* p. 72. Gascoigne approves of the same positions in a passage in his "Certayne Notes of Instruction" (*Eliz. Crit. Ess.,* I, 54), upon which Gabriel Harvey comments that 'Sir Philip vseth this kind often: as in Astrophil, Arcadia" (*Marginalia,* p. 170). Jonson's criticisms of Sir John Davies to Drummond may in part reflect the persistence of these metrical conventions. Davies's "Nosce Teipsum" (*Complete Poems,* I, 50), for example, employs a current diction and clear syntax, despite a good deal of inversion, and is dedicated to the Socratic ideal of self-knowledge. What his

style lacks is precisely the urbanity and idiomatic flexibility of the *sermo,* which has the power to suggest the extent of particular experience substantiating each generalization. This can be illustrated, in terms of prosody, by a lack of caesural variation:

> Againe, if *soules* doe other *soules* beget,
> 'Tis by themselues, or by the bodie's power;
> If by themselues, what doth their working let,
> But they might *soules* engender euery houre?

Rhythmically, these lines are lifeless and in a long poem could not but be monotonous. Their order and connection are lax. Their members might be transposed with little disturbance to the statement (precisely the fault that Jonson made fun of, Drummond twice comments, in the first two lines of Davies's "Orchestra"). The flatness of Davies's epigrams may be a result of these same faults, and there may be an analogy between this rhythmical laxness in verse and the defective style peculiar to the *genus tenue* called the meager or arid style (*Ad. Here.* IV.16 and Demetrius, *On Style,* 236). In long narrative poems such as Daniel's *The Civil Wars* it may have been such stiffness that led to the criticism of prosiness.

20. Daniel, for instance, who finds that "continuall cadences of couplets vsed in long and continued Poemes are verie tyresome and vnpleasing," suggests that "sometimes to beguile the eare with a running out, and passing ouer the Ryme, as no bound to stay vs in the line where the violence of the matter will breake thorow, is rather gracefull then otherwise. Wherein I finde my Homer-Lucan, as if he gloried to seeme to haue no bounds, albeit hee were confined within his measures, to be in my conceipt most happy." *Eliz. Crit. Ess.,* II, 382. Lucan, of course, does not run out, although he breaks the line up abruptly.

21. I am citing the epitaph from *M. Annaei Lucani Pharsalia,* ed. P. A. Lemaire (Paris, 1830–32), I, xviii–xix.

22. *Pharsalia,* Loeb ed., trans. J. D. Duff (London, 1928). Charles Bathurst comments: "Lucan appears to have done in Latin poetry what Jonson did in English; introduced a harsh, dry, artificial system of dividing the verses; and, what made it worse, generally stopping after the long syllable." *Remarks on the Differences in Shakespeare's Versification* (London, 1857), p. 217. Sir Ronald Syme comments on the similarity of the lines, translated by Jonson, to the style of Tacitus, *Tacitus,* I, 143.

23. *The Art of English Poesie,* p. 74.

24. *The Works of Ben Jonson,* ed. W. Gifford with Introduction and Appendices by F. Cunningham (London, 1875), IX, 317. Gifford is following the text of the 1692 and subsequent editions of the *Grammar,* which the Oxford editors agree is a preferable reading of this passage (XI, 210).

25. "Periodus sententiam Commatis & Colis juste perficit. Comma seu Incisum est sensus non expleto numero conclusus, a duabus syllabis ad septem usque aut circiter extensus. e quibus Periodus non raro constat: . . . Colon seu Membrum sensum numeris conclusum obsolvit, sed a Periodo avulsum suspendit auditoris expectationem, ut non perficiens sententiam progrediturque a duodecima syllaba ad decimam octavam, quandoque ad vicesimam quartam." *Index Rhetoricus et Oratorius . . . Thomae Farnabii* (London, 1640), pp. 32–33. The translation is mine. Cf. *Ad. Here.,* IV, xix.

26. See Morris Croll's description of the six characteristics of Lipsius' style, given in Chapter I, n. 59. See also Thomas Wilson's description of "Like ending, and like falling" and "Egall members," *The Arte of Rhetorique,* pp. 202–4.

27. *De Rat. Dic.,* I, vii; *Opera Omnia,* II, 117.

28. *On Literary Composition,* ch. XXVI, W. R. Roberts trans.

29. *Exempla Latina*, p. 43, app. to *Dionysii Halicarnassi de Structura Orationis* (London, 1747). My translation.

30. See also the experiments of Thomas Campion in his *Observations in the Art of English Poesy*, especially the introductory poem, "The Writer to his Booke."

31. Without relating it to the classical plain style, Yvor Winters accurately describes the caesural movement of "To Heaven": "The rhythmic structure of the line is of the post-Sidneyan variety: that is, the accented syllables (and the unaccented also) vary widely in degree of accentuation, so that the line is flexible and subtle, rather than heavy and emphatic. The cesuras are managed with great skill: they fall most often after the second foot or the third, or in the middle of the third, but in line twenty the cesura falls in the middle of the fourth foot; and in many lines the secondary pauses complicate the cesural structure greatly, for example, in ten, eleven, and twelve, and there are other less obvious examples." Winters goes on to describe the relationship of syntax to line, which, as it changes, affects "not merely the sentence but the rhythm of the line and of groups of lines" ("Poetic Styles, Old and New," *Four Poets on Poetry* [Baltimore, 1959], pp. 65–69). For a tabulation on Jonson's increased caesura in relation to the later seventeenth-century couplet, see F. E. Schelling's "Ben Jonson and the Classical School," *PLMA*, XIII (1898), 221–49. The study is valuable largely for its tables.

32. *Paradise Lost*, ed. Merritt Y. Hughes (New York, 1935), pp. 80–81.

33. *"Sublimis,* verborum tum singulari delectu, tum audaci pondere, atroci figurarum dignitate, gravi sententiarum magestate, periodorum respiratione crebra, validioribus vibrata numeris, rapido affectuum aestu, conglobatarum amplificationum acta impete, non fulgure tantum coruscet, aut tonitru terreat, sed & fulmine feriat . . . neque in senses irrepat, sed irruat: iustar rapidi torrentis hybernis nivibus aut montano flumine aucti, pontemque aggeremque indignati, sternat agros; saxa devolvat; viam ubi non invenit, faciat; secum auditorem vel contra nitentem, ferat, cogatque ire quo rapit." *Index Rhetoricus*, pp. 58–59. The translation is mine. Farnaby, the distinguished editor of Martial, seems almost to have his tongue in cheek even though all the details can be found in earlier descriptions of the *genus grande*.

34. *Crit. Ess. of the Seventeenth Cent.*, II, 132.

35. *Lives of the English Poets*, ed. A. Waugh (Oxford, 1946), I, 40.

36. *The Poems of John Donne*, ed. Grierson, I, 325.

CHAPTER SEVEN

1. In his *Index Rhetoricus* Jonson's friend Thomas Farnaby gives a succinct summary of the distinctions between the three styles: *"Humilis* itaque Idea, erit elegans, pressa, verecunda, leniter, fluens, simplex munditiis: non tamen inculta aut sicca, non enervis aut arida. *Media,* insurgat aliquanto altior, translationibus crebrior, sed modestis; figuris florida, egressionibus amoena, sententiis fluens, lenius tamen, ad modum lucici amnis crepante pede per calculos defluentis, pictas utrinque floribus & inumbratas sylvis ripas lambentis." Farnaby's eloquence in describing the high style, quoted in Chapter 6, n. 33, sounds ironic in its inclusion of such details as the breath of full lungs which trembles with strong meter, since they were used so often by the satirists to criticize the style. The plain style he describes is the language in common use among educated men, not the base urban or rustic dialects of the uneducated.

2. An extended version of the epigram was written for John Stephens's *Cinthias Reuenge* (VIII, 383):

Who takes thy volume to his vertuous hand,
Must be intended still to vnderstand: . . .
Who reads may roaue, and call the passage darke,
Yet may as blind men sometimes hit the marke.
Who reads, who roaues, who hopes to vnderstand,
May take thy volume to his vertuous hand.
Who cannot reade, but onely doth desire
To vnderstand, hee may at length admire.

These lines are not nearly so good as the epigram, but they are interesting for showing Jonson's belief that the reader's intention to understand is sufficient to overcome other handicaps.

3. *De Conscrib. Epist.,* Intro. Ep.; *Opera Omnia,* II, 263.

4. Cf. Lipsius, *Inst. Epist.,* viii, *De Perspicuitate*: Virtvs altera, *Perspicuitas*; de industria a me Breuitati subtexta, quia periculum magnum huic ab illa. Quam ardua, quam rara illa Breuitas, quae non praeteruolet aures aut defraudet? in qua legentis sensus non opus sit intendi? Atqui semel hoc imbibe: summum in sermone vitium esse, non solum non capi, sed etiam aegre capi. In quo peccant quidam Natura, qui ipsi obscuri & reconditi talia efferunt: plures, Studio; qui nihil doctum aut laudabile putant, nisi reconditum, & quod fugiat vulgares mentes. Stulti! quia male ingeniosus ille, ad quem capiendum opus est ingenio; praesertim in Epistola, quae arbitrum aut interpretem non quaerit. Clare ergo scribito, si potes, & breuiter, sed ita, vt hoc laudis esse scias; illud necessitatis. Clarus autem sermo erit, praecepto triplici: Si verba in eo propria; si vsitata; si collocata.

5. Cf. Lipsius, x: *Decentia* . . . quod fiet aspectu duplici: *Personae* & *Rei. Personae* dupliciter; si tuam respicis, & eius ad quem scribis.

6. Compare "It is not every mans way to hit. They are men (I confesse) that set the *Caract,* and *Value* upon things, as they love them; but *Science* is not every mans *Mistresse.* It is as great a spite to be praised in the wrong place, and by a wrong person, as can be done to a noble nature" (*Disc.,* ll. 170–74).

7. The Senecan maxim was a favorite of the anti-Ciceronians. Nashe, for instance, translates it in *The Anatomie of Absurditie*: "That which we thinke let vs speake, and that which we speake let vs thinke; let our speeche accorde with our life" (*Works,* ed. McKerrow, I, 46). It is in this context, I believe, that Drummond's remark that "of all stiles he loved most to be named honest" (*Conv. Dr.,* l. 631) should be understood.

8. Pliny's description of Titius Aristo (*Ep.* I.xxii), cited by W. D. Briggs as a source for Jonson's epigram "To William Camden," fits Selden equally well: Quam peritus ille et privati iuris et publici! quantum rerum, quantum exemplorum, quantum antiquitatis tenet! Nihil est, quod doceri velis, quod ille docere non possit; mihi certe, quotiens aliquid abditum quaero, ille thesaurus est. Iam quanta sermonibus eius fides, quanta auctoritas, quam pressa et decora cunctatio! quid est, quod non statim sciat? Et tamen plerumque haesitat, dubitat diversitate rationum, quas acri magnoque iudicio ab origine causisque primis repetit, discernit, expendit. "Source-material for Jonson's *Epigrams* and *Forest,*" *CP,* XI, No. 2 (April 1916), 170–71.

9. This may offer another way of stating the resolution of the conflict between content and expression, since flexibility, almost by definition, is subservient to a purpose.

10. The *Prologue* to *Every Man in His Humour* is Jonson's declaration of independence from dramatic conventions, which Shakespeare had used without embarrassment and with great financial success, in favor of presenting "deedes, and language, such as men doe vse." No matter how well Shakespeare used the conventions, Jonson's

claim to dramatic originality is the stronger, for he introduced a new theory, as far as the English stage was concerned, and perfected it. In the *Induction to Bartholomew Fair* (1614), the same year that he writes the epistle to Selden, he criticizes certain of these conventions specifically, by saying that any spectator "that will sweare, *Ieronimo,* or *Andronicus* are the best playes, yet, shall passe vnexpected at, heere, as a man whose Iudgement shewes it is constant, and hath stood still, these fiue and twentie, or thirtie yeeres" (ll. 106–9). He goes on to say that he is sorry that "there bee neuer a *Seruant-monster* i' the *Fayre,*" since "Hee is loth to make Nature afraid in his *Playes,* like those that beget *Tales, Tempests,* and such like *Drolleries*" (ll. 127–30). In 1619 he remarks to Drummond that "Shaksperr wanted Arte" (l. 50) and was foolish enough to bring "jn a number of men saying they had suffered Shipwrack jn Bohemia, wher y^r is no Sea neer by some 100 Miles" (ll. 208–10). The famous passage in the *Discoveries* (ll. 647–68), pretty surely written after 1623 for "posterity," since it alludes to the address of Heminges and Condell "To the great Variety of Readers" prefixed to the First Folio, criticizes Shakespeare for writing too quickly and for not revising sufficiently. He praises him primarily for his personal qualities and for his "excellent *Phantsie*; brave notions, and gentle expressions"; he "redeemed his vices, with his vertues," and there "was ever more in him to be praysed, then to be pardoned." His enthusiasm for him as a person was "on this side Idolatry" but as a writer it was circumspectly controlled. All of these considerations should be kept in mind when thinking about Jonson's problem of what to praise Shakespeare for in a commendatory poem for the First Folio in 1623.

11. In his commendatory verses to Shakespeare's *Poems,* 1640, Leonard Digges not only contrasts certain of Jonson's plays unfavorably with some of Shakespeare's but also implies the distinction, later to become a commonplace, between Shakespeare's reliance upon "Nature" and Jonson's upon learning. One will find, he says, that Shakespeare did not borrow

> One phrase from Greekes, nor Latines imitate,
> Nor once from vulgar Languages Translate,
> Nor Plagiari-like from others gleane,
> Nor begges he from each witty friend a Scene
> To peece his Acts with, all that he doth write,
> Is pure his owne, plot, language exquisite, . . .

Whatever the inaccuracies of Digges's enthusiasm, it may represent an attitude which Jonson might regard as antihumanistic. Although Jonson attempts to praise Shakespeare by locating him in the humanistic tradition, he may have felt that there was some justification for the popular attitude, and, as a result, one can perceive a certain uncertainty in the tone of his poem. Digges's lines are cited from E. K. Chambers, *William Shakespeare* (Oxford, 1930), II, 232.

12. Cf. *Und.* 69, "Epigram To a Friend, and Sonne." The epistle to Weston is based on Horace's ode IV, 8. Horace, however, is simply amplifying the proposition *Dignum laude virum Musa vetat mori.*

13. *De Satyrica,* p. 229.

14. *Epig.* 97, 115, 129. For the editors' argument that they refer to Jones, see *Works,* X, 689–92.

15. In the epigram Jones is "A subtle thing, that doth affections win / By speaking well o' the company' it's in" (ll. 7–8), and is one of those who "Doe all, that longs to the *anarchy* of drinke, / Except the *duell*" (ll. 12–13). These lines are repeated as the twentieth and the tenth lines, respectively, of the epistle.

16. Jonson's "Prologve for the Stage" for his play *The Staple of Newes* demands from the audience the attention of their minds as well as of their eyes:

> For your owne sakes, not his, he bad me say,
> Would you were come to heare, not see a Play.
> Though we his *Actors* must prouide for those,
> Who are our guests, here, in the way of showes,
> The maker hath not so; he'ld haue you wise,
> Much rather by your eares, then by your eyes: . . .
>
> (ll. 1–6)

In the second epilogue of *The New Inne* Jonson says he has written for "men that haue more of eares, / Then eyes to iudge vs" (ll. 6–7).

17. In his epigram on Donne's satires (VIII, 60) Jonson affirms this purpose: "Yet, *Satyres*, since the most of mankind bee / Their vn-auoided subiect, fewest see" (ll. 7–8).

18. A related danger in the Horatian method is the use of a particular situation to introduce a moral essay, written in a series of precepts which have only an incidental relationship to the situation itself. "An Epistle to Sir Edward Sacvile, now Earle of Dorset" (VIII, 153) is a letter to thank Sackville for his patronage. It is modeled on Seneca's moral epistles and versifies a good deal of his *De Beneficiis*. Since the occasion of the poem is only nominally related to its subject, there is no real situation, either stated or implied, from which to take details or to derive feelings, and the extended discussion becomes the most arid didacticism. The poem is one of Jonson's longest epistles, and the precepts do not develop in any logical order with enough consistency to sustain the structure. The result is repetitious and strained moralizing on the art of giving, with an occasional magnificent line such as "Men have beene great, but never good by chance" (l. 124). It can be said about the method generally that the Horatian satire or epistle is structurally most successful if it is short or if it deals directly with its given situation throughout. It is for this reason that, among his poems, the epigram, the ripest of Jonson's studies, is perhaps the most successful genre of the three traditionally employing the plain style.

19. The situation of an Horatian satire occasionally includes several persons instead of simply the author and the person addressed. Such a situation is presented like a small scene from a play, and the style of the *sermo* is similar to the conversation of dramatic dialogue to which the treatises habitually compared it. The ease with which the *sermones* could actually be adapted to the stage can be seen in Jonson's use of Horace's *Sat.* I.ix in *Poetaster*, III.i–iii. Such situations were presented in other satirical genres such as the epode. An interesting example of what can be done within the limits of the plain style by the inclusion of a speaker can be seen if one compares Jonson's epistle "To Sir Robert Wroth" (VIII, 96) with his translation of Horace's second epode (VIII, 289). Both poems are on the virtues of the country life. They treat their didactic theme almost identically until the speaker in the epode reveals himself in the last four lines:

> These thoughts when Usurer *Alphius,* now about
> To turne mere farmer, had spoke out,
> 'Gainst th'Ides, his moneys he gets in with paine,
> At th'Calends, puts all out againe.

Modern editions of Horace sometimes set off the earlier part of the poem in quotation marks. Whereas the letter to Wroth is a kind of moral meditation on the simple, rural way of life, the epode complicates the situation by the irony of the last four lines, and the direct didacticism becomes an urbane satire on the speaker. This type of urbanity, as well as colloquial address, accounts for what has been called dramatic immediacy.

Such a conversational tone was characteristic of the classical *sermo* from the beginning, and neither Donne nor Jonson needed to have gone to the Elizabethan stage for a stylistic model, as some have suggested. See Patrick Cruttwell, *The Shakespearean Moment* (London, 1954), pp. 41–49, and F. R. Leavis, "English Poetry in the Seventeenth Century," *Scrutiny*, IV, No. 3 (December 1935), 238.

20. "Jonson's Literary Record," *Works*, XI, 356.

21. *The Times' Whistle*, ed. J. M. Cowper (London, 1871), pp. xi–xii.

22. R. M. Alden, *The Rise of Formal Satire in England* (Philadelphia, 1899), pp. 199 ff.

23. *Poems*, II, 15.

24. Compare its structure with Jonson's "To Play-wright," cited earlier. The last two lines of Jonson's epigram add a completely new point, which develops from and thrusts home the simply stated distinction in the fourth line.

25. *The Letters and Epigrams of Sir John Harington*, ed. N. E. McClure (Philadelphia, 1930), pp. 232–33, Epig. 206. Harington, however, wrote a number of epigrams that were not entirely buried under "narrations"; many have charm, such as those to Mall, his wife, and many have the urbanity of the classical epigram, such as the famous one on treason (Epig. 259):

> Treason doth neuer prosper, what's the reason?
> For if it prosper, none dare call it Treason.

Harington's epigram "Of Faustus the Fault-finder" (Epig. 208) is one of the few poems describing the difficulty of writing in the plain style in the Renaissance. Jonson saw in the popularity of the narrative epigram a decadence which was comparable to that of the mythological poem.

26. Somewhere between 1613 and 1616 Drummond called Donne the best epigrammatist in England (David Masson, *Drummond of Hawthornden* [London, 1873], p. 80), and in 1619 Jonson repeatedly quoted "Phryne" to Drummond (I, 150). Of Donne's few epigrams, however, some certainly needed an interpreter, although this is against the manners of the genre. One in particular shows an extremely elliptical complexity:

> *Pyramus and Thisbe*
> Two, by themselves, each other, love and feare
> Slaine, cruell friends, by parting have joyn'd here.

Poetical Works, ed. Grierson, I, 75. The style of this epigram is no more the spoken language, save in diction, than the most ornate speech of Euphues. The syntax is "laboured" and shows the license of composition which Seneca, Quintilian, and Tacitus had criticized in the first century and to which Jonson alludes in his comparison of Sallust with Donne.

27. The second line is repeated in the epigram to the Countess of Rutland (VIII, 224). In a letter to Junius, Casaubon gives a similar description of an English traveler, Sir Henry Wotton: "A noble Englishman, . . . a youth adorned with all the virtues, who has lived many years abroad in order that, returning home at length, he might truly recall the account of Ulysses, that he had seen the cities of many men, and known their minds. Wherever he comes, therefore, his first care is to meet with those from whose company he may depart a better and a wiser man." *The Life and Letters of Sir Henry Wotton*, I, 25.

28. Grierson cites several instances in discussing the phrase in *Donne's Poetical Works*, II, 70.

29. These instructions are divided into twenty-four laws; the Latin text gives each

as an imperative. My translation is literal except where I have been able to combine two laws plausibly with a connective. The models for the epigram are Catullus 13, Horace *Ep.* I.v, and Martial V.78, X.48, and XI.52. Line 24 of the epigram and *Leges* 18–19 either depend upon or recall Martial XI.52.16 and V.78.25; ll. 35–42 and *Leges* 17, 23, 24 are derived from Horace *Ep.* I.v.24–25 and Martial X.48.21–24.

30. T. K. Whipple, for example, says that Martial writes "in the most finished style and with the most finished art, yet without imagination and without emotion," and "is wanting in poetic feeling." The fact, he comments later, "that Jonson has kept his epigrams on so low an emotional level" shows how much he was influenced by Martial. *Martial and the English Epigram from Sir Thomas Wyatt to Ben Jonson* (Berkeley, 1925), pp. 298, 404.

31. *Life and Letters,* II, 311. This letter was pointed out to me by J. V. Cunningham.

CHAPTER EIGHT

1. Bacon, *Works,* IV, 315.

2. Sprat's essay on Cowley relates technical observations similar to those of Dionysius to freedom of subject matter and the flexibility of the *sermo*: "If any are displeas'd at the boldness of his Metaphors and length of his Digressions they contend not against Mr. *Cowley,* but *Pindar* himself. . . . If the irregularity of the number disgust them, they may observe that this very thing makes that kind of Poesie fit for all manner of subjects: For the Pleasant, the Grave, the Amorous, the Heroic, the Philosophical, the Moral, the Divine. Besides this they will find that the frequent alteration of the Rhythm and Feet affects the mind with a more various delight, while it is soon apt to be tyr'd by the setled pace of any one constant measure. But that for which I think this inequality of number is chiefly to be preferr'd is its near affinity with Prose: From which all other kinds of *English* Verse are so far distant that it is very seldom found that the same man excels in both ways. But now this loose and unconfin'd measure has all the Grace and Harmony of the most Confin'd. And withal it is so large and free, that the practice of it will only exalt, not corrupt our Prose, which is certainly the most useful kind of Writing of all others, for it is the style of all business and conversation." Spingarn, *Crit. Ess. of the Seventeenth Cent.,* II, 131–32.

3. *Poetices,* p. 388.

4. This poem, like many of Jonson's, is largely an adaptation of classical sources, especially of Martial III, 58. It is not, however, for this reason a less accurate description of his personal experience. The context of feeling in Martial was one in which Jonson could participate to such an extent that he could borrow the details and make them take hold of his personal situation without distorting it. Had there been no source, the judgments made and the feelings conveyed would have been the same even if all the details were not. The definition of the feeling, and hence the poem, is his own.

5. In his thirty-second epigram Jonson mentions Roe's "two braue perills of the priuate sword" and his participation in the Netherlands campaigns. Jonson's editors cite a letter of Philip Gawdy (XI, 12), dated October 28, 1605, which describes Roe's bravery in terms that imply a kind of reckless bravado. In a letter dated October 5, 1605 (*Sidney Papers* II, 315), Sir John Throckmorton mentions "Sir *John Rooe* sore hurt in the Heade, but he cam of, and recovereth." Any of these actions might have occasioned Jonson's ode, but the last one suggests the possibility of a pun in the lines "Yet doth some wholesome Physick for the mind, / Wrapt in this paper lie," after

"The Cure of that, which is but corporall." Your physical wound in the head is now cured, still you can apply a little advice to it: don't be so reckless in the future. The guess cannot be verified, however, and there is no way to answer the question why Jonson did not include the ode in the *Forest* or *Epigrammes* in 1616.

6. The editors gloss "aspire" as "inspire" (*Works*, XI, 61), which does not make sense. The *New English Dictionary* lists two obsolete transitive meanings for the verb, *aspire* 4. and 8., both of which remove the syntactical difficulty. It cites the meaning "to aim at," as in "He aspired the Empire" (1623 Cockeram *Dict.* III. s.v. *Cleopatra*), and also the meaning "to mount up to" or "attain," as in "That gallant spirit hath aspir'd the clouds" (1592 Shaks. *Rom. & Jul.* III.i.122). The second meaning seems to me preferable and occurs often at the end of the sixteenth century; the *New English Dictionary* cites four instances between 1581 and 1596.

7. Henry Peacham, *The Garden of Eloquence*, p. 22.

8. *The Arte of English Poesie*, p. 152.

9. *Inst. Epist.*, v, 8.

10. *De Rat. Dic.*, II, xvi; *Opera Omnia*, II, 175–76.

11. *De Rat. Dic.*, III, vii; *Opera Omnia*, II, 220.

12. Jonson's funeral elegies, "On the Lady Jane Pawlet" (VIII, 268) and "Elegie on my Muse" (VIII, 282), on Venetia Digby, are both long and contain a good deal of material that might be called religious. They treat their respective ladies much as Donne treats Elizabeth Drury, and they suffer, like Donne's poems, from a lack of structural coherence and too much irresponsible hyperbole. It is strange that Jonson, after telling Drummond "that Dones Anniversarie was profane and full of Blasphemies" and "that he told Mr Donne, if it had been written of ye Virgin Marie it had been something" (I, 133), should proceed to beatify Lady Digby.

13. Herbert states his own rejection of the ornate style in his two poems entitled "Jordan" in terms almost identical to those used in the rejection of Ciceronian and Petrarchan models.

14. Winters offers a good description: "There is a recognition of reality here, distinct from a literary convention (as in Shakespeare) and from a gift for personal drama, or perhaps melodrama (as in Donne), which is very impressive. Much of the power of the poem resides in one of the elementary facts of life: the fact that a middle-aged man of intelligence is often readier to die than to live if he merely indulges his feelings. Jonson deals with the real problem, not with a spurious problem." *Four Poets*, pp. 68–69.

15. For the essentially syllogistic structure of the Elizabethan lyric see J. V. Cunningham's excellent short essay, "Logic and Lyric," *Tradition and Poetic Structure*, pp. 40–58.

16. Aneau's poem is quoted in Jonson's *Works*, XI, 38. Among Jonson's adaptations and translations, which should be mentioned with the love poems, are the three songs to Celia (VIII, 102, 103, 106), "The Houre-glasse" (VIII, 148), and Horace's first ode of the fourth book, "To Venus" (VIII, 292). Despite the figurative devices used in these poems, the language retains its idiomatic directness. This gives the commands of the Celia lyrics a certain blunt force, present in the Latin, which later translators of Catullus' poems often dissipated in an effort to reproduce the sensitive delicacy of the original. The classical place names of the second lyric to Celia have been replaced by local names with the result that the tone of plainly spoken English is in no way decorated by allusions to anything foreign, and therefore exotic, or to anything outside of normal experience. The same things may be said about the song "Drinke to me, onely, with thine eyes," although the details, which are pieced together from the epistles of Philostratus, are more ornate in themselves. The shifting of the

degrees of stress and of the caesural positions makes its rhythm extraordinarily subtle. It is primarily the rhythm that distinguishes this song from the more conventional song "Oh doe not wanton with those eyes" (VIII, 144), which might be considered a kind of prototype for the Cavalier lyric. "The Houre-glasse," which Jonson sent to Drummond, is borrowed from Girolamo Amaltei's *Horologium Pulverum,* and illustrates Jonson's skill and delight in using an intricate stanza with the conversational caesura. It is the intricacy of the conclusion which gives the poem much of its humor:

> Yes; and in death, as life, unblest,
> To have't exprest,
> Even ashes of lovers find no rest.

By using the triple rhyme Jonson calls attention to the humorously stiff and quite superfluous pedagogical emphasis upon the meaning of the poem "To have't exprest." The translation of Horace's ode, blaming Venus for bending "a man, now at his fiftieth yeare," is very fine. Compare especially these lines:

> Sed cur, heu, Ligurine, cur
> manat rara meas lacrima per genas?

> But why, oh why, my *Ligurine,*
> Flow my thin teares, downe these pale cheeks of mine?

Jonson's conclusion is also particularly beautiful in rhythm and phrasing:

> Hard-hearted, I dreame every Night
> I hold thee fast! but fled hence, with the Light,
> Whether in *Mars* his field thou bee,
> Or *Tybers* winding streames, I follow thee.

17. A recent essay by P. M. Cubeta, " 'A Celebration of Charis': An Evaluation of Jonsonian Poetic Strategy," *ELH,* XXV, No. 3 (September 1958), 163–80, is the only study I know of the poems as a group. It is the difficulty of relating the first poem to the explicit satire of Petrarchan conventions in the later poems, I think, that leads the author to interpret the first poem as a parody. In the first four lines Jonson is a "stuffily pompous lover"; lines 13–20 are an arrogant parody of sonnet conventions; and lines 7–12 "give the surface reasoning and veneer of seriousness an ironic undertone as the rhythms rock along in a sing-song fashion which only enhances the stereotyped banality of 'the Language and the Truth.' " For purposes of parody Jonson has put together a "jumble of clichés crystallized out of Petrarchan traditions" (pp. 164–66).

18. Although Neoplatonism was often associated with Petrarchanism, originally their connection was accidental. Petrarchanism referred to the literary forms, the style, and the attitudes which sixteenth-century poets adopted from Italy and France; Neoplatonism, to a system of thought which attempted to synthesize Platonic and Christian doctrine and which, flourishing in the fifteenth and sixteenth centuries, was available and widely discussed at the time when poets were seeking new literary conventions. In his monument to Petrarchanism, George Puttenham never mentions Ficino, Castiglione, or Sir Thomas Hoby, even though he deals with the general function of the poet at Court, who must conduct himself so as to "worthily retaine the credit of his place, and profession of a very Courtier" (*The Arte of English Poesie,* p. 299). It is John Hoskyns, on the other hand, who inserts an appreciative reference to Castiglione into his adaptation of Lipsius' *Institutio Epistolica* to show where the reader may find *adagia, allusionesque ad dicta aut facta vetera, versiculos aut argutas*

sententias, mixed in with *iocis salibusque*, which are the strength and sinews of writing. Jonson transcribes the passage in his *Discoveries*, including the allusion to *The Courtier*, following the warning "not to cast a Ring for the perfumed termes of the time" (VIII, 632). The ethical psychology of Neoplatonism, furthermore, was often cited as a corrective for the materialism of Petrarchan extravagance.

In contrast to the English rhetoric books, concerned mainly with amplification, the courtesy books, such as Henry Peacham's *The Compleat Gentleman*, in their brief treatment of style, because they criticized affectation in all its forms, were usually sensible and advocated a simple directness in speech and writing. Marston and other satirists called their fops Castilio, but Castiglione gives nonetheless a clean description of good prose in *The Courtier*. It is amusing to compare Guilpin's view of the man in his recommendation "Come to the Court, and Balthazar affords / Fountains of holy and rose water words" with Castiglione's hardheaded assertion of independence in rejecting the "literary" Tuscan dialect: "and I say that I have written it in mine owne [dialect], and as I speak, and unto such as speake as I speake: and so I trust I have offended no man" ("The epistle of the Author," *The Book of The Courtier*, trans. Sir Thomas Hoby, *The Tudor Translations* [London, 1900], p. 22). Many of his further statements on writing are commonplaces of the plain style: that content is soul of language and knowledge is the most important thing in speaking and writing well (p. 69), that words "ought to be apt, chosen, clere, and wel applyed, and (above al) in use also among the people [*sopra tutto usate ancor dal populo*]" (pp. 69–70), and that one should speak "with suche conveiaunce of easinesse, that whoso heareth him, maye conceyve a good oppinion of himselfe, and thinke that he also with very litle a doe, mighte attaine to that perfection, but whan he commeth to the proofe shall finde himselfe farre wide" (p. 71). The last quotation is an allusion to Horace's central maxim concerning the *sermo* (*Ars Poet.* 240–42), and it was cited repeatedly to justify the exclusion of ornament in the interests of simplicity; compare Du Bellay, *Les Regrets*, ii:

> Aussi veulx-je (Paschal) que ce que je compose
> Soit une prose en ryme ou une ryme en prose,
> Et ne veulx pour cela le laurier meriter.
> Et peult estre que tel se pense bien habile,
> Qui trouvant de mes vers la ryme si facile,
> En vain travaillera, me voulant imiter.

See also Isocrates *Panathenaicus* 3; Cicero *Orator* 76; Quintilian *Inst. Orat.* IV.ii.38; William Webbe, *Discourse of English Poetrie, Eliz. Crit. Ess.*, I, 300; John Dryden, *Essay on Satire, Works*, XIII, 33–34.

19. The opening lines of the eighth lyric suggest the presence of other people from the beginning of the sequence: "*Charis* one day in discourse . . . of Love" lightly promised to tell what kind of man she could love well, "And that promise set on fire/All that heard her, with desire."

20. For a summary of the extensive use that Jonson, in his masques, makes of a variety of Neoplatonic sources, such as Ficino's *Commentary*, see *Works*, X, pp. 422–28, as well as his own notes and those of his editors to the masques themselves.

21. Lord Gaspar in *The Courtier*, for instance, proposes as his "device" for the evening that "thys nyghte to have everye manne open what vertues he would principally the persone he loveth should be indowed with all" (p. 35). This device was not chosen, but the subject was throughly covered by the one that was.

22. The point is that a man that old making love could expect to be ridiculed, and Jonson, in order to forestall laughter, makes "His excuse for loving." To be sure,

the old man in love is one of the most common targets for comedy in classical and medieval times, especially the old man with the young wife, but the context of this poem is that of the lengthy discussions of the propriety of such a love in the *questioni d'amore* and the courtesy books, and the terms of the excuse are the Neoplatonic ones of Lovel, "A compleat Gentleman, a Souldier, and a Scholer" ("The Persons of the Play," l. 7), in his description of "what *Loue* is."

23. To Phaedrus' praise of Lysias' demonstration that the non-lover should be accepted rather than the lover, Socrates responds, "And I wish that he would say a poor man rather than a rich, and an old man rather than a young one; he would meet the case of me, and all of us, and then his words would indeed be charming, and of public utility." *The Works of Plato,* trans. B. Jowett, 4 vols. in one (New York, n.d.), III, 380.

24. *Marsilio Ficino's Commentary on Plato's Symposium,* reprinted and trans. by S. R. Jayne, *The University of Missouri Studies,* XIX, No. 1 (1944), 50. This entire chapter of the commentary is a necessary gloss on the logical structure of many Elizabethan songs and love poems; it may serve, for instance, as an actual paraphrase of Sidney's song "Who hath his fancy pleased," a brief and tightly argued statement of the Neoplatonic system. See also *The Courtier,* pp. 362–63, which Sidney would have been even more likely to know well.

25. *The Works of Plato,* trans. Jowett, III, 347.

26. W. D. Briggs in "Source-Material for Jonson's *Underwoods* and Miscellaneous Poems," *MP,* XV (1917), 85, comments that "the central situation is supplied by Hieronymus Angerianus, *Carm. Illustrium Poet. Ital.,* 1719, I, 292:

De Caelia, & Cupidine
Vidit Amor dominam, stupuit; cecidere sagittae.
Armavit sese Caelia, fugit Amor."

The situation, of course, is not identical. Jonson knew, and probably liked, Angerianus' collection of erotic poems, but they are entirely different in subject and tone from the "Celebration," despite this and other possible borrowings which I shall refer to later.

27. Ficino, *Commentary,* pp. 217–18. "Numquid optimi viri illud in superioribus animadvertistis, quod dum Plato ipsum fingit Amorem, Socratis omnem pingit effigiem, ac numinis illius figuram ex ideo ille prae caeteris verus sit legitimiusque amator? Agite iam Amoris picturam illam in animum revocate. Videbitis in ea Socratem figuratum" (p. 105). In the same chapter, "Socrates Fuit Verus Amator et Cupidini Similis," there is another detail suggesting that Jonson may have identified himself with Socrates: "Who does not know that Socrates was the son of a stonecutter and a midwife, and that even up to his old age he made his living by his own hands in sculpturing stone, and that he never had enough to feed himself and his family?" (p. 219).

28. Silenus was Socratic in mind as well as in body, and Jonson would in some ways have enjoyed being compared to him. In a marginal note to the masque *Oberon* he compares him with the satyrs. "But in the *Silenes,* was nothing of this petulance, and lightnesse; but on the contrarie, all grauitie, and profound knowledge, of most secret mysteries. Insomuch as the most learned of Poets, *Virgil,* when he would write a Poeme of the beginnings, and hidden nature of things, with other great Antiquities, attributed the parts of disputing them, to *Silenus,* rather than any other. . . . To this see the testimonies of *Plato, Synesius, Herodotus, Strabo, Philostratus, Tertullian, Etc.,*" (VII, 343 n.). This is interesting in view of Jonson's attitude toward his own physical appearance; he could joke about it with some impunity, even in matters of love, for Silenus' way of living was gracious, if not graceful, and above it all he had his

wit to recommend him. The humanists were fond of Plato's comparison of Socrates with Silenus; see Abel Lefranc's extensive notes to Rabelais's prologue to *Gargantua, Œuvres de François Rabelais* (Paris, 1913), I, 3–18. See also Casaubon, *De Satyrica, passim.*

29. *The Minor Poems,* Variorum edition, ed. C. G. Osgood and H. G. Lotspeich (Baltimore, 1943), I, 201.

30. Plato, *Works,* III, 302. For Castiglione's close adaptation see *The Courtier,* p. 264. Ovid develops the comparison between the lover and the soldier in much more detail and gives more emphasis to its erotic connotations. Every lover is like a soldier, he says, and their advancing age is a hindrance to both, for " 'Tis unseemly for the old man to soldier, unseemly for the old man to love." The soldier goes on long campaigns; "Send but his love before, and the strenuous lover, too, will follow without end." He will climb mountains, cross rivers and snow plains, and "when about to ride the seas he will not prate of swollen East–winds"; the soldier besieges towns, the lover the house of his mistress. *Amores* I.ix.1–20, Loeb ed., trans. G. Showerman (London, 1931).

31. Ficino, *Commentary,* pp. 71–72. Compare Castiglione's description of beauty, which "when it findeth out a face well proportioned, . . . therinto it distilleth it self and appeereth most welfavoured, and decketh out and lyghtneth the subject where it shyneth wyth a marveylous grace." *The Courtier,* p. 343.

32. Angerianus uses the name in several different ways. It is the singular form of Charites and hence can refer to one of the Graces, as in "Veneri tum Charis una refert . . ." (*Carmine Illustrium Poetarum Italorum* [Florence, 1719], I, 266), or to the fusion of the three Graces in one person, "Tres Charites; tribus una Charis connecteris; illae/Tres Charites teneant ut Dea, te Charitem" (p. 274). The latter usage was perfectly conventional: see the epigrams of Georgius Anselmus and Franciscus Apostolius in the same volume, pp. 299, 320. Angerianus also seems to equate Charis with Venus when Cupid complains, "Linquo sales, ludosque meos; atque omnia pulchra./Quaeque Charis docuit, quaeque venusta parens" (p. 295), and he occasionally uses the name for a single agent, "Factus Amor mitis, transfixo clausit amanti/Lumina; collegit corporis ossa Charis" (p. 298). See also "De Caelia," p. 254. Jonson, however, could be drawing on the widely diffused usage of the name in neo-Latin poetry just as well as on Angerianus specifically.

33. Jonson used some of these details in *Underwood* 19, in *The Divell is an Asse* II.vi.70–87, and in *The Gypsies Metamorphos'd,* ll. 522–43, a song which includes details and echoes from several of the poems in the "Celebration."

34. See Ficino, *Commentary,* II.vii. Jonson's editors cite the passage in the *Symposium* as the central context for Lovel's definition of love in *The New Inne,* III. ii.60–200 (*Works,* X, 318–19). In his commentary, VI.vii, *De Amoris Ortu,* where he describes the Platonic allegory of Porus and Penia (which Jonson refers to in *Loves Triumph through Callipolis*) from whose union Love was born, Ficino says that the Venus Urania is a specific attribute of the Angelic Mind, and, unless one keeps his system well in mind, his statement is momentarily startling: *habet insuper intelligendi potentiam, quam esse Venerem, arbitramur.* Jonson may well have borrowed these last three lines, as Gifford suggests in his edition, from Angerianus (*Carm. Illust. Poet. Ital.,* I, 265):

> Hoc majus; tres uno in corpore: Caelia ridens
> Est Venus, incedens Juno, Minerva loquens.

This possibility, however, does not invalidate their Neoplatonic implications in the "Celebration." There is nothing in the collection of epigrams, which, although the author, Cupid, and the lady converse throughout, are but fragmentary explorations of conventional conceits, to suggest the narrative structure, the theme, or the feeling of Jonson's sequence.

35. "Knots" refers specifically to love affairs. Ficino for one discusses the difficulties involved in tying the *nodi* between people of similar and dissimilar temperaments, described in terms of the humours. See *Commentary*, VII.ix.

36. *The Courtier*, p. 120. Vittorio Cian, in his biographical notes to *Il Cortegiano*, gives a picture of Morello: "Egli ci appare come l'unico cavaliere anziano, quasi un Nestore dongiovannesco e non rassegnato del Rinascimento, in mezzo al brio e alla gaiezza giovenilmente mondana della Corte urbinate, alla quale i suoi vani rimpianti del bel tempo passato e un certo ridestarsi di fiamme e di velleità galanti offrono materia di motteggi e di sorrisi maliziosi." *Il Libro del Cortegiano*, ed. Vittorio Cian (Florence, 1947), p. 524. It is interesting to compare this hypothetical portrait with Jonson's representation of himself in the "Celebration." There is less resemblance than there appears to be on one's first reading of the sequence.

37. *Shakespeare's "Histories"* (Pasadena, 1947), p. 7.

38. J. C. Scaliger, *Poetices*, p. 389.

39. These figures, of course, commonly occur in love poetry no matter what its philosophical attitudes may be; Jonson's context here, as in the "Celebration," however, associates them specifically with Neoplatonism, where they are commonly found. For the temple and altars burning with "Diviner heat," see Ficino's *Commentary*, VI.ix, *in divini splendoris aedem,* etc.

40. It is a coincidence that in the beginning of the *Arcadia* Sidney describes a maiden Urania in phrases which Jonson almost echoes in the first stanza of the elegy: "Let us in such sorte thinke, I say, that our poore eyes were so inriched as to behold, and our low hearts so exalted as to love, a maide, who is such, that as the greatest thing the world can shewe, is her beautie, so the least thing that may be praysed in her, is her beautie." *Works*, ed. Feuillerat, I, 7.

41. For a general discussion of the elegy see Yvor Winters, *Four Poets*, pp. 62–65. Winters describes the poem as "a fusion of two kinds of poetry: the song and the didactic poem."

42. Jonson's echo of popular ballad meter is slightly less obvious, but it is there. I shall quote the first four lines of the triumph and then a quatrain from Ralegh's imitation of a popular ballad, "As you came from the holy land."

> See the Chariot at hand here of Love,
>   Wherein my Lady rideth!
> Each that drawes, is a Swan, or a Dove,
>   And well the Carre Love guideth.

> Such an one did I meet, good Sir,
>   Suche an Angelyke face,
> Who lyke a queene, lyke a nymph, did appear
>   By her gate, by her grace.

Ralegh's poem, like many of the popular carols, is in the ballad 3-2-4-2 accentual pattern. Jonson echoes the movement in the first and third lines, but then pulls it up sharply by returning to his iambic norm in the second and fourth lines.

43. See Jonson's editors, *Works*, II, 391; Douglas Bush, *English Poetry*, p. 53; and the comment of R.L. Sharp, which implies the misleading assumptions behind the attitude, that "Emotion is always subordinated to the artistic whole: poetic poise sel-

dom succumbs to a passion, and never loses itself entirely. Jonson always kept poetry on the leash, so to speak." *From Donne to Dryden* (Chapel Hill, 1940), p. 8.

44. Jonson's best qualities are even more apparent if one compares his less successful love poems in which, like the unsuccessful odes, the didactic statement does not arise out of his own experience and has the aridity of poor occasional verse. The long "Epithalamion" (VIII, 252) for the marriage of Jerome Weston resembles a royal progress which accidentally happened to take place in a chapel; Charles and his retinue are given considerably more attention than the nuptial pair. Jonson's earlier epode "Not to know vice at all, and keepe true state" (VIII, 109) is also a formal compliment on a specific marriage. It was written before 1601 and was printed with Robert Chester's *Love's Martyr* as one of the tributes to Sir John Salisbury and his wife. Despite the fine opening lines and fine concluding line, little can be said for its overtly didactic treatment of love. The poem tediously works out the old allegorical analogy of the senses as entrances to the mind which must be guarded from the assault of blind desire (ll. 7–43). True love, however,

> No such effects doth proue;
> That is an essence, farre more gentle, fine,
> Pure, perfect, nay diuine;
> It is a golden chaine let downe from heauen,
> Whose linkes are bright, and euen,
> That falls like sleepe on louers, and combines
> The soft, and sweetest mindes
> In equall knots: This beares no brands, nor darts,
> To murther different hearts,
> But, in a calme, and god-like vnitie,
> Preserues communitie.
>
> (ll. 44–54)

The listed adjectives, "gentle," "fine," "pure," "perfect," and "diuine," are too general to take hold, and try, rather, to surround their quarry. They serve, like the golden chain, as Neoplatonic ornament. The chain itself is not sufficiently realized as a metaphor to help with a definition of love. The poem goes on to repeat the distinction between blind desire and true love, using the terms of luxury and chastity (ll. 65ff.), and ends with an application of the phoenix and the turtle to the marital happiness of Sir John Salisbury (ll. 91–116). The epode is a good example of overt didacticism plus ornament, and it fails either to teach or to delight. Jonson has not succeeded in achieving the satisfactory relationship between content and feeling which his later mastery of his style enables him to do. Better than either of these marriage poems are the epistolary couplets Jonson addressed "To the most noble, and aboue his Titles, Robert, Earle of Somerset" on his wedding, especially lines 1–6 and 23–26 (VIII, 384).

45. *Rhetoric,* 1410b, trans. R. C. Jebb (Cambridge, 1909).

46. *Poetics,* Loeb ed., trans. W. H. Fyfe (Cambridge, Mass., 1953).

INDEX TO JONSON'S WORKS

GENERAL INDEX

son's use of, 105–6, 133; pentameter, in "Inviting a friend to Svpper," 185–90

Court of love, and "A Celebration of Charis," 211

Cowley, Abraham, 132–33, 135, 243, 260, 278

Cowper, J. M., 168f.

Croll, Morris, x, 45–46, 111, 179, 239, 253, 269; on *sermo*, 6, 11; on Stoic use of Attic style, 19f.; on Senecan style, 33–34, 86; on Lipsius, 48 n., 248–49

Cruttwell, Patrick, 277

Cubeta, P. M., 280

Cunningham, J. V., x, 271, 278f.

Daniel, Samuel, 110, 267–68, 272

Dante, 99, 119

Davenport, A., 263, 267

Davies, Sir John, 170, 172, 266ff. 271–72

Day, Angel, 60, 259

Demetrius, 18, 25, 74, 84, 107, 139, 190, 199, 240f.; on classical plain style, 8–10; on epistolary style, 60–62; on subject matter of letters, 68; on clauses, 122–23, 126; on forcible style, 112, 243–44

Denotation (of language), 235f.

Dialogue, style of, 61

Diction, in Attic style, 6–7, 20, 60

Digby, Lady, poems to, 102–3, 137–38, 158–59

Digges, Leonard, 275

Diogenes, Laertius, 258

Dionysius of Halicarnassus, 25, 128, 132–34, 191–92, 195, 232, 240, 244, 278

Donne, John, 21, 36f., 39–40, 70, 109, 112, 115, 129, 135, 141, 193, 207f., 210, 227, 239, 243, 245f., 252, 269f., 276; Jonson's estimate of, 4–5, 27, 30–31; style of, 22ff., 259; poems to (*Epig.* 23, 96), 176; obscurity of, 250–51; on verse epistles, 260; epigrams of, 277; "Anniversaries" of, 279; prosody of, 133–34

Drama: of Shakespeare and Jonson, 149, 274–75. *See also* Comedy

Drayton, Michael, 229, 263, 265, 267

Drummond, William, 81, 243; book list of, 168; conversations with: 4–5, 96, 99, 105–6, 124f., 133, 152, 170, 173, 176, 207, 209, 221, 227, Notes, *passim*

Dryden, John, 80, 89, 243

Duport, James, 260–61

Duff, J. W., 39; on Livy, 245

Du Bartas, Guillaume, 98–99, 264–65

Du Bellay, Joachim, 281

Earle, John, 33

Elegies: 103; funeral, 279; love, 108f., 228–29

Elyot, Sir Thomas, 30, 246, 253–54

Enjambement, 135

Epic, 264; projected, of Jonson, 96–97, 104

Epigrams, 191; plain style of, 8; of Martial, 18–19, 262; in Nicole's definition, 84–85; of Jonson, 103, 139–40, 167–90; compared to sonnet, 107; occasional, 113, 185–90; compared to epistles, 167; structure of, 170–71; subject matter of, 171–72; complimentary, 175–76; satirical, 176–80; epitaphs as types of, 180–83; as successful genre, 276; of Donne, 277

Epistemology, 31, 144–45

Epistles, 8, 9, 13; of Jonson, 136–59; on moral character, 138–39; Jonson's self-portrait in, 154–56

Epistolary style, 60–75, 145–46, 257; candor and brevity in, 62–64; simplicity in, 64–65; subject matter of, 68–70, 74; plain style, 259; poetic, 260

Epitaphs, of Jonson, 180–83

Epodes, of Jonson, 276, 285

Erasmus, vii, 28, 35, 42, 45, 69–70, 72–73, 76, 78, 191f., 244f., 253, 265

Euphuists, 20–21, 43

Farnaby, Thomas, 126, 132, 190, 241, 272–73

Ficino, Marsilio, 40, 211, 215–16, 217, 221, 282, 283–84

Fiske, G. C., 12, 239, 241

Fletcher, John, 152–53

Forcible style, 243–44

Fraunce, Abraham, vii, 244

Friendship: duties of, 141–42; qualities of, 156–57; false, 162–63; definition of, 187–88

Fullwood, William, 60

Fustian, 101, 111–13

Gascoigne, George, 114ff., 207, 234; on satirical genres, 270f.

Gellius, Aulus, 43, 242f., 250, 253

Genus familiare, 69. *See also* Epistolary style

Genus floridum, see Middle style

Genus grande, see High style

Genus humile, see Plain style, classical

Genus medium, see Middle style

Genus tenue, see Plain style, classical

Gnomic verse, 119

Grant, M. A., 12, 241

Gregory of Nazianzen, 257

Greville, Fulke, 114f., 244, 269

Guarini, G. B., 245, 268

Guicciardini, Francesco, 246–47

Guilpin, Edward, 112